Moderate Realism and Its Logic

Moderate Realism and Its Logic

D. W. Mertz

yale university press   new haven and london

Designed by Sonia L. Scanlon
Set in Bodoni type by Keystone Typesetting, Inc.
Printed in the United States of America by BookCrafters, Inc.,
Chelsea, Michigan.

Library of Congress Cataloging-in-Publication Data
Mertz, D. W. (Donald W.), 1947–
Moderate realism and its logic / by D. W. Mertz.
p.   cm.
Includes bibliographical references and index/
ISBN 0-300-06561-2 (c : alk. paper)
1. Realism.   2. Individuation (Philosophy)
3. Logic, Symbolic and mathematical.   I. Title.
B835.M37   1996   95-44390
149′.2—dc20   CIP

A catalogue record for this book is available from the
British Library.

The paper in this book meets the guidelines for permanence
and durability of the Committee on Production Guidelines for
Book Longevity of the Council on Library Resources.

10   9   8   7   6   5   4   3   2   1

To Polly, Emily, and Ryan

The topic of relations may prove a peculiarly rewarding one for the theory of universals as a whole. For it may be expected that important classifications and distinctions which can be made at the level of polyadic universals will vanish, or become merely notional, in the limiting monadic case.

D.M. Armstrong

A Theory of Universals

contents

Preface

The following is a work in analytic ontology with a focus on the perennial ontological doctrine of *unit* attributes—the thesis that attributes are themselves as individual and unrepeatable as the particulars that possess them. Despite its persistence in Western philosophy, the doctrine of unit attributes has remained obscure in its defining details and, because of this, undeveloped in its broader ontological and logical implications. A further consequence of this relative obscurity has been the absence of a basis on which both to build direct, convincing arguments for the thesis and to answer challenges to it in a compelling manner. My intention here is to address these deficiencies.

In describing this effort as one of analytic ontology, I use the adjective 'analytic' not only in its usual methodological sense of implying that the insights of contemporary logic will be brought to bear in generating sustained formal analysis and arguments in ontology, but also in the extended sense of referring to a mutual symbiotic influence between logic and ontology, whereby the relationship of tool to subject is interchangeable and seen to be reciprocally refining. Indeed, a thesis I shall attempt to substantiate is that in order to be nonarbitrary, linguistic predication must be motivated by ontic predication, and that it is the formal characteristics of the latter that determine the inference relationships that are the subject matter of the former.

A principle argument is that among the factors contributing to the underdevelopment of the unit attribute thesis has been its occurrence within dominant ontologies that are antithetical to insights necessary to give content to the doctrine. Underlying these variants has been the classic substance/property ontology with its mutually reinforcing subject/predicate logic. Underlying and linking these two areas has been the mostly implicit and insidious *containment model* of predication, whereby predicates are conceived as somehow 'in' their subjects. Despite the fact that subject/predicate logic has subsequently been subsumed as but a fragment of modern predicate logics, on the side of ontology, the uncritical adherence to the mis-analogy of containment as a model of predication continues to have a distorting influence. Complacent in, or unwitting of, the naive containment model, both traditional and contemporary ontology have, for the most part, left unanalyzed the combinatorial nature of predication and in this have confused and retarded both ontology and logic, respectively the 'semantics' and 'syntax' of a coherent account of reality. In particular, a consequential, telling error of the containment model of predication is that it forces the reductive elimination of full multi-subject (polyadic) *relations* to monadic properties only. With this reduction we have the loss to ontology and logic of insights 'writ large' in the case of polyadic relations but hidden in the limiting case of monadic properties.

Fundamental to these insights, I shall argue, is the particularization of relations (including properties) to unrepeatable instances insofar as relations are predicative among specific sets of relata. Universals are retained as the abstracted, nonpredicative content of predicative, hence individuated, instances of universals. The result is a form of the classic scholastic ontology of moderate realism. With this at its core, my analysis will provide an account of the historically long association of instance ontology with the topic of relations, show the specious nature of prominent arguments against instance ontology and the plausibility of a one-category ontology of relation instances, yield a clarification of the ontology of moderate realism, provide an analysis of Bradley's classic regress argument, and demonstrate the telling fact that nominalism is committed exclusively to monadic predication.

Under pressure to formalize the reasoning inherent in mathematics, logic was revolutionized in the late nineteenth century, in part by incorporating the logic of relations. It was then that traditional subject/predicate logic was seen to be but a fragment of the now standard predicate logics. Of course, the present predicate logics themselves have several well-known limitations, among them one that is not generally recognized or correctly appreciated as a flaw: namely, their minimal ontological motivation. Traditional subject/predicate logic was motivated by the containment model of predication inherent in substance/ property ontology, but there is no ontic analysis of predication currently motivating 'predicate' logic. My contention is that this is a flaw, and that the warrant for classifying it as such is evident in the analytic power of a logic observed to be inherent in instance ontology. Taking advantage of the ontic analysis of relations and the resulting combinatorial model of individuating predication that I shall defend, it is possible to formalize a refined instance predicate logic with some extraordinary features and problem-solving potential. Such a logic proves to be a consistent, extended, predicate logic without type distinctions, yet retaining all the classic deduction rules, a system in which it is possible to distinguish legitimate from illegitimate impredicative reasoning; it provides a uniform diagnosis of classic self-referential paradoxes; it is not subject to classic limitation theorems such as Gödel's and Tarski's theorems; it provides the underlying logic for a provably consistent system for the derivation of arithmetic construed intensionally; and it allows identity to be formally distinguished from indiscernibility, something which standard predicate logics cannot do. These formal results are offered as inductive warrant for the veracity of the motivating instance ontology.

The following locutions have been adopted in what follows. First, depending on the context, either 'infix' (e.g., 'aRb') or 'prefix' (e.g., '$R(a,b)$') notation is used to symbolize the assertion that a relation exists among a given set of relata. I employ both, because both continue to be used in the literature, and also because, despite the fact that infix notation is appropriate only for dyadic relations, whereas prefix notation is useful for any polyacity, infix notation has the psychological advantage of reinforcing the concept that relations entail a linking between their relata. Secondly, as regards quotation marks, double quotation marks are used in the normal way for direct, exact quotation, whereas single quotes have two uses: to name the expression inside them and as 'scare quotes', to alert the reader to the fact that what is inside them has associated with it a special or expanded meaning relevant to the context of the quote, one that I do not always endorse. Finally, as is standard, corner quotes, as in '$\ulcorner R(x,y) \urcorner$', are used as variable expressions to range over quoted sentences, and will be used here specifically to name single quoted expressions resulting from the substitution of constants for variables within the corner quotes, with single quotes substituted for the corner quotes themselves.

This book has been ten years in the making. During this period, the philosophers whose work has most strongly influenced my views are, on the side of ontology, D. M. Armstrong, Reinhardt Grossmann, Keith Campbell, James Moreland, and Guido Kung, and on the side of logical analyses motivated by ontological considerations, Nino Cocchiarella, Charles Chihara, George Boolos, Alonzo Church, Gottlob Frege, and Bertrand Russell.

Portions of the book have evolved from papers presented at various philosophical conferences and have benefited from critiques by a number of respondents, including Reinhardt Grossmann, Panayot Butchvarov, Michael Detlefsen, and Terence Parsons. Some of their suggestions were well-taken and have resulted in improved arguments or in some cases deletions. Others missed the mark in my estimation, with the result that I have retained my original position but attempted to clarify it. In any case, all errors are my own. Work on topics in the philosophy of mathematics greatly benefited from participation in a 1988 National Endowment for the Humanities Summer Seminar on Frege, under the direction of Michael Resnik. I am grateful to the Endowment and especially to Professor Resnik for his generous instruction and hospitality.

Small portions of this work have been published previously. Chapter 7 is a modified portion of an article entitled "Particularism, Exemplification, and Bradley's Regress," published in the *Journal of Speculative Philosophy* 1, no. 3 (1987): 177–205, copyright 1987, Pennsylvania State University, reproduced with permission of Pennsylvania State University Press. The section of chapter 4 on Avicenna is substantially the article entitled "Instance Ontology and Avicenna's Argument," published in the *Modern Schoolman* 70, no. 3 (1993): 189–99, reproduced by permission of the editor.

My thanks also go to the University of Missouri at St. Louis for a 1990 semester development leave, during which much progress was made on the book. I am grateful to the University officers and to colleagues for their material and moral support, especially Marguerite Barnett, Blanche Touhill, Sally Fitzgerald, Dorothy Gotway, Ronald Munson, Paul Roth, and Frederick Fausz. I also wish to acknowledge two of my former teachers, Gary McGrath in mathematics and Steven Bartlett in philosophy, who through their rigor, breadth of interest, and generous spirit, inspired and advanced my intellectual world view.

Special thanks also to the editors at Yale University Press: to Judith Calvert and Noreen O'Connor for their diligence in shepherding the manuscript through the publication process and to Jean van Altena for her excellent suggestions to improve the manuscript.

Finally, it is with much pride that I acknowledge the loving support of my wife, Polly, and daughters Emily and Ryan, whose encouragement has been unwavering.

part 1

The Ontology of Particularism

chapter one

Instance Ontology

Introduction

In traditional ontology there is an ancient but recurring doctrine which asserts that attributes are as individual and unrepeatable as the individuals that possess them. This doctrine, referred to as *instance ontology*, or *particularism*, is defined most succinctly in terms of the inclusive category of relations. Its claim is that relations, which include properties as the limiting case of monadic relations, exist as individuals among the individuals they relate. More precisely, relations are particularized to numerically distinct instances as they relate numerically distinct ordered sets of relata (n-tuples). For example, in the facts or states of affairs corresponding to the assertions 'Napoleon loves Josephine' and 'Antony loves Cleopatra', there are said to exist two numerically distinct instances of the Love relation. Symbolically, $Love_1(n,j)$ and $Love_2(a,c)$, $Love_1 \neq Love_2$. Likewise for the limiting monadic case of properties, corresponding to the true assertions 'Apple a is red' and 'Apple b is red', $a \neq b$, are, 'inhering in' a and b, distinct instances of (the exact same shade of) Red, Red_1 and Red_2 respectively, where these instances (or 'unit properties'), Red_1 and Red_2, are not identical.

For some modern philosophers, one motivation for admitting unit relations is the apparently irreducible reference to them in ordinary language. By way of introduction to the doctrine, consider Peter Strawson's observation that we make this reference in assertions such as:

John's anger cooled rapidly.
John's cold is more severe than Mary's.
The wisdom of Socrates is preserved for us by Plato.[1]

Strawson's point would seem to be the following. In the example 'John's anger cooled rapidly', the property corresponding to 'cooled rapidly' (here synonymous with 'dissipated rapidly') can be construed sensibly only as a predicate of anger, or of John's anger, not as a predicate of John. But if it is a predicate of anger, then, relevantly, it cannot be Anger in general—that is, Anger as the universal—that has the property of dissipating rapidly. Not only is it nonsensical to attribute 'dissipating rapidly' to a fixed universal, but with the simultaneously true statement, 'Mary's anger did not cool rapidly', the universal Anger would have to both dissipate and not dissipate rapidly. A straightforward way to avoid these difficulties is to construe the predication of anger here as specific to John—that is, as an *instance* of Anger proprietary to John. Then it is *this* anger that dissipated rapidly. One cannot avoid this alternative by claiming that anger is predicated of the complex but individual *fact* corresponding to 'John's anger' or, more correctly, to 'John is angry'.[2] For in this case we would have the prima facie absurdity of a fact dissipating. Facts either obtain, full and constant, or they do not. They do not evaporate over time; nor do they support corresponding propositions such that the latter are first true, then less than true, then slide down to the status of false. There is nothing initially absurd, however, about an instance of Anger having the property of dissipating. Similar observations apply to Strawson's other two examples.

Prior to Strawson, John Cook Wilson had argued in a similar way that when we say 'Motion is either uniform or irregular', we cannot mean that the universal Motion is uniform or irregular.[3] What is uniform or irregular is not Motion in general or particular bodies that are in motion, but only particular motions, Motion$_i$, as attributed to particular bodies. Likewise, in the attribution 'Covetousness is a disgrace to a man', it is not the universal Covetousness that is disgraceful, but the particular covetousness of any covetous man.[4]

Other examples of apparent attribution of unit relations in ordinary language are easy to find. For example:

The cleanliness of the room was unusual.
John's height is a greater asset to the team than Bill's.
All of Wellington's leadership qualities were superior to Napoleon's.

In order to display the relevant issues, let us analyze a further example:

John's love for Mary is stronger than his love for Ann.

Here it cannot be the universal Love that is stronger than itself, but it is plausible that one instance of Love may be stronger than another.[5] The inclination to admit unit relations becomes stronger when this last example is embedded as a premise in the following intuitively valid argument:

John's love for Mary is stronger than his love for Ann.
John's love for Ann is stronger than his love for Betty.
John loves only Mary, Ann, and Betty.

John married only the person he loved the most.
Stronger-than is a transitive, asymmetric relation.
_____
John married Mary and did not marry Ann.

Establishing the validity of this argument would require at least second-order predicate logic with nominalized first-order predicates, thus allowing relations among individuals to occupy subject positions; yet it seems not to be possible for current second-order or, for that matter, standard higher-order logic generally to formalize this argument successfully. If we attempt to translate the first premise in a straightforward way as

$\text{Love}(j,m) \cdot \text{Love}(j,a) \cdot \underline{\quad\quad}$,

then the blank must be filled in with the translation of the application of the Stronger-than relation. But what would this be? The only possibility is that of

Stronger(Love,Love).

But this will not do, since, in being asymmetric, the Stronger-than relation is also irreflexive.

A more creative approach might be to merge the Stronger-than and Love relations into two relations, Strong-love and Weak-love. The asymmetric character of the original Stronger-than relation translates into a logical relation of contrariety between the Strong-love and the Weak-love relations—that is, they cannot both obtain. So construed, the first premise translates into

$\text{Strong-love}(j,m) \cdot \text{Weak-love}(j,a)$.

But then the second premise would translate as

$\text{Strong-love}(j,a) \cdot \text{Weak-love}(j,b)$,

so that between John and Ann there are the relations of both Strong-love and Weak-love, which violates their character as contraries.

A third alternative, one that raises issues which will be central later, is to quantify over relations (including monadic properties) in the following manner. Translate the first premise as:

$(\exists X)(\exists Y)[X(j,m) \cdot \text{Love}(X) \cdot Y(j,a) \cdot \text{Love}(Y) \cdot \text{Stronger}(X,Y)]$.

The other premises could be translated analogously, and by standard derivation rules the conclusion would be formally derivable. But then the fundamental question arises: What is the implied semantics and, in particular, the theory of predication assumed by such a derivational system? Under the proposed translation schema, rendering the fact that John loves Mary as '$X(j,m)$ · Love(X)' involves two distinct levels of predication, one binary—'$X(j,m)$'—and the other monadic—'Love(X)'—and similarly for relation Y. Now, either X and Y are identical to the intension Love, or they are not. But neither X nor Y can be identical to Love, for otherwise we would have the nonsense of Love(Love)—that is, 'Love is love' ('is' in the sense of predication, not identity). Moreover, in this case a binary predicate, X in '$X(j,m)$', would be identical to a monadic predicate, Love in 'Love(X)', which is precisely the classic error of attempting to reduce polyadic relations to monadic properties, an error about which much will be said below. But according to the alternative, where neither X nor Y is identical to the Love relation, in asserting 'Stronger(X,Y)', we would seem not to capture the meaning or sense of the first premise. The sense of this premise is that the Stronger-than relation is between, in some sense, applications of the same relation, Love. It is cases of Love that are being compared in the first (and second) premise, not two totally different, unspecified relations.

What these brief considerations seem to indicate—at least as I will argue below in advocating the doctrine of individuated attributes—is that in some sense the relations X and Y are identical to the Love relation, but that in some other sense they are not. It is precisely an ontology of relation instances that can provide the distinctions that satisfy these demands. On this ontology the first premise above is rendered simply as:

$$\text{Love}_1(j,m) \cdot \text{Love}_2(j,a) \cdot \text{Stronger}_1(\text{Love}_1,\text{Love}_2).$$

The remaining premises are rendered in analogous fashion, and within a refined predicate/instance logic—for example, as developed in chapter 9—the conclusion is formally derivable. Much of this book is devoted to clarifying and defending an instance ontology that can supply the motivating semantics for such a refined and, as will be seen, powerful logic.

Though linguistic considerations provide suggestive (and sometimes misleading) motivation for ontological analysis, reference to unit relations in ordinary language appears to have had little influence upon the perpetuation of the ancient doctrine in Western philosophy. Rather, the doctrine arose as a response to the traditional problem of universals and a central (if not *the* fundamental) problem of ontology, namely, that of providing a coherent assay of the ubiquitous, fundamental epistemic given of apparently *unrepeatable* entities *possessing* apparently *repeatable* attributes.

It is definitionally necessary that ontology explicate (and possibly explain away some of) the natures of all *three* of these aspects of the pre-critical given. Of the three, traditional ontology has dealt least satisfactorily with explicating the predicative link (the 'possessing') between subject entities and their attributes. Rather, the focus has been primarily upon the repeatability/unrepeatability dichotomy that divides the classic realist from nominalist ontologies. Characteristically, realists posit commonly shared entities to account for the truth of repeatable linguistic predication, whereas nominalists deny the theoretical necessity of such entities. Hence, historically, particularism has divided into either realist or nominalist versions, according to whether or not repeatable universals (e.g., Love, Red, Right-of) are admitted *along with* their corresponding unrepeatable instances. Realist instance ontology further divides into transcendent ('Platonic') and immanent varieties. For the Platonic realist, universals have an existence independent of both the existence of their instances and their apprehension by a mind. For the moderate realist, the universal *qua universal* exists only in the intellect, though it exists 'in' things as an individual.

Evidence for a realist theory of unit properties can be found in Plato and less explicitly in Aristotle. Indeed, it is controversial whether Aristotle held the doctrine; though, interestingly, it is to glosses in Aristotle's *Categories* and *Metaphysics* that the theory owes much of its historical influence. In the Middle Ages this Aristotelian line of influence branched, coming to an early end in the Latin West with Boethius, but being retained by Muslim scholastics—for example, Avicenna and Averroës—and through them returning to the Latin West in the moderate realism of Christian scholastics such as Aquinas, Duns Scotus, and Suarez. Later, this scholastic influence is evident in, for example, Leibniz's theory of 'individual accidents'. Reemerging more recently, the realist conception of unit properties and relations has been advocated in the theories of 'moments' of Edmund Husserl,[6] of 'relating relations' of the early Bertrand Russell,[7] of 'particularized qualities' of John Cook Wilson,[8] of 'cases' of Nicholas Wolterstorff,[9] and of 'particularized qualities' of Peter Strawson,[10] to name only some.

By contrast, nominalist theories of unit properties have been advocated by William of Ockham[11] and more recently in the 'abstract particulars' of G. F.

Stout[12] and the 'tropes' of D. C. Williams and Keith Campbell.[13] Also in the same line, but with a subjective status, as Campbell notes, are the 'sensa' of the empiricist tradition (e.g., Hume's 'impressions' and Locke's 'ideas'). Campbell is perhaps the foremost contemporary advocate of a nominalist version of unit *properties* (relations are excluded as necessarily eliminated in terms of properties) and has argued for the theory indirectly, both by demonstrating its economy and coherence in response to the weaknesses of classical two-category substance/attribute ontology and by showing its explanatory value in such areas as causation, perception, and the philosophy of mind. Because of his clarity and depth of understanding of the issues involved, I shall often return to Campbell's arguments below, and though I shall reject his nominalism, I am in agreement with him when it comes to the power of instance ontology to solve otherwise intractable problems and to provide an ultimate one-category ontology.

Part I will consist of arguments for, and attempts to make precise, a general ontology of attribute instances. Under the general doctrine I shall provide additional arguments for a more specific immanent realist version. The novelty of the direct arguments for attribute instances offered here lies in their association with an ontic analysis of *relations*, specifically insofar as they have the sui generis, defining status of 'actually relating' their relata. It is interesting that, historically, despite the long-prevailing, distorting eliminativist view of relations, arguments for attribute instances are often found associated with discussions of relations. I will examine several of these connections in my lengthy historical overview in chapters 3–5, where I will also raise related ontological issues clarifying to the subsequent 'relational' analysis. Because of the key role of relations in the arguments for unit attributes that I shall be offering and also for the veracity of ontology generally, it is crucial that relations be defended against certain reductionist arguments recently revived by Campbell. That Campbell seeks such a reduction is no tangential matter, for in chapter 2 I will argue that both nominalism generally and the positing of the special compresence relation among unit attributes in particular imply the classic property reduction of relations. Chapter 6 will be devoted to demonstrating that all such eliminativist arguments are non sequiturs. Turning specifically to relation instances, in chapter 7 I shall observe the specious nature of certain prominent arguments against particularized attributes advanced by Russell, Armstrong, and Gilbert Ryle. This will open the field for a set of positive arguments for unit relations in chapter 8: arguments from contrary higher-order properties, from an analysis of Bradley's regress, and from the implications of the concepts of complex structure and 'structural universals'.

I shall also put forward some indirect arguments for an instance ontology. Both to clarify the fundamental issues and to motivate the body of the work, chapter 2 will consist of a critique of classical ontologies and an indication of how instance ontology can provide solutions to both long-standing and newly presented problems. Perhaps more powerful, however, are the indirect arguments from technical fertility. These will be generated in Part II, first by formalizing axiomatically the logic inherent in instance realism, then by applying this logic and the broader ontology it entails as a refined analytic tool for generating solutions to fundamental problems in logic, foundational mathematics, and the theory of identity. The resulting intensional logic ('intensional' in the literal sense of quantifying over intensions) possesses a number of remarkable characteristics. First, the provably consistent system is a simplifying refinement of standard higher-order predicate logic, one that obviates the need for an imposed, complicating theory of types. Its consistency follows from the incorporation of instance predicates and therewith the power to distinguish legitimate from illegitimate (truly self-contradictory) impredicative definitions. By means of this now transparent distinction, not only are the classic self-referential paradoxes avoided, but they are also *uniformly* diagnosed. The representative sampling includes Russell's set paradox, the generalized Fitch–Curry paradox, the liar paradox together with its strengthened and cyclic versions, as well as Patrick Grim's recent extrapolation of the divine liar paradox. I will then show how a language incorporating instance ontology can, for example, contain its own truth predicate (i.e., be a 'closed' language in Tarski's sense) and, significantly, how consequential limitation theorems—for example, Gödel's incompleteness theorems and Tarski's theorem—are defeated in it. The related Cantorian diagonal-type arguments are likewise non sequiturs in the developed logic. So that the reader does not misunderstand these claims and dismiss them as pretentious squaring of circles, I should make clear what is being asserted: I am not claiming that these classic theorems are erroneous *in* (and *about*) their own standard predicate logics; what I *am* claiming is that in the radically refined instance logic that I develop here, these theorems are defeated as not derivable. Significantly, in the absence of Gödel's second theorem, we shall see how it is possible to extend the 'finite' syntactical consistency proof of the developed instance logic given in chapter 9 to an axiomatized 'intensional' version of the arithmetic of natural numbers in chapter 10. Concluding chapter 10 will be a demonstration of how instance ontology provides a means of solving the persistent problem of identity theory—namely, how to distinguish absolute identity from mere indiscernibility.

The success of instance ontology in the above areas gives further warrant as to its truth. For instance ontology and its formalized logic, like all theories, are to be judged on how well they accord with the intuitive conceptual/semantic given and other accepted theories and on how extensive and important their applications are, particularly in solving long-standing problems. Part II will provide a sampling of their problem-solving potential in areas other than basic ontology.

The remainder of the present chapter will be devoted to clarifying the tenets of realist instance ontology and the role of relations taken intensionally in motivating it. Central here is an appreciation of the inadequacies of the classic conceptions of predication and the weakness of theories that attempt to model predication extensionally.

Characterizing Instance Ontology

At its neutral core, instance ontology holds that any relation (again, including monadic properties) exists as numerically diverse individuals, one each in or among the distinct sets of subjects of which the relation can be truly asserted. Also included in the doctrine, though left for the most part unstated, is an assumption of nonredundancy: that is, the same n-tuple of subjects cannot have multiple instances of the same relation. For example, there cannot be two or more instances of the Greater-than relation between the natural numbers 2 and 3.

These theses are rendered precise in the following two principles. For instances R_i^n and R_j^n, of the same n-place relation type R^n,

Principle of subject uniqueness (SU):
If $R_i^n(a_1, a_2, \ldots, a_n)$ and $R_i^n(b_1, b_2, \ldots, b_n)$, then $a_1 = b_1, \ldots, a_n = b_n$, and

Principle of instance uniqueness (IU):
If $R_i^n(a_1, a_2, \ldots, a_n)$ and $R_j^n(a_1, a_2, \ldots, a_n)$, then $R_i^n = R_j^n$.

The phrase 'of the same n-place relation type R^n' is ambiguously neutral and can of course be interpreted either nominalistically or realistically, depending upon whether 'type R' is eliminated in favor of some other theoretically satisfactory but unrepeatable entity or taken as itself a real, unreduced constituent numerically identical across multiple entities—that is, as a universal.

As subject-unique (SU), no relation instance can have more than one distinct n-tuple of relata. It is not the case, for example, that Red_1 inheres as numerically the same in both apple a and distinct apple b, for otherwise Red_1 would have the nature of a universal, not an unrepeatable instance. The principle of instance uniqueness (IU) states the nonredundancy thesis: for example, that apple a cannot have (at the same time and corresponding to the same spatial region) numerically different instances of the property Red. The doctrine of instance uniqueness can be supported not only by an argument from ontic economy ('Ockham's razor'), but also by an argument from the identity of indiscernibles: namely, that there is simply nothing that could serve to intrinsically differentiate two relation instances if they have numerically the same relata n-tuple and are of the same relation constant R^n. The central problem for particularism is to produce cogent arguments for the existence of instances that satisfy the requirement of subject uniqueness (SU). It is a primary purpose of this book to offer such arguments, both direct and indirect.

Instance ontology can be further refined so as to distinguish immanent from Platonic realist versions, and these from nominalist theories. As a defining characteristic, an *immanent realist theory* of relation instances adopts, in addition to principles SU and IU, the thesis:

Principle of immanent instance realism (IR):
For distinct relation instances R_i^n, R_j^n, ... there exists an entity R^n which is a numerically identical aspect of each of the instances R_i^n, R_j^n, ...

IR makes explicit the realist interpretation of 'the same type R^n': namely, that R^n is a common, qualitative content of each of its instances—what I shall call their *intension*—and that this intension is an essential, *numerically the same* aspect of each instance, or 'token', of the type R^n. This is the *identity theory* of predicate intensions, so, by definition, makes the claim that these contents are universals. It is the intension R^n that determines the kinds of relations that can have R^n or its instances as relata: for example, logical relations (properties of symmetry, transitivity, etc., and proposition-forming relations) and physical relations (space-time, causation, etc.).

To anticipate, in chapter 9, in formalizing a logic inherent in realist instance ontology, it will be IR, together with IP, the principle of instance predicates (see below), which will be built into the distinguishing, refined formation rules given. Specifically, the syntax of the logic will contain quantifiers ranging over both attribute instances and their corresponding universals, and where, under a new, simplifying device of 'extending binding', universal quantifiers will bind the operator variables of like instance quantifiers within their scope.

The conjunction of principles SU, IU, and IR constitutes, in part, the *moderate realism* of the scholastics and as such represents a *via media* between the poverty of nominalism and the excesses of Platonic realism. According to the scholastics, the intension R^n, the *metaphysical* or *potential* universal, is neither universal nor particular. When conceived in relation to an additional act of intellectual reflection to be predicable of many, intension R^n is described as the *logical* or *formal* universal and as such exists only in the mind. Yet, identically the same content R^n exists individuated 'in' each subject of predication. The weak point in classical moderate realism has been explaining how intension R^n can be predicated of only one set of relata when 'individuated in (or among)' them, yet, when abstracted from the set, is universal, in being potentially predicable of an indefinite number of sets of relata. The relational analysis that follows will provide such an explanation.

Turning to Platonism, though risking the charge of redundancy, it is possible for a Platonic realist to adopt a theory of immanent unit properties in addition to positing separated Forms. In chapter 3 I shall examine evidence that Plato held such a theory insofar as he subscribed to at least SU, though possibly not IU. In any case, by definition, the Platonic realist rejects IR on account of its requirement that the universal R be a *constituent* of instances of its 'kind'. Rather, the universal is individuated as a Form (e.g., MAN) and raised to the status of a perfect, unchanging, separate exemplar to which, by a relation of 'participation' or 'imitation', concrete, changing individuals (e.g., Plato) approximate. The flaws in Platonic realism, particularly the difficulties in explicating the 'participation' relation, are well known and powerful and need not be reviewed here.[14]

Nominalistic instance theories—for example, contemporary 'trope theory'— subscribe to principles SU and IU but, like instance Platonism, must reject IR. Characteristically, these theories deny any real identity across instances and attempt to account for the apparent sameness of type R^n by various maneuvers: by making R^n a shared linguistic predicate or a shared concept or by replacing

R^n with either a class of R_i^n instances or a resemblance relation between R_i^ns.[15] Specifically, predicate and concept nominalism hold that some individuals, ordinary or relation instances, are related to a shared entity—in the one case to a spoken or written token of a linguistic type, in the other to a mental construct. However, in neither case is the relation a function of the natures of the relata; hence, in the final analysis, it is only an arbitrary association, even if, in some mysterious way, it is reliable, predictive, and true. In light of the explanatory weakness of unfounded association, other nominalists take the shared entity R^n to be an encompassing class or mereological whole and replace exemplification by the element-of relation. The weakness of this approach will be considered shortly. Still others, the resemblance nominalists, eliminate the shared entity R^n entirely and substitute for exemplification the resemblance relation among the otherwise exemplifying individuals.

There exist what I take to be compelling, defeating critiques of all versions of nominalism (predicate, concept, class, mereological, and resemblance), found, for example, in the detailed analyses of D. M. Armstrong, Reinhardt Grossmann, Herbert Hochberg, and others.[16] These arguments all constitute various ways of substantiating the thesis that apparent commonality can be accounted for only by real commonality, and this only by 'sharing' a single entity. I shall not recapitulate these arguments here. More germane to my study are the arguments of chapter 2 to the effect that instance nominalism requires the property reduction of relations, a necessity recognized (albeit for a different reason) and attempted by Campbell. It is my intent here, and in more detail in chapter 6, to show, by strengthening standard arguments and supplying new ones, that this reduction is impossible, and hence that we have in this fact a further *reductio* against nominalism.

Whether as an apparent sameness of nature for ordinary individuals or their property instances, nominalists deny any numerically identical commonality, a position said to be motivated by ontic economy and a reaction against the exaggerated hypostatizations of Platonic realism. The realist, however, can be likewise motivated, without rejecting universals, but rather holding them to be a necessary part of a coherent, integrated explanation of the ontic given. This is the case with the moderate realist, who agrees with the nominalist that every entity that exists extra-conceptually is individual but differs in also holding that at least some of these individuals—specifically, relation instances—have a distinguishable content, which, when abstracted from the individuating aspect of an instance and as such possessed of a conceptual mode, is identical across all like instances. More specifically, then, moderate realism is a via media between Platonic realism and what in the literature has been described as the third ontic 'ism'—namely, conceptualism, a doctrine that is in fact but a form of nominalism. However, beyond simply postulating entities or principles that account for the two characteristics of uniqueness and sortedness, the instance realist, on the basis of the argument from the nature of relations, can offer a theory of how unit relations are unrepeatable yet have a repeatable content.

It is nominalism's explanatory poverty that accounts most, perhaps, for its contemporary waning and for the increasing appeal to universals (relations taken 'intensionally') that one finds in the recent literature of metaphysics proper. In addition to numerous journal articles, this includes, to mention but a few relevant examples, the recent books by D. M. Armstrong and Michael Tooley, in which causation and the laws of nature are explained as relations between universals,[17] and the books by Penelope Maddy and John Bigelow on the foundations of mathematics, where it is argued that natural numbers are properties—for Maddy, properties of sets; for Bigelow, properties of properties.[18] Yet, as Tooley notes, outside metaphysics proper, many philosophers have remained reluctant to appeal to relations conceived intensionally. A wide segment of recent Anglo-American philosophy—in particular, naturalism[19]— has based its rejection of intensions largely on a nexus of arguments from linguistic considerations; classic here are the arguments of W. V. O. Quine and the later Ludwig Wittgenstein.[20] A detailed response can be found in the works of Jerrold Katz, who argues that the central arguments of Quine and Wittgenstein are non sequiturs and that a Platonist construal of intensions is the best explanation of certain features of natural language.[21] (Readers who find the linguistic arguments of Quine and Wittgenstein persuasive are referred to Katz.) The arguments that I shall offer in the sequel against nominalism will be directed at some of the less discussed inadequacies of explanations exclusively in terms of extensions. Beyond this, the argument that is perhaps most persuasive against nominalism/extensionalism is the indirect one of a developed intensional logic quantifying over intensions that has demonstratively wide, profound problem-solving potential in philosophy. The operative meta-principle is: "By their fruits ye shall know them." This will be the program of Part II.

It should be noted from the start that the positing of unit properties or relations does not of itself solve the problem of apparent repeatability; it merely postpones the solution. On this account, certain realist critics—for example, D. M. Armstrong[22]—reject instance realism, arguing that, as made clear by principle IR, it introduces an unnecessary duplication of entities. According to these critics, to further posit relation instances—for example, Red_1 and Red_2— as somehow useful to an account of the repeatable/unrepeatable aspects of the given is simply to push the situation to be explained up a level, to that of the posited instances themselves. How are we to explain that Red_1 and Red_2 are two unrepeatable instances of identically the same repeatable property Red? By positing further instances of some kind? Here we begin the slide into vicious regress. On the other hand, if both the unrepeatable and the repeatable aspects of a relation instance, say Red_1, are accounted for by the particularity of the instance plus its containment of some universal, Red, then this same explanation would suffice at the level of an ordinary individual a and its universal attributes—for example, Red. It is then concluded that relation instances are ontically idle.

However, such realist replies make two mistakes: (1) they fail to understand the proper nature of relation instances, and (2) they do not appreciate the severity of the arguments against the background realism they assume, for which instance ontology offers a solution. In regard to the latter, the crucial assumption is that the individuality of any ordinary entity is to be explained by positing an underlying particular and that the commonality of its attributes is to be explained in terms of possession of universals by that particular. Abetting this view is the further, more subtle assumption of the

Thesis of predicable possession:
Any possession of a characteristic or content P by an individual x is that of predication; i.e., P is a predicate of x, $P(x)$.

Together, these assumptions form the core of a pre-critical, commonsense view—what might aptly be called 'naive realism'—and the model for classic Aristotelian 'substance/attribute' ontology. But, despite its commonsense appeal, naive realism harbors an insidious error. When the subject entity is an individual, it leads to the incoherent notion of a 'bare particular', a stumbling block for many a would-be reform ontology. For any attempt to assay a thick individual under the dichotomous, exhaustive division of a nonpredicative particular on the one hand and universals (or particulars) as its predicates on the other must, when all repeatable determinations are analytically separated and tallied on the side of the predicates, yield as an inevitable residue an underlying 'bare particular'. But the concept of a particular stripped of all content is incoherent. Arguments for this incoherence will be given in detail in the following chapter.

Of course, the same problem affects relation instances—for example, Red_1—if they are misconstrued as but limiting, single-intension analogs of ordinary particulars, each consisting as such of a bare particular of which *is predicated* a single universal, say Red. Yet, as I shall argue, it is precisely relation instances whose proper analysis provides a means of understanding universals as non-predicative constituents.

Ontic Predication and the Containment Model

The crucial issue of ontic predication concerns the remaining third of the tripartite explanandum fundamental to ontology—unrepeatables/*possessing*/repeatables—and it is this aspect of predicable 'possession', and unification in general, which, historically, has remained the explanatory weak link. The problem of predication is but the limiting case of the more general *problem of complexity*:

> What account can be given of the unity of a *complex* which as such is a heterogeneous whole, a one and a many, whose constituents each remain distinct yet are unified into a further distinct whole, itself with new supervening properties and relations not possessed by the elements, singly or as a class?

Like the repeatable/unrepeatable aspects of our experience, which have a fundamental ontic status, complexity too is a primitive datum, prior to, and at the same time a component of, all reflection and theorizing. Complexes are ubiquitous, from the predication of a property to a subject, to the structure of atoms, to the neuro-network making up a central nervous system, to the universe and every subpart of it as spatiotemporal, causal micro- and macro-structures. The analog is likewise true of conceptual/propositional 'space'. It is incumbent upon ontology to account for this pervasive diversity-in-unity.

Victimized unwittingly, perhaps, by the methodology of analysis, with its decompositional drive toward conceptually separated components, traditional ontology has tended to focus primarily upon some proposed atomic, noncombinatorial 'entities', together with their relative categorizations. Explanations of the combinatorial, the unity of complexes formed from entities, whether of the same type (e.g., material compounds) or across classical ontic categories (e.g., between an object and its properties) have often been in terms of the noncombinatorial entities themselves: for example, the 'substances' of pluralism or the 'One' of monism. Combination is explained in terms of what is combined, the predicative by the nonpredicative. One sees this tendency in a widely held view of the ontology of classes or sets, according to which the unity of a diversity of elements that constitutes a class is tacitly assumed to be accounted for by specification of the elements alone. This view is reinforced by the axiom of extensionality, which states that sets are identical if and only if they have the same elements. The victory of the noncombinatorial is complete with the further adoption of the extensionalist position that properties and relations considered intensionally are to be eschewed in favor of their set surrogates. By contrast, 'intensional' logicians, among whom Frege counted himself in this regard, as well as the later Russell, hold that the unity constituting a class is a function of an intension or class concept of which the elements of the class are the corresponding extension.[23]

Another example of this propensity to explain unification in terms of what is united, though now in terms of the resulting whole, is Armstrong's proposal that the 'nexus' or 'tie' of predication between a property F and its subject a is to be explained in terms of the resulting, unpredicable complex—the state of affairs corresponding to Fa.[24] As it were, the container explains the unity of the contained, a model for predication that has a long history. Armstrong's reversal of the direction of explanation is made under pressure of the failure of traditional ontology to adequately explicate predication, central to which is a failure to reach a satisfactory resolution of the classic quandary known as Bradley's regress. Indeed, as I shall argue, essential to the plausibility of the regress is the treatment of the predicative as nonpredicative.

By contrast with this tendency to account for the predicative in terms of the nonpredicative, I shall argue that it is the proper, nonreductive assay of predication that will provide solutions to several classic problems. These include the general problem of complexity and the problem of bare particulars. The assay will yield the further bonus of a positive argument for unit relations: specifically, that what is ontically predicative must be individuated.

Before taking up these issues, it is necessary, in order both to avoid confusion and to bring into relief the problems being addressed, to make explicit certain distinctions that will be assumed concerning entities within, and relationships among, language, thought, and extra-conceptual reality. These distinctions are in accord with common experience and language (the pre-critical given) and theoretically have a long, persistent history, going back at least to the Stoic theory of *lekta*.[25] First is the distinction between *ontic* and *linguistic/grammatical* predication or, in scholastic terms, between 'formal' and 'material' predication. Formal predication refers to the syntactical composition of a declarative sentence (e.g., '*a* is to the left of *b*'), analyzed as consisting of one or more referring terms, the grammatical subject(s) ('*a*' and '*b*'), together with a verb phrase, the grammatical predicate ('is to the left of'). Plato pointed out in the *Sophist* (261d ff.) that a statement—that is, an expression that is capable of being true or false—must consist in at least a noun and a verb ('signifying actions'). (Cf. Aristotle *De Interpretatione* 16a ff.) A list of nouns—for example, 'lion stag horse'—or a list of verbs—for example, 'walks runs sleeps'—do not make statements; only combinations of nouns and verbs, because they 'fit together' properly, make statements. Distinct from, but related to, formal predication, ontic predication refers to the unifying aspect of the corresponding extra-grammatical, though not necessarily extra-conceptual, fact (*a* and *b* as spatially related). Relatedly, we have the common distinction between three levels of complex entities: sentences, propositions, and facts, or states of affairs. Sentences fall on the side of syntax, propositions and facts on the side of semantics, with propositions occupying the central epistemic position of being complex senses that in one direction guide syntactical composition of otherwise arbitrarily associated symbol types and in the other refer to the constituents of the corresponding facts (if any). For example, to the correct grammatical predications '*a* is P' or '*a* R's *b*' there correspond the propositions $P(a)$ and $R(a,b)$, to which in turn, if true, there correspond the states of affairs designated ':$P(a)$' and ':$R(a,b)$'. A colon will be used thus throughout the book to distinguish facts, or states of affairs, if any, from corresponding propositions. Ontic predication pertains to the unity of the corresponding fact :$R(a,b)$, though it could, of course, refer to the unity of the proposition $R(a,b)$, if in the context the latter was the subject of analysis. The grammatical/ontic distinction carries over to the dual use of the term 'subject', both for a grammatical entity and, derivatively, for the corresponding referent. Which is intended is generally left to the context. By the term 'predication' I shall intend ontic predication, sometimes adding the adjective 'ontic' as a reminder or for emphasis.

Specific to the instance ontology advocated here, when a general term, say 'red', is used as a linguistic (formal) predicate, as in 'a is red', where the corresponding proposition, $Red(a)$, is true, then the truth condition for the latter is a fact containing an instance of the intension Red, Red_n, which is ontically (materially) predicative of a—the fact $:Red_n(a)$. In short, it will be argued that the proposition $Red(a)$ is true because the proposition $(\exists Red_i)Red_i(a)$ is true, and this because the fact $:Red_n(a)$ obtains for some instance Red_n.

Though he does not make it explicitly, Aristotle was aware of the predicate distinction, jumping back and forth from formal to material predication in the *Categories* but focusing exclusively upon material predication in the *Metaphysics*. In both cases, as Aristotle realized, predication is essentially a kind of 'tie', an inherence (Latin *inhaereo*: 'to stick, cling to'). At its core it entails the forming of a compound out of elements that nevertheless sustain their identity and existence in the subsuming whole, and it is for this reason that predication has an absolute, indispensable role in ontology. Commenting on attempts by his predecessors to describe the unification of ontic predication, Aristotle writes:

> Yet the same account applies in all cases; for being healthy, too, will on this showing be either a 'communion' or a 'connection' or a 'composition' of soul and health, and the fact that the bronze is a triangle will be a 'composition' of bronze and triangle, and the fact that a thing is white will be a 'composition' of surface and whiteness. The reason is that people look for a unifying formula, and a difference, between potency and complete reality. . . . Therefore, it is like asking what in general is the cause of unity and of a thing's being one. [*Metaphysics* 1045b11–20]

The problem of predication is how we are to understand this 'composition' ('attachment', 'cohesion', etc.) of a predicate to a subject.

A commonsense, but misleading, model is that of *containment*, according to which a predicate is 'present *in*', 'inheres *in*', 'is immanent *in*' (Latin *immanere*: 'to inhabit') its subject. Here the subject is conceived on the model of a whole that subsumes its predicates, the relation between subject and predicate being that of whole to part. In its naive form, the model might be spatial containment as by a vessel, whereas in its more sophisticated, abstract form, it might be that of the relation of elements to a containing class.

Containment is Aristotle's model for predication in the *Categories*, being most evident in one of the two forms of predication he distinguishes there: that of being 'in' a subject, as distinct from being 'said of' a subject. The details of this distinction will be observed in chapter 3. Under the more sophisticated, hylomorphic theory of the *Metaphysics*, the containment model has less sway, though it is nevertheless part of a nexus of explicit, but undifferentiated, concepts that make up the analytic tools (as well as in part the self-applied subject matter) used there to do metaphysics. Central to this short list of concepts,[26] and coming closest to an *explanans* for predication, is the relation of part to whole. That the containment model remains a paradigm for predication is evident in Aristotle's brief lexicon of terms in *Metaphysics* V (Δ). He states that 'have' or 'hold' means many things, among which is "that in which a thing is present as in something receptive of it is said to have the thing, e.g., the bronze has [as a predicate] the form of the statue, and the body has [as a predicate] the disease." Then he goes on to say that these terms can equally mean "as that which contains [as it] holds the things contained; for a thing is said to be held by that in which it is as a container, e.g., we say that the vessel holds the liquid . . . , and so too that the whole holds the parts" (*Metaphysics* 1023a7–24).[27]

After Aristotle, Leibniz stands out as the most consciously systematic advocate of the containment doctrine and its consequences, asserting as an explicit axiom that all truth rests upon the fact that *praedicatum inest subjecto*: "in every true affirmative proposition, whether universal or singular, necessary or contingent, the predicate inheres in the subject or that the concept of the predicate is in some way involved in the concept of the subject."[28] Leibniz clearly intends the material uses of the terms 'subject' and 'predicate'. He was also explicit in observing that the intensional containment model of predication, where for veridical 'S is P' the intension of P is part of the intension of S, is paralleled, albeit in reverse, in its extensional modeling—that is, the extension of S is included in the extension of P. In both cases the relationship between subject and attribute is one of *inclusion*, and we have the nonproblematic subset relation among extensions, with its success in interpreting traditional syllogistic subject/predicate logic, thereby bolstering by association the posited containment model of predication.

Despite its pre-critical appeal, the containment model represents a serious error on two accounts. First, as emphasized by Russell,[29] endemic to the containment model is the mis-analogy of forcing all predication into a monadic mode, and in such a way as to lead either to an all-encompassing single substance monism or to an atomistic pluralism of totally isolated, unconnected entities. The reasoning is as follows. Let it be the case that $:a\,\mathrm{R}\,b$ obtains, where a and b are any two distinct individuals, and R is any relation between them. On the containment model, predicate R would have to be contained in the relevant sense in each subject simultaneously. This implies that subjects a and b must themselves 'overlap' at R: that is, that a and b mutually contain a part of each other, namely, R, in the relevant predicative sense of 'contains'. But if a and b share a part, they must together compose a larger whole, one that again contains R in the predicative sense. R is then a predicate of the subsuming whole (in Russell's notation '$(ab)r$'). Extending this reasoning to its limit, since any two entities whatsoever are related in some way or another, all entities 'overlap' and thus go to compose a maximal whole, the One, which has every monadically reduced relation and every property in general as a predicate. F. H. Bradley, the best-known modern monist, adopts the containment model of predication and, consistent with it, the necessity of the 'internal' conception of relational unity. Indicative is the following:

> Every relation does and again does not qualify its terms, and is and is not qualified by them. . . . The terms and the relation must 'enter' one into the other, and yet again are ruined if they do so. You cannot . . . alter one or both of the terms and leave the relation unaltered, or alter the relation without making a difference to the terms. . . . And to combine the above requirements without contradiction is impossible so long as relations are accepted as something which is ultimately real and true.[30]

The terms of a relation and the relation itself are required to 'enter' into each other according to the containment model of predication, to 'grow together' or 'overlap' as Bradley states elsewhere; this is how the relation qualifies its terms. Yet precisely insofar as it does this, the relation loses its identity as a separate entity 'between' its terms, the 'external' conception of relations. According to Bradley, since relations must be both internal and external in nature, both a 'together' and a 'between', and because these are contradictory, the concept of relation is incoherent.

As to the second alternative, recall that monism follows from the containment model of predication on the assumption that a relation R is polyadic—something shared by both relata, a and b. One can avoid monism and maintain a pluralist ontology by denying that relations are in truth polyadic—by reducing a relation R to separate monadic properties of each relatum. Aristotle, Leibniz, and the majority of Western philosophers up to the last century adopted this last position. The containment model is behind Leibniz's famous critique of relations: that it is impossible for an attribute to straddle two subjects, for this requires it to have a foot in each term, as it were.[31] These philosophers were rarely cognizant of, or at least were not forthright in drawing, the extreme ontic consequences of the property reduction of relations: namely, that all real *connection* between entities is eliminated. Again, Leibniz was a resolute exception. For him, the ultimate existents were perfectly isolated monads (Greek *monas*: 'that which is one') and their internal perceptions, and even though the content of these perceptions included physical objects standing in various relationships (e.g., spatiotemporal relations), in keeping with the tradition, these relations were said to be reducible to nonrelational properties of the relata.

Returning to Aristotle, it is worth noting that, with regard to the containment paradigm, a tension arises in the middle books, VII (Z) (1040b5–10; 1041b11–33) and VIII (H) (1043b5–14; 1045a6–19), of the *Metaphysics*. Here Aristotle comes to the realization that to account for what constitutes *structure* in a complex substance (e.g., Socrates), what is needed is not another constituent resembling the other parts in its ontic status, but rather a unifier, which in his view is predication. The single substantial form is then said to be predicated of a plurality of matter (Socrates' bodily organs). But substantial form is then functioning as polyadic, as a single predicate among multiple subjects—that is, as a full, unreduced relation. The best that Aristotle could say was that, rather than a substantial form being a predicate contained in its subjects, the form is the organizing container of its subjects. That is, contrary to standard cases of predication in which the subject contains the predicate, in the special case of substantial forms, these forms, as predicates, must contain their (multiple) subjects.

In addition to leading to one of two equally unacceptable extremes, monism or isolated atomism, the containment model entails a second insidious error, in that it reinforces the ontology of bare particulars. The concept of an entity some aspect of which is a container for, but distinct from, *all* its predicates forces this aspect to be itself totally devoid of any characteristics, specifications, qualifications, or quantifications, and such a concept is incoherent, as I shall argue. Aristotle was aware of the problem, observing when considering prime matter as the primary subject of predication that, after conceptually

separating off (Greek *aphairesis*: 'stripping away') all predicates, one necessarily ends up with a completely indeterminate substrate, which he rightly
rejects (*Metaphysics* 1029a19–30). For in this we have an entity devoid of
content, a nothing, not even a bare 'this', as primary subject, a subject that has
now evaporated into a nonentity. The problem here is how to give an account of
ultimate ontic subjects each of which has a content or nature, as such repeatable (universal), but a content that is not a predicate of that subject. To separate
the repeatable determinations of an entity and then make them predicates of a
single, individuating substratum is to require the latter to be a fraudulent bare
particular. It is my thesis that this problem can be solved by relation instances;
but what are required for this solution are insights that are blocked by the
property reduction of relations.

The structuring characterization of predication that Aristotle glimpsed but
did not elaborate comes closest to the analysis that I give below. In this context,
Frank Lewis has recently proposed that the predicative composition of form and
matter in the *Metaphysics* is best viewed as analogous to Gottlob Frege's theory
of the saturation of a concept by an object.[32] Just as it is the 'unsaturated',
incomplete nature of Fregean concepts that is the source or cause of the unity of
a Fregean fact,—subjects saturating what would otherwise be a 'gappiness' of
concepts; so for Aristotle, form is not just some other thing alongside the matter
that composes an individual substance but rather the 'principle' or cause of the
composition. In this regard, both Frege and Aristotle reverse the direction of the
containment model of predication—for here subjects are 'contained in' the
predicate. In the *Categories*, for example, Aristotle asserts that nonsubstances
are 'present in' substances, but he immediately qualifies this type of presence
as "in something, not as a part" (*Categories* 2. 1a24–25; 5. 3a31–32). As
Aristotle became aware, what is needed is a constituent with the unique status
of multi-subject unifier and structurer; to hold otherwise is to fall victim to an
explanatory infinite regress (*Metaphysics* 1041a33–b33, 1043b5–14). I shall
look closely at Aristotle's point in chapter 3 and will attempt to reinforce it in
chapter 8. Further, however, Aristotle, and many other philosophers subsequently, insist that only the universal is predicable. "I mean by universal what
is such by nature as to be predicated by many" (*De Interpretatione* 17a39–40).
As indicated above, I shall argue that this is an error. Stated metaphorically in
terms of Aristotelian hylomorphism (an ontology I shall argue against), the

contradicting thesis that I shall advance would say that form, precisely as predicative of its matter, individuates itself and so is the principle of individuation of the composite of matter and form. The unit form would thus be a candidate as a subject for further predicates. Interestingly, there are in the *Metaphysics* texts that have been interpreted as asserting that substantial form is individuated as predicative of matter and is, as a particular, 'primary substance'. So interpreted and without further elaboration, these texts are at odds with Aristotle's often repeated theses that (a) form is universal and (b) no universal is a substance. These issues will be discussed in chapter 3.

Relations: Individuated as Combinatorial

The classic containment model of predication is a primary source of the historically long aversion to treating relations as a category ontically and, subsequently, logically as significant as that of monadic properties. Against this dominance of the monadic, I will argue that the proper analysis of predication is that of the defining characteristic of polyadic relations—that predicates link to or among subjects. In other words, grammatical predication is motivated by ontic predication, and the latter and its implications are understood correctly only when ontic predication is seen in terms of the linking nature of relations. It is the combinatorial nature of predication that accounts for the common observation that, on the corresponding level of formal predication, one can sensibly negate a grammatical predicate (e.g., 'Socrates is not bald') but not a grammatical subject (e.g., 'Not Socrates is bald'). To place negation on a subject (in the same sense in which it can be placed on a predicate) is to assert of the ontic subject that its potential for predicational linking does not obtain in this context. Yet ordinary individuals—for instance, Socrates—do not possess this ontic potential, and to make an assertion to the contrary is to commit a category mistake. Note that if it were the ontic subject that had the status of combinator in the context of predication, as in the containment model of predication, then there would be no accounting for why a subject cannot be negated.

Historically, and despite the long-prevailing property-reduction thesis, relations were held by a variety of philosophers to be the proper and only candidates for solving the problem of complexity. It has been a widely held tenet—and is a basic thesis here—that it is relations that bridge ontological space, by holding their relata as linked both *together* and *apart*, united and distinct. As Bradley put it, relata 'hold together distantly'. In a relational fact, :R(a,b), the natures of the individual relata ('subjects') delimit what intension R can be (e.g., if a and b are geometric figures, then R cannot be the relation Is-Stronger-than), but it is the *relating* of a to b under R that accounts for the unification constituting the emergent fact complex. From this perspective, monadic properties are merely the limiting, single-subject case, so 'attach to' but are not 'present in' their subjects. *It is the nature of relations, including monadic relations, to be combinatorial among their relata, and in this they are the fundamental ontic principles of connectedness and system, accounting for all that requires a unity-indiversity.* As the antagonist Bradley himself put it, a relation is nothing if not both a 'between' and a 'together'. As rigid connectors, relations account for the unity and therefore the being of plural wholes or complexes ('manys')—both the simultaneous connectedness and the identity-saving distinctness of the elements. In this both unity and diversity are saved, and the opposed counterfactual extremes of a distinctionless, homogeneous monism or an unorganized, chaotic atomism are avoided.

Relations are the sine qua non of a plural universe, of connectedness, structure, order, and form. To coin a term, relations are *ontoglial* (Greek for 'the glue of being'). Of fundamental significance, relations, left full and intensional, explain the existence of distinct wholes of the same elements. It is the combining order (or 'direction') together with the intensions of the relations making up the interlinking unification of a complex, which in turn is a function of the nature of the elements linked, that constitute the explanatory bases regarding why a resulting complex may be the subject of emergent properties and relations that the subsumed constituents, singly or as a class, do not have.

Thus, with Frege, I am claiming that cutting across the traditional ontic categories of individuals and their characteristics is an equally fundamental bifurcation of entities into those that account for the nexi or ontic liaisons among terms, the ontoglial, and those that do not. Further, I claim that this distinction has significant ontic consequences: relevantly here, *that each nexus or linking is necessarily occurrent.* Insofar as a relation performs its distinguishing, defining role of what Russell termed 'actually relating' a particular ordered set of relata—that is, as *predicative* among these relata (e.g., Napoleon and Josephine)—it is unique to this ordered set (the $Love_1$ in the fact :$Love_1$(Napoleon,Josephine)). Yet, each such unrepeatable instance—for example, $Love_1$— has a content or intension, Love, that, when abstracted from interconnecting a specific set of relata, is (at least potentially) identically repeatable—that is, universal. Universals are not ontically predicative, but their instances are. These theses are rendered formally as:

Principle of instance predicates (IP):
Only unrepeatable relation instances, R_i^n, are *ontic predicates*—that is, exist as *predicative* among specific subject n-tuples; the universal R^n is not ontically predicative.

Principle of relata-linking (RL):
No n-adic relation instance R_i^n exists except as ontically *predicative* among, and hence necessarily presupposing, some n-tuple of entities which as such it relates.

When the logic of instance ontology is formalized in chapter 9, IP will be incorporated in the formation of rules of the symbolic language in such a way that only relation instances occupy predicate positions; for example, '$R_i(x,y)$' will be a well-formed expression, whereas '$R(x,y)$' will not be.

The conjunction of IP and RL, along with the previous principles SU, IU, and IR, completes an ontology that I understand to both embody and clarify the core of scholastic moderate realism: namely, that an attribute (instance) is individual 'in' (predicated of) a subject but, when separated through being abstracted from the subject (as the nonpredicative content), is universal. Instance ontology— and moderate realism in particular—inverts the relationship between the predicative/unpredicative and the repeatable/unrepeatable distinctions assumed by its traditional rival. In traditional ontology the proportion is:

$$\frac{\text{predicative}}{\text{unpredicative}} = \frac{\text{repeatable universals}}{\text{unrepeatable individual substances}}.$$

By contrast, for instance ontology under IP the proportion is:

$$\frac{\text{predicative}}{\text{unpredicative}} = \frac{\text{unrepeatable relation instances}}{\text{repeatable relation intensions}}.$$

Principles IP and RL also distinguish the particularism I am advancing from that of trope theory, called by some 'moderate nominalism', whose property instances 'free-float' in being posited as unattached to, and not dependent for their existence upon, any relata. With its nonpredicative unit properties, trope theory avoids the untoward consequences of the thesis of predicable possession but, by the same token cannot solve the problem of complexity. By contrast, the emphasis in IP and RL is that relation instances are combinatorial, bridging connectors among otherwise isolated terms. This is true a fortiori of the limiting monadic case of properties. If, on the contrary, the defining *relating* of relations is ignored, and what is affirmed is only the truism that relations are ontically dependent upon some relata, then the classic error of reducing relations to properties of each relatum becomes plausible. By extension, if monadic properties are not seen as the limiting case of relating relations, hence as not dependent as predicative upon some subject, they likewise stand on their own, in need of no subject to which to attach. Hence 'subjects' are eliminated as well. Multiply these free-standing properties into unrepeated but exactly resembling instances, and we arrive at a nominalistic trope theory.

Indicative of the general confusion over predication is the fact that the principle of instance predicates (IP) has been adopted (or rejected) by philosophers on both sides of the instance realist/nominalist divide. It has been adopted, for example, by realist scholastics and by the nominalists Ockham and Stout but denied by the realists Wolterstorff and Strawson and the nominalists Williams and Campbell. Wolterstorff holds that it is the universal (e.g., Wisdom) that is predicative of a subject (e.g., of Socrates), an instance or 'case' of the universal (Socrates' wisdom) being a nonpredicative aspect; whereas Williams and Campbell in their trope theory deny that any entity, universal or instance, is predicative. Closer to trope theory, Strawson holds that neither universals nor their instances are predicative but that there is a third category of fundamental entities, 'attributive ties', one subtype of which connects in parallel the corresponding instances to the same subjects. Though a refinement upon commonsense realism, I will argue that the standard instance realism exemplified by Wolterstorff and Strawson cannot avoid, in light of its assumptions, the inevitable positing of bare particulars as the ultimate individuators, whereas trope theorists, for their part, cannot account for the *unity* of a complex thick particular. To anticipate in regard to trope theory, there is with respect to the problem of unity a defeating circularity. Tropes have no 'attaching' aspect; their unity or 'togetherness' in constituting a thick particular must be accounted for by positing some uniquely ordained relation of 'compresence', which, to perform its ontic duty, must be predicative—that is, actually relating. Yet, as required of all relations in trope theory (as I shall argue), compresence reduces to monadic properties of the subject tropes so related and hence can be but further tropes, which, by the theory, are nonpredicative. Consequently, thick particulars dissolve back into disjoint atomistic tropes, and the goal in positing a compresence relation is defeated.

The unification problem is avoided if properties and relations are assayed as *predicative individuals*, for which both individuation and status as unifier reside, as it were, in the predicate rather than the subject(s). The principal difficulty for the instance realist is to account for the individuation of an instance and for how this unrepeatable aspect can be linked to a repeatable intension. I shall take up this issue at the appropriate place, after rehearsing the arguments that expose the bare-particular-plus-universal conception of particulars as specious. For what the dialectic leading to bare particulars shows, as I shall attempt to make clear, is that although it is true that for every individual it is possible to distinguish the two aspects of unrepeatability and repeatability, nevertheless, this must be, as Armstrong puts it, "a distinction without a relation."[33] The particular and the universal are dual aspects of a single entity and are not separate, albeit linked, relata of some further, subtle ontic relation. But, metaphorically, to collapse the ontic space between the repeatable (universal) and the unrepeatable (individual) is necessarily to effect the fusion that I here call a 'relation instance'.

With regard to scholastic moderate realism, the instance ontology developed below turns out (though this was not anticipated) to have aspects that are remarkably close to, and an explanatory extension of, the theory of *haecceitas*, or 'thisness', advanced by Duns Scotus and in an allied form by Francisco Suarez. For Scotus, a substantial form, or *natura* (the 'such that' [Greek *toionde*], or 'whatness' [Latin *quiddity*])—for example, Man—is 'contracted' and made unrepeatable by the haecceitas of the individual substance—for example, the thisness of Socrates. Though the universal and the individuating thisness of substances are 'formally' distinguishable in the intellect, they are necessarily inseparable extra-conceptually, constituting two aspects of a single entity. This is in keeping with the scholastic maxim that only individuals exist extramentally. In a parallel fashion, I will argue that relations are 'contracted' when they are predicative and that, when abstracted from any individuating relata, are nonpredicative intension residues that are (potentially) repeatable—that is, universal. The contents of the latter are half-truths, in that relation universals do not relate and that, insofar as they do fulfill their relating role, they are 'contracted' to instances.

Predicate Senses and Intensions

The principle of relata linking (RL), which asserts that the existence of a relation instance R_i^n presupposes the existence of n relata among which R_i^n is predicated, must not be confused with the thesis that for each n-adic universal R^n there is at least one n-tuple of entities that exemplify R^n. That is, RL is not to be identified with the thesis that every universal is exemplified. The later, widely held thesis (e.g., by Armstrong, Grossmann, and Hochberg) is said to be justified on the grounds that the alternative is exaggerated Platonism with its hypostatized universals. This, I propose, is a mistaken implication, one that turns upon too narrow a conception of the term 'universal'. Armstrong, for example, uses it to refer to repeatable, extra-conceptual aspects of reality: specifically, those contents which are the properties of and relations between spatiotemporal particulars.[34] By contrast, the conceptual *sense* of grammatical predicates, or 'general concepts', does not, for Armstrong, coincide with that of extra-conceptual universals, it being the job of total science ot determine which concepts so correspond. If a universal, in Armstrong's sense, were unexemplified, then it would be a separately existing Platonic Form, a posit that both Armstrong and I would reject.

More generally, Armstrong seeks emphatically to avoid the thesis that "has been a disaster for the theory of universals": namely, that universals are the meanings of general terms.[35] If this were the case, then along with exemplified concepts, including the logically concocted, 'Cambridge properties' (e.g., the notorious 'grue'—the property of being green if examined before time t and blue thereafter), the intensions of general terms with empty extensions (e.g., 'unicorn', 'philogiston', 'the prime between 13 and 17') would all have to exist extra-conceptually as universals if the term 'universal' were interpreted in Armstrong's sense. I concur in rejecting this theory as well. Yet, I would propose that there is a more accurate and theoretically adequate way of construing the relationship between senses and intensions (universals), one that cuts reality closer to its joints. Though the particular view of intensions offered here has no direct bearing upon the main arguments for relations and their instances that follow, it does go some way toward providing an ontological and epistemological synthesis, which the prevailing alternatives, as I understand them, do not. Included here is a clarification of the conceptual components of moderate realism.

In what follows, the term 'sense' will be understood in a standard, non-

Fregean way as designating what is known by, or the cognitive content of, meaningful linguistic expressions. In other standard terminology, the sense of an expression is said to be its *connotation, meaning*, or corresponding *concept*— what was apparently intended by the *lekton* of the Stoics and the *significatio* of medieval logicians. The sense of a term is the means whereby the denotation or reference, if any, is determined. Synonymy is the identity condition for senses.

Advocates argue that senses are the subjects of conceptual psychology and are an essential element in the semantics of any natural language, their theoretical necessity being brought to the fore particularly in the areas of propositional attitudes, identity statements, and vacuous reference. It is held that any plausible philosophy of mind must quantify over senses and theorize their combinations into complex senses. Weighing against the well-known Quinean critique of senses as lacking an acceptable identity criterion is the psychological datum, not explained away by extensional semantics, that extensionally equivalent general, multiple-reference terms like 'equilateral triangle' and 'equiangular triangle' or 'renate' and 'cordate' or singular reference terms like 'Evening Star' and 'Morning Star' are not identical in content. For, understanding the language, it is possible for a person to know (believe, desire, hope, etc.) that the first of each pair is predicated of or denotes an individual a but not to know (etc.) the same for the extensional partner. I shall return to Quine's critique of senses and of intensions generally below.

Senses can be subdivided in the following manner. As described previously, to declarative sentences, say of the forms 'F(a)' or 'aRb', there correspond as complex senses the propositions F(a) and R(a,b). These complex senses decompose into senses for the subject terms 'a' and 'b', the so-called individual concepts, and into the predicate senses designated by the incomplete (Frege's "unsaturated") expressions 'F(..)' and 'R(.,.)'. Though again not central to what follows, by positing individual concepts, I am advocating a description theory of names (Frege, Searle, Katz) over a direct reference theory (Mill, Kripke), one for which I take there to be strong arguments.[36] The link between the individual concept (or whatever is taken as its substitute) and the predicate sense, which unifies the two into a proposition, is a function not of the predicate sense but of an implicit proposition-forming relation.[37] This is how for true negative propositions—for example, ¬F(a)—it is possible to avoid the embarrassment of having to posit corresponding 'negative facts': that is, ':¬F(a)'; negative proposition ¬F(a) is true precisely because predicate sense F(..)—specifically, a corresponding instance—is not predicative of a, so does not serve to form with a a fact complex. Now, by an abstractive process, it is possible to 'nominalize the predicate senses'; corresponding to predicate senses F(..) and R(.,.) are the 'nominalized' senses F and R, respectively. For example, corresponding to the true sentences 'Apple a is red' and 'a is to the right of b' are the abstracted predicate senses 'is red' and 'is to the right of', from which in turn can be abstracted the nominalized senses Red and Right-of. This process is marked in English by the transition from predicate adjectives—for example, '(is) wise', '(is) happy'—or transitive verbs—such as 'is in love with', 'is the cause of'—to the abstract nouns 'wisdom', 'happiness', 'love', 'causation', and so forth. A similar abstractive process is evident in going from some verbs to their gerunds: for example, 'swims' to 'swimming', or 'thinks' to 'thinking'. The abstractive process from the more complex predicate senses F(..) and R(.,.) to the less complex nominalized senses F and R is one of conceptually removing the combinatorial, or linking, aspect from the richer and, in one sense, more accurate predicate senses. The predicate senses F(..) and R(.,.) are more accurate, not in the sense that contents F and R are not contained exactly in the contents F(..) and R(.,.) respectively, but only in the sense that F(..) and R(.,.) are closer to the combinatorial status than these senses have in the corresponding facts (I say only 'closer', since it is my contention here that in the actual facts the predicate senses, as predicative, are individuated).

A standard, non-Fregean interpretation of the ontic status of senses is that they are psychological entities, identical to concepts, and are subjective insofar as they are dependent for their existence upon the individual mind that possesses them. This, I take it, is Armstrong's view when he seeks to distinguish what he takes to be subjective, conceptual predicate senses, some of which are arbitrarily generated, from objective universals. It is possible, however, that the boundaries between the conceptual/extra-conceptual and the objective/subjective do not coincide. For example, Aristotelian/scholastic realists would not accept Armstrong's bifurcation, holding instead that there are universals—for example, Red, Round, Man—that exist both as such, conceptually, when known, and extra-conceptually 'in' things. This overlapping of extensions of conceptual predicate senses and extra-conceptual 'universals' is not necessary for either a coherent ontology or an epistemology, but it is a strong candidate for both. Because of this possibility, but more particularly because there are both conceptual and extra-conceptual facts (i.e., relation complexes), each with ontic predicates consisting in a predicative aspect and a repeatable content, I will use the term 'intension' (which I take to be synonymous with 'universal') to cover both types of contents. Hence, predicate senses are the subclass of intensions that exist conceptually as known but may also exist per se, extra-conceptually and independent of any cognition. The latter are an objective of total science and may never be known ultimately.

According to the moderate realism advocated here, extra-conceptual intensions exist outside the intellect only as aspects of their instances, individuated to the specific relata among which they are ontically predicative. On the other hand, the contents of relations existing conceptually as known cannot only be abstracted from their instances—for example, as Red can be abstracted from a red percept—but in some cases can be freely constructed prior to, and independent of, any instances, whether motivated by romantic fancy, as with the senses of 'unicorn' and 'fountain of youth', or by serious scientific theorizing, as with the senses of 'ether', 'natural place', 'bodily humors', 'spontaneous generation', and so forth.

I note that, in addition to obviously arbitrarily concocted senses, there are predicate senses such as truth, identity, and exemplification that are not arbitrary but fundamental to our understanding, yet nevertheless exist only conceptually. An inventory of extra-conceptual reality would find nothing corresponding to these otherwise redundant relations; rather, they arise internally in response to our need for concept management and assessment in order to negotiate reality successfully. Outside the workings of finite intellects, facts simply obtain. An assertion that certain subjects exemplify a relation adds nothing to the corresponding fact. Likewise, for the assertion of truth of the proposition stating the fact, as Aristotle observed, "Falsity and truth are not in things, but in thought" (*Metaphysics* 1027b25). As regards identity, meaningful identity statements like '$a = b$' (by contrast with '$a = a$') convey the epistemically useful information that two distinct intensions have the same extension.

In adopting the view that predicate senses form a subset of intensions (= universals), I am rejecting the aforementioned thesis that every universal is exemplified. This thesis is true only when the term 'intension' is restricted to the extra-conceptual, as Armstrong would have it. In either case, when an n-place intension is exemplified by an n-tuple of entities, the effect is a complex whole, a fact—in the one case conceptual (e.g., a proposition), in the other case extra-conceptual (e.g., a physical complex).

The epistemic problem is to determine which predicate senses (conceptual universals) correspond to extra-conceptual contents, a job for total science. I cannot here invest the considerable time necessary to defend a detailed epistemology; arguments for the proposed instance ontology will require effort enough. I will, however, discuss briefly the epistemology of *structural realism*, which is a natural concomitant of the one-category ontology of *instance structuralism* advocated here. First, the realist maintains that there must be a 'real'—that is, nonconceptual—universals in order to account for the nonarbitrary commonalities of our experience. However, it is not necessary for the realist to maintain that these repeatables be identical with the intensions of which we are or can be aware—predicate senses. Predicate senses may be completely idiosyncratic to the apprehending subject. The contrary position is that of naive classical realism. The standard 'arguments from illusion', as well as established science, tell us that corresponding to many concepts, both those that are simple and non-inferentially given (e.g., secondary sense qualities of smells, tastes, colors, sounds, and tactile sensations) and those that are complex and constructed theoretically (as above), there exist no extra-conceptual contents; for example, there is no existence independent of the intellect of a content we refer to by the general term 'red'. Any immediate experience of an instance of Red—for example, that of an observed apple a—is the supervening phenomenal effect of a certain state structure of the brain, which in turn is the end effect of a long causal chain of functionally related physical event structures (involving light and physical space, the eyes, and the nervous system), starting from a particular molecular surface structure of apple a, but where the monadic property Red or any instance of it forms no part of any link in this chain of 'objective' structures. If this sequential structure is duplicated in the observation of apple b, then we shall have the experience that b is red and the reflective knowledge that the reds of a and b are identical, hence the theoretical knowledge that the particular surface structures of a and b are identical in a certain respect—that is, isomorphic in the relevant respect. It is identity or isomorphism of *structure* (or substructure of subsuming larger structures), whether dynamic or static, physical or logical, that is central here and whose epistemic importance was once emphasized by Russell.[38]

Taking issue with the conceptualist view, some philosophers (e.g., Frege and Church) have maintained that in order to account for the fact of objectivity exhibited in the use of a common language as a medium through which different minds communicate, reason, and come to agreement (or meaningful disagreement), particularly in mathematics and science, one must posit a third realm (not conceptual and not physical) of objective 'senses' or 'thoughts'. In learning and using a language, individual minds become aware of these objective intensions as associated with the same terms, a kind of mental seeing of a single, independent, publicly knowable entity, and it is this awareness of numerically the same shared content that accounts for our mutual understanding. Of course, against this view is the fact that it suffers from the same severe epistemological problems as standard Platonic realism. Moreover, it is possible to account for the objectivity of communication and thought without positing a 'third realm' of objective concepts. Sense experience, whether in the context of communication or in nonlinguistic perception, is transference of structure, and it is structure that accounts for the intersubjective. Russell emphasized this point, saying:

> It appears generally that if A and B are two complex structures and A can cause B, then there must be some degree of identity of structure between A and B. It is because of this principle that a complex of sensations can give us information about the complex that caused them. If you see something hexagonal, then, since hexagonality is a structural property, the physical object which has caused your visual sensation must be hexagonal, although its hexagonality will be in space which is not identical with visual space.[39]

It is plausible, then, that all that is necessary to account for the objectivity of thought and language is isomorphism of structure. The nodes and the content of the relations (instances) between the nodes in one structure need not be identical with the respective nodes and relation contents of a second structure; yet, in their higher-order formal properties, the two structures can be identical—that is, isomorphic. Take the example of color concepts. For effective communication and the negotiations entailed in practical living, it does not matter if the qualitative content of my concepts of individual colors is identical to that of your concepts. What matters is that, in our respective conceptual color schemes, what I know as 'red' corresponds to the same position as what you know as 'red'; that is, that they occur in the same color-wheel relationshps with the other respective color concepts—for example, the concept we are conscious of when perceiving the top light of a traffic signal. In general, the view here broached is that a world of sensa proprietary to a single mind is stimulated into existence by, and constantly augmented and corrected against other like worlds through, the shared structure endemic to language and sense experience, including shared sensory/neural apparatus. These brief remarks are sufficient to indicate what I take to be a highly plausible epistemology of structural realism. I would add that the explanatory concepts of structure and isomorphism remain opaque to many philosophers, especially those who have not consciously persuaded themselves of the erroneous nature of the property reduction of relations and the containment model of predication. (Russell had the advantage of an intellectual formation shaped by study of the relational logic intrinsic to foundational mathematics and logic.) It is my claim, further, that epistemological isomorphisms presuppose ontological structure, and that neither can be understood properly apart from the conception of structure as a unity-in-diversity, a composition of 'roads and nodes', in which the unifiers, the 'roads', are individuated relation instances.

As promised above, it is appropriate to end this section with a limited, but relevant, discussion of Quine's critique of intensions, one that will afford an opportunity to consider some central issues concerning spatiotemporal relations. These issues go to the heart of Quine's 'naturalistic' ontology, an empiricist/nominalist rival to the instance realism advocated here. For a different, but extensive, critique from the perspective of linguistics, the reader is referred to the previously cited negative analyses by Katz of Quine's arguments against intensional semantics.[40]

Quine and others with nominalist proclivities take issue with the notion of intensions on the grounds that intensions lack reputable identity conditions, a disadvantage said to be absent for *bona fide* individuals—for example, concrete physical objects and abstract classes. According to these philosophers, what is required for the admittance of an entity of kind N into one's ontology is a criterion for reidentification of such an entity as an entity identical-as-kind-N. The identity criterion sought is that of the more specific identity-of-a-kind-N, not what would be a definition of the general identity relation. Quine asserts that "we have an acceptable notion of class, or physical object, or attribute, or any other sort of object, only insofar as we have an acceptable principle of individuation for *that sort of object*. There is no entity without identity."[41] For Quine, a paradigm example of such a specification is that of the kind *physical object*:

x is-identical-as-a-*physical-object*-to y if and only if x occupies the same space-time positions as y.

For objects to occupy the same space-time positions means that they occupy the same spatial points at the same temporal moments. A second proposed paradigm example is that of classes:

x is-identical-as-a-*class*-to y if and only if x contains the same elements as y.

Of course, as Quine observes, the latter criterion is dependent upon the existence of acceptable identity conditions for the elements. If the elements are physical objects, then we have the right to admit the sets that include them to our ontology. According to Quine, since proffered entities like intensions and propositions do not occupy space-time and have resisted noncircular identity criteria, they are best avoided. For intensions generally the criterion of identity would be:

x is-identical-as-an-*intension*-to y if and only if x is synonymous with y.

For Quine, synonymy is one of a nexus of concepts, including analyticity and necessity,[42] that he finds suspect as vague, obscure, and definitionally inbred, unlike familiar, public, scientifically fundamental physical objects and extensional aggregates thereof. This is the motivation for Quine's thesis that first-order logic is canonical; whereas second- and higher-order logics, quantifying as they do over intensions, are committed to intensions, given Quine's adoption of the objectual (or 'range') interpretation of quantifiers. Put as a slogan: To be is to be the value of a bound variable.[43] Quine will not allow a linguistic predicate to refer (for the referent would then be a universal), hence its semantic relation to the referent of linguistic subjects (entities over which quantifiers are officially to range) is what Quine proposes to be the primitive relation *of being true of.*[44]

In defense of intensions, however, we can make the following observations. First, Quine's objection to intensions as lacking acceptable identity conditions has as one of its grounds the restriction of conceptual explication to definitions of the standard material biconditional form, as exemplified above. This restriction is consonant with nominalist extensionalism, so, to that extent, stacks the deck in Quine's favor. But biconditional definitions are not the only form of concept explication; nor, in fact, in the case of absolutely fundamental concepts can they be very informative—a weakness Quine can exploit only by misinterpreting it. Quine impugns intensions by arguing that the identity conditions for them require the notion of synonymy and that there can be no definitional explication of any of the concepts in the inter-definitional circle of synonymy, analyticity, necessity, self-contradictoriness, and so forth that does not presuppose the very explication it intends. There is no definitional explication that does not appeal to members of the tight kinship circle, each of which is in as much need of explication as the next, according to Quine. The implication is that the explanatory circle is vicious, each concept in the closed chain being equally obscure and when taken together mutually suspect, and so to be rejected. But this conclusion is too hasty. As Strawson and Grice pointed out in their classic reply to Quine, a point reiterated subsequently,[45] it is an unwarranted inference from 'x does not make satisfactory sense (there being, at least at present, no satisfactory explanation of it)' to 'x does not make sense'. At a deeper level, however, constituting a pillar of Quine's circularity argument, is his assumption that conceptual explication is restricted to biconditional definitions, in particular those that do not require appeal to the same family of concepts as that to which the *definiendum* belongs. By contrast, there is the widely used alternative of explicating concepts by specifying their place in a system or network of *relationships* with other concepts. The most obvious examples are the formalized axiomatic systems of mathematics and logic. As Strawson elsewhere observes, "For philosophical explanation is not a steady reductive movement in the direction of the intrinsically clear, but rather an exhibition of connections and relations between notions none of which is immediately transparent to philosophical understanding. The clarity is in the connections."[46] We cannot, for example, define any of the geometric concepts of point, line, space, boundary, and so forth without calling upon some of the other concepts from this geometric family; but this is no reason to reject geometry. Katz makes the same point with regard to propositional logic.[47] None of the standard propositional connectives can be biconditionally defined except in terms of one or more other connectives, but this does not mean that we have to reject propositional logic. The connectives are defined by their context within the system of their basic relations with other connectives, which is made most perspicuous in a formalized system. Note, however, that to allow for this type of *systemic* explanation is to presuppose relations existing intensionally and unreduced, something Quine seeks to avoid and indeed does avoid (ostensibly) by his restriction of explications to biconditional form. But then Quine's circularity argument is not an argument with neutral premises whereby intensions have been discredited, but rather one that simply draws out the implications of assumptions consonant with nominalism.

Identity conditions for intensions are bound to be less ostensibly informative than those for nonintensions, yet this does not impugn intensions; rather, it goes to their fundamental status. Implicit in the informative use of identity is the essential appeal to intensions, a point I shall make both here and in another way in chapter 10. Our best account of identity is that when we assert 'a = b' for ordinary objects a and b, we are saying that what was understood under two different 'guises' is really the same entity or, as Frege would put it, the same entity "even though it is given in a different way."[48] What this amounts to in more precise language is that the referents of the terms 'a' and 'b', as determined by the semantically associated intensions, are the same. Two different intensions—for example, that of the 'Morning Star' and that of the 'Evening Star'—can have the same referent. What makes true identity statements of the form 'a = b' informative is not only the new knowledge that the referents of 'a' and 'b' coincide in a single entity, but the newly established fact that the corresponding but distinct intensions of 'a' and 'b' can be conjoined to form a single, more complete, integrated, and implicationally richer set of descriptions of the same entity. The latter is the real epistemic boon of true identity statements.[49] There is no epistemic gain in statements of the form 'a = a', not only because the referent is obviously the same, but also because there is no net aggregate increase in the descriptive knowledge of a resulting from integrating distinct intensions. Now, when we move up to the level of true identity (synonymy) statements among intensions themselves, A = B, we have the limiting case of the referent of each term being the intension of that term; so, in coinciding, there is again no aggregate increase in knowledge concerning the single referent intension. Such statements are informative only insofar as they establish that linguistic tokens of types 'A' and 'B' refer to the same intension (e.g., intension of 'bachelor' = intension of 'unmarried male'); though this is useful, it does not clarify the single intension involved but merely presupposes it. Yet again, this is no flaw of intensions; rather, these observations concerning identity go to show the fundamental, presupposed role of intensions in the concept of identity and in the limiting case of synonymy itself.

I will make this point concerning synonymy another way. We said above that, for Quine, the criterion for identity of intension was to be stated in the form

(i)   x is-identical-as-an-intension-to y if and only if x is synonymous with y.

For Quine to think that he can discredit intensions through their identity conditions by discrediting synonymy implies that he holds (i) to be true. Now, the very fact that we are able to understand and assert as true statement (i), prior to any analysis or warranting procedure, stems from the fact that we understand and recognize as true the asssertion

(ii) 'is synonymous with' is synonymous with 'is identical as an intension with'.

That is, Quine, at least in this case, must treat 'if and only if' in (i) not as material equivalence, but as intensional equivalence. This is why, if we reject the notion of synonymy, we must likewise reject the notion of 'is identical as an intension to' and so abandon hope of explicating the identity relation for intensions. Observe, however, that to have come to this point, we must in statement (ii) *use* and understand in the metalanguage the very term 'synonymy' that we reject as too obscure when *mentioning* it as a term of the object-language. Synonymy has been used to reject synonymy. Again, what I propose this points to is the inescapable fundamentality of intensions and their synonymy. I shall make this same point presently with regard to the specific concepts of space-time.

As a second response to Quine, I would maintain that he is correct insofar as he observes what is the practical matter of fact that we do continually rely upon space-time position as a means of reidentifying objects. The question is how we are to understand this. There are two alternatives: (1) the substantivist view that space-time consists of a plenum of individual space-time points which, as relata, sustain a set of supervening spatial and temporal relations between them (however these relations are ultimately construed); (2) the relationist (Leibnizian) view that space-time is the total spatial and temporal relations that exist among physical objects as their relata. In the first case, two physical objects are said to be identical if and only if they 'occupy' the same set of space-time points, the spatial and temporal relations of the latter being attributed in a secondary sense to the occupying objects. In the second sense, physical objects are identical if and only if their relations to all other objects are in sum the same. Traditionally, this latter view was thought to give a certain unreality to space because of the prevailing reductionist view of relations. This perception disappears, however, when relations are maintained in their full reality as existing 'between' objects, the more so when conceived as existing as unrepeatable instances, as advocated here. The physical universe consists in a structure of physical objects with an inter-network of spatiotemporal relation instances between them. It has been asserted that modern relativity physics provides strong evidence for the relationist view.[50]

But for Quine the relationist alternative will not do, because it requires that the specifying spatiotemporal relations among objects be taken intensionally. To take the relations extensionally in a nominalist, set-reductionist manner is to reduce these relations to sets of their relata—that is, to physical objects. But now, having argued in a circle, these objects remain without identity conditions. To achieve his purpose, Quine must take space-time to be composed of point-individuals among which exist spatial and temporal relations, but which are independent of physical objects which may or may not occupy identifying sets of these underlying points. But Quine must now require of these space-time points the same ontic standard to which he holds all other kinds of entities. Specifically, he must be able to replace the ellipsis dots in

x is identical-as-space-time-point-to y if and only if $x \ldots y$.

There is apparently only one way: with some spatiotemporal relation R. But if we replace the ellipsis dots with such a relation, we cannot assay it extensionally. For otherwise, we have a difficulty analogous to the one just mentioned: namely, that if R is taken extensionally, it must reduce to a certain set of sets of its relata, x and y; yet it was precisely for these entities that we were seeking a reidentification criterion. Again, Quine's extensionalist/nominalist program is circularly thwarted, analogous to the circularity that he finds in the identity conditions for intensions.

There are further issues here worth exploring. One that I shall mention in passing is the difficulty of explicating the 'occupying' relationship between an object and a set of space-time points that singly or collectively are nonidentical to the object. Rather, I shall turn instead to the weakness inherent in the concept of space taken as composed of atomistic points. This, of course, is a well-worn line of argument, going back to Zeno and reemphasized in modern times by Bradley and the early Russell,[51] but one whose relevance to the irreducibility of relations taken intensionally is not generally appreciated. The assumption on the first, remaining alternative, (1) above, is that any spatial extension, no matter how small, is made up of a plurality of individual point-atoms, each of which is a relatum for spatial relations with other points of that extension. Now either these points are extended, or they are not. If they are extended, then they are themselves composed of points; but this is contrary to the assumption that points are the ultimate quanta out of which space is built. Space was to be composed of points, not points of space. Hence, points cannot be extended; they are dimensionless atoms. But now space and any part of it are composed of sets of points, each of which is not extended. From where does extension as a characteristic of the whole come if it is not a characteristic of any component? Extension does not supervene upon *classes* (or *sets*) qua classes. We cannot identify extension with a mere collection of points, any more than we can identify a house with a mere pile of bricks. The unity of a class is not the unity of space; extension requires a relatedness among objects other than that of mere collection. This kind of relatedness is spatial relation, and thus we arrive again at the necessity of nonreduced spatial relations. The same argument can be repeated mutatis mutandis for moments of time. The upshot of both arguments is that, *pace* Quine, the appeal to space-time as an identity criterion for objects does not succeed in avoiding spatial and temporal relations taken intensionally; indeed, it requires appeal to relation intensions, the very entities Quine seeks to avoid.

Beyond the fact that space-time relations taken intensionally cannot be eliminated, the above argument highlights a further weakness in the point-plus-relation conception of the composition of space. At a minimum, points are to be individuals that support spatial relations as relata. But what can these points be? If they have any content or intension, this content must be spatial in nature, for otherwise a point would be a nonspatial entity occupying space, not the space occupied. Yet, if the content of a point is spatial, this can only mean that it is extended, and, as we saw above, this is impossible. But then we have the problem observed by Leibniz: "Space is something absolutely uniform, and, without the things placed in it, one point of space does not absolutely differ in any respect whatsoever from another point of space."[52] In other words, points reduce on analysis to a subclass of bare particulars: namely, those reserved to be the relata of spatial relations. But the concept of bare particulars, however they are called into service, is incoherent (as I have already argued and will argue further in chapter 2), which means that we are forced to replace the point-plus-relation conception of space with the simpler relation conception—Leibniz's view. The relata for spatial relations are not geometric points manufactured theoretically for the purpose, but physical objects that 'occupy' space. Indeed, here we have a straightforward, coherent way of understanding what it is to 'occupy space': namely, being the relata of spatial relations. But with all this,

Quine's gambit for avoiding intensions by appealing to space-time becomes even weaker. With regard to identity conditions, physical objects are no better or worse off than intensions themselves, it being a delusion to claim the contrary.

Parenthetically, Campbell, in his defense of trope theory, extends with regard to space the implications of Quine's nominalism. Campbell finds himself forced to conceive of space as a plenum of points, relations under his nominalism having been consistently reduced to their 'foundations'—that is, properties of points. Now, as Campbell observes, points must each be unique and distinguishable from other points; yet, as Leibniz noted, in themselves and without regard to their relations to other points, there is nothing intrinsic to one point to differentiate it from another—there is no entity that can be appealed to in order to identify point x and distinguish it from some other point y. In order to save space-time, Campbell must posit an individuating entity C for each point. He observes:

> If we do not opt for pure individuality [= a bare particular(?)], whatever it is that distinguishes them [points] from one another will serve as a foundation for position. . . . We do not need, fortunately, any very precise idea of what such a distinguishing characteristic might be. For our purposes, we can fancy each point carries a unique label (its name in the mind of God, or its coordinate numbers in some arbitrarily selected coordinate scheme). We can be even more circumspect and say only that each point is distinguished from every other point by the distinguishing characteristic C required by absolutism about space-time.[53]

This is, on the face of it, a desperate, ad hoc maneuver, necessitated ultimately by the reductive elimination of spatial relations. Granted the same license, we could make a parallel claim for bare particulars: that each one is distinguished from others by the posited assignment to each of a proprietary entity, by God or otherwise. Campbell rightly refuses to salvage bare particulars in this manner, but the fact that he is led to a conception of points analogous to bare particulars should give him and like-minded nominalists pause. Points are useful geometric fictions, but they disappear into pure relatedness upon ontological analysis.

Finally, with regard to Quine, there is what is perhaps the most damaging observation that could be made concerning his reidentification criterion for ontological admissibility, which I shall wait until chapter 10 to lay out fully. It is that Quine's canonical first-order logic cannot provide a definition that is sufficient for the identity relation itself, let alone for the concept of identical-as-kind-N, of which it must form an essential component. The best that can be achieved is indiscernibility, or indiscernible-as-kind-N, and this defeats the intent of Quine's criterion, which was to be a criterion of reidentification. This point has been made by Peter Geach and will be generalized in chapter 10, where I will show that a logic that quantifies over both intensions and their instances can distinguish identity from indiscernibility. The above arguments all support the thesis that in the explanatory enterprise one cannot avoid an appeal to intensions.

The Property Reduction of Relations

It is interesting that, historically, the combinatorial nature of relations was explicitly defended by many philosophers, including several of those previously named. A standard, recurring argument, advanced both by proponents, as displaying the definitional linking of relations, and detractors, as showing the absurdity of the very concept of relations, is what is now called *Bradley's regress*.[54] This classic argument, which I will outline presently, is crucial and enlightening in many respects and will be analyzed in depth in chapter 8. What is equally interesting is that, until the late nineteenth century, relations were almost universally (with a few exceptions—e.g., Peter Aureoli (1280–1322)[55]) held to be reducible to properties, a specious reduction whose distorting legacy includes a tension with the understanding that, definitionally, relations are 'between' two or more entities. Frequently repeated is Aristotle's description of relations as the "least of all things a kind of entity or substance" (*Metaphysics* 1088a22). From the perspective of the ontology that I am arguing for, Aristotle is both right and wrong. He is wrong in holding that relations are least of all *entities*. To the contrary, relations and their instances can sustain a viable one-category ontology, whereas the traditional two-category individual/universal ontology proves to be fundamentally flawed. On the other hand, Aristotle errs in saying that relations are not 'substance' in the sense of the *Metaphysics*; indeed, in the latter, relations fill the explanatory bill exactly: relations (as instances) are both a 'this' and predicative among, hence structure, a diversity of subjects (the 'matter'). Aristotle is right in saying that relations are not substances in the sense of the *Categories*, because in the final analysis nothing is 'substance' in this sense, for the ultimate ontic atoms are not the nonpredicative subjects of other predicative but lesser entities; rather, they are all predicative relation instances. Higher-level complexes formed from the latter come closest to Aristotelian substances.

Under the monadic reduction of relations, the special, limiting case of properties is treated as paradigm, and the more general polyadic case is reduced to properties of each relatum, though each with a characteristic mode of being 'toward' other relata. Finding a home for this uneliminable toward aspect, which is prima facie a specific, second-order asymmetric relation induced by analysis from the given first-order relation, proves to be an embarrassing problem. In preliminary form the monadic reduction thesis is formally stated as:

Thesis of Property Reduction of Relations:
For any formal (binary) relation $\ulcorner R \urcorner$ and relata x and y, there exist relation properties R′ and R″ such that the proposition that $\ulcorner R(x,y) \urcorner$ is true $\equiv [R'(x) \cdot R''(y) \cdot R''$ toward $y \cdot R''$ toward $x]$.

In such a reduction the characteristics of the binary case are reinterpreted to conform to the unique characteristics of the monadic case—the monadic tail wagging the polyadic dog, so to speak. Here the combinatorial, 'between' nature of relations is eliminated and replaced by properties whose status is to be 'in' their singular subjects, yet somehow point to their correlatives without this pointing being a further binary relation.

Note that the property reduction thesis yields as a consequence the common assertion (e.g., advanced by Bradley) that relations imply diversity among their relata; that is, there are no truly reflexive relations (there are no relations R such that $R(x,x)$ for any x). By the above reduction thesis, if one assumes $R(x,x)$ for some R and x, then

The proposition that $\ulcorner R(x,x) \urcorner$ is true $\equiv [R'(x) \cdot R'(x) \cdot R'$ toward $x \cdot R'$ toward $x]$,

which is a redundant equivalent of

The proposition that $\ulcorner R(x,x) \urcorner$ is true $\equiv [R'(x) \cdot R'$ toward $x]$.

But the right bijunct can only be interpreted to mean that R′ is a monadic property of x. Hence the assertion $\ulcorner R(x,x) \urcorner$ is equivalent to the assertion of the monadic property R′ of x. Thus a reflexive relation reduces to a single property of a single subject, so is not truly relational in involving multiple subjects.

The spurious bifurcation of the nature of relations under the property reduction thesis has had far-reaching and insidious effects. The easy illusion is that
the intension of a relation R, taken to be what is officially relational, dissipates
within one or more relation-properties, while to account for the characteristic
linking aspect of the relation, there remains a pale, contentless 'toward'—a
blank connection. The toward aspect is an intensionless association, a connection obtaining independently of the natures (i.e., the intensions) of the relata.
With the presumed elimination of polyadic intensions, it is the nonrelational
toward component that remains as the uniquely identifying characteristic of the
relational fact. It is then an easy step—indeed, a necessary one, I think—to the
thesis that relational facts characterized as 'blank associations' are in every
case a product of minds (ens rationis). The conceptual status of relations was the
expressed view of many philosophers, including Spinoza, Leibniz, Gassendi,
Hobbes, Locke, and Hume.[56]

It is instructive to consider Hume in this regard. For Hume, the 'free association' conception of relations abets his skepticism concerning possible referents
for the concepts of 'self' and 'substance' and, in particular, renders plausible his
counter-intuitive 'constant conjunction' reduction of causal relations. Hume
was rightly critical of the implication of the containment model of predication
that the truth condition for 'A is the cause of B' is the fact that *in* A is the
property of the Power-to-Produce-B. He observes, "For the effect is totally
different from the cause, and consequently can never be discovered in it,"[57] and
that if it were otherwise, then by pure thought alone we could analyze A and
know that effect B must follow.[58] Moreover, as others have observed, if all effects
were *in* their causes, then the existence of a cause would make for the simultaneous existence of its effect, and thus the entire causal network constituting the
universe would collapse into a single event-moment—not the 'Big Bang', but the
'Big Fizzle'.

Despite his rejection of the contained status of effects, Hume nevertheless
retained the implication of the containment model that relation intensions are,
in effect, to be eliminated. He held that relations arise "from the comparison
which the mind makes";[59] yet, as one of his fundamental principles, he also
held that "the mind never perceives any real connexion among distinct exis-
tences."[60] Perceptions can be "conjoined but not connected." I think it is clear
from the text that, by denying 'real connexion', Hume is denying connection-
under-an-intension, a connection that would not be arbitrary and would obtain

only if the natures of the relata were in agreement with the relation intension (as, say, Is-Brighter-than obtains between two color sensa but not between two odor sensa). It is, for example, the intension of the causal relation that conveys the notion of nomic necessity; hence, with this intension abstracted away, no sense of production remains. Similarly, for the independently real complexes that constitute 'self' and 'substance', when the multifarious intensions that are the contents of the web of relations constituting these structural entities are deleted conceptually, only a skeleton of groundless associations is left—a loose system of externally imposed, unfounded, if constant, conjunctions.

Pace Hume, however, the general denial of 'real connections' is counterfactual. We don't simply experience sensa; we experience them linked under various intensions—that is, related in the proper sense. We experience sensa as related. Likewise in pure conceptual thought, we apprehend concepts connected by 'real' relations—for example, 2 is less than 3, and 7 is a prime divisor of 21—connections that, being more than blank associations, have intensions (e.g., Is-Less-than) that determine the relations' obtaining nonarbitrarily among relata of specific kinds. Of relevance here, both Armstrong and Evan Fales have recently restated the case that among the real connections we experience are certain kinds of causal relations.[61]

The blindness to the relational aspect of experience evidences a prior theoretical bias that selectively filters the epistemic given. In Hume's case it is his 'scientific' program of explaining *all* our concepts in terms of atomic sensa, where, significantly, these sensa are restricted to *monadic* intensions of the external senses (colors, sounds, tastes, etc.) or of reflections (passions and emotions). Such a theory acquires its plausibility from the received tradition, where the polyadic is held reducible to the monadic together with the residue 'toward'. But Hume appears more insightful with regard to relations when he substitutes for the strained toward aspect of traditional reduction the notion of 'conjoined', with its clear sense of being both between and equally dependent upon multiple relata. Though, like the 'toward' of tradition, arbitrary conjunction is not a 'real connection' in Hume's sense of existing as a function of the natures of its relata, it is nevertheless a polyadic intension, albeit a remote, abstract one. Conjunction has formal properties dependent upon this fact: it is symmetric, irreflexive, and nontransitive. The question then arises: Where do we acquire the concept of this, or any other, polyadic intension if the material we have from which to build our concepts ('ideas') consists strictly of monadic sensa? Hume cannot account for his pale theoretical reductum of 'conjunction' any more than he can account for ordinary relations in general. Nor would he think it necessary to give such an account if, with other philosophers of the tradition, he was under the illusion that the elimination of 'real connection' was the elimination of the polyadic—of relations.

Moving on to other issues, we note the historical preoccupation with two-place relations. Until relatively recently, it has been dyadic relations that have received exclusive attention in ontological contexts, and even now in the work of some ontologists (e.g., Campbell[62]). This myopia reenforces the monadic reduction, a maneuver that loses much plausibility with polyacities that are triadic and higher. The reader may find it instructive to attempt a property reduction of the four-place relation in 'John paid a dollar to Bill for a pen'. Unfortunately, whereas the combinatorial aspect is 'writ large' in polyadic relations, in the case of single-subject properties it is far less evident and is easily lost in favor of other analogies, such as the containment model.

We have previously observed that the containment theory of predication is one, if not the principal reason for the classic property reduction of relations. It is therefore worth expanding briefly on what appear to be its background presuppositions. The containment theory is an implication of a more general, subtle inclination that has found various modes of expression in philosophical thought. What could be termed the 'doctrine of the primacy of the unit', it is simply that all ontic explanations are to be given in terms of the posited internal natures of isolated units. The underlying equation is: being = unity = unit (classical substance). Or, as Leibniz would have it, *ens reale* and *unum per se* are equivalent. This equation is in contrast to the one advocated here: namely, being = unity = unification (relation complexes).

A corollary to the primacy of the unit doctrine is the thesis that unification follows from the unit, from the single-subject monadic, not the multiple-subject polyadic. All unification is accounted for by imposing what is already a distinct singularity, and only in that aspect of which it is one, and in no respect in which it is heterogeneous, is it a principle of unification. Unity flows from a prior *one*. Indicative is the description given by the Neoplatonist Plotinus in the *Enneads*, VI. 4. 8:

When we affirm unity in multiplicity we do not mean that the unity has become the multiples; we link the variety in the multiples with the unity which we discern, undivided, in them; and the unity must be understood as forever distinct from them, from separate item and from total; the unity remains true to itself, remains itself, and so long as it remains itself cannot fail within its own scope (and therefore does reach over the multiple).[63]

In sum, *from the unit, unification comes.*

In this regard, one is again reminded of Leibniz, who was stoutheartedly persistent in drawing out the consequences of the unit doctrine. He states: "Only simple things are true things, and the rest are beings by aggregation . . . existing . . . by convention but not by nature."[64] Here Leibniz follows the classic distinction going back to Aristotle (*Metaphysics* 1015b16ff.) between unity *per se* and unity *per accidens*, the former being substantial unity, the latter the lesser unity of an aggregate such as a herd or an army. Consistent with the primacy of the unit doctrine, Leibniz holds that true unity, unity per se, is necessarily internally simple, hence indivisible. He then argues that, since ultimate substances may be true units and all extension is divisible, no such substance is extended. Hence Leibniz's substance monads become nonphysical, ontic points.

Leibniz also allows for complex substances to have unity per se; these are 'organisms' such as humans and animals. Though again, consistent with the unit doctrine, that these complexes are per se unities is because there is a 'dominant monad' that unites other monads by means of a 'substantial chain', the latter a concept borrowed from scholasticism.[65] By contrast, a unity per accidens is "merely a phenomenal unity or a unity in thought, which is insufficient for the reality within the phenomena."[66]

When the unity-is-from-the-unit doctrine is applied to the unification effected by predication, it follows that there must be a single, prior subject that is the source and cause of the possession of it by diverse predicates. This is the motivation for Leibniz's *praedicatum inest subjecto* doctrine. Even the term 'property' derives from the Latin *proprius*, meaning 'one's own'. Aristotle, for example, takes this tack in the *Metaphysics*, where individuated substantial form (e.g., Man) is the principle of unification and the source of emergent properties in an otherwise unorganized 'heap' of secondary matter (e.g., a group of bodily organs). He recognizes that he needs an ingredient in the whole with an ontic status different from that of being just another element and, significantly, uses a version of Bradley's regress to prove this (*Metaphysics* 1041b11–30). As individuated, a substantial form has the status of a subject, since predicates are, for Aristotle, of the nature of universals. Yet, as individuated, substantial form has the requisite oneness necessary under the unit doctrine to account for the unification of the subsumed matter. In this manner, an external, superimposed substantial form is somehow the source of an *intra*-structure. But how a monadic form, individuated or not, can effect such a polyadic complex remains a mystery. What is needed is something that is predicative and, more important, predicative among, *inter se*, a plurality of elements. This is precisely what we know as relations. However, once relations are monadically withdrawn into their relata, then, pace Aristotle, these disconnected relata must collapse into a mere heap. The elimination of relations in favor of properties (including as a special case substantial forms) renders an explanation of structural entities ultimately impossible.

In general, there is a fundamental tension between the primacy of the unit doctrine and *any* pluralist ontology, for a pluralist ontology requires relations of many kinds, starting with the most general 'is coexistent with' and proceeding down to the more specific, here germane subsumption relations of 'participation' and 'exemplification' or the reductionist surrogate for the latter, 'resemblance'. This is to say nothing of spatiotemporal and causal relations. Moreover, even if relations are relegated to the 'just mental', they are still polyadic. Now, because relations are inherently polyadic and so on the side of multiplicity and plurality, from the perspective of the unit doctrine, relations are seen as having the same status as any element in any unification among diverse things—as something requiring the *intra*-unification imposed by a subsuming 'one', not something that causes connectedness and wholeness as *inter*-unifier. Hence, the doctrine requires a telescoping reduction of polyadic predicates to monadic predicates and the latter to a state of containment in a single subject—the property reduction of relations.

There is a second, historically recurring argument that on one interpretation is also said to force us to reject relations as self-contradictory, an argument that, so interpreted, reinforces the containment model of predication. This is the aforementioned Bradley's regress, which, for present purposes, can be summarized as follows. Compare the class $\{a,R,b\}$ and the relational fact $:R(a,b)$. The two wholes are not identical: the class exists necessarily and 'eternally', whereas, for contingent R, the fact $:R(a,b)$ may or may not obtain. What distinguishes the fact from the class is that the unity of the fact is a function of the relation R as it relates a to b, whereas the unity constituting the whole of the class is not a function of R. There is a problem here, however; for it appears that the fact and the class have exactly the same constituents, no more, no less. Hence, the difference between the two wholes cannot be accounted for by any of the shared elements, a, R, b. Consequently, the supposed relating of a to b under R that is to account for the fact :R(a,b) and distinguish it from class $\{a,R,b\}$ cannot be accounted for by R. The only alternative is to posit some implicit, further relation R$'$ such that :R(a,b) = :R$'$((R,a,b). But now, the argument goes, relation R$'$ succumbs to the same analysis given above to R and so requires the posit of a further relation, R$''$, to account for the unity that the relatedness of relations in the previous complexes could not account for. But then, repeating the above reasoning, a third relation, R$'''$, is required, and so on to infinity. The unity of the initial and all subsequent relation facts remains unexplained, despite the fact that this is precisely the defining characteristic of relations as they 'actually relate' their relata. Relations are thus declared illusory as self-contradictory.

Russell, in his famous exchange with Bradley over internal versus external relations, states "that whenever we have two terms x and y related by a relation R, we have a 'complex' or a 'unity'. . . . A complex differs from the mere aggregate of its constituents, since it is one, not many, and the relation which is one of its constituents enters into it as an actually relating relation, and not merely as one member of an aggregate."[67] To this Bradley replied: "My difficulty as to 'unities' remains. Is there anything, I ask, in a unity besides its 'constituents', i.e., the terms and the relation, and if there is anything more, in what does this 'more' consist? . . . What is the difference between a relation which relates in fact and one which does not so relate? And if we accept a strict pluralism, where, I urge, have we any room for this difference?"[68] Russell sees the use of relation terms in natural language as equivocal; corresponding to relation terms used as grammatical predicates (he calls them 'verbs'[69]—for example, 'is in love with' in 'a is in love with b'—are actually relating relations, whereas corresponding nominalizations of the former phrases name inert class concepts—for example, 'love'.

As rendered above, Bradley's regress reinforces the containment theory of predication in the following way. For a fact :F(a), the predicational composition of F and a cannot be a relation between F and a, as suggested by the use at the level of grammar of the *copula* (Latin for 'to bind together'), 'is'—that is, 'a is F'. For, contrary to the definitional promise of relations, the above regress has purportedly shown that no relation can bridge the ontic distance between F and a. It follows that in the complex fact :F(a) there can be no such ontic distance, so either F is 'contained in' a or, conversely, only 'F in a' is plausible.

Bradley's regress is no trivial sophistry, any more, say, than the liar paradox, though they are equally easily presented; and just as any general semantics must come to terms with the liar paradox, so every serious ontology must provide an answer to the regress. To avoid the viciousness of the regress, several philosophers (e.g., Bergmann, Wisdom, Strawson, and Hochberg) have posited a special 'nexus of exemplification' or 'non-relational tie', to use Strawson's telling description,[70] as the source of unity in the fact :F(a). There is merit here, depending upon how one understands this nexus. According to Hochberg, the realist must admit the predicational nexus as a unique type of *universal* in order to act as the glue that binds particulars to other, standard universals, whether properties or relations.[71] I take Hochberg to mean, by referring to the nexus as a universal, that it is itself an intension, albeit a unique one. However, to describe the required nexus as an intension that simultaneously binds several terms is precisely to describe a *relation*, as ordinarily understood. Yet, how is it that this special relation avoids Bradley's regress when all other, ordinary relations do not? To avoid the regress, the predicational nexus must be conceived of as intensionless—that is, as blank connectedness—and this, I take it, is what Strawson intends in referring to it as a 'non-relational tie'. As I shall argue later, the error of Bradley's regress is to make the predicational nexus of relation R as it occurs in the fact :R(a,b) identical with the intension R or some other relation intension. To the contrary, and in line with Russell's response to Bradley, it is an instance of R that is predicative solely among a and b, the universal R being the nonpredicative content abstracted as a residue from the predicative instance consisting of both the aspects of intension R and the predicational nexus. In our pre-critical conceptions we do not distinguish the nonpredicative universal R from its combinatorial, unrepeatable instances R_i. In this confusion Bradley's argument for the absurdity of relations becomes plausible; in a posited relation complex the relation both relates and does not relate its relata.

The Surrogate Unity of Classes

Pluralist ontologies must explain the *union*, in various forms of composition, of distinct singletons and must do so without annihilating the constituents into homogeneity within the subsuming whole; they must explain diversity-in-unity. The stock-in-trade for nominalists (e.g., Stout, Goodman, and Quine) is the class or set, or 'looser' mereological whole, considered strictly extensionally.

Thus Stout proposed a nominalist theory of unit properties and relations in which the universal is replaced by the extension of a general noun whose nonarbitrary unity is accounted for by a sui generis 'distributive unity of the class'.[72]

More commonly, the nominalist/extensionalist tactic is to 'eliminate' completely relations taken intensionally in favor of certain sets of sets according to the standard Wiener–Kuratowski extensional modeling. Here the unity of the relational fact :R(a,b) is replaced by the unity of the set $\{a,\{a,b\}\}$. Notwithstanding certain advantages as a formal modeling, however, this extensional reduction of relations fails as an ontological analysis, a point that I will argue in detail in chapter 6. This failure traces back ultimately to the basic flaw in the nominalist/extensionalist program for reducing intensions to sets or classes: namely, that the reduction program enforces explicitly an extensional version of the erroneous containment model of predication. Thus the predication in :Prime(3) is modeled by the element-of relation in the fact that $3 \in \{2,3,5,7,11, \ldots \}$, which is to say that 3 is a prime is equivalent to the fact that 3 is *contained in* the set of primes. The relevant mis-analogy of the containment model is that, just as in the intensional version a subject is made to be the cause of the unity it has with its properties and of their collected togetherness, so in the extensional version a set is made to be the source of the unity it has with its elements and of their specific gathering within it—the supposed sui generis 'distributive unity of the class'. Here we have adherence to the extensional version of the primacy of the unit doctrine. Such a view of sets is apparent in an assertion that Gödel once made to the effect that sets and physical objects play similar roles in our conceptual world views, having as their functions "the generating of unities out of manifolds."[73] But surely this conception of sets or classes reverses what must be the order of explanation: for the *unification* of the elements constitutes a set, not vice versa. That is, a set does not exist ontically prior to this unification of elements, so cannot be the cause of it. Some aspect of a class, distinct from its elements and not the effect of the resulting class, must be an essential *constituent* of the class.

The necessity of taking into account the unifying aspect of classes was not lost on Georg Cantor, the father of modern set theory. According to Cantor, a set is "a collection to a whole M of definite, well-differentiated objects m of our intuition or our thought," a "many that can be thought of as one." A set is a "totality of definite elements which can be united to a whole through a law," a multiplicity that "can be thought without contradiction as 'being together' so that their collection into '*one* thing' is possible."[74] It was Cantor's position that the unity constituting a set is conceptual, imposed upon otherwise diverse elements by some intellect and objectified as existing (especially for completed infinite sets) in the Divine Intellect.[75] I will say more on this point later.

It is precisely this *unity* of a class or set, a 'unity *per accidens*', that proves to be a profound problem for any ontology, but acutely so for an extensionalist ontology. Among philosophers who are willing to recognize the problem, the response has been varied—witness, for example, Armstrong's account of sets as aggregates of certain states of affairs[76] and Bigelow's two accounts, initially that sets are certain relations among their members, more recently that sets are higher-order properties of their members.[77] Central to each of these accounts is an appeal to the predicative nature of properties or relations (as such, necessarily taken intensionally). The wide variation in these accounts is attributable, I suggest, to a lack of understanding of the precise nature of the predicative aspect of relations. By contrast, nominalists/extensionalists either conveniently fail to recognize any problem as regards the unity of a set or claim that this unity is sui generis. Indeed, these are the only options available to them, for the argument that I will give in chapter 2 showing that nominalism implies the property reduction of relations eliminates the only possible source of unity for wholes of any kind.

Max Black puts the problem of the unity of a set humorously in saying: "A set having three members is a single thing wholly constituted by its members but distinct from them. After this, the theological doctrine of the Trinity as 'three in one' should be child's play."[78] In complete seriousness, Russell in the *Principles of Mathematics* worried about how a set could be both a one and a many, observing that the problem centered on the fact that since, by definition, classes are exhausted by their elements (axiom of extensionality), classes can have no unifiers inter se that might account for the unity among their elements.[79] Later, in *My Philosophical Development* (1959), Russell summarized his mature views on this subject, saying: "Although from the point of view of a formal calculus one can regard a relation as a set of ordered couples, it is the intension alone which gives unity to the set. The same thing applies, of course, also to classes. What gives unity to the class is solely the intension which is common and peculiar to its members."[80]

Frege was likewise unwilling to identify *extensions of concepts* with sets, considering the latter to be mere collections lacking the essential unity possessed by the former, a unity that accounted for extensions having the ontic status of 'objects'. Describing himself as an 'intensionalist logician', Frege asserted that "the concept is logically prior to its extension; and I regard as futile the attempt to take extension of a concept as a class, and make it rest, not on the concept, but on single things."[81]

Without further elaboration, the claim that the common intension is the source of unity of a class is hardly satisfying. It would appear to be but an application of the unexplanatory primacy of the unit doctrine, that from the common unitary intension comes the unity of the class of exemplifying elements. In this case the analogy would not be the containment model but the 'necklace' model, according to which the intension is the common thread running through and connecting the exemplified terms as beads. But if we strip away the mis-analogies, what remains is only the notion of the intension functioning as an n-adic relation with the exemplifying terms as relata, which is, of course, an error—Red, for example, is monadic, not polyadic. What is needed is a relation between the intension and its exemplars, the obvious relation of exemplification. I shall return to this point below.

As Russell observed, the peculiar nature of sets becomes acute in the cases of the empty or null set and the unit set.[82] If sets are constituted entirely by their elements, then no members, no set. There are extensionless intensions—for example, the property of being a prime number between 2 and 3—but there are no extensionless extensions. Aptly called a logical "fiction" by Russell[83] and rejected as a confusion by Frege,[84] the null set borrows whatever plausibility it has from the notion of an uninstantiated intension, an embarrassing fact to diehard extensionalists.

As for the unit set, what is there internal to the nature of set $\{a\}$ that distinguishes it from a? If a set is identified with its collective elements, then set $\{a\}$ is identical with a.

To respond by declaring classes or sets sui generis wholes is again to evade the problem of complexity, not to solve it. Indeed, class theory and mereology are to ontology as kinematics is to dynamics; the former simply prescind from considering the causes of the complexes they take as given. But if the problem of complexity is answered only by relations, a thesis that Russell always maintained and one with which I concur, requiring all plural entities to be complexes with an interrelatedness, conceptual or otherwise, among their constituents, then this would imply that sets, by their very extensional definition, are necessarily abstractions in the literal sense of 'leaving something out'. Sets must be complexes in which the simultaneously unifying and separating relations among the elements are simply *ignored* conceptually, though in fact they are ontically irremovable and always presupposed. It would thus seem that Cantor was right in saying that sets are a priori and conceptual and that Russell was too reserved in not insisting that all sets are logical fictions. In this we have a rationale for the traditional parallel with intension universals as the abstracted content of property and relation instances—for example, as Red is the abstracted, nonpredicative content of some predicative instance Red_i.

The issues here can be sharpened by returning to the last statement by Russell quoted above, which, if taken literally, presents a difficulty for his theory of relations. He states that it is the 'actual relating' of relations that accounts for the unity of any complex entity, and in the above quote he would apparently now identify the linking aspect of a relational fact $:R(a,b)$—for example, a is to the right of b—with the intension R, Is-to-the-Right-of. But what if at some subsequent time it is the case that $\neg R(a,b)$—that is, that a is not to the right of b. What warrants the change in truth-value of $R(a,b)$ from true to false is presumably not a change in a or b or the intension R (especially for Russell, who took spatial relations to be external); rather, it is the 'actual relating', or tie, that R formerly effected between a and b but no longer effects. Hence, it would seem that the relating-of-R and the intension R cannot be identical. Indeed, in an early unpublished paper (1900) in which Russell argued for relation instances, he held that intensions abstracted from a combinatorial mode, a mode necessarily among specific relata to which the intensions were particularized, were mere 'class concepts'—that is, nonrelating universals.[85] But if this is the case, then, with regard to classes, an intension universal—say Red—cannot itself provide the requisite unification sufficient to sustain the existence of a class as a whole—for instance, the class of red things. If the class of red things is to be, at least in part, a function of the class concept Red, then it would seem that what is required in addition is the implicit actual relating of some relation, presumably the exemplification relation, between the class concept (intension) Red and the things that exemplify it. If, in turn, the exemplification relation is a relation with a conceptual status only, an artifact of intellectual analysis, as I claim, then classes or sets exist only conceptually. From this perspective, set theory becomes what has recently been suggested by Philip Kitcher: namely, the logical consequence of specifications on the iterated collecting and ordering powers of an ideal mind, powers extrapolated and removed from the limitations of our collectings and orderings.[86] In any case, sets defined strictly extensionally (i.e., as identical with their 'collective' elements but not with their *collected* elements) exist nowhere, whatever the ontic status of their elements; they exist neither spatiotemporally, accessible through sense experience (Maddy), nor in some abstract realm, accessible by nonsensuous intuition (Gödel), nor even conceptually.[87] Only *collected* elements—complexes—exist as plural wholes. Sets are half-truths, the residue of a process of intellectual abstraction, with a conceptual status analogous to that of nonrelating relation universals. Or, stated otherwise, sets defined as identical with their elements without remainder are misleading abstractions easily misinterpreted as the illusion that we are getting something (unity-in-diversity) for nothing (no unifier). In real life, whether ontology generally or our economic relations specifically, there is no such thing as a 'free lunch.'

To extend this point, under the theses defended here, all unification requires relations in the precise sense of instances each of which is a linking-under-an-intension. When the intensions of relation instances unifying a *complex* of entities are abstracted, however, we have the illusion that the elements continue to form a unity, now as a *class*, under the anemic instance residue of 'bare linkings'. Further, having no intension contents, these bare linkings easily evaporate from 'between' the elements, and we end up with the miracle of a unified whole of diverse elements with no unifiers. Plato maintained that art is twice removed from reality; so too is set theory, in that sets are logical fictions; moreover, set theory is especially so in projecting as the powers of an idealized human mind the ability to form complexes by collecting and ordering and then the power to abstract ('leave out') the intensions of the relations involved in the collecting and ordering. In order to objectify classes, Cantor was right to place them in the Divine *Mind*.

The mereologist (e.g., Nelson Goodman) is justified in objecting to the extravagance of the class 'Platonist' who, in starting with two individuals, a and b, claims in addition to the class $\{a,b\}$ the proliferating classes of classes of . . . of classes: $\{\{a\},\{b\}\}$, $\{\{a\},\{b\},\{a,b\}\}$, $\{\{a\},\{a,b\}\}$, $\{\{a,b\}\}$, and so on. If there is no internal structure at any level to constitute the distinguishing nature of these sets, then they are all, at best, identical to the being of the mereological whole ab. Though misinterpreting its implications due to his nominalist presuppositions, Goodman is correct in insisting upon the principle: No distinction of entities without a distinction of content.[88] The supposed multiple sets generated by a and b only represent a distinction without an internal difference. Any illusion to the contrary is perhaps the result of surreptitiously attributing the accidental, extrinsic punctuational/spatial ordering involved in the names of these sets to the sets themselves. With the proliferation of different classes, some with the same basic 'Urelements', the set theorist attempts to achieve the closest thing to *structure* that is extensionally possible. Yet these classes are structures whose very nature *as structures* cannot be accounted for by anything intrinsic to the concept of a set—an entity completely exhausted by its elements—but whose nature nevertheless is supposedly delineated through various, competing axiomatizations. Our intuitions are confused, and the mereologist is forthrightly honest in this regard. Unfortunately, however, the mereologist must succumb to his or her own criticism, since even the association or 'fusion' essential to mereological wholes is unavailable in a strict ontology of mere isolated atoms. Nothing—not even structureless 'heaps'—can be built from isolated atoms of any kind. For the loosest whole requires some minimal association (conceptual, spatial, etc.), however feeble, of its elements, and this association is surreptitious, since it cannot be explained in terms of the disjoint elements alone. With regard to physical atoms, even the ancient atomist Lucretius saw that, to explain our experience, a whole (*concilium*) must be more than its elements. Different kinds of atoms must have different kinds of 'hooks' in order to be welded together in varying degrees of solidity and hardness corresponding to the properties of observed bodies (*On the Nature of Things*, II. 380ff.). At one place he goes beyond this crude, spatio-mechanical linking and holds that the spatial relations among *atoma* effect complexes among whose supervenient properties is the potential for effecting color experiences in those with the proper sense organs, a property that the atoms do not have singly or when spatially related in other ways (ibid., II. 757–71). What are required for any complex, whether it be a set, a mereological whole, or whatever, are ontic combinators; but for the extensionalist, these are officially precluded from being constituents of the posited wholes because of the extensional definitions of the latter—the elements are admitted, but not their connecting relations. It is no wonder that Quine was led to what must necessarily be the extensionalist's assessment, that "the notion of a class is so fundamental that we cannot hope to define it in more fundamental terms."[89] Analogous as fictions to the grins of the

Cheshire cat in *Alice in Wonderland*, set theory is like a 'theory of grins' in which the grins become fundamental because the supporting cat has fictitiously been made to disappear.

It is ironic that mathematics, which is widely described as the 'science of structure', should be said to *rest* upon the explanatory foundation of set theory, whose entities have a structure that the theory cannot account for but can only stipulate variously through its generating axioms. Here we have the primacy of the unit doctrine in reverse: the whole is to be explained completely in terms of disparate *ones*.

As already observed, a point yet to be substantiated is the parallel mode of existence of nonpredicative universals, which are abstractions from their full existence as aspects of predicative, individuated instances. In this regard, intensions have the status of Frege's 'concept correlates', the latter being the nonpredicative residue of a predicative concept. In arriving at our conclusion, however, we shall avoid Frege's error of assuming that ontology parallels the syntactical requirements of natural language, an assumption that forced him to countenance such embarrassments as 'The concept of a horse is not a concept'.[90]

In sum, there exists a genuine philosophical problem concerning the unity of classes, a problem about which nominalists/extensionalists are prudently silent. Sets, the surrogate unifiers for extensionalists, are at least as obscure and in need of explanation as intensions are made out to be; hence, in the order of explanation, we have gained nothing by replacing intensions with extensions or modeling the predication relation by means of the element-of relation. To the contrary, and as broached above, relations taken intensionally provide a means of accounting for the plural unity of a set, and in this, relations contribute fundamentally to ontology. I shall turn next to establishing how instances of relations can provide the basis for a one-category ontology generally.

chapter two

Traditional versus Instance Ontology

> It is not possible to give an account of properties and relations purely in
> terms of particulars. That is the error of Nominalism. It is not possible to
> give an account of particulars purely in terms of (universal) properties. That
> is the error of Universalism. We must admit *both* particulars and universals.
>
> —Armstrong, *Nominalism and Realism*

The Problems of Individuation, Universals, and Predication

Given the broad contexts established in chapter 1, we are now in a position to
examine in depth some of the telling weaknesses of rivals to instance immanent
realism in responding to the fundamental ontological problems of individuation,
universals, and predication and their answers to the thesis of predicable possession. By contrast, we shall observe how unit relations provides a solution to each
of these problems. The effort will yield a clear conception of the nature of
relation instances proposed here, for which detailed arguments will be offered
in subsequent chapters.

Relations are central to structure, and structure is ubiquitous. Consider the
fact that much of what we apprehend as our immediate cognitive given, both
from internal and external perception as well as from abstract thought, consists
in structures of multiply interrelated entities, conceptual or concrete. The epistemic given, the content of consciousness, is almost always a complex, a
'gestalt' in the broad sense, whether it be the contents of perceptual fields, of
dreams, or the rarefied content of abstract thought. The atomistic 'sensa' or
'impressions' of classical empiricism are not the ordinary, pre-critical given,
but the mediated result of a considerable amount of attention, abstraction, and
theorizing upon actual perceptual complexes. It is a case of what Whitehead
called 'the fallacy of misplaced concreteness' to think that the epistemic problem is to explain how complex sensory fields (visual, tactile, auditory, etc.) are
identical to only a *class* of atomic sensa—an impossible task. On the contrary,
we arrive at the theoretical resultant and explanatorily impoverished sensa from
an analysis of structurally rich sensory fields. The epistemology is backwards,

because the ontology is backwards—as if it were possible to form a complex from isolated atoms only.

Ontology requires that we give an account of both the encompassing structures and the entities forming the nodes of these systems. To the neglect of the synthesizing relationships, traditional ontology has focused primarily upon the separated nodes, ordinary, mid-sized, concrete individuals of everyday experience being the paradigm (e.g., Aristotle's 'substances'), and in this neglect of structure has tended to be reductionist and atomistic. One is here again reminded of the empiricist program of constructing experience out of atomistic sensa, though an individual sensum, 'this red', even when abstracted from its spatiotemporal structural complex, 'this here now', is still a duality of both the repeatable, 'red', and an unrepeatable 'thisness'. The distinction of these primordial dual aspects of a single entity solves the problem of predicable possession, and it is the proper assay of relations and their instances that renders this distinction intelligible.

In traditional ontology, with its focus on the individuals of common experience, three fundamental ontological aspects must be mutually accounted for: the fact of being an apparently *unrepeatable* 'this', numerically distinct as such from other individuals, and at the same time in *possession* of what are apparently *repeatable* characteristics, being a 'what' or a 'such'—that is, having properties and relations that render the given as tokens of encompassing types, sorts, or kinds. Each ordinary individual is pre-critically a unified 'this-such', an unrepeatable composition of repeatable characteristics—hence the three interconnected classical problems: (a) the *problem of individuation*—what accounts for the unrepeatability of particulars, the *principium individuationis*; (b) the *problem of universals*—what accounts for the apparent sameness of characteristics over diverse particulars; and (c) the *problem of predication*—what accounts for the *union* of repeatable relations with their (in some cases, unrepeatable) relata or, according to various theories, their posited substitutes. The meaning of the term 'union' is the problem of predication, which is a problem for both nominalism and realism. It is worth emphasizing that, since ontic predication is the most elementary *structure*, it is hardly surprising that, with the neglect of structure in general, traditional ontology has focused on the problems of individuation and universals and has dealt least satisfactorily with the problem of predication. The naive containment model of predication and the reductive elimination of system mutually reinforce each other and, when consistently pressed, must lead ultimately to isolated monads between which is an unbridgeable void. Laboring under these assumptions, if plural wholes and their supervenient properties are to be retained as nonillusory, the ontologist must resort to some ad hoc maneuver, a *deus ex machina*, to impose the needed ordering from without. One might account for the ordering (necessarily external and 'between' what is ordered) by attributing it to the associations of a mind (recall Cantor's conception of sets), if mind is somehow exempted from the atomistic reduction (which Hume was consistent in denying); or by positing, as Leibniz did, a harmony pre-established by the Divine Intellect; or by positing, as does Campbell, a unique 'compresence' relation between otherwise isolated tropes, a relation whose tonic effect mysteriously survives the all-pervasive property reduction of relations in his theory. Plural unity at macro- or micro-levels requires more than isolated terms; it requires connections as equally present and in need of a viable ontic account.

As background to the following analysis, it is useful to have ready at hand the sharpened definitions of 'universal', 'nominalism', and 'moderate realism' afforded by the work of chapter 1. The following, I propose, gives the most general characteristics of the concept of a universal. An entity X is a universal if and only if it satisfies the following conditions:

(U1) X is a distinct content (intension, quiddity, or nature), where synonymy is its identity condition.

(U2a) X is intrinsic and essential to ontic predication and in this is representative of the reality of the whole having X as a predicate.

(U2b) numerically the same content X can be an aspect in ontic predication across a diversity of subjects.

How these conditions are further interpreted and then accepted or rejected gives rise to the various standard ontologies. The philosophical tradition of Aristotelian realism construes U2a and b as:

(U2a′) X itself is ontically predicative, and

(U2b′) numerically the same content X can be ontically predicative of a plurality of subjects.

Note that U2a′ restates the thesis of predicable possession. By contrast, the moderate (immanent) realism I am proposing construes U2a and b as:

(U2a″) X is an aspect of *unit* attributes, where the latter, not X, are ontically predicative, and

(U2b″)   this same content X can be an aspect of diverse unit attributes, each
of which is predicative among diverse subjects.[1]

Concept nominalism (e.g., Ockham's) and resemblance nominalism (e.g.,
Campbell's) both allow for entities satisfying U1, though class and predicate
nominalism need not. Definitional, however, is the fact that all forms of nominalism deny U2b (and hence the narrower U2b′ and U2b″), rejecting the supposed commonality features of entities. In addition, the term is often extended
to cover the rejection of U2a as well, though this need not be the case. In the
hylomorphism of Ockham, for example, form would satisfy U1 and U2a. U2b is
pivotal, and in rejecting it, nominalists reject the concept that numerically the
same content can be involved across multiple ontic predicates. The alternatives
are to either reject ontic predication, and so U2a as well (tropism), or require
that all ontic predication be individuated to unit properties, where the emphasis
is on properties as *monadic* predicates (I shall clarify this point presently). The
rejection of U2b is also the implicational meaning of the thesis sometimes given
as definitional of nominalism:

> Reality (conceptual or extra-conceptual) consists only in particulars; that is,
> reality is homogeneously particular.

As homogeneously particular (unrepeatable), there is no aspect of an entity that
could be shared. To avoid possible confusion, note that when U2b is construed as
the naive U2b′, its rejection by moderate realists is sometimes erroneously used
as grounds for classifying the latter as a form of nominalism. Under U2b″, moderate realism allows for shared intensions but denies that they are predicative.

It is typical of every form of nominalism to give a strategy for eliminating
predicativity from proposed universals. For nominalism of the predicate, concept, class, mereological, resemblance, or trope types, a true assertion of the
form 'F(a)' is treated, respectively, as equivalent to 'a falls under predicate 'F'',
'a falls under the concept of 'F'', 'a is a member of the class of Fs', 'a is a part of
the aggregate of Fs', 'a appropriately resembles a paradigm case of F', or 'F$_i$ is a
trope compresent with other tropes constituting a'.[2] In every case, F's prima
facie predicative status in :F(a) has changed to the nonpredicative, F or its
surrogate having been reduced to the status of a Fregean 'object'. The predicative role of F has been removed and given to some stand-in relation. However,
this strategy of substituting a relation for predication will not work, for reasons
that I shall specify shortly.

Nominalism

As previously stated, there exists against nominalism a battery of developed arguments with considerable warrant, arguments we need not rehearse here. Rather, I will offer two further arguments against nominalism that, to my knowledge, have gone unnoticed and that turn upon the fact that nominalism implies the erroneous property reduction of relations. As a backdrop to these arguments, let us examine modern trope nominalism, considered by some to be the most defensible form of nominalism. We need to make explicit exactly what categories of entities trope theory is committed to and hence the proffered 'economy' of the doctrine. For trope nominalism its categories are (i) two types of 'individuals', unit properties and ordinary thick particulars, the latter composed of the former; (ii) a relation of *resemblance* to account for the known 'sameness' of individuals, but posited as existing between two resembling individuals without the existence of anything numerically identical and internal to the relata to found this relation; and (iii) a relation of *compresence* to account for the existence of thick particulars as the unification of some unit attributes but not others. Compresence is a trope nominalist's surrogate for predication.

Note that what are addressed here are the problems of universals and predication, not that of individuation. It is characteristic of nominalists that they do not see individuation as a problem at all. Ockham is explicit in saying that it is not individuation but commonality that is the ontological problem (*Ordinatio*, 2, 6).[3]

The above inventory is not that of the classical nominalism of Ockham and his scholastic followers, though, as I now argue, it should be that of any nominalism worthy of consideration. In regard to (ii), an account of apparent commonality must be given, and the only resource that seems to be available to the nominalist is the relation of resemblance. In regard to (i), the alternatives to positing the compresence relation are to think of ordinary particulars as either form/matter composites or structural complexes. In either case relations become central. In the traditional form/matter complex, the form is, in effect, *polyadic* (i.e., a relation), precisely because, as such, it is predicative of multiple matter (a point that I will expand on when considering Aristotle's hylomorphism in chapter 3). In structural complexes, we have entities that are networks of multiple relations among variously shared relata. Yet, neither of these alternatives can prove satisfactory for the nominalist; for, in addition to the weakness of form/matter ontology, with its slide to bare particulars, there is the subtle but absolute demand on any form of nominalism that it *eliminate the category of polyadic relations.* This is a crucial, but not widely appreciated, point. The necessity of the rejection turns upon the fact that a polyadic relation is simultaneously predicative of multiple subjects. But simultaneous inherence is, in the requisite sense, precisely what nominalists seek to deny in eschewing universals as 'one over many'—that is, in their rejection of U2b. For both relations and universals (classically conceived as predicative), there is, by definition, one intension which functions as a single predicate among multiple subjects, and nominalists reject this possibility. It might be objected that this represents a confusion—that the universal Red, for example, is of such a proposed nature as to be whole and complete in each apple in the bowl, whereas a relation—for example, Is-a-Father-of—is not whole and complete in each relatum, say, Philip and Alexander. But this is to miss the point—an error abetted by the containment model of predication and the mis-analogy of the 'in' metaphor. The relevant issue here is the multi-subject *predicativity* possessed equally by classically conceived universals and by relations, and this nominalists cannot allow.

Restated, the objection of nominalists to universals is their supposed simultaneous 'inherence' in numerically diverse subjects. Removing from the concept of 'inherence' the deceptive irrelevances of the containment model of predication and allowing predication to be seen as an 'attachment', not a 'containment', what the nominalist actually rejects in denying U2b is seen to be the predicative tie of a single intension to two or more subjects. Irrelevant here is the number of fact complexes over which this predicativity is distributed. Historically, monadic predication was the focus, and for monadic facts :$F(a)$ and :$F(b)$, $a \neq b$, the objection by the nominalist was to F being simultaneously predicative of distinct subjects a and b. The same objection, however, must apply to, say, binary relation R in the single complex :$R(a,b)$, $a \neq b$, since here too we have a single intension R predicative of distinct subjects a and b. The long-presumed monadic reduction of relations eliminated the necessity of treating relations as a separate case and thereby obscured a source of critique of nominalism.

Consequently, with the consistent nominalist rejecting polyadic predicates—as witnessed historically both early (e.g., Ockham) and late (e.g., Quine and Campbell)—the possibilities of assaying ordinary particulars as either form/matter or structural composites, with their implicit or explicit appeal to polyadic relations, are likewise eliminated. The remaining alternative is to assay complex individuals as composites of unit properties. But then, in order to explain the nonarbitrary composition of the latter, something equivalent to the specially empowered compresence relation of (iii) must be posited. In sum, any adequate nominalism must adopt the above ontic inventory. Hence we conclude with Armstrong that trope, or 'moderate', nominalism is the most defensible form of nominalism.[4]

Of course, resemblance and compresence are themselves relations, and thus for their explanatory benefits to be retained, their offending multi-subject polyacity must be eliminated in favor of monadic predication. Hence nominalism is forced to adopt the property reduction of relations. Because this reduction is impossible, however, as will be argued later, we have ultimately a *reductio ad absurdum* of all forms of nominalism.

In addition to the above argument showing that nominalism in general requires the impossible property reduction of relations, there is a further argument available to demonstrate that any nominalism adopting the compresence relation will necessarily require the property reduction of relations. Consider first what would be the paradigm case of attribution for a compresence nominalist: a monadic property F—for example, 'a is round' or 'a is red'—predicated of a thick individual a—a colored disc, say. The thick individual a is said to be a complex consisting of several (perhaps infinitely many) property instances—say $F_1, G_3, H_2, \ldots$—each related by the binary compresence relation to the other instances and so collectively making up a and extensionally distinguishing it from any other thick individual, b. The 'repeatable component', 'F', of the attribution 'a is F' is said to stand for an unrepeatable part of a compresent whole making up the subject a. That is,

> The proposition that 'a is F' is true $\equiv a$ is a compresence complex of which an instance F_i is a constituent.

Note that compresence is necessarily a *binary* relation, since otherwise it would have variable—possibly infinite—polyacity, which is impossible. Now let us attempt to extend the compresence analysis of the monadic case 'a is F' to a relational proposition that 'aRb'—e.g., 'a is taller than b'. Let a be the compresence complex consisting of instances $F_1, G_3, H_2, \ldots$, and let b be the complex consisting in $K_1, L_4, M_3, \ldots$ Then, paralleling the monadic case, the 'repeatable component', 'R' ('is taller than'), would have to correspond to some instance R_i and be related by the binary relation of compresence to some other *single* entity

X as a second relata—i.e., R_1 compresent with X. What could this single subject X be? Since R_1 is a relation with two subjects, the missing subject X must involve both a and b, and within the compresence theory there are only two possibilities. The first is that X is a single compresence complex corresponding to the subjects *a and b*. This latter, compound subject would have to consist in instances F_1, G_3, H_1, . . . *and* K_1, L_4, M_3, . . . , each connected pairwise to the others by the compresence relation. That is,

> the proposition that 'aRb' is true $\equiv$ there is a compresence complex consisting of all the instances making up a and b and having an instance R_i as a constituent.

But this is absurd, for in cases where a and b are distinct, as with asymmetric relations like 'is taller than', there will be instances of properties making up the two compresence complexes that are contraries—for example, instances for 'is six foot tall' and 'is five foot tall', respectively. But there cannot exist a self-contradictory compresence complex, hence there is no such X corresponding to a compound subject 'a and b'.

The second possibility is that mystery subject X is a compresence complex consisting in a compresence relation (instance) existing between the compresence complex making up a, abbreviated 'CCa', and the compresence complex making up b, 'CCb'; that is, X = CCa-compresent-with-CCb. Then,

> the proposition that 'aRb' is true $\equiv R_1$ is compresent with CCa-compresent-with-CCb.

The fatal difficulty here is that in the cases where R is asymmetric or nonsymmetric, as with 'is taller than', the order in the attribution 'aRb' must be distinguished from that in 'bRa'. However, the symmetric character of the compresence relation founding the truth conditions for 'aRb' cannot distinguish this order. The complexes corresponding to 'CCa-compresent-with-CCb' and 'CCb-compresent-with-CCa' are identical, but the propositions that 'aRb' and 'bRa' need not both be true. Hence, the needed subject X cannot be treated in the second way either. The only way for the nominalist to avoid the above absurdities is to declare relations reducible to monadic properties of their relata and hence amenable to the compresence–complex analysis.

The property reduction of relations was ready-made for Ockham: he inherited it serendipitously from the philosophical milieu. He himself explicitly rejected polyadic relations on the grounds that, in effect, they are inconsistent with the containment model of predication[5] and that, in addition, they succumb to Bradley's regress argument.[6] After disposing of polyadic relations with Bradley's regress, Ockham states that we can account for the unity of predication as Aristotle did in Book VIII (H) of the *Metaphysics* (1045a22–25): that form is to its matter as act is to potency.[7] Though Ockham, like Aristotle, saw clearly the necessity of a 'cause' for the unity of ontic subject and predicate, the act/potency analogy is far from enlightening on this issue. I will expand on this point when considering Aristotle's views in chapter 3.

Unlike Ockham, Campbell is motivated to adopt the property reduction of relations primarily because properties can apparently stand alone without the need of a subject, whereas it is clear that relations cannot.[8] The existence of a relation (instance)—say, Is-Right-of$_i$—presupposes as logically prior the existence of relata, whereas it is plausible, he claims, that trope properties—for instance, Round$_i$—can stand predicatively unattached to anything. With 'stand alone' tropes, Campbell seeks, by implication, to avoid the ill effects of the thesis of predicable possession. He further contends that since relation instances would require relata, these relata would ultimately have to be monadic tropes (though I shall argue presently that this is not the case). He thus concludes that tropes are the most fundamental category of ontic entities.

The property reduction of relations adopted by Ockham and Campbell, for whatever reasons, is not only untenable in itself, but pyrrhic in applying equally to the key nominalist relations of resemblance and compresence themselves. In particular, without the existence of the compresence relation as a real, multi-subject combinator providing for the unity among unit tropes, there can be no account of complex thick particulars and how they differ from other particulars. In this regard, Campbell and like-minded nominalists attempt to have it both ways, though in the end they cannot.

Universalism

At the other extreme from nominalism and emphasizing the repeatable, some philosophers have advocated *universalism*, the thesis that nothing but universals exist and that particulars are bundles of universals. Bundles are then distinguished extensionally. Like the trope nominalist, the universalist rejects the thesis of predicable possession by theorizing that all determinations of an entity are not predicable of that or any other entity. Yet, as with nominalism, the problem is how we are to understand the *unity* of a bundle? For one thing, the unity cannot be that of a *set*, for the following reasons:

(a) There would be a thing for every set (e.g., even for {round, square}).
(b) Individuals would be necessarily eternal, since properties exist necessarily, and a set exists necessarily if its members do.
(c) Exemplification would become the converse of membership, and so for x = {round, . . .}, we would have the absurdity that the set {round, . . .} is round.[9]

In addition to these, there are two further, particularly relevant objections to bundles as sets. First, assume the individual x = {F, G, H, . . .}, where F, G, H, . . . are property universals. On this assumption, it is *necessarily* the case that no two distinct individuals can have the same properties. Said positively, on this assumption we assert the necessity of the principle of identity of indiscernibles: if x and y have the same properties, then x is identical to y—that is, $(P)[P(x) \equiv P(y)] \supset x = y$. But strong arguments have been put forward (e.g., by Max Black and A. J. Ayer[10]) against the necessity of this principle. It is logically conceivable that two distinct entities could have the same properties. These issues are important, and I shall return to them when illustrating the advantage of unit properties in distinguishing identity from indiscernibility in chapter 10. What is important here is that this criticism is removed if an individual is equated with its set of *property instances*: x = {F_1, G_3, H_2, . . .}. By the thesis of subject uniqueness (SU), no two distinct individuals can possess the same property instances; though, by the principle of immanent instance realism (IR), two instances can have the same intension universal. Hence, two individuals-as-sets-of-instances could each have distinct instances, though one instance each from the same list of shared universals. The identity of indiscernibles is then rendered not necessarily true.

However, a second objection to identifying an individual with the set of its properties, one that applies whether the set is one of universals or of instances, is that it makes every property that an entity possesses *essential* to it. Let F, G, K, . . . be either universals or instances. Now every predication of the form 'x is K' becomes either necessarily true or necessarily false, depending upon whether K is an element of the set {F, G, . . .} or not, respectively. We thus end up with the extreme, untenable position that every property that x has is now essential to x; for example, Socrates becomes essentially white, bald, snub-nosed, tall, short, and so forth. Any change in the properties of x produces a nonidentical individual y. The deeply intuitive, though admittedly problematic, distinction between essential and accidental properties is lost.

If the unity of a bundle is more substantial than that of a set, what is it? The only alternative theory would seem to be that of the more sophisticated related-bundle theory. An individual is its properties as related in some unique binary relation, say C (again Russell's and Campbell's 'comprescence', Goodman's 'to-getherness'[11]). That is, for thick individual x, all of whose properties are F, G, H, . . . , the special relation C exists pairwise among the constituent properties of x and hence forms the facts :C(F,G), :C(G,H), :C(F,H), and so on, which together constitute x as a type of structure. The argument of the previous section that the comprescence relation (or its explanatory equivalent) implies the erroneous property reduction of relations carries over mutatis mutandis to when the relata are universals. Moreover, the related-bundle theory does not escape the essentialist problem of the set conception, for the relation C is here posited as having the virtue of being *contingent*, hence it is not necessary that properties F, G, . . . have been together as related. Hence, unlike the situation when x is identified with a set of properties, which as a set is atemporal, here x can at least have the degree of changeability of coming into or going out of existence. Unfortunately, this is the only alteration that x as x can endure. The properties F, G, H, . . . are just as essential to x as when it is identified with its *set* of properties. Additionally, there is the objection that the C-complex is a single entity but not an *individual*—that is, not unrepeatable. C is a universal among universals, F, G, H, . . . , and the net effect can only be a complex universal. Hence, if x is truly an *individual*, it is not identical to any C-complex.

Finally, recall that thick individual x is supposedly a structure consisting of the network of facts :C(F,G), :C(G,H), :C(F,H), and so on. But then we have the following problem. If it is true that C(F,G), it cannot simultaneously be the case that not-C(F,G). If F is comprescent with G in any individual x, then if y is a distinct individual simultaneously containing G, y must also contain F, for F and G are universals numerically the same across x and y. In other words, no two distinct individuals can share *any* properties, and this is absurd.

The moral of these and the other deficiencies pointed out above is, I think, clear. The nature of material predication cannot be adequately modeled by any of the Element-of, Part-of, Is-Comprescent-with, or like relations that have been proposed as fundamental and sui generis yet supposedly less opaque conceptually. Rather, I will lay the foundations below for the view that these relations, as well as the exemplification relation itself, are conceptual and derivative and presuppose wholes whose unities are a function of the predicative nature of properties and relations generally.

In sum, with nominalism and universalism, we have errors of two extremes, each adopting a solution to one of the problems of individuals and universals which precludes a solution to the other. Nominalism cannot account for property and relation universals (the repeatable) in terms of particulars (the unrepeatable), and universalism cannot account for particulars in terms of property and relation universals. An individual has identically repeatable aspects, but it cannot be said to be constituted by these aspects as universals.

The Error of Predicable Possession

By contrast with both nominalism (where every aspect of an entity is unrepeatable) and universalism (where every aspect of an entity is repeatable), immanent realism in its various forms attempts to reconcile the two extremes. Here the universal (repeatable) and the individual (unrepeatable) are held to be both equally real and aspects of single entities. In its simplest, naive form this analysis would run:

(A) Ordinary individual = individual subject + its universal properties (construed as U2a').

This is the undifferentiated analysis of Aristotle in the *Categories* and the simplest embodiment of the predicational doctrine of predicable possession: that every intension or content of an entity is a *predicate* of that entity. Socrates, for example, is taken as the ontic subject (Latin *subjicere*: 'to place or put under') of all his properties. But this confuses Socrates as constituted by his properties (the 'thick' Socrates) with Socrates as distinct from, but the subject of, his properties (the 'thin' Socrates). A better approximation would be:

(B) Ordinary individual = individuating substratum + universal properties.

One version of this level of refinement is Aristotle's hylomorphic ontology in the *Metaphysics*. A particular substance—say, Socrates—consists in a specific set of individuating bodily organs, his (secondary) matter, and these consist ultimately of prime matter, informed by a repeatable essence or substantial form from the *infimia species* Man. Of this whole are predicated Socrates' accidental properties. As a formula,

(C) Ordinary individual = (substantial form + [proximate] matter) + accidental properties.

The fatal difficulty with (B), as Aristotle saw in his version (C), is that it leads to the incoherent notion of a bare particular. Socrates' collective organs are not a mere heap but rather constitute a functioning system or structure, and according to Aristotle, this dynamic structure is the effect of the form upon the relatively formless proximate matter. The matter at this level is 'relatively formless', because each organ that is systematized with the others to make up Socrates' body is itself an individual substructure of the whole and itself is assayed as a composition of matter (e.g., tissues of certain types) and form (a certain functional structure among the tissues). The substantial form Man is posited as the systematizing 'principle'. However, and as was stressed above, continuing this analysis consistently downward, we must arrive at some truly 'atomic' level of form/matter composition where the matter is absolutely without quality or 'bare', all determinations being reserved to and having been eliminated on the side of form. Significantly, for reasons to be given presently, Aristotle explicitly and rightly rejected the conception of ultimate or 'prime matter' as being a bare individuator. He often asserts that secondary matter individuates, but in *Metaphysics* VII (Z) he makes clear that prime matter as totally indeterminate cannot do so. Some metaphysical principle or cause of particularity is of course needed, and Aristotle can be interpreted as asserting at one point that this cause is the form (in which case form becomes an individuated universal, a property instance). In this regard, Duns Scotus would later criticize Aquinas's view that matter particularizes by observing that, being purely indeterminate and potentially anything, ultimate matter *is* nothing in particular and so cannot be what distinguishes one individual from another. For this reason, matter as well as form, as well as the composite of both, are all universal, hence not the *ultima realitas entis*. Scotus concluded that some positive principle of thisness is required.[12]

Independent of the hylomorphic version, if an individual is assayed according to (B) and thought to consist strictly of a group of repeatable properties over and against an unrepeatable individuator that bears them, then, since any quality, determination, or characteristic whatsoever is (potentially) repeatable, the posited individuator must be completely devoid of any specificity. I shall now make good upon promises made earlier and examine in detail why the concept of such a bare particular, so understood, is incoherent, considering first the defects summarized by Campbell. First, if a bare particular, say a of thick individual A, has absolutely no properties, no nature or content, is of no kind or sort, then it is indistinguishable from any other supposed bare particular b of individual B. That is, all bare particulars are identical. Hence, there is at most one bare particular, and thus, absurdly, there exists in the world at most one thick individual that is individuated by it.

Secondly, the-capacity-to-have-properties would seem to be a higher-order property and hence something that bare particulars cannot have. Yet, this is equally part of its ontic role, to support various properties that together constitute the total individual.

Thirdly, the causal powers of a particular, both passive and active, are a function of its properties and relations. Having none of the latter, a bare particular is causally inert, and, specifically, it cannot be destroyed. But, as Campbell puts it, this is to introduce an "a priori natural philosophy of the most discreditable kind."[13]

In addition to the weaknesses pointed out by Campbell, consider two further points. First is the fact that relations (e.g., 'is taller than' or 'is a mover of') are such that their existence among relata is a function of the existence and intensions of their relata (e.g., spatial intension or position, momentum, etc.). It is the intension of each of the relata that determines the kind of intensions or natures of the relations that can exist between them, various relations obtaining only when the prerequisite contents exist in the relata. Between two apples, for example, various spatial and causal relations could exist, but no logical, filial, (most) legal, and so on, relations. The closest one comes to an exception is the relation of 'blank', 'free', or 'arbitrary association', captured in English by the nonlogical 'and', as when freely chosen items are rendered in a list: 'a and b and c and . . .'. Only the existence, not the content, of the relata is required for this relation to obtain. I take the completely arbitrary nature of blank association to be indicative of its conceptual status, but I shall set this issue aside so as to turn directly to the following argument. Assume p is a bare particular supporting some property F—for example, Round. Because p is completely devoid of intension or content, the only relation that can obtain between p and F is that of free association, any other more qualitative, content-determined relation between them requiring at least some minimal content in p to found the relation. Consequently, at the level of bare particulars as subjects, the predication relation becomes merely arbitrary association. But if this is the case, then there are no other than ad hoc reasons why a property contrary to F—for example, Square—cannot likewise be arbitrarily associated, 'predicated', of p also. On the same grounds that p can be Round, it could equally be both Round and Square, which is absurd.

Finally, if bare particulars are causally inert, it would seem that we could have no sense experience of ordinary thick particulars, precisely *as particulars*, which bare particulars are supposed to individuate. Rather, data would have to consist in bundles of property universals that are themselves universal—that is, repeatable. Yet, as a fact, we are given in perception individuals that are at once individuals-of-a-kind, each a 'this-such'. We could not know the 'this' of an individual if it were identical to a supposed bare particular of that individual, since the latter could have no causal effect, direct or indirect, upon our senses. Rephrasing Locke, bare particulars are 'we can not know what'.[14]

As Russell at one place wrote, "We experience qualities, but not the subject in which they are suppose to adhere."[15] This is again the common maxim that we have no epistemic access to individuals except through their properties and relations. With the failure of both bundle theory at one end of the spectrum and bare particulars at the other to account for the brute unrepeatability of experienced particulars, the alternative is to attribute unrepeatability to the phenomenal properties and relations themselves; they are perceptually given as instances.

Summarizing this section, if the concept of bare particulars is incoherent, then the thesis of predicable possession is an error, albeit a natural one. Bare particulars are the fruit of the predicable possession assumption, and their incoherence demonstrates that the ultimate individuals of any ontology must possess a content that is not a predicate of that individual.

The Explanatory Value of Instance Realism

It has been argued that neither nominalism nor universalism can solve the problems of both individuation and universals and that only a form of realism offers a viable alternative. Further, the problem of complexity requires that there be entities that are 'predicative'—that is, combinatorial, binding to single subjects or across multiple subjects. It is the claim of this section that an immanent realist theory of unit relations provides a single category of entities that successfully answers all these problems.

In brief, the proper assay of relation instances is:

> A relation instance R_i is a particular having two aspects: a repeatable inten-sion (= universal) R and an unrepeatable nexus which under the intension links a specific n-tuple of relata.

The central argument that the predicative aspect of a relation instance, the nexus, is unrepeatable is part of the content of chapter 8. Once this is secured, we have the analog of Armstrong's recipe for the 'victory of particularity' (i.e., particularity plus universality yields particularity), which becomes on our anal-ysis: predicativity under an intension yields particularity. Specifically, predica-tion (which necessarily carries an intension) among an n-tuple of relata is individuated to the n-tuple. The individuated predicative aspect of a relation instance solves for the fundamental category of relation instances the problems of both individuation and complexity, while the intension aspect solves the problem of universals. This analysis of relation instances avoids the error of predicable possession in that, for an instance R_i^n, intension R^n is not a *predicate* of the nexus aspect of R_i^n (characteristic U2a''). A relation instance R_i^n of some fact :$R_i^n(a_1, \ldots, a_n)$ is a simple, unrepeatable entity with two aspects which are separable in thought but are not separate components of R_i^n. That is, the nexus and intension aspects of R_i^n are not two entities united by some further, subtle relation into a relation complex identical to R_i^n. If they were, this would be the first step to Bradley's regress. A further reason why in a relation complex :$R_i^n(a_1, \ldots, a_n)$ the combinatorial nexus aspect of R_i^n is not itself a relation between intension R^n and relata $a_1, \ldots, a_n$ (R^n thus treated as a special relatum) is the fact that the number and order of relata for a relation are functions of the intension R^n (e.g., Red determines one relatum, Left-of determines two relata), and a nexus considered separately from any intension aspect (as a 'bare link-ing') would be indeterminate as to the number and order of relata, hence no re-lation at all. The notion of a bare linking is as incoherent as that of a bare partic-ular. A relation instance R_i^n is not internally complex in the intra-relational sense in which the term is used here; rather, its nexus and intension aspects are distinguishable as abstracta, analogous to viewing a single object from two different visual perspectives. More accurately, an intension R^n is a 'residue' abstraction in the sense that, if we come to know an instance of a relation—say, R_i^n in $:R_i^n(a,b)$—as actually relating two relata, and we conceptually remove these relata—that is, we attentionally ignore the linking of R_i^n among anything— the remainder is intension R^n. The instance R_i^n is particular, whereas the residue intension is universal (characteristic U2b″).

So considered, a relation intension R corresponds to the scholastics' *direct* or *metaphysical* universal—what they referred to as 'the nature considered in itself'. When the scholastics said that this nature is 'neither common nor individual', they can be interpreted as saying that an intension *is not itself predicative* ('not common') but that it can be an aspect of an instance that is multiply predicative ('not individual', in that, for them, individuals by definition are not predicative). As abstract, these intensions have only a conceptual existence— *universale est formaliter in mente*. The nexus, or predicative, aspect of a relation instance corresponds to and, indeed, gives content to Scotus's notion of a positive individuator of an entity, its haecceitas. Moreover, the above conclusion that the separation between the intension (the *quidditas absoluta* or *natura*) and the predicative aspect (the *haecceitas*) is outside the instance and represents no real *relational complexity* within it but nevertheless is objective in that both are realities in the whole corresponds to Scotus's *distinctio formalis a parte rei*.

An instructive analogy here is to think of a relation distance R_i as similar to a circle $\bigcirc$, which can be considered, by abstraction, as having as real aspects the curves $\cup$ and $\cap$, the latter corresponding to the intension and nexus aspects of R_i. Both curves represent 'components' of the circle, yet one cannot identify either one of them as preexisting anywhere distinguished within the continuous circle prior to an external act of segmentation. The circle is simple in its continuity, whereas the complexity of the two component curves is subsequent to abstraction (*post rem*), though each represents an aspect of the reality of the circle. In an obvious sense, each curve is 'in' the circle, and together they constitute it; but in the unbroken circle one does not find these representative aspects, and in this sense the circle is simple prior to an external division by an intellect. The two curves represent a distinctio formalis a parte rei of the circle. A similar relationship exists between an instance R_i and its intension and nexus aspects.

Relation instances represent within a single category of entity a predicative 'intension/extension' minimum. As the fundamental ontic unit, instances resemble their classical forebears, substances, in that they can both be conserved through change and be causally efficient; but, by contrast with substances, instances must always exist as predicates (though they can also be subjects) and can never exist independently of some relata among which they relate. The theory of relation instances retains the spirit of Aristotelian ontology in recognizing no uninstantiated extra-conceptual universals and (at least as Aristotle intended) no bare particulars; the repeatable and the unrepeatable are abstractions from single relation instances, which, in turn, are abstractions from complexes consisting of instances and the relata they combine.

The implications of the above analysis for an ontic account of ordinary concrete particulars (e.g., classical 'substances') is straightforward. An ordinary individual cannot be assayed thinly as something over and against its properties, for, in the final analysis, this reduces it as unrepeatable to an incoherent bare particular. If an ordinary individual is not something distinct from its properties, it must *be* its (essential) properties and relations, but, as we have seen, not the latter *as universals*. The ontology of relation instances shows how ordinary individuals can be assayed precisely as such and in such a way as to solve the problem of complexity. Individuals are complex *structures* and, in general, hierarchies of structures of structures. Relational complexes—say, $:R_1(a,b)$ or $:P_3(a)$—are atomic facts. When relata are shared among atomic structures—for example, as with $:R_1(a,b)$ and $:S_2(a,c)$—there is a derivative heterogeneous whole whose unity consists in the integrated network of such facts. These networks or complexes are themselves individuals, nonrepeatable, and the bearers in turn of (instances of) properties and relations and thus are possible relata in higher-level relations and structures. At any level, the substructures are 'matter' for the relation instances, the 'forms', that subsume them. In sum,

Ordinary individual = a hierarchy of structures each one of which is a complex consisting of relation instances among mutually shared relata.

Emerging at various levels of complexity are properties and relations of these structural individuals that do not exist at lower levels of complexity—for instance, as truth-value is emergent upon the structure constituting a proposition, or as cognition is emergent upon a certain neural structure.

The same analysis applies to complexes with a conceptual existence. Hence, if we combine the analysis of chapter 1 concerning intensions with the theory of

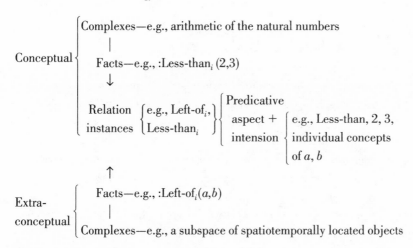

Conceptual
- Complexes—e.g., arithmetic of the natural numbers
  |
- Facts—e.g., :Less-than$_i$ (2,3)
  ↓
- Relation instances $\left\{\begin{array}{l}\text{e.g., Left-of}_i,\\ \text{Less-than}_i\end{array}\right\}$ $\left\{\begin{array}{l}\text{Predicative aspect} +\\ \text{intension}\end{array}\right.$ $\left\{\begin{array}{l}\text{e.g., Less-than, 2, 3,}\\ \text{individual concepts}\\ \text{of } a, b\end{array}\right.$

↑

Extra-conceptual
- Facts—e.g., :Left-of$_i$(a,b)
  |
- Complexes—e.g., a subspace of spatiotemporally located objects

Fig. 2.1. Instance ontology

instances advocated here, full instance ontology can be represented schematically as in figure 2.1. The conceptual status of arithmetic will be a topic of chapter 10.

Significantly, relation instances can form a single fundamental ontic category because, at the lowest level of complexity, it is possible for there to exist only a web of predicative relation instances among other such instances. Some philosophers have rejected this thesis as absurd, however, asserting that relations require relata and that to make these relata further relations is to precipitate a vicious regress. That this is not in fact the case can be seen effectively by returning to Max Black's allusion to the unity of the Trinity mentioned in the previous chapter. Medieval theologians proposed that the best way to understand the doctrine of the Trinity was in terms of pure relatedness, each Person being understood as a relation to the other two. Since each Person is an individual, this would presumably require that the respective relations be individuated—that is, be instances. So understood, they would together constitute the interlinking, self-contained whole described discursively as :Father$_1$(Son$_1$,Spirit$_1$), :Son$_1$(Father$_1$,Spirit$_1$), and :Spirit$_1$(Father$_1$,Son$_1$). By contrast with the standard Aristotelian intra se unity of substantial form on matter constituting ordinary individuals, for the scholastics, at least the Divine Unity must be inter se. In the resulting Divine Complex *all* constituents are predicative relation instances, with no relata that do not have the combinatorial role of such instances. Not only is this state of interwoven connectedness possible logically; it is also possible to construct a simple physical model to represent it. Given modern physics, it is increasingly plausible theoretically that the physical universe is, at its most fundamental level, a system of instances of force relations. What critics confuse is the requirement that relations have relata with the separate assumption, which is not implied, that the relata be nonrelations, a confusion abetted by the lack of refinement of relation instances. Parenthetically, I note the interesting logical truth that if we restrict ourselves to instances of *binary* irreflexive relations, then *three* is the minimum number of instances such that each can be a relatum for one instance while being a link between two others.

As well as giving a coherent account of concrete individuals, instance ontology integrates well the ontology of *events*, a point made by Campbell. It has been argued forcefully by Donald Davidson and Barry Taylor that events are needed in order to provide a workable semantics for natural languages.[16] In striving for an event ontology, it has become clear that among the central challenges to any such ontology is that it provide an identity criterion for events and that it solve the problem of recurrence (viz., that events are unrepeatable, but exactly the same *kind* of event can occur at different times and different places). John's walk at time a is as individual and unrepeatable as John is, yet it is identical *as a walk* with John's walk at a different time, b. Instance ontology provides an elaboration and both material and formal simplification of the version of event ontology known as the 'property exemplification' account advocated by Jaegwon Kim and others.[17] According to this, an event is construed as a structure consisting in an n-tuple of subjects x, an n-adic relation P^n, and a time t, abbreviated as '$[x,P^n,t]$'. By simplifying contrast with what on the face of it is a logical construct, according to instance ontology an atomic event is an n-adic relation instance P_i^n, which, by the principle of subject uniqueness, SU, is uniquely identified with an n-tuple x, and which, as an instance of a relation and not the relation intension (universal), can have temporal relations and come into and go out of existence. Equally important, events can recur, in their being distinct instances of the same event intension. The identity criteria for events are simply those of relation instances generally—having the same intension and being predicative among the same relata n-tuple. Complex events are structures composed of atomic, one-instance events. Otherwise stated,

> An event = a structure, more or less complex, whose substructures consist in temporal or causal relation instances that are sequentially related.

For example, the complex event called a walk would consist in a sequence of a repeated set of specific motions by appendages of an animated body. The event of a collision, C, of two billiard balls consists in one temporal-causal relation instance, say C_1, existing between the two complex structures comprising the billiard balls. Precisely as relation instances of a specific kind, events are nonrepeatable. Whereas bodies are complex spatiotemporal structures of 'matter' (itself a complex structure), events are complex temporal-causal structures, whether of matter or nonmaterial entities (i.e., conceptual or spiritual). In this light and *contra* its critics, event theory does not enlarge the world's ontic inventory but simply classifies one subspecies of complexes whose only constituents, like all complex entities of any kind, are of the single ontic type relation instances.

Related to an ontology of events is the power of instance ontology to solve problems in the *logic* of causation. Consider Armstrong's prominent theory of causal laws, a variant of what is known as the Dretske–Tooley–Armstrong theory of causality. Here, by contrast with the Humean 'constant conjunction' reduction of causation, which cannot account for the accident/nomic distinction, Armstrong proposes that causality is best accounted for as a nomic relation between universals.[18] That is, according to Armstrong, the causal laws between particular events or occurrences (*a* having property F causing *a* to have property G) stem from a relation of nomic necessitation, N, between the universals involved (F and G)—that is, N(F,G). Hence, from the causal law N(F,G) and the obtaining of Fa, it follows that Ga. Yet this inference is precisely the problem, as pointed out by Bas van Fraassen.[19] To secure the entailment, Armstrong proposes that the second-order state of affairs :N(F,G) be considered a first-order relation universal capable of instantiation—for example, N(Fa,Ga). If we then accept as following from the nature of N the two principles

(a) $N(F,G) \supset (x)[Fx \supset N(Fx,Gx)]$

and

(b) $N(Fx,Gx) \supset (Fx \cdot Gx),$

it follows that

(c) $[N(F,G) \cdot Fa] \supset Ga.$

The objection is that a second-order state of affairs cannot also be a first-order universal, any more than, correspondingly, a statement can be a predicate.[20] Moreover, for N(F,G), N is a relation whose relata are universals, whereas for N(Fa,Ga), N is a relation whose relata are from the entirely different category of unrepeatable states of affairs. How can this be the same relation N? The problem is solved if we take instances of properties ('particular causes') to be what the causal law N exists among—that is, the causal law 'N(F,G)' is to be particularized to

$$(F_i)(G_j)(\exists N_k)N_k(F_i,G_j).$$

So conceived, N is an abstraction from its instances, which exist among instances of F and G, the latter, like the states of affairs which they each go to make up, are unrepeatable. The abstraction N is not a predicate of anything, including the pair F and G, and (instances of) a relation R that would exist among N, F, and G because instances of N obtain between instances of F and G is a derivative, secondary relation nonidentical to N (i.e., $R \neq N$). From the refined perspective of instances, relation N would imply a single principle replacing (a) and (b) above:

$$(F_i)(G_j)[(\exists N_k)N_k(F_i,G_j) \supset (x)[F_i(x) \supset G_j(x)]],$$

from which it follows that

$$[(\exists N_k)N_k(F_i,G_j) \cdot F_i(a)] \supset G_j(a).$$

The desired result is arrived at naturally, without any confounding of states of affairs with universals.

In summary, the theory that is supported by the analysis offered here is a one-category ontology of *instance structuralism*. Relation instances are the atomic individuals out of which the world, conceptual and extra-conceptual, is composed. All other individuals are complexes or structures composed of networks of relation instances among other individuals as relata, the latter themselves being relation instances or further complexes ultimately decomposable into instances. The hierarchical iteration and emergence of instances of relations assayed as ontic combinators account for the structurally rich world of our experience. This contrasts with the explanatory poverty of the instance atomism of trope theory. In the latter, property instances as nonpredicative, isolated atoms are compositionally inert; hence the universe as in fact a structural plenum goes unexplained. Campbell, for example, must interpret the fields of contemporary mechanics as single, spatially extended tropes, as opposed to a conception common in modern physics that they are complex relational structures.[21] Classical physics arose out of a background that included at its core a subject (substance)/predicate (dependent property) metaphysics. It was atoms on the billiard ball model that were the primary subject matter, and between them physical properties and relations existed in a secondary, dependent sense. In modern physics, by contrast, it is relationships that are real and primary, particles being networks of relations.

A. N. Whitehead's sweeping metaphysics of organism, principally in *Process and Reality*, is one example of an instance structuralism composed with the modern physics of relativity and field theory in mind.[22] For Whitehead, *nature is relatedness*,[23] where the *res verae*, his 'occasions', are each a nexus, an unrepeatable 'individual facts of togetherness',[24] which go to build up other occasions and ultimately the nexus that constitutes the actual world.[25] Also advocating the value of structural ontology is the cross-disciplinary general systems theory.[26]

> The systems approach . . . proceeds from the fact that the specific features of an object (system) are not exhausted by the peculiarities of its constituent elements, but are rooted first and foremost in the character of the connections and relations between its elements. Moreover, a complex object is usually a hierarchical, polystructured and multi-level formation whose various aspects are studied by different sciences, and the nature of the structure, connections and relations distinguished in it by a certain science and constituting its subject-matter essentially depends on the level of its development and the means of investigation used in it.[27]

A system is defined as "a *connected* set of elements possessing *wholeness* owing to its connectedness."[28] Yet, it has been pointed out that general systems theory lacks a general account of this relatedness among elements so as to constitute a system, an account that, among other things, needs to distinguish systems from sets. I offer such an account here, one that requires the relatedness to be individuated, as Whitehead saw that it must be.[29]

In this book, no grand, encompassing synthesis in the spirit of Whitehead or general systems theory will be attempted. Rather, my analysis has a different goal, that of securing a needed foundation for such a work, both in establishing securely the existence and properties of relation instances and in formalizing the concomitant logic as a precise medium of analysis and as an inference engine. From the multitude of arguments provided for the ontic primacy of relations and their instances, I will establish a foundation for a one-category ontology.

chapter three

Plato and Aristotle on Instance Ontology

In this and the next two chapters we shall examine some of the more historically prominent appeals to attribute instances. My intent is not only to provide further insights into fundamental ontological problems and to determine the role that unit attributes were given in their solutions, but also to examine the pattern of association one finds existing between unit properties and the concept of *relation*. It is generally overlooked that as a historical recurrence, the association between attribute instances and ontological analyses of relations, though spotty, has been persistent and continues into contemporary times. It is a primary thesis of this work that the association is no accident. Moreover, cognizance of this link provides a perspective from which to clarify controversies over interpretations of relevant texts, as we shall observe in regard to passages from Plato, Aristotle, and Leibniz.

Plato

Though not without controversy, there are texts that are traditionally interpreted as implying that Plato and Aristotle each subscribed to a doctrine of unit properties. Though less influential in the tradition, the textual evidence is strongest for the Platonic ontology. Dispersed across at least four dialogues, Plato makes statements, and at one point gives an argument, which imply that, in addition to the invisible, abstract transcendent Forms, there are corresponding immanent forms that are individual, visible, concrete, and in created things.[1] That is, contra the standard textbook ontology attributed to Plato of dual realms of concrete individuals and abstract Forms (and possibly an intermediate realm of mathematical entities), on this reading Plato proposes a tripartite ontology of concrete individuals, quality instances, and transcendent quality universals.

Summarizing the textual evidence, in the *Republic* (510d) Plato refers to a class of 'visible forms', and in the *Parmenides* (130b) gives examples of the likenesses that we each possess, in contrast to (the Form) LIKENESS itself. The same is said to be true of the Forms UNITY, PLURALITY, and others. Similarly, in the *Phaedo* (102d–3b) OPPOSITENESS, LARGENESS, and SMALLNESS are distin-

Transcendent realm:

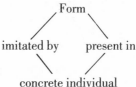

World of ordinary experience: concrete individual

Fig. 3.1. The common view of Platonic ontology

guished from cases of oppositeness, largeness, and smallness that are 'in us', and the latter, in turn, are explicitly distinguished from the concrete objects in which they adhere. In the *Theaetetus* (209a–d) it is argued that unit properties are needed to individuate what would otherwise be just bundles of universals. The textual evidence is thus from both the middle dialogues (including the *Phaedo* and the *Republic*), in which Plato separates the Forms from the participating individuals, and the later dialogues (including the *Parmenides* and the *Theaetetus*), in which he has second thoughts about the ontology of the Forms.

It has been argued (e.g., by R. Demos, R. Bluck, and G. Vlastos[2]) that the unit property reading of Plato not only is faithful to the text but also solves fundamental problems within Plato's ontology. I shall amplify this thesis in analyzing the two major supporting passages from the *Phaedo* and the *Theaetetus*. In the *Phaedo* we see for the first time the establishment of an implicational relationship between the existence of property instances and the ontic assay of relations.

According to the dual realm interpretation of Plato's ontology, Plato is said to have proposed a theory of truth whereby, for example, the statement 'Socrates is white' corresponds to a fact consisting of the changing, ephemeral, individual Socrates and a separated, unchanging, and multiply instantiable Form, WHITE-NESS. The difficulty here, as in all versions of 'Platonic realism', ancient or modern (e.g., current mathematical realism with regard to numbers, sets, structures, etc.), is to account for the ontological relationships, including causal efficacy, between separated universals and the entities that participate in them. The causal relationships among individuals are a function of the properties (and relations) they possess, and because of these causal relationships, we have epistemic access to extra-conceptual individuals through our sensory apparatus. How, then, are we to understand the 'participation' of an exemplifying par-

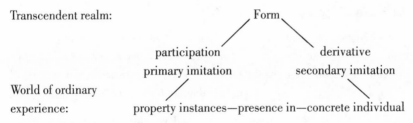

Fig. 3.2. Unit attributes in Platonic ontology

ticular in a repeatable Form? With admirable honesty, Plato in the *Parmenides* points out the problems inherent in trying to give a coherent account of the participation relation. More recently, Gilbert Ryle has argued that participation conceived of as any sort of relation is incoherent. We shall examine this argument in detail in chapter 7.

It has been proposed that Plato's adoption of unit properties represents an effort to reconcile at least two of his attempts at explicating the participation relation. Offering proposals by means of analogy, Plato in places speaks of the Forms as *present in* things and in other places of things *imitating* the Forms. As the standard presentation of Platonic ontology, we would have the schema illustrated in figure 3.1 (reading down). So interpreted, there is an apparent contradiction, for, as Demos observes, relations of imitation and presence-in exclude one another. Imitation implies bridging a gap between the abstract and the concrete, whereas presence-in implies an identity in concreteness of nature between Forms and empirical objects. By contrast, if quality instances are admitted, the relationship of imitation, or 'participation', between concrete individual—for example, Socrates—and transcendent Forms—for example, WHITENESS—becomes derivative and secondary. It is based upon a primary imitation relationship between contained unrepeatable forms and their ideal archetypes—for example, between *this* Whiteness and WHITENESS. Here the schema is as shown in figure 3.2. Thus construed, the Platonic ontology consists in individuals composed of unit properties, where these individuated, immanent forms are the primary effects of, and imperfect approximations to, their transcendent exemplars. The qualitative content of the property instance is in some sense an imprecise, vague copy of the content of the corresponding Form, where recollection of the latter is occasioned by experience of the former.

Unit Relation-Properties

A more important advantage of interpreting Plato as seriously proposing a theory of 'immanent forms' relates to a proposal he makes for analyzing relations and the implications he thinks this could have for an account of the fact of *change*. Because of its importance, I shall quote *Phaedo* 102b–e in full:

Phaedo: I think that when Socrates had got this accepted, and it was agreed that the various forms exist, and that the reason why other things are called after the forms is that they participate in the forms, he next went on to ask, If you hold this view, I suppose that when you say that Simmias is taller than Socrates but shorter than Phaedo, you mean that at that moment there are in Simmias both tallness and shortness?

Echecrates: Yes, I do.

Phaedo: But do you agree that the statement 'Simmias is bigger than Socrates' is not true in the form in which it is expressed? Surely the real reason why Simmias is bigger is not because he is Simmias but because of the height which he incidentally possesses, and conversely the reason why he is bigger than Socrates is not because Socrates is Socrates, but because Socrates has the attribute of shortness in comparison with Simmias' height.

Echecrates: True.

Phaedo: And again Simmias' being smaller than Phaedo is due not to the fact that Phaedo is Phaedo, but to the fact that Phaedo has the attribute of tallness in comparison with Simmias' shortness.

Echecrates: Quite so.

Phaedo: So that is how Simmias comes to be described as both short and tall, because he is intermediate between the two of them, and allows his shortness to be surpassed by the tallness of the one while he asserts his superior tallness over the shortness of the other. . . . I am saying all this because I want you to share my point of view. It seems to me not only that the form of tallness itself absolutely declines to be short as well as tall, but also that the tallness which is in us never admits smallness and declines to be surpassed. It does one of two things. Either it gives way and withdraws as its opposite shortness approaches, or it has already ceased to exist by the time that the other arrives. It cannot stand its ground and receive the quality of shortness in the same way as I myself have done. If it did, it would become different from what it was before, whereas I have not lost my identity by acquiring the quality of shortness—I am the same man, only short—but my tallness could not endure to be short instead of tall. In the same way the shortness that is in us declines ever to become or be tall, nor will any other quality, while still remaining what it was, at the same time become or be the opposite quality; in such a situation it either withdraws or ceases to exist.[3]

The problem that Plato is here attempting to solve is how to reconcile the two true statements 'Simmias is taller than Socrates' and 'Socrates is shorter than Phaedo' with his ontology of the monadic Forms.[4] The two relevant ontological principles are (a) that all true predication is based on the participation of an individual in a Form, and (b) that all characteristics of an entity are, appearances notwithstanding, monadic properties. When, under (b), relations are reduced to properties, the latter are often referred to in contemporary literature as *relation-properties*. I shall adopt this designation below. Hence, under constraints (a) and (b), the given relational sentences would imply that Socrates participates in both the Forms TALLNESS and SHORTNESS. Because these relation-properties are contraries, however, simultaneous participation in both is impossible. To solve this problem, Plato introduces unit properties as a third type of entity and a second type of (unrepeatable) individual. It is implicit that the posited unit properties conform at least to the minimum principle of subject uniqueness (SU). The participation relation is now between an instance and its Form, and only secondarily and in a derivative sense between the concrete individual and the Form. In our relation sentences there is implicit reference to Socrates' Tallness, T_i, and Socrates' Shortness, S_j, which as such are unique to Socrates but participate in, though imperfectly according to Plato, the content of their respective universals (hence the denial of the principle of immanent instance realism, IR). Plato is proposing that Socrates as the containing whole participates only indirectly in the Forms, doing so by means of the contained unit properties T_i, S_j, and so on, none of which ever participate in opposite Forms. To see why this is the case, we must look more closely at Plato's reduction of relations to relation-properties.

As a preliminary, it is instructive to note the following. Much has been made of the above text by H.-N. Castañeda, who proposes that, in addition to asserting unit properties, it shows that Plato had a sophisticated ontological analysis of relations.[5] This is contrasted with the 'standard view' of recent commentators that Plato simply confused relative with nonrelative terms. (Parenthetically, Castañeda has pointed out that an examination of the young Leibniz's abridgement and notes on the *Phaedo* and the *Theaetetus* shows that he is in agreement with Plato's monadic reduction of relations and an internalist theory of predication, both fundamental to the nature of Leibniz's ontology of isolated monads.) But, regardless of whether the contemporary majority interpretation of Plato's conception of relations is in error, I think Castañeda is correct in his analysis of Plato's concept of relations, and I shall amplify it below. Moreover, and significantly, the part of this assay that does not involve unit properties but is unique to relations is the core of Aristotle's doctrine and subsequently that of Neoplatonic and Islamic commentators, was passed on with refinements and variations by medieval philosophers, and hence adopted by much of Western philosophy up to the second half of the nineteenth century.[6]

Let us now examine Plato's analysis of relations, the theses implicit in the above quote from the *Phaedo* and those that form the basis of what became the classic monadic reduction of relations. According to Plato, the statement 'Simmias is taller than Socrates' corresponds to two states of affairs and a *referring* of each to the other: Simmias has *his* Tallness, Socrates has *his* Shortness, and Socrates' Shortness is 'in comparison with', is 'towards' Simmias's Tallness, as Simmias's Tallness is 'towards' Socrates' Shortness. For Plato, as for Aristotle later, a relation has the identifying characteristic of being a *to pros ti*, literally 'that which is towards something'.[7] Using scholastic terminology, the relation Is-Taller-than, insofar as it applies to Simmias, has two aspects, a *being in* (*esse in*), which is its inherence in a single subject—here Tallness predicated of Simmias—and a *being toward* (*esse ad*)—that is, a pointing to the correlative Shortness in Socrates. And similarly for the correlative fact involving Socrates and his Shortness. Though Plato is attempting to force multi-subject relations into the mold of single-subject properties, he does see as an essential ingredient of relatedness a being toward, or a 'with respect to another', aspect of the terms of the relational proposition. Intuitively, relations are essentially *conjunctive*; they are a linking together of relata under a specific intension (e.g., Is-Taller-than, Is-the-Father-of). Plato recognizes this by asserting that Simmias does not have

Tallness *simpliciter* but has it *with respect to* the Shortness of Socrates, and it is to the latter that the conjunctive aspect of the relatedness has been relegated. However—and this is crucial—in an ontology that admits only single-subject attributes, the aspect of being toward cannot itself be treated as a relation in the intuitive, unreduced sense of 'a between', but only as a modification of a single subject. But how are we to understand the esse ad aspect?

There are two problems here, one endemic to the attempted monadic reduction of relations in general, one peculiar to Plato's ontology. As regards the first, Plato and all who follow in the tradition want and need unification within what is diverse but cannot admit relations as the principle of this *linking* of entities as relata. Here we see the Pythagorean influence and what was termed earlier the primacy of the unit doctrine. Only the monadic can unify what is diverse. Relations, as polyadic, are but one more element along with their relata whose unity with the latter is to be explained. But if relations do not *link* relata, they cannot be *between* relata, so are necessarily withdrawn into each relatum as an aspect of it, but with a peculiar esse ad to make up the definitional loss. The esse ad aspect is somehow thought to establish reference to another without being a relation in the defining sense of having multiple subjects. It is as if, in being referentially coy, one can accomplish implicitly what one would abjure were it made explicit. For example, it is as if by pointing to a third person instead of shaking his hand, I can, without contacting him, indicate to you the person to whom I wish to refer. If there is any plausibility to such an analogy, it evaporates when it is realized that, though in hand shaking there is a relation of spatial contact that does not obtain in the case of pointing, the semantic reference *relation* that it was our goal to achieve is established in either case. Put more succinctly, Russell observed against Leibniz that, futile as regards all evasions to the contrary, the being-toward-another aspect of a relation-property is itself nothing but a further relation, albeit one with a different content or intension; hence no eliminative reduction of the 'between' of relations to the 'in' of relation-properties has been achieved.[8] This may have been one of the reasons why Leibniz sought to de-emphasize the esse ad aspect of relations by making it a being of reason (*ens rationis*).[9]

The second problem with this reduction of relations is peculiar to Plato and concerns the impossibility of fitting the esse ad aspect of relations into his ontology of individuals and Forms, or even into an ontology enlarged to include individuated forms. Returning to Plato's example in the *Phaedo*, Simmias's

Tallness has the added aspect, S, of being-toward-Socrates'-Shortness. Now S is not an unrepeatable individual but seemingly a multiply instantiable property—for example, an aspect of Phaedo's Tallness, in lambda notation $\lambda x(x$ toward Socrates). It must be, then, a universal or Form. Yet such a Form would have as a *constituent* a changing particular, Socrates, imperfectly participating in its own Forms. That is, S would be mutable. But this would be anathema to Plato, since for him the Forms are perfect, unchanging exemplars. Hence, as neither an individual nor a Form, the esse ad of relations has no place in Plato's ontology. Plato evidently saw none of this, but he did see in his analysis of relations the benefit of positing unit properties as a means of solving problems involving change. Let us now turn to the implications of this.

Given Plato's assay of relation statements, the import of introducing unit properties in the above text can be understood as follows. We have three relation statements:

(a) Simmias is taller than Socrates.
(b) Phaedo is taller than Simmias.
(c) Phaedo is taller than Socrates.

The last statement is implicit in the transitivity of the Taller-than relation. These correspond, respectively, to the following triplets of facts and their necessary coordination:

(a′) Simmias is Tall_1; Socrates is Short_1; Tall_1 is toward Short_1.
(b′) Phaedo is Tall_2; Simmias is Short_2; Tall_2 is toward Short_2.
(c′) Phaedo is Tall_3; Socrates is Short_3; Tall_3 is toward Short_3.

Note that by the fact that Phaedo, for example, can have two instances of the property Tall, Tall_1 and Tall_2, Plato is here denying the principle of instance uniqueness (IU).

With regard to the above problem, taking the extreme case of change, if Simmias ceased to exist, then presumably so would the instances Tall_1 and Short_2. Because the latter are necessarily connected to Short_1 and Tall_2, respectively, then the latter would also cease to exist. Yet Tall_3 and Short_3 would remain, and so Phaedo would continue to be taller than Socrates. On the other hand, if we were to delete the subscripts, then, by parallel reasoning, upon Simmias's demise, Phaedo would cease to participate in TALLNESS and Socrates in SHORTNESS, and so Phaedo would cease to be taller than Socrates. We have in this case the annihilation of properties by associated opposites, the association being a function of the relations. This counterfactual result is circumvented by introducing unit properties and the subsequent refinements of distinct opposites. We can now say how it is that Plato thinks Simmias can participate in opposite relation-properties. The participation is indirect, through their instances, and, though $Tall_1$ and $Short_1$ are opposites, because they are connected and so change in one brings change in the other, $Tall_1$ and $Short_2$ are not so connected and are not excluding opposites.

An exact analogy of Plato's argument applies to spatial relations—for example, Is-Above, Is-to-the-Right-of. Thus, Plato implies that a correct account of change of place can be given only by introducing unit properties. Indeed, he proposes that this account of change applies not just to relational properties but to 'any other quality'. When a leaf changes from green to red, it is not that Green is transformed into the contrary Red, but rather that an instance $Green_1$ 'withdraws' or 'ceases', and an instance Red_1 takes its place. Instances of Forms go in and out of existence, whereas the Forms themselves remain immutable.

This is an appropriate place to consider a recent argument by Reinhardt Grossmann concerning the irreducibility of relations to monadic properties of their terms.[10] Using as a base the above passage from the *Phaedo*, Grossmann first excludes the 'towardness' aspects of all pairs of $Tall_i$s and $Short_i$s. As he points out, to retain this esse ad aspect in any attempted reduction of a relation is simply to reduce one relation to *another* relation. For a true reduction of the relation Is-Taller-than to monadic properties, the above three relation facts must reduce to the following set of monadic statements and nothing more:

Socrates is $Short_1$, and Socrates is $Short_3$.
Simmias is $Short_2$, and Simmias is $Tall_1$.
Phaedo is $Tall_2$, and Phaedo is $Tall_3$.

Now, the reductionist might want to claim that, for example, the statement 'Phaedo is taller than Simmias' is equivalent to the conjunction 'Phaedo has two tallness and Simmias has one tallness'—that is, he might want to allow for a subject to have more than one instance of a property (which is a denial of the principle of instance uniqueness, IU). Use of the relation Taller-than is then but a manner of speaking and is eliminable without loss to quantitative aspects of its terms. But, as Grossmann observes, implicit in this move is an appeal to the quantitative relation Is-Greater-than existing between the numbers 3 and 2.

The sense of the relation statement can be maintained only if the latter numerical relation is added to the monadic conjunction. Hence no reduction of relations has been achieved. Of course, this argument could have been framed in the more commonsense terms of units of height rather than in sums of instances of TALLNESS or SHORTNESS, but the conclusion remains. There is also the fact that the conjunction 'and' is a logical relation, which is the source of its complexes having certain logical properties and relations that those of other logical connectives do not have. Labeling such connectives 'syncategorematic' does nothing to reduce their status as *relations*. Finally, Grossmann makes the general observation that any attempt to reduce a relational fact of two or more terms must end in the production of a logical or ontological *complex*: a whole with internal diversity. But "there can be no complex without some kind of relation."[11] The plural nature of a complex requires relatedness among its elements. But this must be understood correctly. It is not simply the case that a preexisting complex implies ontically secondary supervening logical relations among its constituents—for example, Is-Co-member-of-Complex-A-with—but, more fundamentally, the very existence of a complex is a function of a relation or relations existing among distinct but so unified terms. It is relations that simultaneously unify and diversify their relata.

Returning to Plato, at *Theaetetus* 155a–c, in the context of a discussion of a theory of sense perception, Plato alludes once again to the Taller-than relation and the puzzle it engenders for a coherent account of change. The puzzle is the fact that it appears that an individual can gain or lose relations with other entities without undergoing any change in itself, that is, that some relations at least are *external*. Theaetetus can grow taller than Socrates, so Socrates can lose the property Taller-than-Theaetetus and gain the property Shorter-than-Theaetetus while retaining the same foundation for both properties—namely, his specific height and his remaining the same individual. Commenting on this passage, the young Leibniz asserts that changes in relations do indeed effect change in the individual—that is, all relations are *internal*, and that, because of this, "everything is in a certain way contained in everything."[12] In an influential passage in the *Physics* (225b11–13) Aristotle simply asserts: "Nor is there motion in respect of Relations: for it may happen that when one correlative changes, the other can truly be said not to change at all, so that in these cases the motion is accidental." Stoics and, later, some scholastics used this position of Aristotle to argue that relations are not distinct from their foundations and, because of this, are strictly subjective conceptual entities.[13] In the *Theaetetus* Plato may be offering a solution to his puzzle, one that follows from the theory of perception proposed there. According to this theory, an object can become white *for* a percipient without itself suffering any internal change. F. M. Cornford suggests that by the time of this third-period dialogue, Plato had given up the view that instances of qualities (e.g., hot, white, large) reside in and perish with change in individuals.[14] Change can now be thought of as occurring not in, but *between* and external to, individuals. Plato even speaks of change itself as inherently 'toward something' (*Theaetetus* 160b–c) and hence as relational, but without being reducible to a modification of its foundation or its relata. By implication, though Plato nowhere draws it out, relations could be strictly between their relata without being properties of them. If relations were so treated, the initial puzzle of how Socrates can simultaneously have the opposite properties of tall and short would evaporate. But this is, of course, to give up a strict ontology of only monadic properties.

In any case, Plato has argued that to give an account of change within the restrictions of an ontology of monadic properties forces the introduction of unit properties. Note that Plato's argument turns on his use of asymmetric relations (e.g., Is-Taller-than), because symmetric relations (e.g., Is-Similar-in-Respect-A-to) would not rest on contrary opposites in their relata. Asymmetric relations have also been used by modern authors to demonstrate the nonreducibility of polyadic relations to monadic properties, arguments I shall reinforce below. Interestingly, we shall see the medieval philosopher Avicenna demonstrating how the monadic reduction of any symmetric relation, in itself and independent of the problem of change, requires the introduction of unit properties. Relevant to Plato, unit properties imply that repeatable universals must be 'separated' in the sense of being nonidentical with their instances, which are 'in' their particulars. This is what Plato proposes in the middle dialogues, including the *Phaedo*. Aristotle and his followers accept this separation of the universal, but only in a conceptual mode achieved by abstraction. The content or intension of the universal is universal only in the mind.

Unit Properties and the Problem of Individuation

Perhaps the strongest evidence for the thesis of property instances comes at the end of the *Theaetetus* (209a–d), where Plato is apparently arguing for their use in providing a solution to a fundamental ontological problem, that of individuation. Addressing the problem in the context of the epistemological subject matter of the *Theaetetus*, Plato argues that to have knowledge of the person Theaetetus, one must know more than a set of general properties (i.e., having a nose and a mouth and . . .) that Theaetetus possesses. An indefinite number of other men may possess these properties. Indeed, even if we could know *all*, even the more distinctive properties of Theaetetus (i.e., his snub-nosedness, etc.), this would be insufficient for knowing the specific, unrepeatable individual Theaetetus. For it is possible that other individuals could possess all these identical properties, since, by definition, each can be commonly held. To know *this* individual as Theaetetus requires knowing it *as individuated*, hence knowing what individuates it—its 'differentness', to use Plato's term. "The correct notion of anything must itself include the differentness of that thing" (*Theaetetus* 210d). In translating "differentness," Cornford notes that Plato appears deliberately to avoid the Greek term whose technical sense he uses for the *differentia* of a species.[15] This is further evidence that Plato is referring to the unrepeatability principle of concrete individuals and not to the repeatable differentiating constituent (e.g., Equilateral) of some species universal (Equilateral Triangle) with respect to its genius universal (Triangle). Now, according to Plato, this individuating differentness is known when one knows property instances qua instances that inhere in the concrete individual. Plato suggests that there will be no notion of Theaetetus in his mind, "I suppose, until *this particular* snubness has stamped and registered within me a record distinct from all the *other cases* of snubness that I have seen, and so with every other part of you" (*Theaetetus* 209c, my emphasis). To know the snub-nosedness-of-Theaetetus is to know a quality instance that has the dual aspects of unrepeatability in quantity but a repeatable quality or content and, through it and other inhering property instances, to know Theaetetus *as this individual*.

It is instructive to elaborate Plato's implicit argument, because of the fundamental issues it raises and the implications it has for instance ontology in particular. As mentioned previously, there is the often repeated maxim linking epistemology to ontology which asserts that nothing is known except through its properties. Stated with the relevant precision, there is no epistemic access to a particular over and above, prior to or independent of, at least some of its properties—knowledge of an individual qua individual and knowledge of some of its properties are simultaneous. On the purely ontological side, it follows that an individual cannot be something underlying and distinct from all its properties. We have seen the insuperable difficulties of postulating an underlying but completely indeterminate individuator—'bare particulars' or Aristotle's prime matter conceived likewise. Such a hypothetical posit is devoid of all properties and hence is unknowable in itself. If our only epistemic access to individuals is through their properties, and an individual is its properties-as-universals somehow together with an individuator, all that can be known of such an entity is its properties-as-universals. To explain the fact of how we know individuals qua individuals, the individuator must serve its postulated function at the level to which we have epistemic access, and this is the level of properties. Hence, an ordinary particular must in some sense be its-properties-individuated; Theaetetus, for example, is somehow his unit properties. Insightfully, Plato is welding both the general and the particular in the same entities, and where both aspects are given simultaneously in the same acts of perception.

Aristotle

The textual evidence that Aristotle held the thesis of property instances is less direct than that for Plato and is mostly embedded in his sometimes obscure, conflicting accounts of substance.[16] The evidence consists of an interpretation of a distinction made once in the *Categories* and a few statements made at various other places, primarily in the *Metaphysics*. On one interpretation of the *Categories*, Aristotle is referring to unit attributes in categories other than that of substance—for example, instances of Whiteness. Though this interpretation is disputed, there are a few texts in works other than the *Categories* that would seem straightforwardly to refer to nonsubstance unit properties. In the relevant texts of the *Metaphysics*, Aristotle describes substantial forms as being each 'a this' (*tode ti*: literally, 'this something'), a technical term which, as commentators have pointed out, he sometimes uses to mean a token of a type (i.e., a particular) and at other times uses only to specify a type within a wider class. Depending upon how one reads the attribution of being a 'this' in certain contexts determines whether Aristotle can be taken to be advocating the doctrine of unit forms there.

Significantly, however, there were, at least at times, two other arguments for unit attributes available to Aristotle, one based upon the theory of predication in the *Categories*, a theory modified to the exclusion of this argument in the

Metaphysics, the other based upon the classical property reduction of relations advocated continuously throughout the *Categories* and the *Metaphysics*. Both these arguments are found in Avicenna and will be examined below.

Though a standard interpretation of the *Categories* passage has included unit properties, Aristotle nowhere explicitly repeats the generating four-way distinction. It has been argued that it is because the *Categories* is an early work, containing doctrines developed during Aristotle's long tenure at Plato's academy, that we find reference to unit properties. This, of course, would give added weight to the interpretation that the author of the *Phaedo* seriously entertained this doctrine. Werner Jaeger makes the case that Aristotle's early dialogue, the *Eudemus*, draws heavily on the *Phaedo* and anticipates the *Categories*.[17] Even so, the *Phaedo* is one of the Platonic dialogues most referred to in Aristotle's writings.

In the *Categories* Aristotle presents a theory of substantial atomism, in which ordinary substances (e.g., men and horses) are taken to be fundamental and unanalyzable, admitting of predicates that are either essential (e.g., being rational and an animal are essential to Socrates) or accidental (e.g., being white). Significantly, a central criterion for primary substance laid down by Aristotle in the *Categories* is what Frank Lewis aptly calls the criterion of 'primary subjects'.[18] An entity x is an element of the set S of primary subjects if and only if (1) all predicates are ultimately of elements of S as subjects, and (2) x is predicated of nothing (cf. *Categories*, chap. 5). This is coupled with a transitivity principle for predication: namely, "When one thing is predicated of another, all that which is predicable of the predicate will be predicable also of the subject" (*Categories* 1b10). Primary substances are the ultimate subjects of all predication. For example, the predication 'Animal is pallor' is true only because there is some primary subject that is both an animal and pale. Other criteria for the status of substance are being an individual, not admitting variation in degrees, and remaining the same through a succession of contrary qualities. The last criterion allows, contra Heraclitus, for accidental change in a substance that does not imply a difference in substance (*Categories* 4a10–22). In addition to primary substances, we also have 'secondary substances', which are the genus (e.g., Animal) and species (e.g., Man) of primary substances (e.g., Socrates).

By contrast, in the *Metaphysics* a decompositional theory of hylomorphic substantialism is proposed. The ordinary concrete substance is analyzed into matter, form, and a composite of both. Predication becomes two-tiered; accidents are predicated of the matter/form composite, internal to which form is predicated of the matter. Aristotle attempts to maintain the same criteria for substance as in the *Categories*, but as we shall see, he is forced to give up the particular criterion of 'primary subjects' when it leads to a concept of prime matter that evaporates upon sustained analysis. This then requires with regard to the remaining candidates, form and the posterior composite of form and matter, that form be declared substance. Hence substantial form must satisfy the remaining requirements for substance, those of being 'separable' and being a 'this'. If being a 'this' is here to mean being an individual, then substantial form—for instance, Man—becomes unique to each composite possessing it—say, Man_1 in Plato and Man_2 in Socrates. It is this interpretation of 'this' that is controversial.

In addition to the last-mentioned reductio, matter introduces a further, profoundly important requirement for substantial form: namely, that it be the *cause* of the organizing unity among what is plural underlying matter. Socrates' proximate matter (his organs, limbs, etc.) is not a mere 'heap'; rather, it is an integrated complex with supervening properties of its own, and this organization can only be the function of the form. Given Aristotle's remarks in this regard, the containment model of predication would seem to be in the process of being abandoned for what, from a modern perspective, is a relational conception. Yet Aristotle resists and, with regard to substantial forms, simply inverts the conception of a predicate from one that is contained-in a subject to one that contains-as-structuring multiple subjects. We shall examine these issues presently.

For context, consider briefly Aristotle's theory of the relationship between universals and the process of abstraction. According to Aristotle, the primary ontic units are substances, each a 'this-such', individuals-as-men or individuals-as-horses, and so on. Pure, separated 'such's' (universals—e.g., Man, Horse) are abstractions with cognitive existence only. Outside the mind, universals exist only in things—*universalia in rebus*. Aristotle's theory of abstraction is apparently that different individuals with the property F cause similar perceptions in the normal observer. These perceptions then give rise to a single concept, F, in the soul of the perceiver (*Posterior Analytica* 2. 19. 100a1–b6; *Metaphysics* 980a30–981a12).

As a schema with the unit property aspect ignored, as in most popular expositions, Aristotle's ontology becomes as shown in figure 3.3 (reading down).

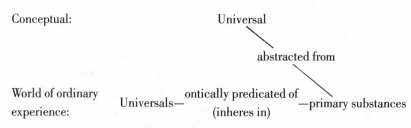

Fig. 3.3. The common view of Aristotelian ontology

This was the predominant interpretation of Aristotle among Europeans from after Boethius (480–525) to the middle of the twelfth century; individuality extends only to substance, and universals are not separable from substances. This is in contrast to what became the majority view in the thirteenth and fourteenth centuries, when both nominalists and moderate realists extended individuality to accidents as well.

Unit Predicates in the *Categories*

Let us now turn to the evidence that Aristotle's ontology included unit properties first in categories other than substance. First, at *Categories* 1a24–b9 Aristotle proposes that all 'things that are' fall within at least one of the following four classes:

> Of things there are: (a) some are *said of* a subject but are not *in* any subject. For example, man is said of a subject, the individual man, but is not in any subject. (b) Some are in a subject but are not said of any subject. (By 'in a subject' I mean what is in something, not as a part, and cannot exist separately from what it is in.) For example, the individual knowledge-of-grammar is in a subject, the soul, but is not said of any subject; and the individual white is in a subject, the body (for all color is in a body), but is not said of any subject. (c) Some are both said of a subject and in a subject. For example, knowledge is in a subject, the soul, and it is also said of a subject, knowledge-of-grammar. (d) Some are neither in a subject nor said of a subject, for example, the individual man or individual horse—nothing of this sort is either in a subject or said of a subject. Things that are individual and numerically one are, without exception, not said of any subject, but there is nothing to prevent some of them from being in a subject—the individual knowledge-of-grammar is one of the things in a subject.[19]

The *said of* and *in* relations follow, respectively, the English language distinction between copulas exhibited in the forms 'X *is a(n)* Y' and 'X *is* Y'.[20] Man is said of Socrates, and animal is said of man, since it is correct to say 'Socrates is a man' and 'Man is an animal' but not 'Socrates is man' or 'Man is animal'. For the in relation, pale is in Socrates, and pale is in man, since we say correctly that 'Socrates is pale' and 'Man is pale', it being ungrammatical to say 'Socrates is a pale' or 'Man is a pale'.

Aristotle, however, intends these terms to mark relationships existing beneath the surface grammar, at the level of 'things themselves'.[21] The term 'subject' translates literally as 'what underlies', and that Aristotle is giving a classification of things, not names, is reiterated at *Categories* 2a19 f. Aristotle assumes that distinctions in linguistic predication provide clues to distinctions within the underlying ontological predications.

Because of this mixture of linguistic and ontological analysis, the *Categories* is a book of exceptional ambiguity, and controversy surrounds exactly what ontological distinctions Aristotle intends to mark by the said of and in relationships. The following is offered as a minimal interpretation consonant with Aristotle's few explanatory remarks and examples and comes close to (though it is not identical with) Ackrill's analysis.[22] As a preliminary, it should be noted that it is extensions of general terms that are ontically fundamental for Aristotle, and these consist in sets of primary substances. The said of and in relations can exist between universals, but this is only because of—and requires—a definition that encompasses the said of or in relations existing between a term and a primary substance. For Aristotle goes on to say:

> For example, animal is predicated of man [the universal] and therefore also of the individual man; for were it predicated of none of the individual men it would not be predicated of man [the universal] at all. Again, color is in body [the universal] and therefore also in an individual body; for were it not in some individual body it would not be in body [the universal] at all. Thus all the other things are either said of the primary substances as subjects or in them as subjects. So if the primary substances did not exist it would be impossible for any of the other things [the universals] to exist. [*Categories* 2a34–2b6]

Thinking in terms of extensions, the *said of* relation would require at least the following. Given terms 'S' and 'P' with non-empty extensions, S and P respectively, for P to be said of S is for *P* to subsume the class *S* as a smaller subclass. What this implies is that 'P' denotes a universal: "Things that are individual and numerically one are, without exception, not said of a subject" (*Categories* 1b5–6). Moreover, as the last quote indicates, P must be a predicate of every entity in *S*. Using Aristotle's examples, the predicate is said of the subject in 'Socrates is a man' and 'Man is an animal'. Then, for denial of the universal, for P 'not to be in any subject', it must be the case that there are no terms 'S' whose extensions are smaller than, therefore subsumable by, *P*. This requires that 'P' be a singular denoting term (e.g., 'Socrates') whose extension is the entity denoted. Here 'P' must denote a particular.

With regard to the *in* relation, Aristotle twice repeats the disclaimer that 'in' here does not mean 'present as a part' (*Categories* 1a22, 3a30), by which he presumably intends to reject the naive conception of spatial encompassment. For a property to be in a subject is, or is based on, a more abstract relation. More important is Aristotle's further explanation: namely, that for something to be *in* a subject means that it "cannot exist separately from what it is in" (*Categories* 1a23). Given this restriction and the examples provided, P is in S if it is impossible for P to exist as an ontic predicate of entities outside the extension of S, *S*. Or, alternatively, P is not in S if it is possible for P to exist in entities outside *S*. Consequently, for denial of the universal, for P 'not to be in any subject', implies that it is possible for P to exist outside the extension of any class—that is, P's existence is not tied to any (other) subject. This is a prime characteristic of substance, which, in the *Categories*, includes both primary and secondary substance. Hence, knowledge is in the soul, since knowledge treated extensionally cannot exist outside some soul. White is in body, though not in Socrates, for the extension of the term 'white' encompasses more than, and so can exist without being, an attribute of Socrates' body. This is why Aristotle can say that "the differential also is not in a subject. For footed and two-footed are said of man as subject but are not in a subject; neither two-footed nor footed is *in* man" (*Categories* 3a22–24). The extension of 'footed', for example, is not a subset of the extension of 'man'. Given that the said of and in relations imply the requirements described, they yield the here relevant subclass (b) of the above quote, entities that are "in a subject but are not said of any subject"—that is, entities P that are not multiply exemplifiable but, for some subject S, are predicable of each element of *S* and cannot exist as a predicate of entities outside S. Since these entities are not multiply exemplified, the subject class (the extension of S) for the predication of any of them must consist of a single entity. That is, the predicable entities P are specific to the individuals that possess them; they are property instances.

Taking a cue from the surface grammar, Socrates' whiteness is not repeatable, because it cannot 'be said of Socrates'; that is, it makes no sense to say 'Socrates is his whiteness' or 'Socrates is a whiteness'. Yet Socrates' whiteness is *in* a subject, since his whiteness does not exist outside him as a subject.

Along this line, it was observed by Wilfred Sellars that, if 'W_1' names the instance of white possessed uniquely by Socrates, then it makes perfectly good sense to say 'W_1 is a white'.[23] Here we have for predication in nonsubstance categories an exact parallel to predication in the category of substance—for example, with 'Socrates is a man' (see table 3.1). Socrates and W_1 are both unrepeatable 'this's', the predicates Man and White being universals.

It is significant that, although unit properties according to Aristotle's cross-classifications as interpreted above are *predicable* entities, in later works he asserts that it is only the universal that is predicated of a subject (e.g., *De Interpretatione* 17a39–40, *Prior Analytics* 43a25–40, *Metaphysics* 1038b15). However, as will be seen, on one reading of certain texts in the *Metaphysics*, Aristotle rejects this thesis and has *unit* substantial forms predicated of matter. Relatedly, as will be seen, Aristotle also vacillates on the cause of individuation; in several places matter is declared to be the cause of the unrepeatability of an entity, yet there are a few texts in which individuation is attributed to predicable form.

Returning to Aristotle's initial classification, the remaining subclasses specified are secondary substances (universals as genera and species of primary substances), which fall under (a); universals outside the category of substance, which fall under (c); and primary substances, which fall under (d). Primary substances, as being 'neither in a subject or said of a subject', have an existence not tied by dependent predication to any other entity and are individuals (unrepeatable). The entities hereby classified are made perspicuous in table 3.1.

This classification of entities, in particular the positing of property instances under (b), is the interpretation of the above text by scholars J. L. Ackrill, W. D. Ross, H. G. Apostle, and others.[24] It has been disputed by G. E. L. Owen, Michael Frede, and Frank Lewis.[25] Below I shall speculate as to why at the time of the *Categories* Aristotle might have felt the need of property instances.

Concerning the principles inherent in instance ontology as identified in

TABLE 3.1 Classifications from the *Categories*

	Never in a subject (substances)	In a subject (nonsubstances)
Said of a subject (universals)	(a) Genus and species as secondary substances (e.g., Man, Animal)	(c) Nonsubstance properties as universals (e.g., White)
Never said of a subject (particulars)	(d) Individual primary substances (e.g., Socrates)	(b) Unit properties (e.g., Socrates' whiteness)

chapter 1, if the above classification is correct, then Aristotle is explicitly committed to the minimal principle of subject uniqueness (SU) as well as to the principle of immanent instance realism (IR)—that distinct instances (e.g., Socrates' Whiteness and Plato's Whiteness) contain a numerically identical universal (Whiteness). Equally clear is Aristotle's rejection of the principle of instance predicates—that only property instances are ontic predicates, since for him genus and species universals are also predicates.

Aristotle goes on to discuss the remaining nine categories apart from substance which constitute the ultimate classificatory divisions and from which all predicates can be taken: quantity, quality, relation, place, time, posture (e.g., 'sits'), possession (e.g., 'is shod'), action (e.g., 'cuts'), and passivity (e.g., 'is cut'). Under the heading 'relation', Aristotle (and, through him, much subsequent Western thought) adopts the Platonic reduction of relations as monadic properties, each with a characteristic 'toward' aspect. Because of the implicit, but fundamental, link that Aristotle makes between relations and substance in the *Metaphysics*, I shall amplify his views on relations shortly.

If Aristotle did in fact adopt the doctrine of unit properties at the time of the early *Categories*, what motivated him to do so? First, as mentioned, there is a straightforward argument for unit predicates, at least from the subclass of secondary substances. Though not found in Aristotle, the argument is later made explicit by Avicenna. Once instances of genus and species were allowed—say,

Man$_1$ and Animal$_1$—it would be natural to extend this mode of existence to unit accidents—for example, White$_1$. The argument can be summarized as follows. At *Categories* 2b38–3a5 Aristotle asserts that every attribute of an individual man—for example, 'skilled in grammar'—is applicable or attributable to the species and genus to which the individual belongs. He is emphatic that "This law holds good in all cases." Now if one man is learned and another man is an ignoramus, then on this theory of predication the species Man as subject would have contrary properties: namely, 'Man is learned' and 'Man is ignorant'. This contradiction is avoided, however, if it is distinct instances of the species that are predicates of the distinct men and if, in turn, these instances of the species—for example, Man$_1$ and Man$_2$—are separate subjects for what are contrary predicates—'Man$_1$ is learned' and 'Man$_2$ is ignorant'. Aristotle presents an argument along these lines in the *Metaphysics* (1039a34–b6) when criticizing the Platonic theory of Forms, and he does so in the midst of texts most easily interpreted as advocating unit substantial forms. He states there that if there were a Platonic Form of 'Animal', as such a 'this', it would have to share in the contrary attributes of being 'two-footed' as well as 'many-footed', and this is absurd.

A second suggestion for why Aristotle adopted unit predicates at the time of the *Categories* has been offered by R. E. Allen.[26] According to Allen, Aristotle's choice of vocabulary shows that he had clearly in mind the dilemma of participation formulated by Plato in the *Parmenides* (131a–c) and mentioned again in the *Philebus* (15b–c) as a notorious crux. The dilemma is: assume that one characteristic is in many things, then it will be in such things as a whole, or parts of it will be in each. If the first case, "what is one and the same will be present, at the same time and as a whole, in many things, and therefore it will be separated from itself" (*Parmenides* 131b1–2). On the other alternative, the "characteristics themselves are actually divided, and the things which partake of them partake of parts of them. . . . (But we cannot say) that we can really divide one characteristic, and that it will still be one" (131c5–10). Aristotle responds to the dilemma by positing two related kinds of entities: universals (e.g., White), which are 'one and the same' but not 'in many things', and separate property instances, which are in distinct individuals and in each as complete, so not 'divided'.

Providing less controversial evidence for the thesis that Aristotle posited individuals in categories other than substance are texts outside the *Categories*.

For example, in *Physics* VIII reference is made to motions that are 'numerically one', as opposed to specifically one—for example, as 'from white to black'. A motion is "numerically the same if it proceeds from something numerically one to something numerically one in the same period of time, e.g., from a particular white to a particular black, or from a particular place to a particular place, in a particular period of time" (*Physics* 242a38–b2). A motion would be specifically one if it were to go from white (as universal) to black (as universal), whereas it is numerically one if it goes from an instance of white to an instance of black.

In the *Nicomachean Ethics* Aristotle criticizes Plato's theory of separated Forms, pointing out that it would be no benefit to the carpenter or the doctor in respect of their crafts to know the 'good itself': "For a doctor seems not even to study health in this way, but health of man, or perhaps rather the health of a particular man; it is individuals that he is healing" (1097a11–14).

In the *Metaphysics* Aristotle questions his thesis, stated elsewhere, that knowledge is exclusively of the universal, saying that this "statement is in a sense true, although in a sense it is not." He explains:

> For knowledge, like the verb 'to know', means two things, of which one is potential and one is actual. The potency, being, as matter, universal and indefinite, deals with the universal and definite; but the actuality, being definite, deals with a definite object—being a 'this', it deals with a 'this'. But *per accidens* sight sees universal color, because this universal color which it sees is color; and this individual *a* which the grammarian investigates is an *a*. [1087a15–20]

Aristotle here seems to be saying that there are instances of color as there are multiple tokens of the same type '*a*' and, more significantly, that we have knowledge of the corresponding universals because we have prior knowledge of the individual instances *as individuals*, this knowledge of the individual being either by 'intuitive thought' for intelligible individuals (e.g., this geometric circle) or by perception for sensible individuals (*Metaphysics* 1036a2–8).

Unit Substantial Forms in the *Metaphysics*

A second textual source for interpreting Aristotle as positing unit properties, though now in the category of substance, is the *Metaphysics*, particularly books VII (Z) and VIII (H).[27] As a caveat, I should remind the reader that the *Meta-*

physics is a notoriously difficult book to interpret; moreover, the relevant parts of the text are written in the style of working notes, with problems posed, solutions offered then criticized, the problem re-posed, and so on. As previously mentioned, when Aristotle wrote the *Metaphysics*, he subjected to scrutiny and refinement in the overall context of an adopted hylomorphism much of the ontology taken for granted in the *Categories*.

In the *Categories*, concrete individuals (e.g., Socrates) were taken as un-analyzed ontic atoms, which, as 'primary subjects', were the ultimate subjects of all predication. But now in the *Metaphysics* we have a two-tiered theory of predication, in which ordinary substances (e.g., Socrates) are subjected to further internal analysis in terms of the subject/predicate distinction (1049a34–36). In the hylomorphism of the *Metaphysics*, accidents are predicated of substances, and substances, in turn, are compounds of substantial forms predicated of matter. Significantly, the substantial form does not simply *attach to* or *inhere in* its matter as subject; rather, it informs or organizes it as elements into a *structure*. Such structures need not only be static spatiotemporal complexes, as in a statue, but can be temporally expansive event structures working themselves out according to their dynamic nature, like the life cycle of a living creature.

On one possible interpretation, Aristotle in book VII (Z) of the *Metaphysics* can be construed as putting forward an argument for unit substantial forms, one that shows the bankruptcy of the idea that every aspect or determination of an individual is a predicate of that entity. Here Aristotle seeks to determine what substance is in its primary sense, "that something definite which underlies them [accidents] (i.e., the substance or individual) which is implied in such a predicate" (1028a26). The principal candidates are form, matter, and the form/matter composite. Criteria mentioned here are self-subsistence or separability, being a 'this', and, important, that substance be a 'primary subject'—that is, "That it is that which is not predicated of a stratum, but of which all else is predicated" (1029a7). As stressed previously, when the subject/predicate analysis is pressed consistently within a form/matter context, a downwardly iterated sequence of form/matter compositions is introduced, down to and through the physical atoms of earth, air, fire, and water, and indeed beyond the minimum matter of space—'intelligible matter' (1035b27–36a12).[28] The matter at any level *n* consists of one or more entities, each with some essential determination (all accidental specifications presupposing an essential form) that functions as form upon matter at the next lower level, $n + 1$. This downwardly ratcheting analysis must either proceed to infinity or stop at some level of ultimate forms and matter. The first option is an explanatory vicious regress which Aristotle does not waste time to consider. If, on the other hand, this process must come to an end, then, having 'stripped off' (*aphairesis*) every determination what-soever on the side of form, all "affections, products, potencies of bodies, length, breadth, and depth,"[29] the resulting matter as ultimate subject will be

> neither a particular thing nor a certain quantity nor assigned to any other of the categories by which being is determined. For there is something of which each of these is predicated, whose being is different from that of each of the predicates. . . . Therefore, the ultimate substratum is of itself neither a particular thing nor of a particular quantity nor otherwise posi-tively characterized; nor yet is it the negation of these, for negation also will belong to it only by accident. [*Metaphysics* 1029a20–25]

Aristotle intends that this matter so construed have absolutely no predicates; it is prior to any specifications, it is completely indeterminate, pure potentiality. Nor can the nature of this prime matter so conceived be determined negatively. What was posited as a primary subject and a 'something' has now dissipated into a *no-thing*. Elsewhere, at several places in the text where Aristotle calls upon matter to be an individuator for concrete composite substances, this mat-ter already has some determination, being what was later termed 'secondary' matter (e.g., bones, flesh, bricks, bronze). But here, as what is left when concep-tually all predicable determinations are removed, this matter cannot be a 'such' or 'what'; it is completely *bare*; and moreover, it cannot even be a 'this' in the sense of a bare *particular*. For Aristotle concludes:

> For those who adopt this point of view then, it follows that matter is substance. But this is impossible; for both separability and *'thisness'* are thought to belong chiefly to substance. And so form and the compound of form and matter would be thought to be substance, rather than matter. The substance compounded of both, i.e., of matter and shape, may be dis-missed; for it is posterior and its nature is obvious. [*Metaphysics* 1029a27–33, my emphasis]

If, then, form is, by default, substance in the primary sense, it must satisfy the remaining criteria—in particular, it must be a 'this'. Elsewhere he says, "No substance can consist of universals because a universal indicates a 'such' (*toionde*), not a 'this'" (*Metaphysics* 1039a15; cf. 1003a5–11, 1033b23, 1038b35). If being 'a this' means being an individual and unrepeatable, then Aristotle is here asserting the existence of unit substantial forms. Unfortunately, however, the technical term 'thisness' is used by Aristotle in some contexts to indicate a particular (e.g., *Categories* 3b10–18) and, it is argued, in other contexts to specify a division of a wider kind[30]—hence the controversy as to whether Aristotle is committed to unit forms. Rather than go into this controversy in detail, I shall consider only some of the more relevant texts.

Before turning to the texts, however, let us be clear about what the above reductio, so interpreted, has established independently of the issue of the individuality of form. As often pointed out by Aristotelian scholars, the very concept of prime matter conceived as the posited ultimate substratum that receives as predicates attributes distinct from itself but can have no characteristics distinct from these, 'of its own', is itself incoherent.[31] If ultimate matter is posited as what underlies, directly or indirectly, absolutely all properties and so in itself is completely devoid of predicates, then we cannot persist in giving characteristics to it, even the sometimes attributed 'ingenerable', 'indestructible', and 'a persistent substrate for generation and corruption'. Joseph Owens, for example, contends that this 'pure potentiality' is a positive characteristic in itself and therefore sufficient to save the concept of prime matter as primary subject from evaporation.[32] But this will not save it, for even the 'capacity' to have a property is a property, and as an ultimate subject, prime matter cannot have even this. As completely devoid of predicates, a bare particular cannot only *not* be a particular, it *is* nothing. To say that such an entity is a Lockean substratum, unknowable in itself (cf. *Metaphysics* 1036a9) yet a legitimate theoretical posit, or, at a minimum, to hold that although it may be ontically idle, it is harmless, is to miss the point. The concept is fraudulent and self-nullifying. This is why Aquinas and some other scholastics adopted as ultimate matter *materia signata quantitate*, matter endowed with an intrinsic capacity to occupy a definite portion of space. Thus we have reiterated the falsity of the thesis of predicable possession—that there are no ultimate individuals every determination (i.e., property) of which is a predicate of them. Prime matter *as ultimate subject* has failed as a candidate for "substance or individual." At some ultimate ontic level there must be individuals with no ontic distance between their individuality and their content or properties. In other words, at the atomic ontic level there is a nonpredicative composite of the repeatable and the unrepeatable, between intension and extension. This is precisely the case with property instances. A unit property—say, Man_1—is predicated of other entities, Man_1 (Socrates), but the intension, Man, is not predicated of some bare individuator that might be thought to be designated by the subscript '1'. If intensions are predicates, they must be individuated predicates—hence a logical motivation for Aristotle to have posited unit substantial forms as individuals predicated of plural proximate matter.

We thus have a demonstration that there are no substances devoid of attributions, though interestingly, and conversely, there are for Aristotle some attributes—the pure forms of the Prime Mover, the lesser celestial intelligences, and the human 'active reason'—which are subjectless—that is, are not predicated of matter. Though Aristotle did not do this, the scholastics later drew the logical conclusion that in order to get something approaching uniqueness, the pure forms of God and angels must be their own infimae species. This, of course, will not do, since a universal is at least potentially repeatable even if, in fact, it is not multiply exemplified; whereas a true individual is, as such, necessarily unrepeatable. Even unit forms would not do here, since though they would account for a plurality of angels, each one a distinct instance of some angelic species, the individuation of each instance of the species could not be accounted for. As the only two candidates, both the matter as subject and the 'state of predication' of form in matter are here precluded. Note, however, that if substantial forms were allowed to be predicated of other forms, not matter, and if predication were the 'principle' of individuation, then angels as complex intelligences would be individuated as networks of individuated properties (and relations). Likewise God. Of course, this is nowhere to be found explicitly in Aristotle and the subsequent tradition, though it is sometimes implied, as we shall see in the next section.

In the relevant text, in book VII, Aristotle, in speaking of predication, states that when the subject is 'the substratum of modifications', modifications being accidents like musical or pale, "the ultimate subject is a substance; but when this is not so but the predicate is a *form* and a 'this', the ultimate subject is matter and material substance" (1049a29–36). In the following book, VIII (H), in discussing sensible substances, Aristotle asserts:

> The substratum is substance, and this is in one sense matter (and by matter I mean that which, not being a 'this' actually, is potentially a 'this'), and in another sense the formula or shape (that which being a 'this' can be

separately formulated), and thirdly the complex of the two, which alone is generated and destroyed, and is, without qualification, capable of separate existence. [1042a25–31; cf. 1070a9–15]

This is repeated elsewhere, in *De Anima* 2. 1:

We are in the habit of recognizing, as one determinate kind of what is, substance, and that in several senses, (a) in the sense of matter or that which in itself is not 'a this', and (b) in the sense of form or essence, which is that precisely in virtue of which a thing is called 'a this', and thirdly (c) in the sense of that which is compounded of both (a) and (b). [412a1–10]

In the *Metaphysics* he goes on to state: "By form I mean the essence of each thing and its primary substance" (1032b1), and "The substance of a thing is that which is peculiar to it, which does not belong to anything else, but the universal is common" (1038b9).

At one place Aristotle states that forms in concrete things are temporally limited: "Since substance is of two kinds, the concrete thing and the formula (I mean that one kind of substance is the formula taken with the matter, while another kind is the formula in its generality), substances in the former sense are capable of destruction" (*Metaphysics* 1039b20–23). Since it cannot be the universal that is destroyed, it must be a form specific to the compound concrete substance that is lost when the compound dissolves.

Aristotle also speaks of a parallel between the composition of universals and their corresponding instances.

It is clear also that the soul is the primary substance and the body is matter, and man or animal is the compound of both taken universally; and 'Socrates' or 'Coriscus', if even the soul of Socrates may be called Socrates, has two meanings (for some mean by such a term the soul, and others mean the concrete thing), but if 'Socrates' or 'Coriscus' means simply this particular soul and this particular body, the individual is analogous to the universal in its composition. [*Metaphysics* 1037a5–9; cf. 1035b28–31]

The apparent parallel is between

(universal) Man = (universal) Soul + (universal) Body

and

Socrates = this particular soul + this particular body.

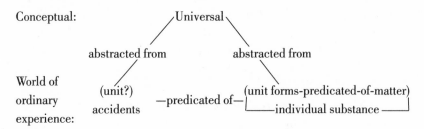

Fig. 3.4. Unit attributes in Aristotelian ontology

Further on, the point is made in another way: "And those things in the same species are different, not in species, but in the sense that the causes of different individuals are different, your matter and form and moving cause being different from mine, while in their universal definition they are the same" (*Metaphysics* 1071a27–29). And again, Aristotle states: "But man and horse and terms which are thus applied to individuals, but universally, are not substances but something composed of this particular formula and this particular matter treated as universal" (1035b28–31).

The last three texts quoted would seem to provide an answer to critics who stress Aristotle's repeated position that only the universal is predicated, and that if form is predicated of matter, it must be a universal. The reply is that Aristotle equivocates on the term 'form', using it sometimes to refer to 'this particular formula', which, like 'this particular matter', is unreplicable—for example, Rational-Animal₁—and sometimes to refer to a formula abstracted from the context of any individuation—for example, Rational Animal. Some of these critics base their doubts concerning a theory of unit forms upon Aristotle's equivocation between 'thisness' and 'particular' (*to hath' hekaston*),[33] and one might make the case, perhaps even a fortiori, that the same is true for 'form'.

Relevant to this possible equivocation is the point that unit forms would render consistent a widely observed prima facie incoherence of *Metaphysics* VII. The familiar problem is that Aristotle there appears to commit himself to three mutually contradictory theses:[34]

(a) No universal can be a substance.
(b) A substantial form is a universal.
(c) A substantial form is that which is most truly substance.

Countenancing unit properties removes the contradiction. Analogous to ordinary particulars, which possess individuality and universality, a property instance is a limiting case of a particular with a single content, intension, or 'class concept' that is common to many. In this way a unit property is not *in the same respect* both occurrent and universal, for this would be a contradiction and is one of the objections that Aristotle brought against Plato's Forms. It is primarily an individual with an intensional aspect that, when abstracted from the instance, can be known as identical across like units. The apparent contradiction of *Metaphysics* VII is resolved as:

(a) No universal can be a substance.

(b) The *intension* of an individuated substantial form is a universal.

(c) The individuated substantial form is that which is most truly substance.

If Aristotle did in fact advocate an ontology of unit substantial forms and possibly also one of unit accidents in the *Metaphysics*, it, together with his theory of abstraction, would be given by figure 3.4 (reading down). The phrase 'predicated of' in figure 3.4 refers to ontic predication. If we affirm the commitment to unit accidents, then the resulting scheme is the interpretation of Aristotle by Avicenna and the view adopted by medieval scholastics under the head 'moderate realism'. It represents a commitment to the principles of subject uniqueness (SU), instance predicates (IP), and immanent instance realism (IR). Aristotle would also be committed to the principle of relata-linking (RL)—that no instance exists apart from its being predicative among a set of relata, this for the same reasons that he gives for rejecting the independently existing Platonic Forms.

Substantial Forms as Principles of Structure

Aristotle does not explicitly or directly tie unit properties to relations, as did Plato, yet he does make an implicit, insightful connection in a paragraph at the end of *Metaphysics* VII (1041a33–b33), which is repeated in VIII. 3 (1043b5–14; cf. 1045a7–19, 1040b7–10). The context is one in which "the inquiry is about the predication of one thing of another. And why are these things, i.e., bricks and stones, a house?" (1041a24–20). In other words, predication is concerned with the fact that "certain elements make up a certain whole" (1041b1). Aristotle observes that a syllable *ab* is more than the mere sum or 'heap' of its elements, *a* and *b*, just as flesh is more than a heap of its physical components, ultimately fire and earth. An ingredient is required to account for the structure, which, as such, has properties that the subordinate constituents, singly or as a class, do not. "For none of them is a unity, but as it were a mere heap, till they are worked up and some unity is made of them" (*Metaphysics* 1040b8–9; cf. *De Anima* 410a20–22). Yet Aristotle observes that the requisite ingredient cannot be a further element similar in ontic status to the rest, for this would lead to an infinite regress of stages, with more and more elements, the collection of which at any one stage would remain nonidentical to the original emergent *whole*. That is, a unifier at the $n + 1$ stage must be posited to account for the unity of the 'heap' at the n level; but if this unifier is but another element with the same status as the rest with respect to the whole, there results a new heap whose unity must be accounted for at the $n + 2$ level. And so on. What is required, according to Aristotle, is a *cause* (literally, 'that which is responsible for') "which makes *this* thing flesh and *that* a syllable. And similarly in all other cases. And this is the *substance* of each thing" (*Metaphysics* 1041b25–26). It is clear that Aristotle is attempting to account for *structure* or system and to do so with his hylomorphic theory of substance.[35] In ancient Greek, *systéma* (derived from *syn-histémi*: 'to [make to] stand together') meant to join together as a connected or composite whole, the *holon*. Paradigm substances—for example, individual men or trees—are dynamic functioning systems of material components. For Aristotle, what gives emergent structure to a set of elements considered as matter, a whole that at its own level has supervenient properties not found at the reduced level of unorganized elements, is individuated substantial form as predicated of the elements. If structure is intrinsic to an entity, then the cause of the structure must be immanent to the entity. Perhaps this fact, along with the observation that, because of the disordering effect of matter, two individuals (e.g., Socrates and Plato) are similar but not isomorphic or exact clones, was a further motivation for Aristotle to individuate substantial forms (e.g., Man). Slightly different structural arrangements require distinctness of the forms that effect the structures, even if each is of the same infimae species.

Frank Lewis has suggested that an insightful way of interpreting Aristotle's position that substantial form is the principle of unification for a complex individual is as an analog to Frege's 'unsaturated' functions, specifically to the monadic case of 'concepts'.[36] According to Frege, of the constituents of every complex whole, "at least one must be 'unsaturated' or predicative; otherwise they would not hold together"[37] It is only entities in this fundamental category—that is, those that are unsaturated—that are "capable of serving as a link," and these, he says, are relations.[38] To treat all constituents of a complex as saturated, as 'objects' in Frege's terminology, is to land in a regress in which no matter how many additional objects are posited, they will "hold aloof from one another,"[39] remaining a class with no direct connectedness inter se. Similarly, for Aristotle, matter lacks the requisite unity that would account for the structure of the composite of itself and form. Matter is 'saturated', and what is required is an 'unsaturated' form (Frege's 'functions') to account for the unity of the complex.

Albeit without Frege's 'unsaturated' metaphor, Aristotle makes a weak but telling attempt to explain emergent unity-in-diversity by utilizing the act/potency distinction (*Metaphysics* 1045a20–25, b16–21). He states that "the proximate matter and the form are one and the same thing, the one potentially, and the other actually. Therefore it is like asking what in general is the cause of unity and of a thing's being one; for each thing is a unity, and the potential and the actual are somehow one" (1045b17–21).

Importantly, it is implied here that the individuality of form *as actual* is ontically prior to the unity it effects among (secondary) matter as only *potential*. Put succinctly, the principle of individuation for concrete substance is a prior individuated form, not the underlying matter. Note that the above quote follows in the same book VII which contains Aristotle's reductio of prime matter as ultimate subject. There it was implied that if individuation of a composite is a function of matter at every level of composition, and that if ultimate matter as the subject for the lowest level of forms in the matter/form hierarchy dissipates into nothingness, then individuation at any level goes unaccounted for. Of the two explicit candidates, matter and form, it must then be form that individuates, and this would seem to be Aristotle's conclusion here. The unrepeatability (the 'thisness'?) of a composite substance is a function of the unrepeatability of the containing form.

Assuming that we have interpreted Aristotle correctly, what is the relationship between form as individual, R_i, and form as universal, R? If form is in—the primary—sense *universal*, its reduction to unreplicated unit forms must have a cause, but one that is not matter in any primary sense. The only, albeit suppressed, candidate in the form/matter composite, one invisible to Aristotle, is the *predication* of the form upon matter. Matter as subject is the 'occasion' for the individuation of form, but it is the *attachment* of the form to matter that renders the former occurrent. What is required, then, is that predication be a distinct, third ontic 'principle', different from, but on a par with, the 'principles' of form and matter, and Aristotle nowhere adopts this line. Indeed, in keeping with the overall conceptual milieu, he consistently presupposes the theses that all predication is monadic (primacy of the unit doctrine) and that the subject is the source of the predicational unity ('unity being from the unit'). When applied to the conclusions reached in book VII, these assumptions require that plural matter (e.g., Socrates' organs) as subject of a substantial form be a 'one', and since this is impossible in the full, direct sense, it must be so in a lesser sense, as 'potential'. Aristotle continues to maintain in several places that it is matter that individuates (*Metaphysics* 1016b32, 1034a5–8, 1035b27–31, 1074a31–34). The tension between matter as a plurality and the requirement that it be a 'one' as subject explains the peculiar assertion in the last quote that matter and form are "one and the same thing," the one potential, the other actual.

There is a second, related reason why Aristotle might have chosen the analogy of act/potency duality to explain the predication relationship between form and matter. Form has been proposed as the *cause* of the unity among diverse matter as subject. With analytic assent, Aristotle now reflects upon the general relation of causality as an analogical clarifier to the specific case of the predication relation. But, unfortunately, the intrinsic weakness of the Aristotelian account of predication is simply reduplicated at the level of causality. Causality, like predication here, is a relation and so, when taken strictly and subjected to the pervasive reductionist presupposition, must be eliminated in favor of monadic attributes. The act/potency dichotomy is nothing but the analytic residue of the property reduction of relations applied to the particular case of the causality relation itself. The relation in 'a is caused by b' reduces to the relation-properties in '$R'a$' and '$R''b$', R' being act and R'' being the corresponding potency. Yet, even to say 'corresponding potency' is to misrepresent the would-be reduction, for the phrase signifies a lingering unreduced relation, though of a more abstract, bloodless form, and all relatedness across terms has supposedly been eliminated in favor of containment within the terms. A potential unity is not a unity, and Aristotle's act/potency analog contributes nothing to an explication of the structural connectedness of predication, because the 'connectedness' that is needed is equally absent at the level of causality. What is essential, but lacking, is a polyadic conception of predication (and causality), predication with simultaneous multiple subjects—that is, relations—and these Aristotle quite consistently eliminates in a manner to which we shall next turn.

Aristotle's Monadic Reduction of Relations

As for Plato, so for Aristotle, relations are *to pros ti*, 'that which is toward something'. He says: "Those things are called relative, which, being either said to be *of* something else or *related to* something else, are explained by reference to that other thing" (*Categories* 6a36). Knowledge is knowledge *of something else*, as a slave is a slave *of a master*. "All relatives as spoken of in relation to correlatives that reciprocate. For example, the slave is called slave of a master and the master is called master of a slave; the double double of a half, and the half half of a double; the larger larger than a smaller, and the smaller smaller than a larger; and so for the rest too" (6b27–31). Like Plato, Aristotle held the thesis of property reduction of relations, and that relations are thus to be treated as monadic properties but with the peculiar, defining characteristic of pointing or referring to another (*Categories* 6a37ff., *Topics* 142a26, *Sophistical Refutations* 181b25ff., *Metaphysics* 1021a27ff.). Ontologically, this reduces relations to the "least of all things a kind or entity." This is for two reasons: first, a relation—for example, Is-Taller-than—presupposes in each relatum a property as a kind of foundation—say, a certain height in Socrates; and second, an entity can change its relations without undergoing change itself—Simmias can become shorter without becoming a different person if Socrates happens to grow taller than him (*Metaphysics* 1088a21ff.). Hence, at least some relation-properties are accidental to their relata; that is, some relations are external. This point is in contrast to Plato's conception of relations in the *Phaedo*. Aristotle summarizes it again in the *Physics* (225b11–13): "Nor is there motion in respect of relation: for it may happen that when one correlative changes, the other can truly be said not to change at all, so that in these cases the motion is accidental." This passage was much quoted by thirteenth- and fourteenth-century scholastics, some using it as support for the position that a real (as opposed to a conceptual) relation is not an entity distinct from its foundation.[40]

Significantly, there are texts which show that Aristotle distinguished within a relational situation the extra ingredient of *foundation-properties* in the terms. That is, in addition to relation-properties in each relatum, there are further properties in each relatum that provide the grounds for the relation-properties. For example, he claims that things are 'alike' or 'equal' because of some underlying quantitative or qualitative identity (*Metaphysics* 1021a10–13; cf. 1055b10–12).[41] At another place he distinguishes three types of friendship, which differ as to the grounds within the parties involved—moral character, wittiness, mutual economic usefulness (*Nicomachean Ethics* VIII; cf. *Physics* 246b3–247a8). Aristotle's analysis of relations can be summarized thus: relational fact :R(a,b)— for example, a is taller than b—entails the following components: (a) the terms of the relation, a and b; (b) in each term, attributes that are grounds or foundations—respectively, F′ (a certain height) and F″ (a lesser height)—for the further attribution of relational properties R′ (Is-Tall) and its converse R″ (Is-Short); and (c) the relation-property R′ associated with subject a is Toward-b, and relation-property R″ associated with subject b is Toward-a. Aristotle's analysis can be symbolized as:

> For binary relation R and entities x and y, there exist relation-properties R′ and R″ and foundation-properties F′ and F″ such that:
>
> The proposition that ⌜R(x,y)⌝ is true ≡ [F′(x) · R′(x) · F″(y) · R″(y) · R′ Toward y · R″ Toward x].

In the later terminology of the scholastics, the relation-properties R′ and R″ are referred to as the 'esse in' of the relation R, while the *toward* aspect is the 'esse ad' of R.

According to Aristotle, relations are of three types, depending on whether the foundations are numerical, causal, or psychological—for example, the relation between the knower and the known (*Metaphysics* 1020b26–1021b11).[42] Many scholastics, including Aquinas, believed that Aristotle intended psychological relations to be nonmutual—that is, for such a relation the relation-properties R′ and R″ are such that R′ is real but R″ is *of reason*, having no extra-conceptual foundation.[43] A relation of reason exists only by virtue of the activity of some mind. The relation R in aRb is nonmutual if and only if one or both of the corresponding relation-properties R′ and R″ are not real but of reason, thereby making no real difference to their relata. For example, R′ makes a real difference to a if, when R ceases to relate a to b, the foundation R′ also ceases to exist. This would produce a real change in a, essential or accidental depending upon the relation between F′ and a. If R″ is of reason, then R″ makes no real difference to b. If fact :aRb ceased to exist, then relation-property R′ would cease to exist, but the corresponding foundation F″ would not change, hence there would be no real change in b. Nonmutual relations exist independent of the existence of one or both of their foundations. For medievals, the relation between the three Persons of the Trinity is nonmutual, as is the relation between creature and Creator.

If the relation-properties are eliminated from the above analysis, consonant with the nonreductive analysis of relations, the issues raised in respect of nonmutual relations are transformed into those discussed under the contemporary debate over *internal* versus *external* relations. Relation R is internal to *a* and *b* if the foundations F′ and F″ change with changes in R, and if these foundations are *essential* in being necessary to the nature of *a* and *b* respectively. It is sometimes said that, as internally related, *a* and *b* are what they are by virtue of R. This is not the case with external relations—for example, Is-to-the-Left-of—where the foundations are accidental to their relata. Some relations are internal to one relatum and external to the other—for example, Is-Knowledge-of. In regard to the relation Is-Knowledge-of, both Aristotle and Aquinas insist that it have this dual character, since otherwise we fall into a subjectivism or 'idealism'. If to know is to alter the known intrinsically, then the act of knowing alters the known and makes it impossible to grasp in itself.[44] A realistic epistemology is then impossible. Holding that all relations are internal, Bradley was willing to accept this conclusion. His antagonist, Russell, was inclined to hold that all relations are external.

chapter four

Some Medieval and Early Modern Views

Both the doctrine of unit properties and the property reduction of relations were carried over into medieval philosophy primarily through translations and commentaries on Aristotle's works. Of early importance are Simplicius's (fl. 527–65) *Commentary on the Categories of Aristotle*, Porphyry's (232–304) *Isagoge*, and Boethius's (480–525) commentaries on the *Isagoge*, on Aristotle's *Categories* and *De Interpretatione*, and his *De Trinitate*. Starting from the middle of the twelfth century, the doctrine of unit properties became the majority view of European scholastics, common to both nominalism and moderate realism. The latter is in contrast to the Platonic realism that flourished in the Latin West from the ninth to the twelfth century.[1] The change occurred with the introduction of translations from Greek and Arabic into Latin of Aristotle's works and those of his Islamic commentators, especially Avicenna (ibn Sina, 980–1037), and Averroës (ibn Rushd, 1126–98). I shall not attempt an exhaustive survey of these views. Of the many medieval philosophers who adopted the doctrine of unit properties, I have selected the following few in order to illustrate an explicit commitment to and expansion of Aristotle's views (Boethius and Duns Scotus) and to display two positive arguments for unit properties (Avicenna and Buridan). Avicenna's argument is of particular relevance, since it involves an argument from relations and, in particular, from the asymmetric character of the 'toward' component of the monadic reduction.

Boethius

My interest in Boethius lies not only in several explicit assertions in his writings of the existence of unit properties and his attribution of this doctrine to Aristotle, but also in the fact that we have here an explicit commitment to both moderate realism and the thesis that properties are individuated by the substances in which they inhere. With regard to moderate realism, Boethius in his commentaries on Porphyry's *Isagoge* offers answers to three questions that Porphyry posed but refrained from answering. They are: (a) Do genera and species exist in nature, or are they purely conceptual? (b) If they exist in nature, are they material or immaterial? (c) Do they exist apart from sensible things or in them? In response, Boethius answers (a') that genera and species are both *subsistentia*, existing in things, and *intellecta*, in the mind; (b') that genera and species are incorporeal by abstraction; and (c') that they so exist both in sensible things and apart from them.[2] "Genera and species are in individuals, but they are thought universals."[3]

On unit properties Boethius is explicit and repetitive, though, unfortunately, most of the relevant comments are in his *Commentaries on Aristotle's 'Categories'* and *'De Interpretatione'*, works that had much less historical influence than some of his other writings. Nevertheless, in commenting on the *Isagoge*, Boethius picks up on Porphyry's reference to a particular instance of white, 'this white', and writes:

> For this [white] which is in this snow cannot be predicated of any other white [thing], because it is forced to singularity and it is constrained to an individual form by the participation in an individual. . . . For as it is said of snow, the white which is present in this snow subject is not a common accident, but [is] proper to this snow which appears to the eyes as a subject. . . . Because Socrates is individual and singular, animal is made individual, since Socrates is an animal. Again, man is predicated of many men indeed, but if we consider the humanity which is in the individual Socrates, it is made individual, since Socrates is individual itself and singular.[4]

In his commentary on the *Categories*, Boethius repeats his view that "every accident which comes to individuals is made an individual."[5] He then presents what he takes to be Aristotle's distinctions in chapter 2 of *Categories*:

> The universal is what is established to be predicated of many; the particular, however, what is predicated of no subject. . . . If particular is united to substance, it makes the substance particular, as it is [the case] with Socrates and Plato, and whatever is found in the substance is individual. . . . When particularity is united to an accident, it makes the accident particular, as [is the case of] Plato's or Aristotle's knowledge. For they make four combinations: universal substance, particular substance, universal accident, particular accident.[6]

Here and in like statements elsewhere, Boethius is not only expanding upon but also contradicting Aristotle's views. According to Boethius, *all* universals are particularized by a cause that is *external* and *individual* prior to them. We have seen that Aristotle, with good reason, rejects this move in the case of substantial forms being individuated by distinct matter. For even if what constitutes a substance's secondary matter—for example, Socrates' organs and bones—are individuals, their individuality must be accounted for by a combination of form and matter and so on, telescoping down ultimately to individuals whose matter is prime matter. And, as Aristotle observed, prime matter as what underlies *all* of an entity's properties is totally amorphous and potentially any individual, not one definite individual. Indeed, there is the argument that individuality—that is, unrepeatability—is a property, one not possessed by all entities (e.g., universals), and hence that, lacking qualities, prime matter cannot possess even this. Perhaps Boethius was cognizant of this point when, in his commentaries on the *Isagoge*, he asserts that substances—for instance, Socrates—are individuated by distinct sets of accidents, the set in Socrates not being exactly identical to that in any other.[7] This is consistent with his position that uniqueness has an external cause, but avoids the mistake of ascribing it to matter.

Avicenna

With the possible exception of the aforementioned texts from *Metaphysics* VII (Z), Aristotle nowhere explicitly argues for the existence of property instances. Yet, two arguments for unit properties, based upon premises that, at least at times, he subscribed to, were available to him. These arguments are given by Avicenna, one in the *Metaphysica* of the *Dānish Nāma-i 'alā'ī* (The Book of Scientific Knowledge), the other in the *Metaphysica* of the *Shifā* (The Healing). In the *Metaphysica of the Dānish*, paragraph 12, Avicenna first rejects Platonic realism—that universals exist separately from the individuals that exemplify them—by asserting that we know, for example, the universal Man by abstracting it from "other instances of humanity external to the universal man," and that all such universals exist only in the "imagination and in man's thoughts."[8] A universal, by the very fact that it is universal, is not an actual existent except in thought; yet it is real to what is external to thought, a distinction taken over by Christian scholastics. Avicenna states: "Its [a universal's] reality, however, both exists in thought and is external to thought, for the reality of humanity and of blackness both exists in thought and is external to thought in things."[9] Avicenna then gives the following argument from contrary second-order properties to show that universals must be particularized in things. He says:

> The identical form of man-qua-man cannot be a knower like Plato and also an ignoramus like someone other than Plato. It is not possible for knowledge to be and not to be in one and the same thing. Neither is it possible for one and the same thing to contain both blackness and whiteness simultaneously. It is similarly impossible for the universal animal to be a particular real animal, for it would then have to be both walker and flyer, as well as not walker and flyer, and be both biped and quadruped.[10]

Conforming to Aristotle's theory of predication in the *Categories*, Avicenna assumes that when a property (e.g., Knower, Ignoramus, White, Black) is predicated of concrete substances (e.g., Plato or Socrates), it is also predicated of the corresponding species (Man) as well as (with, e.g., Walker, Flyer, Biped, and Quadruped) of the genus (Animal). For example, since it is the case that Plato is a man, an animal, and is learned, it is likewise true that 'man is an animal', 'man is learned', and 'animal is learned'. Yet for someone else, say Meno, who is a man, an animal, and is ignorant, it would be true that 'man is ignorant' and 'animal is ignorant'. Hence, from the combined predicates of Plato and Meno it is true that 'man is learned' and 'man is ignorant'. Avicenna concludes that because one and the same genus (Animal) or species (Man) cannot have contrary properties, it is not numerically one and the same genus or species that can be present in multiple subjects. The logical alternative, and Avicenna's implied conclusion, is that genus and species are individuated as property instances, such that, say, Man_1 is predicated of Plato and Man_2 is predicated of Meno, where it is now Man_1 that is learned and Man_2 that is ignorant. Similarly, for the distinct instances of Animal, $Animal_1$ and $Animal_2$, it is possible that $Animal_1$ is biped and $Animal_2$ is quadruped.

That Avicenna intends the last quote above to be an argument for property instances is evident from subsequent comments regarding the prior unity of the subject being the source of the individuation of the predicated properties. In regard to the universal Black, he says:

> Therefore, if it is not the case that a thing becomes a unity due to blackness, and that this unity, though caused by another thing, is in reality associated with blackness, then blackness will not be divided into two due

to blackness itself, but rather due to a cause through which blackness becomes particularized for each of the two entities.[11]

The individuation of instances of Black is a function not of Black as universal, but of the prior individuation of the distinct subjects in which instances of Black adhere. Generalized, there is here an assertion of the principle of subject uniqueness (SU). Avicenna is also explicit in asserting the principle of immanent instance realism (IR). He states:

> It becomes evident, then, that the idea of a universality, for the very reason that it is a universal, is not an actual existent except in thought. Its reality, however, both exists in thought and is external to thought, for the reality of humanity and of blackness both exists in thought and is external to thought in things. That certainly does not exist which supposedly is a single humanity or a single blackness and which exists supposedly like universality in all entities.[12]

The principles SU and IR as expressed by Avicenna—that properties are individuated by their subjects and that a property is universal in the mind but particular in things—are found in Aquinas and other scholastics.

Avicenna's argument would not succeed on the more sophisticated theory of predication embedded in the hylomorphism of Aristotle's *Metaphysics*. There, attributes of an individual are predicated not of primary or secondary forms but of the composite of substantial form and matter that together constitute the individual. Consequently, the individuation of concrete composite substances is sufficient to prevent the same entity (e.g., the substantial form Man) from being both black and white, biped and quadruped, and so forth; hence no individuation of forms is necessitated by the possession of contrary properties. Recall, however, that for Aristotle in the *Metaphysics* a substantial form is itself predicated of an underlying matter, and that when the form/matter analysis is forced down to its ultimate conclusion, we have a matter that is completely characterless, not even a 'this' as unrepeatable. It must be, then, that in matter/form composition it is the form which is a 'this'—that is, a property instance—and thereby accounts for the unrepeatability of the composite.

Elsewhere in the *Metaphysica* of the Shifā, in a chapter on relations, Avicenna gives a second, completely general argument for the individuation of attributes based upon the assumption of the classic property reduction of relations. On this monadic reduction, the special, limiting case of properties is treated as paradigmatic, and the more general binary case (e.g., Is-a-Father-of) is reduced to properties of each relatum, albeit each with a peculiar, characteristic mode of being 'toward' other relata. Avicenna illustrates the reduction with the classic example of the Is-the-Father-of relation:

> Each of two related things has in itself an idea *with respect to the other*, which is not the idea the other has in itself with respect to the first. This is evident in things whose related terms differ, as in the case of the father. Its relation to fatherhood, which is a description of its existence, is in the father alone. . . . The same applies to the state of the son with respect to the father. There is nothing here at all which is in both of them.[13]

Translating the 'with respect to' by the more standard 'toward', the reduction of relations, insofar as it is developed here by Avicenna, can be formalized as:

> For any formal binary relation R and relata x and y, there exist relation-properties R' and R'' such that the propositon that $\ulcorner R(x,y) \urcorner$ is true $\equiv$ [R'(x) · *Toward-y*(R') · R''(y) · *Toward-x*(R'')].

Applying the formalization to Avicenna's example above,

> The proposition that 'a is the father of b' is true $\equiv$ [Fatherhood(a) · Toward-b(Fatherhood) · Sonship(b) · Toward-a(Sonship)].

In scholastic terminology, relation-properties R' and R'' are the 'esse in' of the relation R, while the *toward* aspects are the 'esse ad' of R.

Avicenna now turns specifically to the reduction of equivalence relations. With such relations, the resulting relation-property reducta are identical, and this is the basis for a general argument for the numerical distinctness of these properties in distinct subjects. He states somewhat cryptically:

> If such a state of affairs consists in the fact that each of the two has a state with respect to the other, this is similar to the case of the swan and snow, each of which is white. Nor is this state rendered identical by the fact that it stands with respect to the other; for whatever belongs to each individual with respect to the other belongs to that individual and not the other; but it possesses it with respect to the other.
>
> If you have understood this from what we have given you by way of

example, then know that the identical state of affairs obtains in the rest of the relatives that do not disagree in their two terms.[14]

What Avicenna means by 'relatives that do not disagree in their two terms' are equivalence relations whose separate relation-property reducta are the same universal. In the example of the swan and snow there is the implied equivalence relation of Is-Similar-as-White-to, and its property reduction would be:

The proposition that 'a is similar as white to b' is true $\equiv$ [White(a) $\cdot$ Toward-b(White) $\cdot$ White(b) $\cdot$ Toward-a(White)].

Also, and central to his argument for unit attributes, Avicenna stresses the point that the second-order properties of Toward-a and Toward-b are necessarily contraries. That is, with respect to distinct subjects a and b, the fact that a relation-property is toward b precludes it from being toward a. From this it follows immediately that the white in a must be numerically distinct from the white in b, since otherwise the universal White would have contrary second-order properties. To avoid this, property instances are required, and the last formalization must be rewritten as:

The proposition that 'a is similar as white to b' is true $\equiv$ [White$_1$(a) $\cdot$ Toward-b_1(White$_1$) $\cdot$ White$_2$(b) $\cdot$ Toward-a_2(White$_2$)].

Avicenna makes the same point with a further example of the relation Is-a-Brother-of restricted to males.

In the case of two brothers, one has a state relative to the other and the other has a state relative to the first, and since the two states are of the same species [being a brother], these states have been thought to be one individual [the universal *Brotherhood*]. But this is not the case. To the first belongs the state of being the brother to the second, that is, he has the description of being the brother of the second. Now this description is his, but only with respect to the second. This is not the same description of the second numerically, but only in species, just as the case would be if the second was white and the first was white.[15]

It is the second-order contraries Toward-Brother-b and Toward-Brother-a that require their first-order subjects, a and b respectively, to be individuated in number though one in species. Each brother has his own property instance of the universal Brotherhood.

Avicenna's argument is perfectly general, in that it can be made to show the individuation of any property P. Let a and b be two distinct individuals each possessing property P. Then a and b are related by the relation Is-Similar-in-Possessing-P-to. Once again, the contrary second-order properties of Toward-a and Toward-b require P to be individuated to a and b each. That Avicenna intends his argument to apply to all properties is shown by his succinct conclusion given immedately after the above passages: "You must never think that an accident, one in number, exists in two substrata."[16] It is interesting that this admonition has come to be associated with Leibniz, in whose work it is standardly interpreted to be but the insistence of the property reduction of relations (see below). But Avicenna's intent goes deeper, and he uses the property reduction of relations as a means of demonstrating the nonrepeatability of property reducta themselves.

Latin Scholastics

In the Latin West during the period between Boethius and Peter Abelard (1079–1142) and John of Salisbury (1115–80), the standard view was that individuality extended only to primary substances, not to attributes predicable of them (accidents, properties, or essential features). A bundle theory of individuation was commonly held. From the time of Abelard and John of Salisbury on, however, philosophers of the Middle Ages were almost unanimous in extending individuality to attributes as well. The problem of individuation was itself the focus of a great deal of attention in the thirteenth and fourteenth centuries. There was general agreement concerning the principles (limited to monadic properties) of subject uniqueness, SU (no unit property has more than one subject), instance predicates, IP (only unit properties are ontic predicates), and relata linking, RL (no unit property exists except as ontically predicative). The major disagreement was over the principle of immanent instance realism, IR (that there exists a common entity R which is a numerically identical aspect of instances R_i, R_j, . . .)—nominalists denying it, moderate realists upholding it. The principle of instance uniqueness, IU (that the same subject cannot have numerically distinct instances of the same property) appears to be implied in most of the scholastics, though there is an explicit exception in the work of Francisco Suarez.

In the works of Thomas Aquinas (1224–74) we have a paradigm example of a realist theory of unit properties—that is, moderate realism. In the *Summa Contra Gentiles*, for example, Aquinas asserts:

> That which is common to many is not outside the many except by the reason alone. Thus, *animal* is not something outside Socrates and Plato and the other animals except in the intellect that apprehends the form of animal stripped of all its individuating and specifying characteristics. [I. 26. 5]

> Universals, on the other hand, are not subsisting things, but rather having been only in singulars, as is proved in [Aristotle's] *Metaphysics* VII. . . . Now, the singular essence is composed of designated matter and individuated form. [I. 63. 2–3][17]

Accidents are individuated by the substance in which they inhere, whereas the substantial form of a composite substance is individuated by matter. Immaterial substances (subsistent forms)—for example, angels—are unique to their forms, different angels for different genera. Scotus criticized Aquinas for this non-uniform, dual theory of particularization. For Aquinas, matter individuates composite substances, but not matter simpliciter. What is required is 'designated' matter. In the early *De Ente et Essentia* Aquinas makes clear that the principle of individuation is not just any matter, but only *designated* matter: "By designated matter I mean that which is considered under determined dimensions" (2, 4).[18] The Latin terms *designatum* and *signatum* are equivalent to the demonstrative 'this' and are found in Boethius and the Latin translations of Avicenna, the latter in vogue in Paris in Aquinas's time.[19] Designated matter is anticipated in the *dimensione interminatae* of Averroës. Averroës had criticized Avicenna for considering only actual quantity in accounting for multiplicity within a species. Actual quantity is an accident posterior to a particular substance, hence not a prior cause of its individuality. Thus, adhering to the traditional view that matter individuates, yet understanding with Aristotle that pure indeterminate matter cannot be a principle of individuation, Aquinas posits *materia quantitate signata*.

Commentators from Duns Scotus (1266–1308) on have pointed out the difficulty of this position.[20] It implies that quantity is the actual cause of individuation; yet quantity is an accident, and no substance can be individuated by an accident. Moreover, as Scotus pointed out against Aquinas, materia quantitate signata is not matter in its definitional purity, but matter already informed by a substantial form that gives it quantitative specificity.[21] But one cannot then account for the particularization of this substantial form without circularity. The conclusion that Aristotle drew in *Metaphysics* VII but contradicted elsewhere was likewise passed over by Aquinas: matter in any guise cannot be a principle of individuation.

The confusion endemic to the whole issue is illustrated in the various positions of near-contemporaries of Aquinas. St. Bonaventure (1217–74), for example, held that the principle of individuation is in the union of form and matter. Consistent with Aristotle's one-time insight, Godfrey of Fontaines (1260–1320) held that the substantial was the principle of individuation. Roger Bacon (1212–92) concluded that there is no intrinsic cause of individuation, and that its source must therefore be extrinsic—so positing Divine agency.[22]

While advocating the doctrine of individual accidents and substantial forms, Scotus observed that matter, form, and the *compositum* of both can each be conceived as a universal.[23] Matter in itself, as purely undifferentiated and indeterminate, is potentially everything and nothing in particular, hence cannot be a diversifying principle. What is required in each individual is 'this' matter and 'this' form, which together constitute 'this' *compositum*. To account for this uniqueness, Scotus posited for each particular a haecceitas (thisness) as a positive principle of individuation (*Reportata Parisiensia*, 2. 12. 5, nos. 1, 8, 13, 14; *Quaestiones in libros Metaphysicorum*, 7. 13, nos. 9 and 26). Each particular consists in a natura, which is universal and common to individuals of the same species, and a haecceitas, which is unrepeatable and contracts the natura to its unique inherence in the particular. It is to be noted that even a 'this matter' has a natura, or general content, which is rendered occurrent by a thisness unique to it (*Reportata Parisiensia*, 2. 12. 8, no. 8). Further, between the natura and the *haecceitas* there is a 'formal difference' only (*distinctio formalis a parte rei*); that is, they constitute two realities that can be distinguished in thought but are not separable extra-conceptually. They are different modes or aspects of the same thing.[24] Other examples of formal differences are the distinctions between God's attributes and between essence and existence. According to Scotus, the same distinction does not exist between form and matter, as held by Aquinas, and hence matter can exist by itself—at least, by Divine agency. For Scotus, the haecceitas adds no quantitative determination or content to the nature of an entity. In being only formally, but not actually, distinct from the nature, the haecceitas of an entity does not have the status of a 'bare particular' with its proprietary problems.

The point to note here is that Scotus makes explicit a doctrine only broached in Aristotle: that individuated substantial forms contain their own principle of individuation. Scotus, along with many of the scholastics, was keenly aware that matter, though a principle of continuity through change, was not, nor could be, a cause of individuation. A particular form must be individuated from within. Scotus is proposing exactly this when he asserts that every individuated substantial form (as a natura) consists of two formally distinguishable but extraconceptually inseparable components: the content or intension of the form, which is repeatable, and the principle of individuation, which 'contracts this form to unrepeatability'. Scotus could not explain, however, the connection between the intension and the thisness of a unit property; he simply concluded that both were needed in a single individual. It is my thesis that this connection can be explained by the predicative nature of properties (and relations in general): for a relation has both an intension and a combinatorial mode among its relata, the latter individuating the former, the two aspects being conceptually distinguishable but necessarily inseparable in being definitional of relations in their proper role of relating. Yet Scotus, like all philosophers in the substance/ attribute tradition, conceived of predication as a predicate contained *in* a single subject. But there is nothing in the concept of containment that implies the individuation of the contained. Hence, individuation of a property must be conferred either by an already individuated container, which simply pushes the problem back a step, or one must posit a nonpredicative presence of an individuator in the property—Scotus's haecceitas.

Synthesizing and extending the instance ontology running through scholasticism is the work of Francisco Suarez (1548–1617), often said to be the last great scholastic philosopher. In the authoritative *Disputationes metaphysicae* (which influenced both Descartes and Leibniz) he both summarizes and critiques the views of his medieval and scholastic predecessors and then draws his own conclusions. He first asserts that everything that exists is individual, including, contra Aquinas, God and angels. Rejecting Scotus's theory, interpreted as individual = universal + haecceity, Suarez maintains that an entity is its own principle of individuation (V. 6. 1).[25] Entities individuate themselves, and this extends to form, matter, and even their mode of union in a compound particular, as well as to the accidents of the particular (V. 6. 1; 7. 1). But, if accidents are not individuated by their subjects, it is improper to explain the individuality of accidents, which is something intrinsic and tied to their very natures, by something extrinsic (V. 7). He thus goes on to assert that there is no apparent reason in principle why multiple instances of the same accident cannot be simultaneously in the same subject (a denial of the principle of instance uniqueness, IU), though, as a matter of fact, no such duplicated inherence occurs naturally (V. 8). As we shall see, this is also a problem for contemporary trope theory.

In the *Disputationes* Suarez makes an important distinction between a property and its inherence or union with a subject. The mode of inherence is said to be an aspect of the property itself. He writes:

> Thus in quantity, for example, which inheres in a substance, two aspects may be considered. One is the entity of quantity itself, the other is the union or actual inherence of the quantity in the substance. The first we call simply the thing or being of quantity, comprising whatever pertains to the essence of the individual quantity as is found in nature, and remains and is preserved even if quantity is separated from its subject. . . . The second aspect, the inherence, we call a mode of quantity . . . for the inherence of quantity is called its mode because it is something affecting quantity and, as it were, ultimately determining its state and manner of existing, without adding to it a proper new entity, but merely modifying a pre-existing entity. [VII. 1. 17][26]

Note that the union of inherence of a property is a *mode* of the property, and Suarez has an explicit theory of such things. A mode is neither a substance nor itself a quality of things. A mode does not constitute an entity in reality but is a modification of some entity without which the mode could not exist—for example, the union of body and soul and in the above quote the linking aspect of a property. Suarez argues that to hold otherwise—that is, to take the linking ('inherence') aspect of a property as a further entity—is to deny it the status of actual union between attribute and subject and so require a further 'medium for union' between the initial inherence of an attribute and its subject (VII. 1. 18). What is insinuated here is Bradley's regress, and the lesson to be learned is that inherence "is *per se* and directly joined without the medium of another mode, as, for instance, sitting is joined to the sitter" (VII. 1. 19). Suarez goes on to assert that modes of inherence are themselves just individuals, as are the properties of which they are a mode. "Inherence has a mode of being such that it cannot exist unless it is actually joined to the form of which it is the inherence, and that this *particular inherence* can modify or rather unite only this *particular form* to which it is, so to speak, affixed" (VII. 1. 17, my emphasis).

The distinguishing of an intension from its union of inherence in a subject represents, I propose, a great insight, a milestone in the long intellectual struggle to free ontology from the tyranny of the subject, by recognizing an ontic power legitimate to properties that was traditionally granted only to the subject. Not that Suarez saw it this way—far from it. He concluded that hylomorphism, with its dominating substantial form, was the only reasonable ontology, since only form could provide the essential or per se (as opposed to per accidens) unity required to account for what would otherwise be a collection of properties "merely accidentally congregated in a subject" (XV. 1. 14).[27] Nevertheless, Suarez is anticipating what is an ontic mode of relations, if only in passing and in the limiting case of monadic properties. He observes rightly that it is the predicative nature *of the attribute*, its 'union', whereby it inheres in a subject, and that this union is individuated as is the property instance.

Because of its relevance in interpreting Leibniz's ontology, we shall look briefly at Suarez's distinctions and vocabulary with regard to the topic of universals. Using an unfortunate though then common terminology, Suarez distinguished between 'formal concepts' and 'objective concepts'. A formal concept is an act of the intellect whereby it conceives a thing or common nature, whereas an objective concept is the thing or the nature (intension) that is represented by the formal concept.

> Again, the formal concept is always a singular and individual thing, because it is a thing produced by the intellect, and inhering in it. But the objective concept sometimes can be a singular and individual thing insofar as [such a thing] can be objectified and conceived by a formal act, but often it is a universal or confused, and common, thing, such as man, substance, and the like. [II. 1. 1][28]

The 'objective concept' can be an individual (e.g., Socrates) or a universal (e.g., Man), though in both cases it is real and independent of an intellectual existence only. The objective concept is what is signified by the formal concept; hence in the tradition of moderate realism, the formal universal signifies an objective universal (cf. VI. 5. 1; 2. 9).[29] He states:

It must be said that all things that are actual beings or that exist or can exist immediately, are singular and individual. I say "immediately" in order to exclude the common natures of beings which, as such, cannot immediately exist or have actual entity, except in singular and individual entities. . . .

Universals cannot exist separated from singulars. [V. 1. 4–5][30]

The implication is that universals exist per se 'mediately', as abstracta from an 'immediately' individuated status in actual beings.

In addition to moderate realism, nominalism was also a prevalent doctrine, epitomized in the work of William of Ockham (1290–1349).[31] Ockham criticized Scotus's theory of formal distinction, asserting that "In creatures no extramental distinction of any kind is possible except where distinct things exist."[32] This implies that in a would-be unit form the universal cannot be 'contracted' by an individuator into a single entity, but that both must remain distinct, rendering the individuator a bare particular juxtaposed with a form as an extra-conceptual universal. Ockham rejects the existence of universals (hence IR) by insisting upon the principle that "Every particular is homogeneously particular; there is no constituent of a particular which is not a particular (i.e., unrepeatable)" (*Ordinatio*, I. 2. 5).[33] Note that this is not an argument but a bare assertion. The moderate realist holds, to the contrary, that a universal is precisely the kind of entity that can exist completely in each of multiple entities. The difference between the two theories must be decided on the grounds of how well each accounts for the issues surrounding both the characteristics of individuality and the commonality inherent in our total experience.

Ockham attempts to account for commonality by adopting a conceptual nominalism: "A universal is nothing outside the mind" but, rather, "A universal is an act of the intellect."[34] Certain concepts, or 'states of mind', are, by convention, made to stand for several diverse entities outside or within the mind, on the analogy of arbitrarily assigning a spoken word to multiple things.[35] It is, of course, this characteristic subjective arbitrariness, which is indicative of nominalism, that is at odds with the de facto nonarbitrary classifications of science and everyday experience. By contrast, the realist has no difficulty objectifying his epistemology.

It is worth noting briefly a theological argument prevalent in the thirteenth and fourteenth centuries—found, for example, in both Ockham and Jean Buridan (1295–1356)—which was said to prove that unit accidents could exist without subjects in which to inhere.[36] According to the doctrine of transubstantiation, it was an article of faith that in the Eucharist the bread and wine are changed substantially into the Body and Blood of Christ. In this miracle, all the instances of the quantitative and qualitative accidents of the bread and wine remain, even though the underlying substances no longer exist. Hence, at least by Divine agency, it is possible for unit accidents (e.g., this white) to exist without inhering in any subject. This would imply that individuation of an accident is not a function of a state of inherence in or of the individuality of a subject. The particularity of a unit accident thus comes from within. The modern theory of tropes extends this as the natural status to all property instances, doing away completely with the troublesome posit of underlying substances. Tropes free-float, their compresent coagulation constituting ordinary individuals.

Interestingly, Buridan posited, in addition to substances and unit accidents—for example, this whiteness—'dispositions' of unit accidents which account for the latter's actual inherence in particular subjects.[37] The disposition of a particular whiteness is the ontic glue that accounts for its attachment to a substance, a linking aspect of the whiteness that could be dissolved by God, as in the Eucharist, without destroying either the content of the accident (White) or its individuality. Buridan's 'dispositions' would then seem to anticipate Suarez's 'modes of inherence'. Indeed, like Suarez subsequently, Buridan uses a Bradley-type regress argument to show that the disposition that causes a unit accident to attach to a subject is of a unique combinatorial nature such that, unlike the original accident and its subject, it needs no further disposition to attach it to the original disposition.

Medieval Views on Relations

Returning briefly to relations, consistent with their radical nominalism and materialism, the Greek Stoics held that relations are subjective, their subjects being perhaps real, but the relations themselves having a conceptual existence only.[38] Later, Plotinus adopted this view, as did the Mutakallimum, a school of fundamentalist Muslim theologians. The latter used Bradley's regress to argue that, in order to account for the connectedness inherent in a relational fact, a further relation is necessary between the relata and the original relation. But then, to account for the linking inherent in the new relational fact, a third relation must be introduced between the original relata and the second relation, and so on to infinity. Later, Ockham likewise interpreted the regress as showing the absurdity of the view that relations 'lie between' the things united.[39] By contrast, Avicenna responded to the Mutakallimun by saying that the infinite regress only goes to show that the original relation itself accounts for the connection among the terms.[40] One gets a sense here of what, historically, has been a persistent pattern of divergent interpretations of Bradley's regress argument. On the one side, philosophers like Buridan and Suarez see it as dramatically displaying the sui generis mode or disposition of a property whereby it is ontically predicative of its subject, whereas others like Avicenna extend this conclusion to the general case of relations. On the other side, philosophers like the Mutakallimun, Ockham, and Bradley interpret the regress as displaying the inherent incoherence of the concept of relations. The root cause of this ambiguity will be discussed when the regress argument is analyzed in chapter 8.

As noted, the standard analysis of relations in the Middle Ages was the monadic reduction, though with minor variations. For example, there is evidence that in the reduction of a relation R Aquinas held that the relation-properties R' and R'' are to be identified with their respective foundations, F' and F''.[41] This identification is explicit in the writings of Giles of Rome (1243–1316), who is thought to have been a student of Aquinas. It is also the teaching of Henry of Ghent (1217–93).

Also worth mentioning is Peter Aureoli (1275–1322), who rejected the monadic reduction of relations. Distinct from its terms and foundations, a relation is an 'interval', a 'medium', 'being in the middle' or 'connecting', something existing between two things.[42] Here the would-be relation-properties (esse in) and the 'toward' aspect (esse ad) are collapsed into a single between. Interestingly, however, Aureoli held the common view that no extra-mental entity could have this between characteristic, and so concluded that relations have a conceptual existence only.

Many philosophers argued for the reality of relations, however, the arguments being similar to those offered, for example, by Scotus: (a) that the real unity of the universe requires order among the parts; (b) that all real composition requires relations of union; (c) that the relation of spatial proximity is needed for a real cause-and-effect relation; and (d) that the objectivity of the many relational statements of mathematics requires it.[43]

There were also theological doctrines that had direct implications for the theory of relations. Most important of these was perhaps the doctrine of the

Trinity. It is a tradition going back to Augustine that the three Divine Persons are constituted in some way by real relations, each Person's contribution to the Divine essence being its relations to the other Persons. The formalities of this view were clarified in chapter 1. However, on the prevailing esse in/esse ad analysis, the Trinity, conceived as a network of relations, would seem not only to place the entire nature of at least these relations in their esse ads, but also to make their relata (their subjects) the other relations with the same and only status of esse ads. So conceived, the Divine essence is pure relatedness, which as such provides both the requisite absolute unity and the maximum simplicity consistent with a triune God. Moreover, if individuated as relating, then each relation has a uniqueness deserving of the appellation 'Person'. But this would seem to imply that subject substances, foundation-properties, and even relation-properties conceived as such must be eliminated. However, such a view would give to relations a substantiality and a multiple-subject betweenness contrary to the standard monadic reduction—hence the treatment of these relations as a unique type. Aquinas, for example, held that because the relations of the Trinity are not accidents (God can possess no accidents), these relations do not fall within the nine accidental categories making up the traditional substance/ accident ontology. They do, nevertheless, have the *ratio* of a relation—being a 'toward'.[44] Aquinas claims that the relations of the Trinity have foundations, the situation being unique here, in that the foundation is numerically the same Divine nature.[45] But this will not work. Under the monadic reduction, it is the nature of the foundations that determines the nature or content of the relation—for example, paternity or filiation—hence identical foundations effect identical relations, so paternity = filiation. Once again, we have a collapse into a homogeneous monad effected by the gravity of the monadic reduction of relations.

Leibniz on Individual Accidents

In the ontology of Gottfried Wilhelm Leibniz (1646–1716) one again finds a link between a doctrine of unit properties and a theory of relations, an association that has received little attention. I shall examine this connection below and in the process shall observe or argue for points that serve to resolve controversies over how to interpret Leibniz on the issues of both relations and individual accidents.

Leibniz both recognized relations as fundamental to his ontology and accepted the ontic uneliminability of the defining polyadic characteristic of relations (i.e., their connectivity among multiple subjects). Like the scholastics, Leibniz held it to be fundamental that there is a "real connection of all things." Indeed, he goes further and asserts that "there is no term so absolute or so loose as not to include relations and the perfect analysis of which does not lead to other things and even to all others; so that you can say that relative terms indicate expressly the relation they contain."[46]

Relations are central to Leibniz's explanatory concept of possible worlds, for a possible world is what is *compossible* among comprising substances; that is, a possible world is a set of entities in a network of noncontrary relationships.[47] Yet, more resolute than his predecessors in drawing out its implications, Leibniz was committed to the doctrine of single-subject inherence (monadic predication) and, through this, to an analysis of relations that rests ultimately upon properties of their relata. Consequently, he was committed to the view that the traditional relation-property reduction does not eliminate the still relational 'toward', or esse ad, aspect of relations but simply places it surreptitiously in the relation-property reducta, or what he calls 'extrinsic denominations'. Specifically, a complete polyadic relation is an abstraction from a containing relation-property, where the latter, in turn, rests upon the foundation of a nonrelational property of a relatum, the 'intrinsic denominations'. So understood, unreduced relations imply no conflict with Leibniz's mature ontology of substances and their properties.

As we will see, Leibniz attempts to demonstrate the conceptual status of relations directly on the basis of the ontological principles of individual accidents and monadic predication. He argues that a relation, conceived in the full sense of bridging multiple relata, is neither a substance nor a unit accident; because of this, it must be a conceptual, albeit nonfictitious, entity only.

It is important in interpreting Leibniz's mature views on relations to understand precisely what sense he intended when he classified relations as *ens rationis* or *ens mentale*.[48] As we have seen, it was part of the philosophical tradition to ascribe to relations a conceptual status. In Leibniz's time, for example, the British empiricists Locke and Hume both held relations to be a product of the mind; according to Locke, relations are "not contained in the real existence of Things, but something extraneous and superinduced";[49] and for Hume, relations arise from impressions "connected together in the imagination."[50] But there is in both Locke and Hume an element of arbitrariness and unreality given to relations, especially in comparison with monadic properties, which is not to be attributed to Leibniz. For Leibniz, relations, along with canonical monadic properties and indeed everything except monads and per se unities of monads, are all equally *phenomena* (*L* 445, 531, 617, 623). Phenomena are perceptions of monads, monads and their perceptions being the two ultimate categories of elements comprising all existence. Phenomena are real in the usual sense; indeed, they are objectified in the mind of God, the supreme monad, though Leibniz usually reserves the honorific title 'real' for monads. The adjective 'mere' that Leibniz sometimes uses in his descriptions of 'merely mental' or 'merely phenomenal' only serves to signify the totally dependent status these entities have on monads, the ultimate containing, hence synthesizing substances (*L* 609). At one place Leibniz refers to space and motion, which for him are purely relational, as 'true phenomena' (*L* 270).

Leibniz's views on relations are reflected not only in specifically ontological contexts but also in his formal program of logical paraphrase. As part of a 'rational grammar', relational propositions are to be parsed into forms amenable to traditional Aristotelian logic. Here, in the crucial case of asymmetric relations, Leibniz introduces a non-truth-functional *logical* connective between two subject/predicate propositions designed to do at least some of the work of the esse ad aspect of the thus parsed relation.

That Leibniz adopted the scholastic doctrine of unit properties has only recently been highlighted in the separate works of Laurence McCullough and Kenneth Clatterbaugh.[51] McCullough points out that from his earliest *Disputatio metaphysica de principio individui* (1663)[52] through his mature works, Leibniz adopts key elements of Suarez's metaphysics. These include the thesis that a being's whole entity (*entitas tota*) is its principle of individuation, this extending to substance and accident alike. From here it is a short step to Leibniz's thesis that every property and accident are essential to a thing's identity. Leibniz comments that it is possible for individual accidents to be simultaneously in the same subject but differ only in number, a thesis previously advanced by Suarez. Individual accidents (which include the category of relations) are 'modifications' (Suarez's term) of entities, so cannot exist apart from substances (Leibniz's monads). Important for the emphasis on relations below, McCullough observes how Leibniz adopts Suarez's position that single-subject relation-properties exist extra-conceptually in their subjects, whereas their corresponding relation-universals are concepts only, abstracted from relation-properties. Below I shall offer an interpretation of later Leibniz texts that clarify this position.

In arguing that the theory of unit properties had a pervasive influence upon many of Leibniz's fundamental doctrines, Clatterbaugh cites textual glosses found throughout Leibniz's works as internal evidence for the theory. Leibniz distinguished 'individual accidents' (giving as an example the extension of this particular spatial object) from their corresponding 'attributes' (e.g., extension in general), which are repeatable. Attributes are abstractions and as such are 'merely conceptual', *entia rationis* (*L* 621–22). What is interesting and directly relevant is the fact that, with one exception, the passages cited by Clatterbaugh in which Leibniz makes reference to unit accidents are embedded in discussions of relations. In these contexts Leibniz repeats the particularity principle: that no accident can be in more than one subject. Yet, unlike Avicenna, who, as we have seen, used relations to argue for the particularity principle, Leibniz assumes the principle and uses it to argue for the conceptual status of relations when considered separate from any relata (i.e., as repeatable attributes). This is precisely the ontic status that scholastic moderate realism assigns to any property abstracted from its individuating inherence in a subject.

If McCullough's and Clatterbaugh's scholastic interpretations are correct, then, contra the views of some commentators (G. Martin, B. Mates, and McCullough himself[53]), Leibniz from an early stage in his career was not and, given the avowed, fundamental theses of his mature thought, could not consistently have been a nominalist, except in the loose, inaccurate sense in which the term is attributed to moderate realism (cf. chap. 2, sec. 1). McCullough, for example, has claimed that in the youthful *Disputatio* Leibniz found Suarez's anti-Scotist arguments persuasive and in response adopted a nominalist ontology, which he subsequently retained.[54] In the *Disputatio* Leibniz rejects 'Scotus' position' as misrepresented by Suarez, refusing to accept the 'extreme realist' view that an individual = common nature + haecceity.[55] The rejected view would have the common nature or universal be a constituent of the individual, a thesis that Scotus himself explicitly spurned. Suarez had argued that there is no distinction in an individual itself, *ex natura rei*, between its individuality and its common nature. Hence, there are no common natures as *common* in things. But accepting this conclusion does not make Leibniz a nominalist in a strict sense, any more than Scotus was. As for other evidence that the young Leibniz was a nominalist, I shall not pursue it here but only observe that by 1670, seven years after the *Disputatio*, he was writing as if he was committed to moderate realism. Although Leibniz here speaks admiringly of the nominalists' principles of economy and parsimony, that entities are not to be multiplied beyond necessity and that a simpler hypothesis is a better hypothesis (*L* 128),[56] and comments that "nothing is truer" than the nominalist position that "everything in the world [outside of abstractions from it] can be explained without any reference to universals and real forms" (*L* 128), the context is nevertheless one in which he is commenting upon the modes of reasoning and hypotheses to be used in physical science—in particular, astronomy. He makes it clear that it is "universals and substantial forms," as scientifically sterile, that he objects to. However, in the same text, on the fundamental status of universals, Leibniz goes on to criticize the "nominalist sect" and their "destruction of the reality of forms and universals." Leibniz is explicitly critical of class nominalism, as if "the universal abstracted from all the sheep which graze here were . . . identical with the collective whole of them" (*L* 129). His argument is that "if universals were nothing but collections of individuals, it would follow that we could attain no knowledge through demonstration" (ibid.). The implication is that demonstration is by means of relationships among universals. Leibniz makes the same point, but from a different angle, when, in his *New Essays Concerning Human Understanding* (1701), he responds to the question of whether animals are capable of abstract thought by saying: "They apparently recognize whiteness, and notice it in the chalk or the snow; but this is not yet abstraction, for that demands a consideration of what is common, separated from what is particular, and consequently there enters into it the knowledge of universal truths, which is not given to the animals" (*NE* II, 9, par. 10, p. 145). I shall argue presently that Leibniz's views on unit accidents, the identity of indiscernibles, and 'resemblances being a reality' are further evidence that he in fact did and, to be consistent, must have retained repeatable universals, and so was not a nominalist. Further, I will argue that, for Leibniz, it is universals abstracted from their instances that are 'ideal', and that unreduced, fully polyadic relations can only be such abstractions.

  Leibniz's view of the ontic nature of relations has been variously interpreted in the secondary literature, often following what is taken to be Leibniz's logical program for parsing ('reducing') relation propositions to propositions of subject/predicate form. Obviously, formal considerations have implications for the ontic status of relations, reinforcing some views and eliminating others as incompatible. For example, if one interprets Leibniz as holding that relation propositions are to be parsed as a set of either truth-functionally combined (apparently Russell and C. Broad[57]) or non-truth-functionally combined (B. Mates[58]) propositions containing, in either case, only nonrelational predicates, then the simplest consistent interpretation of the description 'merely ideal' would be that relations are but a matter of surface grammar, *façon de parler.* In an ontologically precise, adequate language, no relation or relation-property terms would appear. No worries concerning the ontic status of relations are thereby engendered. On the other hand, if Leibniz's paraphrase program is interpreted as a parsing of relation propositions into a combination of propositions whose predicates are relation-properties (H. Ishiguro[59]), then multi-subject relations have not been eliminated, and 'merely ideal' must be interpreted as an ontic status that needs to be reconciled with Leibniz's general ontology, resting as it does on an assumption of monadic predication. For either interpretation of the logical parsing program, the explicit textual evidence is inconclusive in my view, hence the controversy. Moreover, there is an aspect of this formal program that has received little attention, but one that, once clarified, is evidence for what would be a more accurate view of Leibniz's conception of relations. This is the 'adverbial' predication of a relation-property. Here a relation-property is predicated of a subject not simpliciter but *under a guise,* specifically, as a subject-insofar-as-it-possesses-a-further-foundation-property. We shall examine this in some detail below. Further, we will observe that Leibniz's argument for the ideal status of relations, rightly understood as involving unit properties, implies the second interpretation above and also shows how relations can be reconciled with his ontology. To anticipate, a relation conceived as separate from any specific relata whereby, like any accident, it would be individuated, is unreduced and polyadic. And, like unary properties abstracted from their unrepeatable mode in their individuating subjects, in such a mode the relation is a universal, so has the conceptual ('ideal') status ascribed by the moderate realist tradition. The intension Is-a-Lover-of is ideal in the same way that the intensions Extension or Red are ideal when abstracted as the common content of instances of extended or red things. This assessment is in agreement with that of Ishiguro, who summarizes Leibniz's idealization thesis as one not about a distinction between relation-properties and nonrelational ones, but about a difference between relation-properties and a reified common intension.[60]

As a preliminary to examining Leibniz's attempted demonstrations of the ideal status of relations and the role therein of unit properties, it is necessary to review some aspects of his novel reformulation of the classic concept of substance. Individual substances are either monads ('simple substances', 'entelechies') or composite substances, the latter being the ordinary objects of the phenomenal world, which are divided into living and nonliving bodies. Monads are minds whose only properties are perceptions, the content of which are phenomena or appearances. As we shall see below, properties, or 'accidents', are individual and can both come into and go out of existence. Monads have no spatial or temporal relations among themselves; indeed, they have no relations of the same ontic status as themselves at all:

> The relations which connect two monads are not in either the one or the other, but equally in both at once; and therefore, properly speaking, in neither but only in the mind. . . . I do not think that you would wish to posit an accident which would inhere simultaneously in two subjects—one which, so as to speak, has one leg in one and another leg in the other.[61]

Composite substances are the ordinary objects of experience, given in experience with their properties and relations. Yet all these attributes are the representational content of perceptions possessed by monads and hence phenomenal, though Leibniz calls them 'true phenomena'. It is as if, in conformity with the terminology, Leibniz here collapses Suarez's distinction between 'objective concepts'—objective, real individuals and properties—and 'formal concepts'—the former as represented within the intellect.

Much of the time Leibniz uses the term 'accident' as the categorical complement to 'substance', so as synonymous with 'attribute' or 'mode', as any characteristic of a substance. He says at one place:

> Besides substances, or ultimate subjects, there are the modifications of substances, which can be produced and destroyed per se; and further there are relations, which are not produced per se but result when other things are produced, and have reality in our intellect—indeed, they are there when nobody is thinking. For they get that reality from the divine intellect, without which nothing would be true.
>
> Bare relations are not created things, and they are solely in the divine intellect, without the addition.[62]

Modifications, or accidents—for instance, a specific height of Socrates—come and go; so too do relations supervening upon them—for example, being shorter than Phaedo. But relations have an objective, nonillusory, nonarbitrary status in two senses: they rest on nonrelational modifications of substances, and they exist independently in the mind of God. Leibniz says elsewhere that "relations and orders are some kind of *entia rationis*, although they have their fundament in things; for one can say that their reality, like that of eternal truths and of possibilities, comes from the supreme reason" (*NE* II, 25, par. 1, p. 235).[63] Like the content of all perceptions—that is, 'ideas' or concepts—relations are concepts in the mind of God that are communicated to lesser minds. Leibniz claims that corresponding to every individual substance is a *complete individual concept*. This concept contains all the properties (as universals), including relation-properties, that the individual will possess throughout its existence. Knowledge of such a concept, which is fully possible only to God, would allow the deduction of all true propositions that could be asserted about the individual. This doctrine follows from the fact that, according to Leibniz, any proposition, necessary or contingent, is true when the predicate concept is contained in the subject concept: *praedicatum inest subjecto*. Hence the predicate of every true proposition concerning an individual must be contained in its (thus complete) concept.[64] An individual concept is *complete* in the sense that it cannot form part of a concept more complex than itself.

The complete concept of a monad contains both intrinsic and extrinsic (relation-property) denominations. "I say that the concept of an individual substance includes all its events and all its denominations, even those which are commonly called extrinsic, that is, those which pertain to it only by virtue of the general connection of things and from the fact that it expresses the whole universe in its own way" (*L* 337).[65] In other words, both relation-properties and non-relation-properties are part of the complete concept of an individual. It is through the relation-properties that an individual 'mirrors' the entire universe (*L* 308).

H.-N. Castañeda has shown how the young Leibniz (1676) was influenced in his strong internalist view of relations by his study of Plato's theory of relations presented in the *Phaedo* and the *Theaetetus*.[66] With regard to the passage in the *Theaetetus* where Plato puzzles over how Socrates can be the same through the change of relations from being taller than Theaetetus to being shorter than Theaetetus, he comments: "This is a remarkable difficulty, and of great importance for other matters."[67] Shortly thereafter, he proposes his solution: "When somebody becomes taller than I, by growing up, certainly some change occurs in me too, since a denomination of mine is changed and in this way everything is in a certain way contained in everything."[68] This anticipates Leibniz's developed view of complete individual concepts and his internalist view of relations. Relations are internal for Leibniz, in that when individual a enters into a relation R with some other entity, this translates into a relation-property whose intension is part of the defining individual concept that a exemplifies. If any relation with a as a relatum might have been different, then the corresponding individual concept for a would be different and so not correspond to a after all. Given aRb, with perfect knowledge of the relation-property intension contained in the individual concept of a (i.e., $\lambda x(xRb)$, using the notation of lambda abstraction), one would also have knowledge of the complete concept of b. By traveling conceptually across the network of relations into which a enters, which is, extensionally, not to leave a, a sufficiently penetrating intellect would achieve knowledge of every other substance.

Some complex ideas constitute propositions; still others correspond to definite or indefinite descriptions. Mixing use and mention, Leibniz calls both the descriptions and any corresponding property referent 'denominations', these being of two types. An extrinsic denomination, as a determination of an individual x, involves reference to some one or more other individuals, y, z, and so forth—that is, it is inherently fully relational. An intrinsic denomination makes no such external reference. For example, 'is a lover of Helen' is an extrinsic denomination of Paris, whereas 'is a man' is not. Extrinsic denomination is a classificatory designation for relation-properties.[69] Again using the notation of lambda abstraction, extrinsic denominations have the forms

(I) $\lambda x(xRa)$ or $\lambda x(aRx)$.

Intrinsic denominations on which properties of form I) are founded have the non-relational form

(II) $\lambda x(F(x))$.

Attributes having this form are sometimes referred to as 'absolute properties'. Unreduced, fully dyadic relations would have the form

(III) $\lambda x \lambda y(xRy)$.

It is relations in this latter, full, multi-subject sense that Leibniz seems to be referring to at places when using the adjectives 'pure' and 'wholly' with the phrase 'extrinsic denomination'.[70] In the context, Leibniz repeats the thesis that "there are no purely extrinsic denominations which have absolutely no foundation in the thing denominated" (C 520). As we will see, Leibniz holds that relations conceived in the manner of form III are merely conceptual. By contrast, his program for logical paraphrase is often interpreted as an attempt to show that the relations of form III are eliminable in favor of logical compounds involving nonrelational properties of form II. Along with Ishiguro, I think the overall textual evidence is that Leibniz intends to reduce relations of form III to combinations of form I, with absolute properties of form II as necessary foundations. More specifically, relations of form III exist in the mind as repeatable abstractions whose basic logical form is that of relation-properties of form I from which they are abstracted, where the latter are individuated to single subjects in which they inhere.

As a preliminary to the ontological argument for these latter theses, we will examine Leibniz's fragmentary project for the paraphrase of relations. This is part of his 'rational grammar' enterprise of translating certain types of sentences into canonical forms amenable to formal inference rules, whether of the standard syllogistic logic or of the programmatic formal calculi whose development he urged.[71] We have seen that in the traditional reduction of relations to relation-properties, the latter absorb both the single-subject mode of inherence, its esse in aspect, and the unique, defining, relational aspect of being-toward or with-respect-to, the esse ad aspect.

Consider, first, Leibniz's example of 'Paris loves Helen'. He states:

> This will be the best way of explaining 'Paris is the lover of Helen', that is, 'Paris loves, and by that very fact (*et eo ipso*) Helen is loved'. Here, therefore, two propositions have been brought together and abbreviated into one. Or, 'Paris is a lover and by that very fact Helen is a loved one'. [C 287][72]

The logical work of linking the specific person Paris to the specific person Helen under the intension of Loves is now to be accomplished by a non-truthfunctional connective between resulting propositions. Symbolizing the new connective 'by that very fact' as '@', our relational sentence becomes

(4.1) Lover(Paris) @ Loved(Helen).

It is now through the logical connective that Paris as a lover is to be linked with Helen and not someone else, and vice versa for Helen as loved.

That Leibniz cannot eliminate the necessity of relation-properties by using the connector @ in 4.1 is seen from the following. What is required for 4.1 to be equivalent to 'Paris loves Helen' is a linking specifically between Paris and Helen, and this cannot be accomplished without relation-properties. First, note that it cannot simply be the ostensible subject of each @-junct proposition that are linked under @, as if 4.1 were identical to

(4.2) The subject of the proposition Lover(Paris) is connected to the subject of the proposition Loved(Helen).

Or, symbolically,

(4.3) [Lover(Paris) · Loved(Helen) · Paris is connected to Helen].

But this will not do, since Paris and Helen could equally be connected as, say, married. So to distinguish the love relation from this case we must add to 4.3 the phrase 'under the intension of Loves'. That is,

(4.4) [Lover(Paris) · Loved(Helen) · Paris is connected under the intension of Loves to Helen].

Yet the last conjunct is but a long-winded way of saying that Paris loves Helen, so we do not have a reduction to absolute properties. Even worse, the proposal requires @ to have a specific intension, so @ is no longer a general connective and could not be used as in the other examples above. To prevent this, 4.1 must be understood as

(4.5) The unspecified correlative of 'Lover(Paris)', i.e., Helen, is connected to the unspecified correlative of 'Loved(Helen)', i.e., Paris.

The cross-reference needed from the connective @ is easily captured in modern logic through the overlapping scopes of quantifiers; that is, 4.1 understood as 4.5 is rendered:

(4.6) $(\exists x)(\exists y)$ [Lover(Paris,x) · Loved(Helen,y) · x = Helen · y = Paris].

In short, 'Lover(Paris)' and 'Loved(Helen)' in 4.1 must be implicit relation-properties, not absolute properties. We shall see that Leibniz's ontic analysis of relations is in agreement with this.

But this example does not completely capture what is apparently intended to be the more complex analysis as found in other examples. In these examples, not only are foundational properties for the given relation made explicit, but it is *through them*, by a mediated predication, that the relation-property is predicated of the given relata. For example, Leibniz parses the sentence 'Titus is wiser than Caius' as:

Titus is wise and as such (*qua talis*) is superior, to the extent that (*quatenus*), Caius qua wise is inferior. (*C* 280)

Or, symbolically,

Superior<Wise(Titus)> @ Inferior<Wise(Caius)>.

The expression '<Wise(Titus)>' refers to Titus under the aspect or guise of being wise The predication of being superior is of wise Titus, and not, say, of athlete Titus, for Titus may not be superior as an athlete.

That Leibniz intends the opaque context of mediated, or 'adverbial', predications in each @-junct comes out in other parsings in the same grammatical texts. For example, the adverbial modification in 'Peter stands beautifully' is to be rendered: 'Peter is beautiful in so far as he is a stander [*quatenus est stans*]' (*C* 244).[73] It is not standing (in general) or Peter simpliciter which is beautiful, but only Peter as he possesses the property of standing; that is;

Beautiful<Stander(Peter)>.[74]

At another place he states:

A ∞ B means A and B are identical, or that one can be substituted for the other everywhere. (That is, if it is not prohibited, as in the case where some term is considered in a certain respect. For example, although triangle and trilateral are identical, yet if one were to say that a triangle by its nature as such [*quatenus tale*], has 180 degrees, one cannot substitute trilateral. For the term [triangle] there is something material [intensional]. [*C* 261][75]

Leibniz is claiming that where 'triangle' is synonymous with 'has three angles' and 'trilateral' with 'has three sides', it is the case that

180 degrees<Triangle(x)>,

but not

180 degrees<Trilateral(x)>.

It is insofar-as-x-is-three-angled that it has the property of 180 degrees. Mediated predication makes perspicuous the reason for the failure of Leibniz's principle of substitutivity *salva veritate* in such contexts. Whether he was aware of it or not, that Leibniz needs adverbial predication in the Paris/Helen example, particularly for the relation of *Loves*, is brought out by the following. To make the contrast clear, I shall substitute the relation *Lusts-after* for the ambiguous Loves. Consider now the propositions

(4.7) Oedipus lusts after Jocasta.

(4.8) Oedipus lusts after his mother.

It is possible for 4.7 to be true while 4.8 is false, even though Jocasta is Oedipus's mother. The reason for this is that Oedipus does not lust after Jocasta independently of any of her properties (to which he has epistemic access), so treating her as if she were a bare or thin particular numerically identical as such to Oedipus's mother. Rather, Oedipus lusts after Jocasta insofar as she has certain properties (e.g., physical beauty) and not others (e.g., being his mother). Lust is a mediated relation, as is love in other senses.

Leibniz's previous two examples involved asymmetric relations and thus required the introduction of a non-truth-functional connective in the paraphrase. Asymmetric relations apparently fall under what Leibniz termed *relations of concurrence*, which involve "some connection, as that of cause and effect, of whole and parts, of position and order, etc." (*NE* II, 9, par. 4, p. 144). These are distinguished from *relations of comparison*, which entail "congruity and incongruity, . . . and comprise resemblance, equality, inequality, etc." (ibid.). This category is apparently that of symmetric relations. By contrast with asymmetric relations, Leibniz says that only the truth-functional connective 'and' is needed for parsing symmetric relations—for example, 'is similar to'. "All oblique inferences—e.g., 'Peter is similar to Paul'—are to be explained by explanations of words. Such may be seen from the logic of Jungius. It is reduced to the proposition 'Peter is A now' and 'Paul is A now'" (*C* 244).[76]

Given the above examples, Leibniz's logical paraphrase program parallels the classical analysis of relations and has the following schema:

(4.9) $x\mathrm{R}y \equiv \mathrm{R}'<\mathrm{F}'(x)> \,\square\, \mathrm{R}''<\mathrm{F}''(y)>$, where, for asymmetric relation R, R' and R" are properties of form I, F' and F" are the requisite foundational properties of form II, and □ is Leibniz's connective, 'by that very fact'. For a symmetric relation R, R' and R" are deleted, F' and F" are of form II, and □ is the standard conjunction.[77] We can now use schema 4.9 as the basis for a brief comparison of prominent analyses of Leibniz's logical program for relations. Jaakko Hintikka emphasizes the asymmetric analysis, though he does not appeal to the properties F' and F", restricting R' and R" to quantified versions of form I—for example, R' = $\lambda x(\exists x)(x\mathrm{R}y)$.[78] Hintikka offers a logical analysis of the connective @. Benson Mates emphasizes the symmetric analysis, replacing ≡ by the weaker conditional ⊃ in the direction of 'F'x · F"y ⊃ xRy'.[79] Russell and C. Broad apparently subscribe to the same interpretation as Mates except that they retain the biconditional.[80] But why, if Leibniz had intended that the truth-functional conjunction be used in all cases, would he not simply have said so and parsed all relation propositions like the 'A is similar to B' example?

Let us now turn to Leibniz's ontological analysis of relations, with his view of universals as a preliminary. He says at one place:

> I do not believe that you will admit an accident that is in two subjects at the same time. My judgment about relations is that paternity in David is one thing, sonship in Solomon another, but that the relation common to both is a merely mental thing whose basis is the modification of the individuals. [L 609]

If we were to read the first sentence in this quote as making the general assertion that no two subjects have the same *property* and import no further refinement of unit properties, then it would commit Leibniz to the nominalist position that no two entities share any numerically identical property; nor, even in some moderating sense, can they exactly resemble one another. For the resemblance relation, being analogous to the similarity relation of the above example, must for Leibniz reduce to properties of its relata; but on the present assumption, these properties are held to be qualitatively distinct, and so cannot resemble in the requisite sense. This construal of 'no property can be in two subjects' could be called the assumption of general property uniqueness and rendered symbolically as the closure of:

(4.10) $[\mathrm{P}(x) \cdot \mathrm{Q}(y) \cdot x \neq y] \supset \mathrm{P} \neq \mathrm{Q}$.

It must be said that 4.10 is true for Leibniz if P and Q are restricted in their range to complete individual concepts. But this application is a function of both the complexity of individual concepts and God's economy of creation. Nevertheless, the fact that the special nature of such complex concepts precludes their multiple exemplification does not prevent contained atomic concepts from being multiply exemplified. In fact, as previously mentioned, there is strong evidence that Leibniz is not committed to the nominalist denial of the identity theory, which holds that there are identical property intensions common to distinct individuals. Clatterbaugh has argued that when Leibniz says that a substance has a certain attribute, this is an abstraction or idea corresponding to the fact that the substance possesses an individual accident.[81] That is, corresponding to the scholastic view, attributes are the content of a property when conceptually removed from any individuated inherence in a specific subject. I will not recapitulate all Clatterbaugh's evidence but only the key texts connecting unit properties and relations, to which I shall add some further considerations which in my view further support Clatterbaugh's thesis.

First, Leibniz holds that the identity of indiscernibles—that is,

$$(4.11) \quad (P)[P(x) \equiv P(y)] \supset x = y,$$

is not a logical truth but a metaphysical one. This follows from the fact that two distinct but indiscernible entities would violate God's standard of metaphysical perfection, which seeks the maximum variety with the greatest economy. "This supposition of two indiscernibles, such as two pieces of matter perfectly alike, seems indeed to be possible in abstract terms, but it is not consistent with the order of things, nor with the divine wisdom by which nothing is admitted without reason" (L 699). Significantly, he here asserts that it is logically possible for two individuals to have the same set of numerically the same properties (i.e., universals), F, G, and so on. That is, it is possible for some x and y that

$$(4.12) \quad x \neq y \cdot (P)[P(x) \equiv P(y)].$$

To capture the contrast intended by Leibniz, the right conjunct must be understood as asserting that it is numerically the same property P that is said to be in both x and y.

Secondly, despite Leibniz's endorsement of nominalist methodological standards in science, he is not committed to a denial of the identity theory to the extent that there is no sense in which two individuals have the same property. In

New Essays, Leibniz comments on Locke's nominalist position that "what is called *general* and universal belongs not to the being (*existence*) of things, but that it is a work of the understanding . . . and the essences of each species are only abstract ideas" (*NE* III, 3, par. 11, p. 313). Leibniz responds: "I do not quite see this consequence. For generality consists in the resemblance of separated things among themselves, and this resemblance is a reality" (ibid.). Further on he says: "As far as you conceive the similarity of things you conceive something more [than only particulars], and the universality consists only in that" (*NE* IV, 17, par. 8, p. 567). But what Leibniz is suggesting cannot be simply resemblance nominalism, where the latter is understood as exact resemblance. For one thing, by 'resemblance is a reality' he cannot be saying that the resemblance *relation* is a reality, since this violates his position that relations are entia rationis. What are real, as opposed to merely ideal, are 'separated things' and their properties.

In addition, there is the general argument against resemblance nominalism, which, on his assumptions, Leibniz would necessarily have fallen victim to. Given the fact that A (exactly) resembles B—for example, a red disc and a red tile—the resemblance is 'real' and, like all relations for Leibniz, internal, and so rests upon the nonrelational foundations F' and F'', the reds, in its relata: $F'(A)$ and $F''(B)$. That is, A (red disc) and B (red tile) resemble one another *because* of the respective foundations F' (say, Red_i) and F'' (say, Red_j). But on the assumption of resemblance nominalism, which denies the existence of universals, $F' \neq F''$ (i.e., $Red_i \neq Red_j$). It is the case that F' and F'' *resemble* one another and in the same way in which the original terms A and B resemble each other. Indeed, A and B resemble one another (as red) *because* F' and F'' resemble each other (as red). But now we have the start of a vicious regress. The resemblance relation between F' and F'' must in turn rest upon some intrinsic foundations G' and G'' in F' and F'' respectively, where again resemblance nominalism requires that $G' \neq G''$. For the same reason as above, F' and F'' resemble each other because of the facts that $G'(F')$ and $G''(F'')$ and that G' resembles G''. But now the resemblance between G' and G'' must be explained by appeal to further foundations in them of H' and H'' and their resemblance, and so on. We have a vicious infinite regress of resemblance facts, each successive one needed to explain the resemblance in the previous case.

Let us now turn to Leibniz's remarks on unit properties, among which is further evidence for the moderate realist interpretation of shared, 'ideal' universals inherent in thus 'exactly resembling' instances. That Leibniz held the view of property instances is clear from at least three texts, including the following, in which he is commenting on issues in Descartes' *Principia.*

> Therefore, since substance and accident depend upon each other, other marks are necessary for distinguishing a substance from an accident. Among them may be this one: That a substance needs some accident but often does not need a determinate one but is content, when this accident is removed, with the substitution of another. An accident, however, needs not only some substance in general but that very one in which it inheres, so that it cannot change it. [*L* 390–91]

Unit properties are here proposed as a criterion for distinguishing substances from the accidents that inhere in them. He is responding to the observation that it is not enough to say that accidents depend upon substances, since equally there are no substances without accidents. Because a particular unit accident is tied to a specific subject substance such that its unrepeatability is a function of this subject, the unit accident would lose its identity if moved to inhere in another substance.

This characteristic of individual accidents is formalized as

(4.13) $[F_i(x) \cdot F_j(y) \cdot x \neq y] \supset F_i \neq F_j,$

which is the principle of subject uniqueness (SU) of chapter 1, limited to the monadic case.

Leibniz refers to unit accidents in the much-quoted fifth letter to Clark, where he makes it clear that a repeatable attribute, which is the common content of multiple unit accidents, is an 'ideal thing'. Here Leibniz is considering the concepts of place and space. He asks us to conceive of an object A, which is fixed spatially by its relations to other given entities, as being replaced by an object B. He says:

> For the place of A and B is the same, whereas the relation of A to fixed bodies is not precisely and individually the same as the relation B (that comes into its place) will have to the same fixed bodies; but these relations agree only. For two different subjects, as A and B, cannot have precisely the same individual affection, it being impossible that the same *individual accident* should be in two subjects or pass from one subject to another. But

the mind, not content with an agreement, looks for an identity, for something that should be truly the same, and conceives it as being extrinsic to
the subject; and this is what we here call *place* and *space*. But this can only
be an ideal thing, containing a certain order, wherein the mind conceives
the application of relations. [*L* 704, my emphasis]

Clearly, Leibniz is distinguishing between relation-property instances and relation-property universals. Further, he claims that the mind is compelled to look
for that which is absolutely identical across distinct individual accidents—for
example, (Being-to-the-Right-of-C)$_1$ and (Being-to-the-Right-of-C)$_2$—and this
is the common attribute or universal Being-to-the-Right-of-C. Because the universal is separated from, hence not individuated to, a distinct subject, it is
conceptual.

The commonality that is looked for by the mind is not invented by it but,
rather, abstracted from the particular. In a dialogue written in 1711, Leibniz is
emphatic in saying that we should "always distinguish between the extended or
extension, and the attribute to which being extended . . . is referred" (*L* 622).
For the "extension is nothing but an abstraction and demands something which
is extended. It needs a subject, . . . some quality, some attribute, some nature in
the subject which is extended" (*L* 621).

Leibniz not only uses the assumption of unit properties to argue for the
conceptual nature of relation-properties abstracted from individuating relata,
but, more important, he also uses it to argue for the ideal nature of relations
taken in the full polyadic sense prior to reduction. This comes out in the
following famous quote, but only clearly when interpreted in light of the doctrine of unit accidents stated explicitly in the above passage, a passage that
slightly precedes the following in the text. I have inserted what I take to be the
correct interpretation in this light.

I shall allege another example to show how the mind uses, upon occasion
of accidents which are in subjects [i.e., unit accidents], to fancy to itself
something answerable to those accidents out of the subjects [abstracted
common content]. The ratio or proportion [R] between two lines L and M
[L ≠ M] may be conceived three several ways: as the ratio of the greater L
to the lesser M [R'(L)], a ratio of the lesser M to the greater L [R"(M)], and,
lastly, as something abstracted from both, that is, the ratio between L and
M without considering which is the antecedent or which the consequent,

which the subject and which the object $[R = \lambda x \lambda y (x R y)]$. . . . In the first way of considering then, L the greater, in the second, M the lesser, is the subject of that accident which philosophers call 'relation'. But which of them will be the subject in the third way of considering them [R]? It cannot be said that both of them, L and M together, are the subject of such an accident; for, if so, we should have an [unit] accident in two subjects, with one leg in one and the other in the other [i.e., $R_i(L) \cdot R_i(M)$], which is contrary to the notion of [unit] accidents [i.e., violates 4.13]. Therefore we must say that this relation, in this third way of considering it [not individuated to a single subject], is indeed one of the subjects; but being neither a substance nor an [unit] accident, it must be a mere ideal thing [abstracted universal], the consideration of which is nevertheless useful. [L 704]

In brief, Leibniz asserts that relations conceived in the 'third way' are fully polyadic and between multiple subjects, having the form $\lambda x \lambda y (x R y)$. He argues that a relation R taken as fully polyadic cannot be in any subjects, for as such, by the doctrine of single-subject inherence, it would have to be simultaneously in both subjects, and this, together with the further requirement that it be a unit accident, leads to contradiction. By 'the notion of accidents', Leibniz means *unit accidents*, as he has just previously explained. If the full relation R inheres in its subjects, then, by the restriction to single subjects, it must do so as R(L) and R(M). Under the restriction of unary inherence, the conjunction 'R(L) and R(M)' is the only sensible way of interpreting 'both of them, L and M together, are the subject'. Now, with the further requirement of unit accidents, we have $R_i(L)$ and $R_j(M)$, and indeed the fact that $R_i = R_j$. This identity is also required again by the fact that, as here interpreted, R is polyadic and unreduced, and as such, if it has relata, it must simultaneously inhere in both, 'L and M together, are the subject'—that is, $R_i(L)$ and $R_i(M)$. However, since L ≠ M, this violates restriction 4.13 above—namely, no unit property can inhere in two distinct subjects. It is the combination of the doctrines of single-subject inherence and unit accidents that shows it to be impossible for relations to straddle their relata.

As indicated in the first sentence of the last quote, a full, unreduced relation is an abstraction obtained from relations 'in subjects', and these must be relation-properties of form I, not absolute properties of form II. Because one cannot get more from less, one cannot abstract a polyadic property with, as

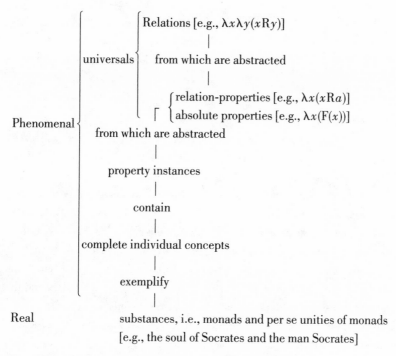

Fig. 4.1. The role of relations and their instances in Leibniz's ontology

such, a multi-subject structure from an absolute property devoid of such a structure. Again, Leibniz's ontic reduction program is not one that eliminates relation-properties.

If the above is correct, then Leibniz's ontology can be diagrammed as in figure 4.1 (reading up).

chapter five

Some Modern Views of Unit Attributes

Like their medieval precursors, modern theories of unit properties and relations divide into realist and nominalist versions. Turning first to realist theories, in more or less detail this doctrine has been advocated by John Cook Wilson, P. F. Strawson, N. Wolterstorff, and the early Bertrand Russell.

The instance realism of both Cook Wilson and Strawson is advanced, at least in part, on the basis of apparent irreducible reference to unit attributes in ordinary language, as reviewed in chapter 1. I note in passing that Cook Wilson also offers the argument encountered previously that the matter/form analysis of entities leads to an infinite regress, and that unit attributes answer this difficulty. "Every existence combines being as this and being as such, and the inseparableness of this from the such might be represented by 'a this such'. . . . This avoids the conclusion caused by matter and form, where matter is inevitably regarded as having again form of its own."[1]

Russell and Wolterstorff

Let us turn to the instance realism of Russell and Wolterstorff.[2] What is interesting and relevant about the positions of the early Russell and later of Wolterstorff is that both argue for the existence of unit relations as a direct consequence of Bradley's regress. Before considering the regress argument, it should be noted that Russell had argued in an early unpublished manuscript entitled "An Analysis of Mathematical Reasoning" (1897) that there are instances of certain properties and relations—for example, good, red, heavy, and causation—based upon the spatial and/or temporal localization of their relata. Russell reiterated the argument from distinctness of spatial occurrence in a 1911 paper "On the Relations of Universals and Particulars."[3] He argued that the fact that it is logically possible for precisely similar things to coexist in two different places but that things in different places cannot be numerically identical shows that 'instances of universals' exist at different points in space, not the universals themselves. In a 1955 postscript to the 1911 paper, Russell rejected the argument for instances, saying that he no longer thought it necessary that spatial or temporal relations necessarily implied diversity of relata.[4]

But there was another, relevant tack that Russell had taken early on in arguing for unit relations, an argument of a more general character utilizing Bradley's regress. In another unpublished manuscript entitled "Do Differences Differ?" (1900), he had argued that Bradley's regress forces a distinction between a relation universal (intension) and its particularized instances. The relation universal is merely a class concept; it relates no terms. To analyze a relational fact $:aRb$ as containing, in addition to a and b, only the universal R is to require further relations to account for the unity—that is, $aR'RR''b$—and the same for the latter, and so on. Consequently, it is particularized relations that 'actually relate' their relata. Interestingly, this argument in a slightly altered, expanded form is considered in the *Principles* (1903), pars. 54–55, just prior to an argument against instances of the exemplification relation, an important argument that will be examined in chapter 7.

More recently, Wolterstorff has likewise proposed that the perplexity of Bradley's regress can be resolved by distinguishing between relations (universals) and 'cases' (i.e., instances of relations).[5] He observes that the regress is stopped by simply admitting a relation that does the work of relating, 'ties which actually tie', or, adopting Bradley's metaphor, "things in relation—objects fitting into one another like the links of a chain."[6] Wolterstorff asserts that it is cases of relations which have this ontological function.

> Loving is a relation. Somebody's loving somebody—John's loving Mary—is a *case* of that relation. . . . A case of a relation consists of things in relation; a relation does not. To get things in relation, we do not need some non-relational links or ties. All we need is *cases* of relations. If we just have relations and things, we do not have things in relation; but we do have things in relation if we have cases of relations. If all we have is the relation of love, and some persons, we do not have persons loving persons. For this, we need cases of loving.[7]

Both Russell and Wolterstorff contend that Bradley's regress forces us to admit what is in effect Suarez's distinction, a distinction between relations-with-a-mode that is combinatorial among their relata *and* relations where the defining linking nature has been abstracted away. It is this very distinction that allows Bradley regress to get off the ground. The nonrelating relation is the intension R, an abstraction common to instances R_1, R_2, . . . which actually exist among and connect relata and as such are individuated. But here we have a large—or at least nonobvious—jump to why relations as actually relating must be individuated, with no argument given. An argument is possible, however, and I will provide it in chapter 8.

Trope Nominalism

Modern versions of nominalistic particularism can be found in the works of G. F. Stout, D. C. Williams, and, most recently, Keith Campbell.[8] I shall examine Campbell's basic theses as both indicating and revealing what, I shall argue, are the weaknesses of instance nominalism in general.

It is telling that Campbell seeks to distance himself from traditional nominalism. He states:

> The great, liberating insight which Stout and Williams offer us is this: properties can be particulars, so the denial of universals need not be the denial of properties. In other words, Particularism (which is economical, plausible and appealing) does not have to take the form of Nominalism (which is economical, but neither plausible nor appealing).[9]

Despite this seeming disclaimer, however, Campbell's trope theory is nominalistic: all entities (including tropes) are homogeneously particular, and on this and other grounds—for example, the monadic reduction of relations—his theory is both implausible and nonappealing.

Campbell's goal is to expand upon Williams's theory of tropes and thereby substitute a one-category ontology for the traditional, problem-plagued two-category ontology of substances and attributes. The single category is that of tropes: simple, nonrepeatable property instances—for example, Red_1, $Round_3$, $Mass_5$, At-Position-A_1. Campbell observes that, ignoring their subjective status, Hume's *impressions* and Locke's *ideas* are abstract particulars, or tropes. A trope is a particular, but not a bare one; it is a particularized simple nature, a particularized intension. "Their role is dual: to be particular natures."[10] In this one category of entities, Campbell seeks to account for the dual ontic givens of both unrepeatability and repeatability. Of course, it is the attempt to explain away repeatability on which all nominalism flounders, and this is equally true of tropism. To account for the apparent sameness of content across tropes—say, the Red in Red$_1$ and Red$_2$, Campbell adopts a standard nominalist ploy, proposing one of two relations that are fundamental to tropism: *resemblance.* The claim 'Red$_1$ and Red$_2$ are both red' is true because there exists a resemblance relation between Red$_1$ and Red$_2$. Further, an ordinary particular is assayed as a bundle of tropes whose internal unity and concomitant external distinctness from other bundles are accounted for by the second fundamental, sui generis relation of tropism: *compresence.* An ordinary object is a set of compresent tropes.

As mentioned in chapter 1, there exists in the literature a set of standard arguments impugning the thesis that the resemblance relation is sufficient to account for the commonality among entities that is the epistemic given. I shall not rehearse these arguments here. Rather, I shall concentrate on what I propose are additional, fatal weaknesses in trope nominalism. These can be summarized as follows. First, it is ironic that though both resemblance and compresence are fundamental to trope theory, the theory nevertheless *requires* that these, like *all* relations, be eliminated by monadic reduction. Campbell is explicit about this, and consistently so—recall the arguments of chapter 2 demonstrating that both nominalism generally and the compresence relation among tropes imply the erroneous property reduction of relations. Motivating the property reduction of relations is the posited free-floating status of tropes— they inhere in *no* subject (so constitute a denial of the principle of relata-linking, RL). For it is Campbell's intent to avoid the difficulties of substance/ attribute ontology, specifically the inevitable reduction of substance to the incoherence of a 'bare particular'. The obvious choice for elimination are substances. But Campbell takes this to be equivalent to the necessity of eliminating any entity with the status of an ontic subject. That is, Campbell identifies the assertions:

(a) Attributes exist only by inhering in or among extrinsic *substances.*
(b) Attributes exist only by inhering in or among extrinsic *subjects.*

Identifying (b) with (a) and rejecting (a) leaves an ontology of unattached attributes. This free-floating status of qualities constitutes the novelty of tropism over traditional nominalism. However, the elimination of entities with the status of subjects not only has the drastic consequence of the necessary reduction of relations to foundational properties, but also, with all subjects removed, there is the a fortiori elimination of the predicative nature of would-be ontic predicates (i.e., properties), the implications of which Campbell appears not to fully appreciate. Further, the elimination of both subjects and the predicate mode of properties puts *all* attributes on the same ontic plane; all alike are tropes. This must apply also to second-order properties attributable to tropes themselves. Consequently, tropes are not simple but are themselves bundles of further tropes. Let us look in detail at each one of these difficulties.

According to trope theory, relations must be eliminated, for relations are in general polyadic and so exist between and presuppose terms whose ontic status is that of subjects. The relation Is-Taller-than exists only between two distinct terms, and to admit its existence is to admit two simultaneous subjects. As Campbell observes, "no terms; no relation."[11] He then states:

> Monadic tropes require no bearer, polyadic ones call for at least two, which will have to be themselves tropes, and in the most elementary cases these terms will be monadic tropes. For this reason the trope philosophy cannot treat qualities and relations as differing only in the number of their bearers, a difference which carries no serious implication as to ontic priority.[12]

Campbell then attempts to show that some classic arguments for the nonreduction of relations are flawed and so, after all, do not stand in the way of a monadic reduction. In chapter 6 I will not only show that the traditional arguments are not flawed but will provide further arguments for the irreducibility of relations.

Secondly, with entities having the ontic status of subjects eliminated, properties are no longer attributive of anything—they are not predicative—hence the characterization of tropes as, in effect, substance atoms, not individuated *attributes*. Tropes have no attachment mode; they have no linking to an extrinsic subject; they are 'saturated', to borrow Frege's metaphor. Ironically, then, we have predicates that are not predicative and so, to all appearances, are subjects, but now existing in a metaphysical space with no true predicates at all; that is, nothing is ontically predicative. All that is combinatorial and are principles of pluralistic unity has been eliminated in favor of a granulated, isolated universe of tropes. If, as Campbell claims, tropes are the bricks out of which every object is built, then, without predicative properties and relations, there is no mortar to hold these materials together in organized complexes. There are no unified states of affairs or facts to constitute the truth conditions for atomic propositions. In general, this is the debilitating position that all strict, reductive atomists put themselves into, whether they advocate abstract atomism of sets or a concrete atomism of physical particles. Complexes of any kind become not simply miracles; they are strictly impossible. Even a posited 'bundle' is a complex, albeit one whose unity must be radically extrinsic—completely independent of any characteristic making up the natures of the constituents, an aggregate-by-listing. All that is presupposed is the existence of the entities. But it would seem that such a unity, if it can exist at all, must be the arbitrary *association* of an extrinsic kind. To account for the existence of objective complex objects (i.e., bundles), it would be necessary to introduce as essential a Divine Mind, similar to Cantor's reliance upon the Divine Intellect to guarantee the objective existence of the hierarchy of infinite sets. Bundles are miracles after all.

Of course, this will not do. First, there are two types of plural unity that trope theory must explain: the apparent sameness of nature of certain tropes and the togetherness of some tropes, not others, so as to constitute complex ordinary individuals that are nonrandom and of a kind. To solve the problem, the *relations* of resemblance and compresence are posited. Yet relations have been necessarily dissolved into the residue of their foundations; moreover, these foundations must be either (a) identical to the natures of two or more tropes or (b) separate, second-order properties of first-order tropes. If (a)—that is, if relations are reduced to the natures of the resembling or compresent tropes—this means that, contrary to their posited role, the relations of resemblance and compresence have in fact no explanatory power; they are ontically empty and idle. Resemblance was to account for the commonality of two tropes of the same type; but resemblance itself is identified with the natures of the resembling tropes— hence the explanation that tropes A_1 and B_2 are of the same kind because of their natures A and B. In other words, A_1 and B_2 are of the same type because they are what they are. But this is no explanation, only a restatement of the data to be explained. The same bogus role is played by the compresence relation: with all relations (including resemblance) retracted to within subsequently isolated tropes, then several tropes can be said to constitute the entity they do only because they each are severally what they are. But how does this explain their conjunction into this entity as opposed to some or all others? It does not. If (b)—that is, if resemblance and compresence are treated as second-order properties of first-order tropes—then we encounter a general weakness of considerable force, as pointed out by Armstrong.[13] What could it mean for a trope A to have a property P? After all, other things can be attributed to tropes, in addition to resemblance and compresence—for example, the relation-properties of spatial, temporal, and causal relations, as well as properties like Simplicity, Has-a-Nature, and so on. In this one-category ontology it could only mean that P is but a further trope. But this implies either that trope A is really a quasi-trope composed of subsumed tropes, contradicting the doctrine that tropes are simple, or that trope P is not a constituent of Trope A but is predicative of the latter as *a subject*, again a situation that trope theory rules out.

With regard to relations, Campbell is right in holding that "there is no way of dispensing with the relational vocabulary and relational descriptions altogether";[14] but the reason for this is that it is impossible to dispense with the entities to which the language makes reference. Campbell wants to retain the benefits of relations, even speaking at places of relations 'supervening' upon their foundations. Yet, at the level of reality, he must deny them because all relations definitionally require multiple *subjects* and a combinatorial status among them; so, once admitted, there is no non-ad hoc reason to deny these conditions to the limiting case of monadic properties as well. But thinking that the only way he can avoid the weaknesses involved in the category of substances is by eliminating the subjects in which properties inhere, Campbell must relinquish the category of relations.

Despite the elimination of relations and the disclaimer that the language of relations that he uses not be taken literally, Campbell makes demands of his trope ontology that require real relations in addition to resemblance and compresence. To account for both our daily and our scientific understanding, tropes must form 'rich complexes'—for example, electromagnetic fields, crystal lattices, the sky. The relation of causality must also be included: "The distribution of tropes is in constant flux, as the causal links among states, events and processes bring forth real changes."[15] At one place Campbell states that causation can be viewed as 'supervening' between cause and effect, and that "where one item supervenes upon another there is no real difference."[16] Even though supervenience is a mode of dependence, it does not obviate the necessity of the question of how something can supervene and still not exist. The ontology that Campbell envisions requires the plural unity and betweenness of real, unreduced relations. In this regard, the austerity of trope nominalism leads to bankruptcy; but, like some governments, it hopes to cover its explanatory deficit by printing relational vocabulary. This language is fraudulent, however, if there are no real relational assets to back it up.

Consider a further endemic weakness of trope theory. Campbell implies that we can formally distinguish two aspects of a trope: its individuality and a nature or content, though in extra-conceptual reality they constitute a single entity. In this he is consistent with a realist theory of property instances. He even mentions in this regard Scotus's 'formal' distinction. Yet he insists that "although the idea here is that all particulars are particulars and each of them has a nature, this does not involve conceding that a trope is after all complex (a union of particularity with a nature-providing property)."[17] But to hold that the individuator and the nature of a trope are only formally distinct—that is, cannot exist separated extra-conceptually—does not imply that there is no internal distinction within a trope. James Moreland has pointed out this inconsistency at length.[18] Each trope has two distinct aspects, each with its own, hence distinguishing, second-order attributes. Like the scholastics, Campbell offers no theory as to how these two aspects can belong to a single entity. However, he is emphatic that the nature of a trope is not universal (i.e., not repeatable), and herein lies a problem. Let T_1 be a trope, let N_1 be the nature of T_1 whereby it exactly resembles some but not all other tropes, and let H_1 be the thisness, or haecceitas, of T_1, the source of the unrepeatability of T_1. To say that H_1 is the principle of individuation of trope T_1 is to imply that the only other metaphysical component, the nature N_1, is itself repeatable (i.e., a universal). If N_1 itself were individuated, then why would a further individuator H_1 be needed? Yet Campbell insists that the nature is itself not repeatable. A trope, then, has two distinguishable aspects, a thisness and a nature, both of which are unrepeatable. But this in turn implies that what individuates the nature aspect, N_1, must be a thisness distinct from H_1, say H_2. With this we have two untoward consequences. First, since the nature of T_1 is now attached to individuator H_2, H_1 has become that dreaded entity, a bare particular. Second, the trope T_1 has two distinct individuators, H_1 and H_2, so should be two tropes, not one. Indeed, we have the makings of a vicious regress, for the individuator H_2 must be distinguished from the nature N_1, which must still be individuated, thereby requiring a third haecceitas, H_3, and so on. The original unitary trope has now dissolved into infinitely many individuals. The moral: the intension component of a unit attribute must be a universal.

Consider as a final criticism of trope theory in this chapter the problem of spatiotemporal location. Campbell has a propensity for wanting to identify the source of particularity with space-time position. However, as he observes, this illegitimately rules out a priori abstract individuals such as sets, numbers, concepts, sounds, tastes, angels, and God.[19] Further, Moreland has shown that if a trope is individuated by its place, it must *have a place*; that is, this place is part of its nature or content.[20] But, since tropes are simple, this place cannot be distinct from the content of a trope at this place, say Red_1. Then, for any other trope compresent with Red_1—say, $Round_1$—it must be the case that the two natures are identical—Red is identical to Round. In light of this criticism, Campbell has abandoned the view that tropes are individuated by their place.[21] He concludes that "to preserve the simplicity of tropes, one must then affirm that *individuation is basic and unanalyzable.*"[22] This, of course, is in keeping with the position of traditional nominalism: there is nothing to individuation to be explained; it just is. Commonality is what must be explained (away). However, Campbell is uneasy enough about this reply to contend that anyone who advances a theory of unit properties that includes an internal individuator as a real aspect (Moreland) is in the same position. He writes: "Now ask: what is it about one of these individuators that makes it the individuator it is and not some other? There can only be the non-informative, but true, answer (not any feature, aspect, or constituent of that individuator but) just being that individuator rather than another."[23] In this, Campbell is wrong. A moderate realist can account for why this specific property or relation is attached to these subjects. For, as I shall continue to argue, if one admits a linking, or predicative, aspect to unit properties, it is this combining which renders occurrent the concomitant intension or nature to a specific subject. This requires both an extrinsic subject and a predicative nature for properties, both of which Campbell denies.

chapter six

The Irreducibility of Relations

Historically, arguments against admitting relations as a fundamental ontic category are of two types. It is argued either that (a) the very concept of a relation is suspect or, indeed, incoherent—the often claimed moral of Bradley's regress; or that (b) relations are reducible without loss to properties, so are ontically superfluous. As observed previously, perhaps the argument most frequently invoked, interpreted by some as for, by others as against, the coherence of the concept of relations, has been Bradley's regress. Because of both the importance of its conclusion and the ambiguity that has existed historically in interpreting the direction of its force, it is necessary to examine the argument in detail. I shall do so in chapter 8. We have also observed in the overview of the previous chapter an almost continual adherence up to the nineteenth century, albeit with some notable exceptions, of a reductive account of relations. Relations were reduced either to relational properties of their terms, which presupposes a foundation in one or more terms, or to foundations themselves. In advocating a trope theory of unit properties, Campbell has recently revived the latter gambit (indeed, necessarily so according to the arguments of chapter 2) and thus has atttempted to parry some classical arguments against the reduction of relations. Here I shall concentrate primarily upon demonstrating that Campbell's arguments, which turn upon formal properties of relations, are non sequiturs. This will provide an opportunity to review and strengthen these classical arguments against reduction of relations, which, because of the precision with which they can be formulated, carry considerable warrant. I shall conclude by taking up three instructive arguments against relations once advanced by Panayot Butchvarov which turn upon nonformal, less precise considerations.

It was not until the middle of the nineteenth century that the importance and irreducibility of relations began to be widely accepted, motivated in part by logical investigations into the foundations of mathematics. Many arguments, particularly those of mathematics, use propositions that are relational and involve monadically irreducible multiple quantification, as in '$(x)(\exists y)R(x,y)$'. On the logico-mathematical side we have the work of DeMorgan, Peirce, Schroeder, Frege, Russell, Whitehead, and others. Russell and Whitehead were the principal advocates of admitting relations on a par with properties, recognizing the ontological advantage of such a move.

The impressive formal results of modern 'relational' logic themselves provide an argument for the irreducibility of polyadic relations to monadic properties. There exist meta-theorems which assert that monadic first-order predicate logic is decidable, whereas relational first-order predicate logic is not. Hence, relations in general are not translatable without loss to properties, for otherwise polyadic logic would be disguised monadic logic and therefore decidable.[1]

Reinforcing Russell's Classic Arguments

In addition to these results from formal logic, the *locus classicus* for arguments against the noneliminability of relations has been Russell's *Principles of Mathematics*.[2] Russell's arguments turn upon the fact that it is *ordering* among relata that is irreducible to properties, and that this characteristic is the function of asymmetric relations. According to Russell, traditional attempts to reduce relations are of two kinds. Monadists—for example, Leibniz and Lotze—reduce the would-be fact $:aRb$ to the joint obtaining of the facts $:Fa$ and $:Gb$, where F and G are monadic properties. By contrast, monists—for example, Bradley and Spinoza—would have the supposed fact $:aRb$ reduce to a single property of a whole composed of a and b, $:F(ab)$. It was observed in chapter 1 that the containment model of predication implies these alternatives. In response, Russell makes short work of disposing of the monist view. Assume that R is asymmetric: if aRb, then $\neg(bRa)$. Yet the whole (ab) to which R is to be reduced as a property, F, is symmetric with regard to a and b; that is, there is no difference between wholes (ab) and (ba), hence there is no difference between $:F(ab)$ and $:F(ba)$. To explain the asymmetry of R, we must proceed from the whole to its parts and a relation between them. In other words, to explain the difference between wholes (ab) and (ba) requires the introduction of an asymmetric relation between a and b; hence no monistic reduction of relations to properties of a whole has been achieved.

Russell's criticism of the 'monadist' reduction is twofold, in effect depending upon whether the 'toward', or esse ad, aspect of relations is retained, though he does not use this language. If it is retained, then, according to Russell, one continues to appeal to the full polyadic relation, though in a circuitous, cumbersome way. For example, if

L is greater than M

is rendered

L is (greater than M),

where the device '(greater than M)' is to emphasize that 'greater than M' is to be treated as an adjective of the single subject, L, then we have not thereby eliminated as a truth condition essential appeal to the relation Greater-than, full and unreduced. The traditional Platonic/Aristotelian reduction assumed that the accurate use of the adjective 'greater than M' with regard to L has as its ontic underpinning the possession by L of a relation-property, the esse in Is-Great, where the latter possesses a concomitant esse ad corresponding to 'than M'. The superficial grammatical structure may give the impression that we have a property Is-Great inhering in L and a property or modification(?) Than-M inhering in Is-Great, at least insofar as the latter inheres in L. (Note that this would seemingly require the 'property' Is-Great to be individuated, for reasons analogous to those appealed to by Avicenna.) Russell's point is that the expression 'is great' is essentially oblique, analogous in this respect to the request 'Please', the context supplying what is necessary to render the expression unambiguously meaningful. In the case of 'is great', what is implicit is a second relatum M, for something is great only by comparison with something else. What is required is an attribute with dual subjects, and this is an unreduced relation. Campbell concurs with Russell in holding that any attempt to eliminate relations on the above grounds is 'pseudo-foundational'.[3]

Having shown that to attempt to retain the esse ad aspect of relations is to retain polyadic relations, Russell then argues that relations cannot successfully be reduced to properties (esse in) of the relata. We shall examine Russell's argument within the context of an example provided by Campbell. Assume it to be the case that A and B are islands and that

A is larger than B.

In a reductionist spirit, assume that this proposition is equivalent to the conjunction of two propositions asserting specific magnitudes of A and B—for example:

A is 20 hectares and B is 15 hectares.

Russell would argue, correctly, that to retain the one-directionality of the asymmetric relation of the original relation proposition, we must admit another asymmetric relation between the magnitudes: namely, that

20 hectares is larger than 15 hectares.

Now, if we attempt to push this reduction further, we must admit yet another asymmetric relation, this time between purely abstract terms:

20 is larger than 15.

In proposing this example, Campbell asserts that the foundationist can go on to find monadic properties of the numbers 20 and 15 that will be adequate foundational reducta for the Larger-than relation. What these properties might be, Campbell does not venture to say. But even if such promised foundations could be achieved, Russell's argument is that this line of analysis must proceed to a vicious infinite regress. To explain the directionality of the present relational proposition '20 is larger than 15', a new asymmetric relation must be introduced between the now posited foundations, and so on. Hence, there is no avoiding what must remain full polyadic predicates.

In response to the regress argument, Campbell makes the claim that, contra Russell, all that is presented here is consistent with his reductionist foundationism. The reasons he gives are obscure and appear to be inconsistent. Campbell would have "relations supervene upon foundations"; yet he claims that "only relations as polyadic properties are here being denied, while relational facts are being accepted."[4] In this he risks inconsistency because, as previously noted, he is sensitive to the fact that there is in the end "no way of dispensing with relational vocabulary and relational descriptions altogether."[5] I will not attempt an exegetical clarification of Campbell's views, for, ultimately, his foundationalist thesis is untenable. To see this, consider the following. Let it be the case that propositions $a\mathrm{R}b$ and $b\mathrm{R}c$ are true. According to Campbell, the truth conditions for these statements are such that

$$a\mathrm{R}b \equiv (\mathrm{F}^1 a \cdot \mathrm{G}^1 b),$$

and

$$b\mathrm{R}c \equiv (\mathrm{F}^2 b \cdot \mathrm{G}^2 c),$$

where the Fs and Gs are the respective foundations in a and b corresponding to the relation R. In the example above these would be the foundations in 20 and 15 sufficient to ground the fact that 20 is larger than 15. Now, by simplification and conjunction, we have:

$$F^1a \cdot G^2c.$$

This conjunction either has a true relation proposition corresponding to it or it does not. If there is such a proposition, aRc, then it is true, given that aRb and bRc are true. But, combined with the previous, like propositions, this requires that every relation be transitive, which is absurd. On the other hand, if $F^1a \cdot G^2c$ does not correspond to a true relational proposition, then the burden is on Campbell to explain why not. After all, F^1 was sufficient as a first-term foundation for R as required by aRb, and G^2 was sufficient as a second-term foundation for R as required by bRc. If these are not jointly sufficient for aRc to be true, then it must be because F^1 and G^2 are *related* differently from F^1 and G^1 on the one hand and F^2 and G^2 on the other, and this relation must be other than logical conjunction. But in this case the monadic reduction of relations can be preserved only by appealing surreptitiously to a further unreduced relation.

Campbell seeks to bolster his foundationism by attempting to defuse a classic demonstration of the irreducibility of relations to properties of their relata. This is Lewis and Langford's argument from mixed multiple quantification.[6] Let R be an asymmetric relation. It is the case that

(a) $(x)(\exists y)x$Ry

is not logically equivalent to

(b) $(\exists y)(x)x$Ry.

(For example, let R be the relation Is-Greater-than, and let x and y range over the integers.) Taking F and G as the requisite properties, the proposed monadic reduction would be, respectively,

(a′) $(x)(\exists y)(Fx \cdot Gy)$

and

(b′) $(\exists y)(x)(Fx \cdot Gy).$

But (a') and (b') are logically equivalent. Hence, we have on the face of it a simple, compelling demonstration that the attempted reduction of asymmetric relations is impossible.

Campbell replies that the last argument does not go through, because it wrongly assumes that every instance of a relation R must have the same pair of foundations, F and G. He asserts that, to the contrary, "the sensible foundation-ist is not proposing any such uniform resolution, but allows there may be cases of $x R y$ where x is not F and/or y is not G."[7] But this will not parry the above argument. Let F^ns and G^ms range over the foundations or, in general, any property reducta for R in x and in y, respectively. Then, conforming to Camp-bell's constraints, (a') and (b') become

(a'') $(x)(\exists y)[(\exists F^n)F^n x \cdot (\exists G^m)G^m y]$

and

(b'') $(\exists y)(x)[(\exists F^n)F^n x \cdot (\exists G^m)G^m y]$.

Yet again, (a'') and (b'') are logically equivalent, whereas (a) and (b) are not.

It is possible to construct a further argument, conforming to Campbell's multiple-foundations constraint, which again demonstrates that relations can-not be reduced to properties of their relata. As above, the argument will turn not upon preserving the formal property of asymmetry, but on preserving intran-sitivity. Assume

(c) $a R b$ and $b R c$, but $\neg(a R c)$.

Let F^n range over reducta of R in the first term, and G^m over reducta of R in the second term. These ranges can, of course, intersect or coincide. Assuming a property reduction for $a R b$ and $b R c$, we have

(d) $(F^1 a \cdot G^1 b) \cdot (F^2 b \cdot G^2 c)$.

Simplifying, it follows that

(e) $F^1 a \cdot G^2 c$,

that is,

$(\exists F^n)F^n a \cdot (\exists G^m)G^m c$.

However, because $\neg(a\mathrm{R}c)$, under the reduction program, it follows that

(f) $\neg(\exists F^n)F^n a \lor \neg(\exists G^m)G^m b.$

But (e) and (f) are contradictory. Again, we have a demonstration that relations cannot be reduced to properties of their relata.

The Noneliminability of Relation Intensions

Nor can relations (or properties) taken as fully intensional be eliminated in favor of extensional constructions. Grounds for this statement were given in chapter 1, and more will be supplied shortly, based on premises established by the following epistemological argument. It is standard in mathematics and extensional logic to model relations as sets of ordered pairs. The relation of Is-Greater-than among the natural numbers is modeled as the infinite set $\{<1,2>,$ $<1,3>, \ldots, <2,3>, <2,4>, \ldots\}$. All the logically relevant formal properties of the relation are inherent in the set. For example, that the modeled relation is asymmetric is determined by the fact that for any element pair $<a,b>$, the pair $<b,a>$ is not a member of the set. Importantly, however, this example illustrates the epistemic peculiarity of extensional modeling—what might be called the 'omniscience' problem. To know if the relation modeled by the above infinite set has a formal property—for example, asymmetry—without knowing the intension of the relation (Is-Greater-than) would require inspecting and comparing an infinite number of pairs. Pythagorean pretensions aside, only the Divine Intellect could accomplish such a feat. Yet even children, innocent of set-theoretical modeling, know from the 'meaning' (the intension) of the phrase 'is greater than' what pairs of numbers are so ordered. The intension, or 'content', of a relation determines its formal properties, and knowledge of the former is knowledge of the latter.

Further, as is often pointed out, an ordered pair, in being ordered, implies an asymmetric relation between its element such that, for example, $<1,2>$ can be distinguished from $<2,1>$; so relations are not eliminated. More subtle, however, are the modelings of ordered pairs by certain sets of sets, as in the Wiener–Kuratowski paraphrase. For example, the ordered pairs $<a,b>$ and $<b,a>$ are each rendered as one or the other of $\{\{a\},\{a,b\}\}$ or $\{\{b\},\{a,b\}\}$. Here we appear to have the elimination of relations but the retention of all the desired formal properties. In response, it can be said, first (and as alluded to earlier), that claims of the complete extensional elimination of relations are false. In this regard, Mario Bunge observes that the relation of elementhood of set theory cannot be reduced to sets of sets; nor, for that matter, can the predication relation of logic or the satisfaction relation of model theory be eliminated in this way.[8] Bunge makes the additional point that not even all mathematical theories are reducible to set constructs—the foundational subject of category theory has basic concepts not so reducible—but that the predicates of set theory are nevertheless definable in terms of them.

Going to the very heart of the matter, Hochberg has shown that the reduction of ordered pairs to unordered sets of sets is only apparent.[9] Let R be an asymmetric relation. The relational fact

(1) $:a\mathrm{R}b$ (e.g., a is larger than b)

can be distinguished from the fact

(2) $:b\mathrm{R}a$ (b is larger than a)

by the fact that

(3) a is the *first relatum of $a\mathrm{R}b$*,

and

(4) b is the *second relatum of $a\mathrm{R}b$* in (1).

These two relations do not obtain for b and a, respectively, in the case of (2). When (1) is 'reduced' to, say,

(5) $\{\{a\},\{\{a,b\}\}$,

as opposed to

(6) $\{\{b\},\{a,b\}\}$,

then the order in (1) is preserved in (5) only with the implicit employment of two ordering relations, *is-a-member-of-the-unit-class-in* and *is-not-a-member-of-the-unit-class-in*. (3) translates to

(7) a is a member of the unit class in $\{\{a\},\{\{a,b\}\}$,

and (4) is rendered

(8) b is not a member of the unit class in $\{\{a\},\{a,b\}\}$.

The appeal to order is not eliminated by the Wiener–Kuratowski paraphrase. Ordering relations between a and b and the class $\{\{a\},\{\{a,b\}\}$ are simply substituted for the ordering relations in (3) and (4), which are themselves derivative from the asymmetry inherent in the intension of the original relation R. All evasions to the contrary, order is not eliminable and requires relations taken intensionally.

On the intension/extension issue, consider the relevant points made by Armstrong.[10] First is the standard observation that it is possible for two intensionally distinct relations to have the same ordered pairs as extensions. Extensions cannot provide the finer distinctions inherent in intensions. Secondly, it is to be observed that any correlation between ordered pairs and unordered sets is completely arbitrary and reversible. Thirdly, unordered sets of sets obtain with the mere existence of their elements a and b. Yet, in general, this is not the case for a relational fact :aRb to which the unordered sets of sets are to function as surrogates. Beyond these observations, we also have with sets the same problem of omniscience that we had with ordered pairs. Anyone who understands the intension Is-a-Father-of knows that it is an asymmetric relation without having to perform the impossible task of examining and comparing all of a certain type of binary sets of human beings going back to Adam and forward to the Last Day. Extensional models must not be confused with the intensional original.

Disposing of Butchvarov's Nonformal Arguments

The responses given above to those who would eliminate relations from their ontologies have been based upon considerations of the formal properties of relations and the inadequacies of extensional surrogates. It will be instructive to end this chapter by considering three additional arguments against relations given by Butchvarov, arguments that call into play issues other than those previously considered.[11] Indeed, it is one criticism of Butchvarov that relations as an ontic category are suspect, because, he asserts, unlike monadic properties, relations do not have nonformal, higher-order properties, their description being limited to the formal properties of transitivity, symmetry, and so on.

Butchvarov's first criticism of the reality of relations is that in an experiential field one can single out and attend to one monadic property of the field (e.g., the shape of this page) without attending to any other property of it (e.g., its color), but it is not possible to attend to a relation without attending to its relata. In response, I observe that there is a confusion here. One certainly can "single out and attend to the shape of this page and not single out and attend to its color," but to attend to the *shape of this page* is to attend to a shape *as a predicate of* a subject (this page) and hence as a property with a single relatum. To attend to the shape of this page and not its color entails a differentiation between properties; this is not a differentiation between a property and its subject of predication (its relatum). On the other hand, if one abstracts the shape from being a predicate of this page, then one will have the universal; but this is likewise possible for relations. If we abstract away the relata in the fact that Napoleon loves Josephine, we have the relation of *Love*, about which we can make second-level claims—for example, that Love is a virtue.

Butchvarov's second criticism of relations is that, even though monadic qualities as such are universals and do not have spatial location, their instances ('quality-objects') must have such locations, whereas there is no sense in which the instances of relations can be said to have spatial location. If a is to the left of b, the instance of the relation To-the-Left-of, L_i, does not itself exist in space. It makes no sense to say that instance L_i is to the left of a or b or anything else. Though this point is correct, it is no criticism of relations. Recalling the response to Quine in chapter 1, space is constituted, at least in part and intrinsically, by spatial relation; an extended entity is extended precisely because it has parts that are spatially related. Spatial relations are not *in* space; they define space. It makes no more sense to ask where an instance of To-the-Left-of is located than to ask where space is located. Moreover, pace Butchvarov, it is not the case that all instances of properties, even properties of spatially extended objects, exist in space. It makes no sense to say that the instance of Wisdom proprietary to Socrates has a spatial relation to Socrates or anything else. On the other hand, instances of color—for instance, Red_1—might enter into spatial relations with other instances of color—say, $Green_2$.

Butchvarov goes on to conclude that though we can perceive physical objects a and b, we cannot perceive the relation To-the-Left-of between them, and that this gives warrant to the classical empiricists' view that relations are 'products of comparison', the result of thought. The response here is the same as above: an instance of the relation of To-the-Left-of does not exist *in* space between a and b; rather, it is part of what constitutes the space in which a and b exist. Moreover, we do in fact perceive instances of the To-the-Left-of relation; in a single, normal perceptual field we can have as given the singular fact complex of a-To-the-Left-of-b. Classical empiricism along the lines of Locke and Hume is factually in error when it holds that the experientially given consists in atomistic monadic qualia, or *sensa*, or perhaps in 'associated groups' (i.e., classes) of sensa whose elements are instances of colors, sounds, tastes, and so forth of the external senses or instances of the passions and emotions of the internal senses. To the contrary, a visual field, for example, is a gestalt, an integrated whole or complex, from which isolated 'sensa' can be abstracted by a subsequent selective attending, the result of a conceptual operation upon the given. For Locke and Hume, the given of experience had to consist in atomistic sensa only, since they were operating with the preconception that polyadic relations are products of the mind, so must be produced subsequent to, and upon, the given as relata. But, for integrated wholes to be given in experience, what are required are unifying relations along with relata as *constituting* the given itself.

Finally, Butchvarov claims that relations are ontically anemic, in having only formal properties, whereas monadic properties can have a wealth of characteristics, a 'character'. He gives the example of a color, which can be a specific shade of pink; it can be darker or purer than another color (note that 'darker' and 'purer' name relations), have aesthetic qualities, and evoke emotions. Yet again, contra Butchvarov, relations likewise have a 'character', in the same sense, possessing higher-order properties and relations. In the example from chapter 1, 'John's love for Mary is stronger than his love for Ann', the (instance of the) relationship of Love between John and Mary is related by the Stronger-than relation to the (instance of the) Love relationship between John and Ann. Moreover, the term 'stronger' could be meaningfully replaced by 'purer', 'more rational', 'more satisfying', and other relational terms. Further, the relation of Stronger-than between the two instances of the Love relation can have aesthetic qualities and can certainly evoke emotions (perhaps especially in Ann), and could even have moral attributions as well.

In sum, relations cannot be reduced to foundational properties of their relata or to a single property of the whole composed of their relata. Nor can relations be eliminated in favor of their extensional models or called into question on the grounds that they do not exist in space or do not have higher-order properties and relations. Relations in their full, intensional sense are not eliminable. Traditional ontology has suffered much from the explicit, and even more from the insidious implicit, distortions to the contrary.

chapter seven

Specious Arguments against Relation Instances

Influential critics of the doctrine of relation instances include Bertrand Russell, D. W. Armstrong, and Reinhardt Grossmann. According to Armstrong and Grossmann,[1] despite its long history, the few developed arguments for particularism are inconclusive. Moreover, particularism leaves the problem of universals unsolved; and to solve it requires admitting relation universals in addition to their instances. But once universals are admitted, it is doubtful whether the intermediary instances have any explanatory power over and above that of universals alone. Finally, even if instances are admitted, according to Armstrong, no coherent account can be given of the link between relation instances and the corresponding universal.[2] Each one of these points will be challenged below.

This last criticism made by Armstrong has to do with a much referenced, paradigmatic argument attributed to Gilbert Ryle, which purports to show that any kind of exemplification relation between universals and particulars is incoherent.[3] The argument turns upon the assumption that the exemplification relation has instances from which there is said to follow a vicious infinite regress of ever higher-order exemplification universals and their instances. Hence, the universal Exemplification and its instances fall together. Armstrong has generalized this argument to one against any relational analysis of what it is for an object (or instance) to have (or be an instance of) a relation and utilizes it repeatedly as a weapon, not only against particularism but also against various forms of nominalism and the doctrine of transcendent universals.[4] Similarly, the later Russell reaffirmed his position against unit properties and relations by referring to a brief, obscure passage in the earlier *Principles of Mathematics* (1903), where he argued that, on the supposition that the relation of Difference had instances, a contradiction would result, and that in this regard it was no different from all other relations.[5] However, as I will attempt to show in the analysis below, Russell's argument depends on the implicit assumption of the impossibility of instances of the exemplification relation. In response to the Ryle–Armstrong argument, I will demonstrate that it is a non sequitur; the supposed vicious regress is stopped by simply admitting instances of relations along with their universals, an admission that is consistent with the premises of the argument.

Ryle–Armstrong against Exemplification

The Ryle–Armstrong argument against instances of relations is admitted to be an analog of Bradley's regress argument, an argument which, as we have seen, is ancient and persistent. This is odd, since Bradley proposed the argument to show the inherent contradictoriness and unreality of all relations, a position that Ryle and Armstrong reject.

Commenting on Plato's *Parmenides*, Ryle proposed an amended version of Aristotle's 'Third Man' argument, which, while assuming instances of relations, was said to prove that there cannot exist a relation (exemplification, participation, etc.) between a universal and its instances.[6] Ryle's argument was re-emphasized, particularly against Russell's analogous use of 'predication', by Alan Donagan in his influential article "Universals and Metaphysical Realism."[7] The Ryle–Donagan version of the argument runs as follows. Consider the examples: Plato exemplifies$_1$ Man, and Socrates exemplifies$_2$ Man. It would be said, then, that there is a universal, Exemplification^1, of which the two examples are instances; symbolically, Exp_1^1 and Exp_2^1 are instances of the universal Exp^1. The Ryle version of the argument assumes that it is necessary to introduce a second-level universal Exemplification^2, whose instances would connect the instances of the first-level universal with their universal—symbolically, $Exp_1^2(Exp_1^1, Exp^1)$ and $Exp_2^2(Exp_2^1, Exp^1)$. The second-level exemplification universal, Exp^2, is thought to be necessary in order to account for the commonality of the first-level instances. What they have in common is that they each second-level exemplify, Exp^2, first-level exemplification, Exp^1. However, this in turn involves two instances of Exp^2; hence we must account for how they are related to their universal, which, by the same line of reasoning, requires the introduction of a third-level universal, Exp^3, and so on. This regress is said to be vicious because, supposedly, to explain how n-level exemplification instances have anything in common requires an $(n + 1)$-level exemplification universal, as well as instances of it, so as to relate the n-level instances to their n-level universal. Because there is no end to the regress, it is concluded that the posited initial relation of exemplification, presupposing as it does the entire hierarchy, cannot express what is in fact a real relationship between a universal and its instances.

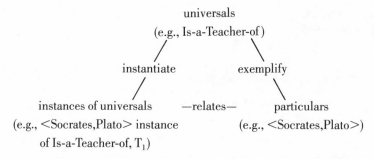

Fig. 7.1. The instantiation and exemplification relations

Wolterstorff has argued that Ryle's regress is not compelling, in that it does not show the necessity of positing further and further *different* exemplification relations.[8] The context of Wolterstorff's remarks seems to imply that instances (his 'cases') show why we need not posit further different exemplification relations, but he does not elaborate. I will take this up below. Though not among his objections, Wolterstorff observes that Ryle confuses the exemplification relation with the instantiation relation.[9] To clarify the issues involved in the Rylean regress and so avoid irrelevant objections, it is necessary to look at this distinction in detail. Particulars such as Socrates or ordered n-tuples like $<$Socrates,Plato$>$ exemplify universals such as the property Man or the relation Is-a-Teacher-of, respectively, which they are said truly to possess; whereas instances of universals such as Socrates' man-ness, Man_1, or $<$Socrates,Plato$>$'s instance of Is-a-Teacher-of, say T_1, instantiate their respective universals. Wolterstorff is correct in observing that these relations are distinct. The situation is illustrated in figure 7.1 (reading up). It is clear that with these distinctions, ordinary concrete individuals such as Socrates, or n-tuples of such, exemplify but do not instantiate the universal. However, instances of relations do instantiate the universal, and it is here that the Rylean regress would supposedly follow.

To be correct, the Rylean regress must be reconstructed as follows, again given Exp_1^1(Plato,Man) and Exp_2^1(Socrates,Man). Now, both Exp_1^1 and Exp_2^1 instantiate but do not exemplify Exp^1—that is, $Int_1^1(Exp_1^1,Exp^1)$ and $Int_2^1(Exp_2^1,Exp^1)$. On the Rylean view, the two instances Int_1^1 and Int_2^1 must themselves instantiate a second-level instantiation universal, Int^2, such that $Int_1^2(Int_1^1,Int^1)$ and $Int_2^2(Int_2^1,Int^1)$. It is clear that the two instances could not exemplify a second-level exemplification relation. Now, for the two instances Int_1^2 and Int_2^2 there must be a third universal, Int^3, which they instantiate, and so

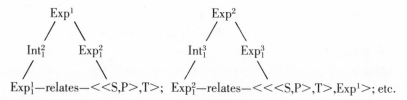

Fig. 7.2. The Rylean view of instantiation and exemplification

on. To achieve the regress that Ryle has in mind, a side step from the exemplification to the instantiation relation must be made.

It is possible, however, to generate an analogous regress for the exemplification relation. From figure 7.1, $Exp_1(<S,P>,T)$. Yet Exp_1 is a particular that itself instantiates the universal Exp^1. On the Rylean view, this would require not only an instance of a second-level instantiation relation but also an instance of a second-level exemplification relation, which in turn would require instances of analogous third-level relations, and so on. This is illustrated in figure 7.2. Hence, if there is a vicious regress for the former, there is also one for the latter. Because neither Ryle nor Armstrong distinguished between instantiation and exemplification but formulated their arguments against both effectively in terms of the exemplification relation only, I shall for the remainder of this section respond to both on their own ground, utilizing the exemplification relation. Though this will make the non sequitur character of their arguments more perspicuous, the reader is advised that an accurate formulation of the supposed regress and a parallel response require a side step from the exemplification relation to the instantiation relation.

Armstrong has adopted the Rylean argument, but in a more succinct, generalized form.[10] If a's being F—that is, $F(a)$—is analyzed as a's having a relation R to a universal U, $R(a,U)$, then the latter is also the sort of situation that the theory undertakes to analyze. Focusing on $R(a,U)$, it must be the case that there is a relation R' such that R has the relation R' to a new universal, U'—that is, $R'(R,U')$. According to Armstrong, we then have the dilemma: "(i) if R and R' are different, then the same problem of analysis arises for R' necessitating the generation of a new universal U'', and so on *ad infinitum*, or, (ii) if R and R' are identical, then the projected analysis of R appeals to R itself, which is circular." Though stated in terms of properties, Armstrong intends the dilemma to apply mutatis mutandis to relations.

In regard to (ii), it is not clear that the circularity involved is vicious, though

Armstrong would seem to be on firmer ground than Donagan or Ryle. Donagan's objection in (ii) to the nonidentity of R and R′ is not that it makes for circularity, but rather that a relation cannot relate anything to itself.[11] Here the topic of self-predication enters. Ryle maintains the same thesis, generalizing from the Third Man argument in Plato's *Parmenides* 132a, where an infinite regress results from the assumption that the Form Large is itself large.[12] Ryle formulates the supposed principle as: It is logically vicious to treat any universal as one of its own instances. By this, he means that for any relation R, it is not possible that $R(..R..)$. Armstrong adopts the same position.[13] In the context of what he calls "the restricted Third Man," he observes that if first-order Forms participate in the Form of Formhood but the Form of Formhood participates in itself, then no vicious regress of further Forms of Formhood is generated. However, he maintains that self-predication is impossible, and hence that the restricted Third Man is successful as an argument against transcendent universals. This, of course, rules out all self-predication, even innocuous, intuitive examples such as that the property of being abstract is abstract.

Returning to the Ryle–Donagan form of the argument against exemplification and its instances, it is a relatively easy matter to show that the conclusion is unwarranted. In fact, all that is needed to answer the above vicious regress are further instances of the first-level exemplification relation Exp^1. To see this, we need only ask the question: Why is it that instances Exp_1^1 and Exp_2^1 cannot be related to their universal Exp^1 by further instances of Exp^1 itself? If one admits that there are two instances of Exp^1 in the examples $Exp_1^1(\text{Plato,Man})$ and $Exp_2^1(\text{Socrates,Man})$, then there can be no consistent objection to there being another instance, say Exp_3^1, relating the particular instance Exp_1^1 to the *same* universal Exp^1. It is the case that instance Exp_1^1 itself *exemplifies* the universal Exp^1, and this is no different from the situation in the above examples. The only criterion that was necessary to assign an instance of Exp^1 to the pair <Socrates,Man> was simply that the particular Socrates exemplifies the universal Man. The situation is the same for the particular instance Exp_1^1 and its universal Exp^1. The same tactic can perhaps be demonstrated more precisely using Armstrong's version of the argument given above. Here one simply lets the universal $U' = Exp$ and R and R′ be different instances of the same universal Exp, respectively Exp_1 and Exp_2. Then, in response to (i), Exp_1 and Exp_2, being nonidentical yet nevertheless instances of the *same* universal, do not generate an infinite regress of further universals, each presupposing the next, though they

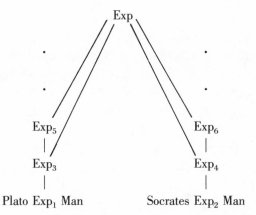

Fig. 7.3. The harmless regress of exemplification instances

do allow for an infinite process of further instances of each harmlessly presupposing the former. Moreover, in response to (ii), since the two instances Exp_1 and Exp_2 are not identical, then the analysis of Exp_1 as $Exp_2(Exp_1, Exp)$ cannot be construed as circular.

Once this line is adopted, we stop the vicious infinite regress of presupposed next-level universals, and in its place find only an innocuous process of instances of one universal, Exemplification. In other words, all instances of Exemplification are related to it by instances of it. The situation is illustrated in figure 7.3. As cautioned earlier, to accurately reflect the distinction between the exemplification and the instantiation relation, all lines in figure 7.3 above the bottom line would have to be replaced by the instantiation relation. In either case, the harmless infinite process here is, as Russell would put it, one of implication, not analysis.[14] It is harmless because any given instance—for example, Exp_5—follows upon and presupposes the lower-level instances, Exp_3, not vice versa. The Rylean regress is stopped, then, by simply extending in a straightforward way what is permitted by hypothesis—instances of the first-level exemplification universal. Likewise, Armstrong's generalized version against instances of any relation is a non sequitur. The difficulty of a vicious regress in explaining how instances instantiate or exemplify their universals is removed by admitting further instances of the latter relations.[15] Thus, pace Armstrong, a coherent account of the relation between a universal and its instances can be given.

Russell and Unparticularized Relations

While accepting universals, Russell argued in the *Principles of Mathematics* (1903) that the added assumption of the existence of relation instances among different sets of relata leads to contradiction. Interestingly, in a 1946 reply to critics, Russell claimed that he had held the view that relations were unparticularized continually since the *Principles*, though, as we have noted, he argued briefly for 'instances of universals' in a paper of 1911, likewise repudiated later. Because of the apparent importance for Russell of the 1903 argument, we shall examine it in detail.

Commenting on Russell's theory of universals, Morris Weitz wrote in 1946 that, at least by 1910, Russell had abandoned his "very curious doctrine, namely, that universal *relations* had no instances."[16] In his reply to Weitz, however, Russell stated that this interpretation was mistaken. With regard to this doctrine, Russell wrote:

> I have held it continuously since 1902. Nor is there any difference in this respect between relations and qualities. When I say "A is human" and "B is human," there is absolute identity as regards "human." One may say that A and B are instances of humanity, and, in like manner, if A differs from B and C differs from D, one may say the two pairs (A,B) and (C,D) are instances of difference. But there are not two humanities or differences.[17]

In saying that he "held it [the denial of relation instances] continuously since 1902," he is presumably referring to the argument in the *Principles* which he still finds convincing. Here it is Russell's thesis that if relations are particularized, the *same* relation cannot hold between different sets of relata. Yet, the argument for this thesis is extremely curt and is mixed with an analysis of the type of unity constituting a relation complex, or what Russell called at this time a "proposition." Concerning propositions like "A differs from B," he presents his argument saying:

> If differences did differ, they would still have to have something in common. But the most general way in which two terms can have something in common is by both having a given relation to a given term. Hence if no two pairs of terms can have the same relation, it follows that no two terms can have anything in common, and hence different differences will not be in any definable sense *instances* of difference. I conclude, then, that the

relation affirmed between A and B in the proposition "A differs from B" is the general relation of difference, and is precisely and numerically the same as the relation affirmed between C and D in "C differs from D." And this doctrine must be held, for the same reasons, to be true of all other relations; relations do not have instances, but are strictly the same in all propositions in which they occur.[18]

This argument can be made more perspicuous by utilizing a paraphrase made by Weitz, one that is presumably accurate, since Russell does not take issue with it in his response to Weitz.[19] For the sake of argument, we are to first hypothesize that the 'differs from' in 'A differs from B' and in 'C differs from D' are two distinct instances of the universal Difference. Now, in order for these instances to be instances of the same relation, they must have something in common with the relation universal. And to have something in common with the universal implies that these instances must have a common relation to the relation universal. But, Russell claims, they cannot have such a common relation to the universal because that would contradict the first hypothesis. Therefore we are to conclude that there cannot exist separate instances of Difference.

Looking at this argument closely, it becomes evident that it turns upon what Russell means by his requirement that the two instances—say, $Dif_1(A,B)$ and $Dif_2(C,D)$—have a *common relation* to the universal, Dif. If he means by *common* one and numerically the same relation of instantiation, Int, between the two instances of Difference and the universal—that is, $Int(Dif_1,Dif)$ and $Int(Dif_2,Dif)$—then indeed there is a contradiction. For the initial assumption—namely, that two distinct sets of relata (e.g., (A,B) and (C,D)) require two instances of a relation (e.g., Dif)—is contradicted at the level of the instantiation relation. In short, separate instances of Difference imply, by the same token, separate instances of Instantiation; but this requirement is taken to be contradictory. Russell is here assuming that the distinct pairs of relata, $<Dif_1,Dif>$ and $<Dif_2,Dif>$, are related by one and numerically the same universal, which would be Instantiation. That this is in fact Russell's assumption is made explicit in a footnote to the argument in the *Principles of Mathematics*, where he comments on Moore's theory of relation instances, saying, "The relation of an instance to its universal at any rate, must be actually and numerically the same in all cases where it occurs."[20] Of course, the key question is why? Russell does not attempt to give an answer but assumes the proposition, and in this he simply begs the entire question. For if we can admit for the sake of argument two instances of Difference, why is it that two instances of Instantiation—say, $Int_1(Dif_1,Dif)$ and $Int_2(Dif_2,Dif)$—cannot be permitted? There is no relevant difference in the situations here; Instantiation and Difference are both universals, and both are applied to diverse sets of relata. If we are permitted instances of the latter, then we should be permitted instances of the former; but if not, we need an argument for why not. Thus Russell begs the question by having it turn upon his assuming for the instantiation relation what he is attempting to prove for relations in general.

Indeed, our conclusion here is like that concerning the Ryle–Armstrong argument: that Russell's initial worry—namely, that if relations are particularized, then the *same* relation could not hold between different relata sets—is answered by simply admitting consistently for all relations (including instantiation and exemplification) both instances and their universals. For though two instances R_i and R_j that hold between different relata n-tuples are not the same, insofar as they each instantiate identically the same universal R, it can be said that in this sense the *same* relation occurs among different sets of relata.

Armstrong's 'Decisive Argument' against Unit Properties

Armstrong has given what he sees as a decisive argument against property (and likewise relation) instances. His presentation is compressed, as is a version of the argument given by Brand Blanshard against Kemp Smith's adoption of instances, or 'characters', which Armstrong cites.[21] I construct the argument as follows. Let F_1 and F_2 be instances of the property F such that $F_1(a)$ and $F_2(b)$, where $a \neq b$. Now, if we abstract away from instances F_1 and F_2 their common intension F, what remains is either nothing at all or else, analogous to 'bare particulars', what could appropriately be called 'bare instances', I_1 and I_2, the respective individuators of F_1 and F_2. If nothing remains, then the instances F_1 and F_2 are constituted in their entirety by the universal F; hence they are not distinct instances after all. If, on the other hand, we are left with bare individuators I_1 and I_2, they will have no intensions of their own but will simply serve to individuate the universal F. But as such, bare instances are indistinguishable from each other and so are identical (universal) across all instances; $I_1 = I_2$. This means that any instance F_1 dissolves upon analysis into a *complex* of two universals: bare instance-ness, I, and F-ness, F. Thus there is nothing 'particular' or unique about instance F_1 that would not be shared by some other like instance, F_2; that is, $F_1 = F_2$. The doctrine of unit properties and relations is, then, nothing but a pretentiously redundant identity theory, one that is more economically replaced by the traditional theory with ordinary individuals and universals, nothing more.

That this argument does not prove what it intends to prove is not difficult to see. The argument turns upon the thesis that the bare instances I_1 and I_2 are indistinguishable and, in so doing, begs the question in favor of the identity theory. It is no argument against the particularist, who holds the here unaddressed counter-thesis that the distinctness of I_1 and I_2 is a function of the distinctness of a and b, the respective subjects of predication of F_1 and F_2. That is, the possibility remains open that it is through the predicative tie that F_1 has to its subject a that F_1 is individuated, this tie being I_1. Likewise, for F_2, it is individuated as predicative of b. Because $a \neq b$, the predicative ties of F_1 to a and F_2 to b are nonidentical; that is, $I_1 \neq I_2$. I_1 and I_2 are not themselves entities like a and b, but rather modes or aspects, along with intension F, of single entities, F_1 and F_2. F and I_1, say, are not two entities forming F_1 as a *complex* by means of some implicit, unmentioned relation between F and I_1. Between F and I_1 is a 'distinction without a relation', as Armstrong calls the distinction between the particularity of any particular and its properties and relations.[22] The above argument depends upon the fact that Armstrong does not extend to instance particulars an ontic distinction that he insists on for ordinary particulars. The counter-thesis, depending as it does on the proposition that the predicative ('actual relating') aspect of relations is unrepeatable, is the focus of the next chapter.

In sum, of the influential arguments against particularism examined, all are non sequiturs. This adds all the more warrant to the aggregate effect of the direct and indirect arguments for instance ontology. To further such arguments we shall now turn.

chapter eight

Bradley's Regress and Further Arguments for Relation Instances

In the previous two chapters it was argued that relations are not reducible to properties and that certain influential arguments against relation instances are specious. The first point completes an indirect argument against nominalism from chapter 2, where it was seen how nominalism implies the property reduction of relations. We also observed arguments for the doctrine in the work of Avicenna (chapter 4) and from the apparent uneliminable reference to unit attributes in natural language (chapter 1). In this chapter I shall increase the warrant for the thesis of unit relations by offering additional arguments based upon the intrinsic nature of relations and the structure they effect. The first argument turns upon the absurdity of contrary higher-level properties. If occurrences of relation R have contrary properties, then, by (the contra-positive of) the indiscernibility of identicals (i.e., $x = y \supset (P)[Px \equiv Py]$), these occurrences of R cannot be identical. I then analyze the Bradley's regress argument and use the insights to construct two further arguments for relation instances. Hereby an intuition pursued by the early Russell (1900) and, more recently, but following a different tack, by Wolterstorff, is substantiated: namely, that there is an intimate connection between Bradley's regress and the necessity of relation instances.[1] The arguments presented here will avoid what I have suggested elsewhere is the crucial lacuna in Russell's and Wolterstorff's arguments—why the instances of a relation have the ontological role of relating relata whereas the universal does not.[2] Next, the important concept of structure will be shown to provide two additional arguments: one from the notion of complex structure, the other from the notion of 'structural universals', both of which have received increasing attention of late. Though I contend that the arguments I give are strong, I do not rest my entire case for relation instances on them. The pragmatic promise of a logic incorporating the refinement of relation instances I develop in chapter 9 also gives indirect weight to the ontic distinction.

Using the Uniqueness of Composition Principle

Consider the following situation described by Armstrong.[3] Let it be the case that the facts :R(a,b) and :R(b,a) both obtain, where R is a nonsymmetric relation—

for example, x loves y. Armstrong points out that we have here two distinct complexes (specifically, atomic structures) and that they are composed of exactly the same parts: a, b, and R. Yet this is impossible. The standard, intuitive observation is that there is an *order* in which R relates its relata. The distinction between the two complexes :$R(a,b)$ and :$R(b,a)$ is a function of the relation and its ordering of relata that characterize R as nonsymmetric. In complex :$R(a,b)$, R relates a-to-b, not b-to-a; whereas in complex :$R(b,a)$, R relates b-to-a, not a-to-b. In the relational complex 'Mary loves John', the loving is from Mary to John, not the reverse, the latter being a separate complex that may or may not exist along with the first. Now, because of the possession of these contrary next-level properties, by the indiscernibility of identicals, the relating of R from a-to-b cannot be numerically the same as the relating of R from b-to-a. There is a sense in which R is the same in both complexes (as intension R—e.g., Loves); yet, as relating distinct specific relata and thus establishing a specific order among them, R is particularized (as instances R_i and R_j). If one fails to make a distinction between the intension of a relation and the actual relating or linking that is unique to a specific ordered n-tuple of relata, then the above argument does away with relation universals, and we end up at best with trope nominalism. The combinatorial state constituting one ordered n-tuple is not the combinatorial state of a differently ordered n-tuple. Yet the intensions under which all relating must take place are repeatable. I shall reinforce this point below.

Armstrong proposed the above case of two distinct complexes having the same constituents as a counterexample to a principle put forward by David Lewis.[4] This is Lewis's principle of uniqueness of composition:

> There is only one mode of composition; and it is such that, for given parts, only one whole is composed of them.

Unit relations render Armstrong's example consistent with this principle. But Armstrong himself, unable to accept any medium between universals on the one hand and nominalistic tropes on the other, rejects the latter and so rejects Lewis's 'attractive sounding principle' as holding in all cases.[5] Lewis advanced this principle in the course of a dispute over structural universals, and I shall take up this topic briefly later. The thesis I wish to advance here is that Lewis's principle is correct if the single 'mode of composition' is understood as *ontic predication*. All composition, all structure (logical, spatial, causal, etc.), has as its cause the predication of a property to its subject in the limiting case or, generally, the relating of a relation among its relata. If relations are not reducible to properties, then, if R is an asymmetric or nonsymmetric relation, the ontic predication of R in :$R(a,b)$ must be distinct from the ontic predication of R in :$R(b,a)$. The parts making up :$R(a,b)$ are in reality a, b, and some instance R_i; whereas the parts of :$R(b,a)$ are a, b, and some instance R_j, where $R_i \neq R_j$. In conformity with Lewis's principle, then, there is only one whole composed of, say, R_i, a, and b.

Resolving the Ambiguity of Bradley's Regress

The intuitive, defining polyadic predication of relations is forced most clearly into consideration upon examination of the historically important argument of Bradley's regress. Once we have seen how the regress reinforces and clarifies our intuition that intrinsic to the nature of relations is a linking, combinatorial status among their relata, we can use this fact to provide an argument for relation instances. The argument is not that positing relation instances clarifies Bradley's regress, but rather the mediated reverse: that the combinatorial nature of relations implies unit relations, and that, when correctly analyzed, Bradley's regress displays the sui generis linking character of relations.

Recall that Bradley himself, like several philosophers before him, proposed the ancient regress argument as showing that relations are self-contradictory. He was quite willing to admit that in a relation complex :$R(a,b)$ there is a 'fact of relatedness', which is "that union of both [relation and its terms] which we experience as a relational fact."[6] This is so because the relation R is a 'bond of union', for "relations are nothing if not conjunctive." In other words, in the relation complex the relation R has the ontic role of *linking* its relata. The regress shows, he claims, that, upon analysis, R cannot have this defining property. According to Bradley, if we analyze a relation complex :$R(a,b)$, we arrive *without remainder* at the *class* of constituents {R,a,b}. Note that the set exists a-temporally and does so whether or not it is now or ever the case that :$R(a,b)$ obtains. Bradley is thus implying that there is a way of conceiving R independently of its relating any relata, yet that in some sense it is the same relation R that is in the complex. But if R is exactly the same in the class as in the complex and does not relate in the former, then it cannot relate in the latter either. Hence we must call upon a relating relation R' to account for the type of unity that distinguishes the initial complex from its constituent class—that is,

R', such that $:R(a,b) = :R'(R,a,b)$. Now, by the same sequence of reasoning, Bradley would have the new complex $:R'(R,a,b)$ analyze into the constituent class $\{R',R,a,b\}$. But then, in turn, R' (in the class) can be conceived as independent of relating any relata, and since R' is in some sense the same in both wholes, the R' as it occurs in $:R'(R,a,b)$ does not relate. We again attempt to remedy the situation by supplying the needed relatedness by means of a third relation, R'', such that $:R'(R,a,b) = :R''(R',R,a,b)$. And so on. This recursion continues indefinitely, each n-step introducing a further relation R^n in an attempt to account for the unity of a relation complex whose relation R^{n-1} has been denied this property, yet R^n is itself denied this role in the $n+1$ step. The result: explanatory bankruptcy.

Characteristically, Bradley sums up the situation more dramatically. When a relation complex is analyzed into its class of constituents, "the diversity here [in the class], while still forming a whole, has hardened itself into a plurality of terms, each so far independent as to have become an individual with a being and character of its own."[7] But then, "if, to remain themselves, our terms retain their character as individuals, there is no legitimate way (we have seen) to their union in fact. We are without the 'together', which (like the 'between') is essential if any relation is to be actually there."[8] Since R both has and does not have the property of 'linking' its relata, "relational experience must hence in its very essence be called self-contradictory" and so "commits suicide" regressively.[9]

Others have interpreted the regress argument as showing exactly the opposite—that it is the relation R in a relation complex $:R(a_1, \ldots, a_n)$ which is the cause of the unity of the complex, and no further relations are needed or will suffice to account for this unity. According to these commentators, the lesson of the regress, to use Grossmann's metaphor, is that relations are like glue among planks as terms, and no further superglue is needed to connect the glue to the planks and so account for the unity of the deck.[10] If, however, the glue is made to have the same role in the deck as the planks, then, as one more 'solid', a further superglue would be required to hold the glue to the planks. As a slogan: *For relations, to be is to bond.* Taking the example of the relation Loves and the individuals John and Mary, it is certainly the case that we can have the class $\{John,Loves,Mary\}$ and not have the fact that John loves Mary. For the latter to obtain, John must be in a relation of loving to Mary, the three not being simply juxtaposed conceptually. As previously observed, Russell responded to Bradley by saying, "A complex differs from the mere aggregate of its constituents, since it is one and not many, and the relation which is one of its constituents enters into it as an actually relating relation, and not merely as one member of an aggregate."[11] Elsewhere he observes that in aggregates that are such that their parts completely determine them (i.e., classes), the parts "have no direct connection *inter se*. . . . But other wholes occur, which contain relations . . . not occurring simply as terms in a collection, but as relating. . . . These are not completely specified when their parts are all known."[12] That is, to know that we have such a complex, we must also know the relation in such a way that it has, not a higher-order relation between it and its terms, but a higher-order *property* of being connective.

Now, despite (and, indeed, as an explanation of) the historical persistence of the contrary conclusions drawn from it, I would propose that Bradley's regress does not in itself establish any of these conclusions. To derive what they claim, each side must attach an additional assumption to what is the only conclusion that can be derived from the regress proper. This core, on which I think all parties agree, is:

(8.1) If the relational unity of a complex $:R(a_1, \ldots, a_n)$ is not a function of the relation R as it occurs in the complex, then this unity *cannot* be a function of some further relation R' as it occurs in the complex $:R'(R, a_1, \ldots, a_n)$, where $:R(a_1, \ldots, a_n) = :R'(R, a_1, \ldots, a_n))$.

In itself the regress establishes neither that the original relation R is the cause of the unity of its relation complex nor a denial of this thesis. The regress only— but crucially—focuses attention upon the necessity and importance of deciding the issue. Furthermore, it is clear, I propose, that the pre-critical presumption is on the side of the thesis that relations are unifiers among their relata—after all, this is what we mean when we say that terms are *related* by a relation R. As Bradley acknowledged, it is definitional of relations that they indicate a connection of a certain sort between terms. What is required in order for 8.1 to be extended into an argument that has any initial plausibility whatsoever in impugning the strong intuition that relations are combinatorial is an added, sufficiently compelling, although thus far confused, insight into the nature of relations. What is this insight? What makes it conceptually plausible for a relation to appear both combinatorial and not combinatorial but, when properly understood, eliminates the contradiction? The answer I have proposed persistently is that the apparent contradiction is due to confusing a full 'relating relation' with a corresponding residual abstraction. Just as the property of being red can be conceived as a class concept, Red, separated from its attribution to any individual (red-in-a), so a relation concept—for example, Is-to-the-Left-of—can be abstracted from distinct complexes in which there are actual relata. The universals Red and Is-to-the-Left-of are half-truths, which leave aside the defining predicative and combinatorial aspect that they have in actual predicational complexes. Bradley and like-minded thinkers make the mistake of *identifying* R-as-actually-relating with R as separated from, and not relating, any relata. This is a contradiction *ab initio*, and the regress simply writes large as a repeated absurdity what is absurd from the start.

My analysis of Bradley's regress does not imply that we cannot conceive of a further relation R′ such that R′(R,a,b), but that R′ is derivative and implies as logically and ontologically prior the relating *by* R of a to b. Indeed, we could introduce a still further relation R″ such that R″(R′,R,a,b), and so on. The resulting nonterminating *progression* is not a vicious regress, because R^n is the ontic ground for R^{n+1}, not vice versa. Avicenna and Aquinas held that this progression of further 'relating' relations is purely conceptual; they are, according to Aquinas, *relato rationis tantum*.[13] Such a progression is analogous to:

p (e.g., the proposition: Hesperus is Phosphorus).
That p is true.
That (p is true) is true.
That ((p is true) is true) is true.
(And so on.)

Each proposition rests upon the previous one, and ultimately, in the example, upon the obtaining of a nonlinguistic astronomical fact corresponding to p. Being true is a logico-cognitive predicate of general practical value, but in the specific case of the above progression, this value falls off rapidly.

As previously noted, some philosophers—for example, Bergmann, Hochberg, and Strawson[14]—contend that for the realist the lesson of Bradley's regress is the necessity of postulating an ontically unique type of universal, a 'nexus', 'tie', or 'exemplification' capable of accomplishing what ordinary property and relation universals cannot: namely, connect a particular with its property and relation universals. They are correct in saying that relations *as universals* do not relate and that to account for this connectedness of articulated wholes something further is needed. But they simply postulate a further, 'correctly behaving' relation, a tack that is only slightly more insightful than Aristotle's postulation of substantial form to account for structure. An explanation must be given of how this unique relation can avoid the vicious regress and why ordinary relations cannot. The 'tie' theory does have the virtue of insisting upon relatedness as the cause of unity, however.

It is now possible to generate a second argument for relation instances incorporating the perspective gained by our analysis of Bradley's regress, an argument, together with the next one, that sustains the intuitions of Wolterstorff and the early Russell. It was maintained that the regress shows that the defining characteristic of a relation R—namely, its relating its relata and hence the cause of the existence of the complex :$R(a,b)$—is not an additional *relation* R' with R as a relatum, R'(R,a,b). This further implies that the relating of R in the complex :$R(a,b)$ is not a relation-property of R, $\lambda x(x$ relates a to $b)$, with a and b as implicit relata. For any such property implies an explicit relation, 'x relates y to z' with R as a relatum. What, then, is the actual relating, or linking, of a to b by R in :$R(a,b)$? It can be nothing but R as it is exemplified in :$R(a,b)$. The relating-of-R is not a relation *of* R or a property *of* R; it is simply R in the complex in which it occurs. Now, let it also be the case that $R(c,d)$, where $a \neq c$ and $b \neq d$. The same reasoning applies. The relating of c to d is simply R as it occurs in :$R(c,d)$. Further, assume that it is numerically the same universal R in both complexes :$R(a,b)$ (e.g., a is to the left of b) and :$R(c,d)$ (c is to the left of d). The sustaining cause of the existence of both individual and distinct complexes as unified wholes is the relating of R. Now what if the complex :$R(c,d)$ ceased to exist as an articulated whole under intension R—that is, if R no longer relates c to d (c is no longer to the left of d)? Since it is hypothesized that numerically the same relating by R obtains in both complexes, the complex :$R(a,b)$ would also cease to exist (a would cease to be to the left of b). The dissolution of the structure-sustaining relatedness in one complex means the dissolution of the structure of the other. But this is absurdly counterfactual! Hence, the occurrence of R in each complex must be numerically distinct—that is, occur as an instance of R.[15]

Again utilizing the points raised in the above analysis of Bradley's regress, I propose a third argument for relation instances. A relation complex is a singular, unrepeatable entity; that is, :$R(a,b)$ is an *individual* fact or state of affairs. Relevant here is what Armstrong calls the "victory of the particular."[16] The predicative combination under a universal R and the particulars a and b results in a particular (unrepeatable) fact. The implication is that it is the particularity of the subject terms that effects the particularity of the encompassing relation complex. But this cannot be the case. A relation complex can have universals as subjects, :R(F,G)—for example, the fact that Loves has more subjects than Red. Substantive (as opposed to attributive) number statements are also of this kind— for example, the fact that $2 < 3$, or :$<(2,3)$. The point is that the particularity of a relation complex is *not* a function of the nature of the subject terms, which may be either individuals or universals. In addition, if the predicative aspect of a relation is conceived as universal, then the individual, unrepeatable relation complex, say :$<(2,3)$, is composed exactly and without remainder of universals. But how is it possible to get unrepeatability from entities that are all repeatable? This is the problem encountered in the bundle theory of particulars. There is no particularity without it being a property (universal) of something particular. What, then, is the source of the individuation of the complex :R(F,G), if not the universals R, F, and G? The only candidate is the fourth 'ingredient' in the complex—that is, the *connectivity* among R, F, and G, which is a function of R as predicative or actually relating F to G. It is *this* relating by R that is unrepeatable and that accounts for the individuation of the resulting complex. We can, of course, abstract away the universal R from any individuating complex as not having (relating) any relata, but such a half-truth gives us only the common intension, not the defining characteristic of this category of entities.

What the above three arguments for relation (including one-place property) instances confirm is the analysis announced in chapter 2: that for any n terms, $a_1, \ldots, a_n$, and n-place relation R^n,

The proposition that $\ulcorner R^n(a_1, \ldots, a_n) \urcorner$ is true $\equiv (\exists R_i^n) R_i^n(a_1, \ldots, a_n)$, where

R_i^n consists in $\left\{ \begin{array}{l} \text{(i)   R, a repeatable intension or content,} \\ \text{and} \\ \text{(ii) an unrepeatable linking among an } n\text{-tuple of specific} \\ \quad\quad \text{entities, } a_1, \ldots, a_n. \end{array} \right.$

The two aspects of R_i are *formally* distinguishable, but they are not, in constituting R_i, relata for some further relation rendering R_i itself a 'complex'. To hold otherwise is to start down the futile road of Bradley's regress. In this sense, R_i is simple. Frege may have had something like this in mind when he asserted that "a concept can be distinguished within, but not separated from, the complex in which it occurs."[17] It is the instance R_i that accomplishes the defining linking of relata under intension R. Analogous to a class concept for properties, the relation intension R is a universal, identical across all instances of its type. The intension determines the formal properties (e.g., symmetry and transitivity) but is an abstraction and does not have the defining role of relating any relata; it is combinatorially inert. It is because we can make these abstractions that Bradley's regress gets started and initially seems plausible: senses in which the 'same' relation both links (as R_i) and does not link (as R) its terms. It is true, then, that a relation (intension) is not a relation (linking instance), and for the exact same reason we can resolve in a way satisfactory to Frege his much commented upon paradox that the concept of a horse (intension) is not a concept (i.e., predicative).[18]

Arguments from Compound Structure

Let us now turn to the fact of compound structure and two arguments for relation and property instances implied by its analysis. As an example of compound structure, consider figure 8.1.

$$a\overset{R}{\rule{1cm}{0.4pt}}b\overset{R}{\rule{1cm}{0.4pt}}c$$
$$S|\quad S|$$
$$d\quad e$$

This might be the structure of a particular molecule or that of a particular configuration of objects, and so on, where R and S are types of relations (e.g., of chemical bonding or being spatially below) among relata nodes. We can imagine this simple case being increasingly expanded—for example, to the structure of an antique mechanical adding machine. In the adding machine the structure is spatial/mechanical, with 'push–pull' causal interconnections. This is contrasted to a contemporary electronic calculator, with its spatial/circuit structure and electromagnetic causal chains.

According to the first argument for relation instances, consider one of the simplest compound structures, as shown in figure 8.2.

$$a\begin{cases} \overset{R}{\diagup}b \\ \underset{R}{\diagdown}c \end{cases}$$

Contrast figure 8.2 with the two disjoint atomic structures shown in figure 8.3.

$$\underset{a}{\overset{R}{\quad}}\!\!-\!\!b, \qquad \underset{c}{\overset{R}{\quad}}\!\!-\!\!d$$

There is no single compound structure in figure 8.3. The question is: What identifies figure 8.2 and not figure 8.3 as a single, articulated compound structure? Intuitively, it is the fact that in figure 8.2 two relation structures *share* a term. In general, the diverse unity of a compound structure is a function of both linking relations *and* shared relata. By the mediation of these two conditions, there are chains of interconnectedness (by 'road and node'), so that any term in the structure is systematically tied to any other. Figure 8.2 is a compound structure because distinct atomic and simple complexes :R(a,b) and :R(a,c) share a term, or node, a. But this gives rise to the following problem: What can it mean for complexes :R(a,b) and :R(a,c) to share a term a? It must mean that

(8.2) a is a relatum of R as it occurs in :R(a,b), and a is a relatum of R as it occurs in :R(a,c).

Now, if it is assumed that R as it occurs in :R(a,b) is *numerically the same* universal R that occurs in :R(a,c), then 8.2 becomes the redundant

(8.3) a is a relatum of R as it occurs in :R(a,b), and a is a relatum of R as it occurs in :R(a,b).

Or simply,

(8.4) a is a relatum of R as it occurs in :R(a,b).

Hence,

(8.5) :R(a,b) and :R(a,c) share term a if and only if a is a relatum of R as it occurs in :R(a,b).

But this yields the contradiction that figure 8.3 is also a compound structure. For the right bijunct of 8.5 is also true of figure 8.3, hence we are forced to conclude that the disjoint structures of figure 8.3 share a relatum and are not disjoint but form a compound structure. The single universal R cannot share a relatum with itself any more than it is possible to clap with one hand. It is only when we see figure 8.2 as involving two instances of R, say R_i and R_j, that we can understand a as shared by these two distinct instances.

Finally, consider a second argument for relation instances based upon the notion of compound structure. It has been argued recently (e.g., by Armstrong and by Bigelow and Pargetter[19]) that any adequate theory of universals must account for 'structural universals'. The methane molecule is a favorite example. Each such molecule consists of one carbon atom and four hydrogen atoms bonded in a certain configuration. In this structure each methane molecule is *isomorphic* with every other. Because this same structure can be duplicated over multiple molecules, 'being methane' is a universal intrinsically related in some way to the three universals Hydrogen, Carbon, and Bonded. Yet there is a structure even in the methane universal: for example, the bonding relation is instantiated four times by carbon–hydrogen pairs, which renders the structural universal irreducible to a class or mereological whole. The universal Methane cannot simply be the universals of Hydrogen, Carbon, and Bonded, since this would make it indistinguishable from Butane (ten hydrogen and four carbon atoms configured in thirteen cases of bonding). Specifically, the important characteristic of structure that must be accounted for in the universal is the possibility of repetition of substructure, but in such a way that any constituent of a complex universal must also be a universal.

Armstrong has offered an account of structural universals which addresses these difficulties and which brings him very close to the theory of relation and property instances advanced here, though he rejects the full theory. He asks us to consider the monadic universal F and the dyadic universal R, from which we could have a possible structural universal: *an F* (e.g., a particular but unspecified carbon–hydrogen pair) having R (e.g., sharing a carbon atom) to *another F* (again unspecified, but different from the previous carbon–hydrogen pair). Note that Armstrong does not say 'F having R to F'. It is not the *universal* Being-a-carbon–hydrogen-pair that shares a carbon atom, R, with itself. Moreover, so construed, there is no numerical repetition of a substructure F. We must have what Armstrong calls 'particularizing universals'. With these, "there is a sense in which such universals enfold particularity within themselves *even when considered in abstraction from their instances.*"[20] Armstrong's particularized universals represent an abstraction one step removed from unrepeatable relation instances. Take, for example, the complex :$Carbon_1(a)$, an individual instance of carbon as predicated of a particular individual a. If we take one abstractive step and detach the instance from the specific subject a, we have a 'universalized instance', $Carbon_j$, whose content includes both its intension Carbon and the notion of the latter's nonrepeatable inherence in a single, albeit unspecified subject. One further abstractive step achieves the full universal

Carbon. Distinguishable 'universalized instances'—say, $Carbon_j$ and $Carbon_k$—can explain structural universals; moreover, they presuppose 'particularized instances' (i.e., relation instances proper), from which they are abstracted. We have, then, an additional argument for relation instances and the moderate realism advanced herein.

With this I conclude the portion of this work dealing with arguments for instance ontology, both direct and to-the-best-explanation, which do not rely upon a formalization of the logic inherent in the doctrine. I have attempted to make the case that the ontic analysis of relations, full and polyadic, implies the existence of relation instances. Supporting this position was the observation that, historically, the connection between unit attributes and relations has been continual, though it has been unfruitful for instance ontology because of the nullifying effects of the prevailing containment model of predication. It is the combinatorial model of predication writ large in polyadic relations that offers the possibility of overcoming the severe weaknesses of the traditional substance/attribute ontology and of yielding a viable, economic one-category ontology of relation instances.

part 2

The Logic of Particularism and Some Applications

chapter nine

Formalization of a Particularized Predicate Logic

The formal relationships of a logistic language picture the ontological structuring of reality.—Küng, *Ontology and the Logistic Analysis of Language*

It is desirable not only to find intuitively acceptable methods for avoiding
the Curry and Russell paradoxes, but also to find intuitively acceptable
systems of logic that can be shown to contain no contradictions whatever.
                    —Fitch, "A Method for Avoiding the Curry Paradox"

Introduction

In the previous chapters an extended case was made for a realist ontology that
includes, in addition to property and relation universals, corresponding unrepeatable instances of each. This ontology, which as such is equally a theory of
predication, follows directly from our ontic analysis of relations, including
properties as monadic predicates. Insofar as relations relate—that is, are predicative of or among entities as relata—they are unrepeatable; and insofar as they
are universal, they are half-truth, nonpredicative abstractions from unrepeatable instances. That is, it was argued that to the extent that a relation fulfills its
ontically defining role and links a specific n-tuple of relata, it is specific to that
ordered set of terms, whether those terms themselves are universals or individuals. Relation instances are predicative and, indeed, are individuated precisely
as predicative. This view of predication stands in direct opposition to the classic
'Aristotelian' theory, which asserts that a universal is predicative and conversely, whereas what is individual is *as such* not predicative of anything.

It is a common, albeit vague thesis that logic is 'topic-neutral'—that it applies
to all reasoning regardless of the subject matter. This is not to be construed,
however, as implying that logic itself has no specific subject matter or that there
are no logical entities. Frege observed that for logic to be more than an arbitrary
syntactical game with symbols, it must be about the relations that follow from
the *senses* (intensions) that attach to the logical symbols, most conspicuously the
senses of the logical connectives, of identity, and of the quantifiers. The scholastic philosophers referred to these senses that were the objects of logic as entities

of second intension (*intensiones secundae*), and their grammatical designators as 'syncategorematic signs'. But as also logically relevant, Frege was persistent in emphasizing the 'unsaturated' character of predicates ('concepts'). Frege knew that underlying the metaphors of 'unsaturated' and his more formally precise analog of mathematical function was the essential notion of the combinatorial nature of predication. And, in contrast to the classic containment model, the theory of the linking nature of predication had the systemically altering implication for logic that it was possible for there to be single predicates with more than one subject. This, coupled with the device of Fregean quantifiers, brought with it a host of insights and a synthesis unavailable to classical logic—for example, the notion of multiple general quantification which integrated precisely and simply what the relevant portion of the complex medieval theory of supposition could not. What Frege did not further observe, however, was that the combinatorial nature of predication implies the individuation of predicates, and that this refinement of instance predicates implies a parallel refinement in logic. Analogous to the advantage of multiple general quantification over the relevant supposition theory, instance logic has at its own more elemental level a power to organize what are, upon standard logical analysis, isolated, partial insights and to solve otherwise intractable logical and ontological problems. It is my purpose in this chapter to demonstrate these claims.

I shall here develop the refined predicate logic which underlies, and is a vehicle for, a formalization of the ontology of particularized predicates. I will take as my guiding principle that the deep semantics of ontic predication is to be the basis of, and structural model for, a parallel system of grammatical predication/logic that encodes it. The rules of symbolic construction of the latter provide a perspicuous medium for conceptualizing both the intuitive underlying notion of ontic predication and the logical relationships that it subsequently generates. Specific to instance ontology, its minimum proto-logical core is the systematization through formation and transformation rules of the principle of instance predicates (IP) and the simple quantificational device implied by the principle of immanent instance realism (IR), which I shall refer to as 'extended binding'. From this core I shall develop a formal language which I will designate 'PPL', short for 'Particularized Predicate Logic', a system which I take to be an approximation to what Gödel once described as a programmatic 'theory of concepts'.[1] PPL is a *logic* in the straightforward sense of being an analog of standard higher-order predicate logic, but with the encumbering distinction of 'orders' or 'types' removed and the resulting system extrapolated to contain the refinement of instance predicates and the concomitant device of 'extended binding' by intension quantifiers. Stated otherwise, PPL is a logic of nominalized predicates and their instances, without a type stratification of predicates.

Once delineated, PPL will be observed to have the following salient features:

(a) PPL is provably consistent. The consistency proof is established by means of a simple modification of a standard syntactical technique found, for example, in Church's *Mathematical Logic.*[2]

(b) PPL is an *impredicative* predicate logic, in that it allows innocuous and seemingly necessary forms of self-reference that are otherwise precluded in higher-order logics under imposed, ad hoc type theories. Specifically, PPL distinguishes legitimate impredicative specifications from illegitimate forms and in this offers the possibility of a uniform diagnosis of the classic self-referential paradoxes. PPL retains global ranges of quantification and hence the power and scope of expression widely held as necessary in the areas of foundational mathematics, semantics, and philosophical analysis. PPL, then, is a candidate for what Frederic Fitch sought as a 'universal metalanguage of philosophy'.[3]

(c) In PPL all of classical logic is retained. Self-referential paradoxes are avoided without such devices as restricting bivalence (Fitch) or rejecting classical negation (intuitionists). Though classical logic and mathematics survives in PPL, key forms of reasoning and limitation theorems of foundational mathematics and metamathematics do not carry over to the refined organon of PPL. The impredicative specifications contained in the Cantor-type diagonal constructions—for example, Cantor's theorem—will be seen to be illegitimate under PPL analysis. Relatedly, the self-referential specifications pivotal to Gödel's incompleteness theorems and Tarski's theorem (and related theorems—e.g., the Halting theorem of recursion theory) are defeated, so that the theorems no longer hold in PPL.

(d) PPL is an analytic tool and inference engine that has much explanatory potential. With the addition of Hume's principle, it has the power to generate Peano arithmetic in a formal system for which there is a finite consistency proof. It also has the power to distinguish identity from indiscernibility, a distinction that standard predicate logics cannot formalize.

On its intended interpretation, PPL is an *intensional* logic in the literal sense, though not in the broad technical sense for which the term is also presently used—encompassing modal, epistemic, deontic, and tense logics.[4] PPL is intensional in the strict sense that, not only are there constants and quantified variables of the language that, under the previously argued 'informal' realist interpretation, name or range over unrepeatable entities—individuals and relations instances—but there are likewise constants and quantified variables naming or ranging over repeatable property and relation intensions—that is, universals. Specifically, PPL is a three-sorted impredicative predicate logic with constants referring to, and variables ranging over, entities within the three mutually exclusive and exhaustive categories of 'individuals', 'intensions', and 'instances of intensions'. In addition, global variables ranging over all three domains are admitted. Under the previously presented ontology as an interpretation, the category of 'individuals' contains, in addition to relation instances, unrepeatable complexes or structures consisting of two or more relation instances sharing various relata—for example, hierarchical complexes of complexes constituting ordinary observable objects. In PPL, however, no distinction among types of individuals will be observed.

As stated, PPL is an impredicative predicate logic in that constants and variables in all three domains (individuals, relation instances, and relation intensions) are allowed in subject position, and there is no stratification into a hierarchical system of types within which predicates of type n are restricted to subjects of type $n-1$ or, as in some systems, to type $n-1$ and lower. It is an extension of second-order predicate logic, in which predicates (and instances) are also allowed to occupy subject positions totally free of any restrictions that are a function of the containing predicates. The motivation for a type stratification is, of course, to avoid the vicious-circle inconsistency that arises from sanctioning certain impredicatively defined entities (relations, properties, or individuals) under an unrestricted *axiom (schema) of comprehension*. The crux of the problem for all the classic self-referential paradoxes is specifying exactly what constitutes an impredicative definition and, within this, distinguishing and permitting cases of innocuous and theoretically crucial self-predication while prohibiting cases that are contradictory.

Russell proposed his famous vicious circle principle as both an inductive diagnosis and a means of eschewing the several offending definitions. Though variously formulated by Russell, the two most relevant statements are:

(a) Whatever contains an apparent variable must not be a possible value of that variable.

(b) No totality can contain members defined in terms of itself.[5]

To enforce the principle within an otherwise unrestricted logic—that is, what was once referred to as 'extended predicate logic'—it is necessary to introduce a system of types of some variety which precludes the global and self-predicative applications of a single, standard axiom of comprehension. Yet all such 'predicative' type theories introduce considerable formal complications and, in one form or another, counter-intuitive limitations. The latter include not only the surrendering of both innocuous and theoretically fundamental self-predication (e.g., the Bolzano–Weierstrass theorem of classical analysis), but also the exclusion of definitions of globally applicable laws of logic (e.g., excluded middle), as well as global definitions of identity, number, mathematical induction, truth, and so on, all for the safe but narrowly local applications within isolated types.

For these reasons type theory has been widely viewed as ad hoc and overly restrictive, reflecting an inadequate understanding of impredicative specifications. The claim to be substantiated here is that this grossness is a product of the lack of a refined instance ontology together with its parallel, more precise formal logic.

Unlike type theory, in PPL terms for individuals, terms for intensions, and terms for instances of intensions can occupy subject positions, all undifferentiated as to artificially imposed types. But only instance terms will occupy predicate positions, for only intension instances are predicates. As we shall see, the advantage of PPL, with its added refinement of both intensions and their instances, is a relatively simple formal system with a positively motivated comprehension axiom, which permits impredicative definitions while retaining intuitively global definitions and laws of classical logic. This formal success is further indirect but strong evidence for the truth of a motivating ontology of property and relation instances.

Because the only intensions admitted in PPL are those corresponding to open sentences, or propositional functions, but none corresponding to individuals ('individual concepts') or to closed sentences (propositions), PPL is a *partial* intensional logic. To do full justice to intensions, one would need to extend PPL to a system paralleling, for example, that proposed by Alonzo Church.[6] A small extension of PPL in this regard will be considered briefly when analyzing the liar paradox below.

Though not a full intensional logic, PPL is nevertheless offered as a fundamental core to such a logic and in this contributes substantially to the fulfillment of a program once described by Kurt Gödel.[7] It was Gödel's view that the intractability of the intensional paradoxes (e.g., Russell's property) are symptomatic and a consequence of our lack of even a moderately satisfactory theory of intensions or 'concepts'. According to Gödel, we must distinguish between mathematics (set theory), which deals with extensions, and logic (the theory of concepts), whose subject matter is intensions. With regard to the latter, Gödel's view is consonant with the scholastic thesis that logic is the study of 'second intensions'. Gödel observed that the set-theoretical, or extensional, paradoxes are eliminated by the iterative concept of set; no set belongs to itself, and there is no universal set. Yet certain concepts can perfectly well apply to themselves, and there is the universal concept (i.e., the concept of being a concept), which applies to itself. A task of the theory of concepts is to find a way to deal consistently but noneliminatively with impredicative specifications—for example, the concept of all concepts not applying to themselves. In this sense, PPL is the core of a theory of concepts.

Although I will present PPL axiomatically and with the minuteness necessary for precision and to guarantee the veracity of the metalogical results (e.g., the consistency proof), PPL in a natural deduction mode is an easy extrapolation from the axiomatization, being a simple, intuitive extension of standard natural deduction systems, a practical tool easily mastered and applied.

Before turning to the formalization of PPL, I should note that there exist other intension logics in the above sense, but to my knowledge none with the refinement of relation instances. For example, there are Nino Cocchiarella's logic of nominalized predicates T^{*}[8] and George Bealer's intensional logic L_{ω}.[9] Interestingly, both systems are syntactically consistent and semantically sound and complete. Cocchiarella achieves this result by means of a special restriction on the axiom of comprehension of T^{*} which requires that the definiens be free of the identity relation. The net effect, besides consistency, includes unintuitive results such as that the identity sign does not stand for a relation in T^{*} and the fact that for some properties indiscernibility is insufficient for coextensionality. Bealer's system L_{ω} is provably complete provided that no predicate is singled out as expressing the predication relation. It is the predication relation, Bealer argues, that is the source of incompleteness in any logic, and he goes on to argue that this is the source of the self-referential paradoxes. The lesson said to be learned is that, to avoid the paradoxes, there must be explicit, contextually invoked limitations on the relevant universes of discourse. With both Cocchiarella and Bealer their maneuvers for avoiding the paradoxes are ad hoc and do not represent a penetrating analysis of the source of illegitimate impredicative specification. This is an advantage of PPL.

Formalization of PPL

In formalizing the logic of particularized predicates, we must first specify the *primitive basis* of PPL as a logistic system, or uninterpreted calculus. This syntactical system is of course intended to be the formalized theory of predication inherent in the semantics of intensions and their instances previously argued for. When this logistic system is taken along with its interpretation, the combination is then said to be a *formal language.* The following axiomatization is an extension and refinement of the predicate calculi found in Church's *Mathematical Logic.*[10] For the sake of brevity, the propositional calculus will not be explicitly formulated as a subsystem of PPL. The primitive basis of PPL consists in (1) specifying what will constitute the primitive symbols of PPL; (2) detailing the formation rules specifying what sequences of primitive symbols constitute well-formed formulas, 'wffs', of PPL; and (3) listing the transformation rules—rules of inference and axioms from which theorems of the system will follow.

Primitive symbols

Improper: ( ) ¬ ⊃ ∃ ∨ · ≡

Proper:

(1) *Individual symbols*: Infinite lists of

Variables: $x \, y \, z \, x_1 \, y_1 \, z_1 \, x_2 \, y_2 \, z_2 \ldots$

Constants: $a \, b \, c \, a_1 \, b_1 \, c_1 \, a_2 \, b_2 \, c_2 \ldots$

(2) *Intension symbols* (constants that name or variables that range over universals):

Variables: an infinite list of one-place variables

$$P^1 \, Q^1 \, R^1 \ldots Z^1 \, P'^1 \, Q'^1 \ldots Z'^1 \, P''^1 \, Q''^1 \ldots$$

An infinite list of two-place variables

$$P^2 \ Q^2 \ R^2 \ldots Z^2 \ P'^2 \ Q'^2 \ldots Z'^2 \ P''^2 \ Q''^2 \ldots$$

Likewise for three-place, four-place, etc., variables. (Under the intended interpretation the superscripts represent the polyacity [number of relata] of the intension over which the respective variables range.)

Constants: an infinite list of one-place constants

$$A^1 \ B^1 \ C^1 \ldots O^1 \ A'^1 \ B'^1 \ C'^1 \ldots O'^1 \ A''^1 \ B''^1 \ldots O''^1 \ldots$$

Likewise, infinite lists of two-place, three-place, etc., constants. Also included among the intension constants of PPL is

$$Id^2,$$

which, under the intended interpretation, has the identity relation as its referent.

(3) *Instance symbols* (constants that name or variables that range over, to various extents, instances of intensions):

Full instance variables: an infinite list of one-place intension variables for each of the one-place predicate-type variables above

$$P^1_i \ P^1_j \ P^1_k \ldots Q^1_i \ Q^1_j \ Q^1_k \ldots Z^1_i \ Z^1_j \ Z^1_k \ldots P'^1_i \ P'^1_j \ldots$$

(where the list continues indefinitely on subscript letters by means of the use of prime marks, e.g., R'^1_j. Likewise below.)

An infinite list of two-place instance variables for each of the two-place intension variables above

$$P^2_i \ P^2_j \ P^2_k \ldots Q^2_i \ Q^2_j \ Q^2_k \ldots Z^2_i \ Z^2_j \ Z^2_k \ldots P'^2_i \ P'^2_j \ldots$$

Likewise for three-place, four-place, etc., intension variables above.

A full instance variable, e.g., P^1_i, ranges over *all* instances of P^1, where P^1 is a variable ranging in turn over all intensions.

Limited instance variables: an infinite list of one-place predicates for each of the one-place intension constants above

$$A^1_i \ A^1_j \ A^1_k \ldots B^1_i \ B^1_j \ B^1_k \ldots C^1_i \ C^1_j \ C^1_k \ldots$$

Likewise for two-place, three-place, etc., predicate-type constants above.

Limited instance variables range over the instances of the *fixed* intension constant named by the intension constant component of the variable symbol, e.g., 'A' of 'A$_i$'.

Instance constants: an infinite list of one-place instance constants for each one-place intension constant

$$A_1^1 \, A_2^1 \, A_3^1 \ldots B_1^1 \, B_2^1 \, B_3^1 \ldots C_1^1 \, C_2^1 \, C_3^1 \ldots$$

Likewise for two-place, three-place, etc., intension constants above, including instances of the identity relation 'Id^2', i.e.,

$$Id_1^2 \, Id_2^2 \, Id_3^2, \ldots$$

Finally, we shall introduce the following Gothic font Latin letters for variables ranging globally over entities of all three ontic categories—that is, intensions, instances, and individuals.

Global variables:
$$\mathfrak{a} \, \mathfrak{b} \, \mathfrak{c} \ldots \mathfrak{z} \, \mathfrak{a}' \, \mathfrak{b}' \, \mathfrak{c}' \ldots \mathfrak{z}' \, \mathfrak{a}'' \, \mathfrak{b}'' \, \mathfrak{c}'' \ldots$$

An example of the use of global variables is given by

$$(\mathfrak{a})(\exists Id_i^2) Id_i^2(\mathfrak{a},\mathfrak{a}),$$

which states succinctly that for any entity whatsoever there exists at least one instance of the identity relation that that entity has to itself. This truth of identity will be seen to follow from the axiom of PPL that characterizes the identity relation.

In the examples and explications that follow, superscripts indicating polyacity (i.e., the number of subject terms) will be left unspecified except in cases of possibly falsifying ambiguity.

So as to contrast the primitive symbols of the object-language PPL with the informal metalanguage, the latter metalanguage will consist of a modified fragment of English containing certain Greek letters and bold Latin letters with or without subscripts and superscripts. These syntactic variables which, as such, take object-language single terms or complex expressions as *substitutens* will be introduced as needed. Symbols of the object-language will be taken over into the metalanguage as names of themselves. For ease of reading, braces and brackets will at places be substituted for parentheses.

Formation rules:

(1) If $\mathbf{R}_i^n$ is a full or limited instance variable or instance constant and if $\mathbf{a}_1$, $\mathbf{a}_2, \ldots, \mathbf{a}_n$ are variables or constants of any kind, then $\mathbf{R}_i^n(\mathbf{a}_1, \mathbf{a}_2, \ldots, \mathbf{a}_n)$ is a wff, and it or its negation is said to be a *literal* of PPL. Literals contain at most one occurrence of negation, $\neg$, those containing $\neg$ are *negative* literals; otherwise they are *positive* literals.

For wff $\mathbf{R}_i^n(\mathbf{a}_1, \mathbf{a}_2, \ldots, \mathbf{a}_n)$, $\mathbf{R}_i^n$ is said to occupy the *predicate position*, and $\mathbf{a}_1, \mathbf{a}_2, \ldots, \mathbf{a}_n$ each occupy *subject positions*.

(2) If $\mathbf{A}$ is a wff, then $\neg \mathbf{A}$ is a wff.

(3) If $\mathbf{A}$ and $\mathbf{B}$ are wffs, then $(\mathbf{A} \supset \mathbf{B})$, $(\mathbf{A} \vee \mathbf{B})$, $(\mathbf{A} \cdot \mathbf{B})$, and $(\mathbf{A} \equiv \mathbf{B})$ are wffs.

(4) If $\mathbf{A}$ is a wff, and $\mathbf{a}$ is any variable, then $(\mathbf{a})\mathbf{A}$ and $(\exists\mathbf{a})\mathbf{A}$ are wffs.

A wff $\mathbf{B}$ is said to be a *subformula* of wff $\mathbf{A}$ if and only if $\mathbf{B}$ is a part of $\mathbf{A}$.

It is important to note that by (1) only instance symbols (full or limited instance variables or instance constants) can occupy predicate positions in wffs of PPL, not individual, intension, or global symbols, though all may occupy subject positions. This is in conformity with the principle of instance predicates (IP) of chapter 1, part of the theory of predication that motivates the present logistic system.

To understand the analytic power of this language, it is important to note that the possible quantifier combinations within PPL extend beyond those available in standard extended predicate logics. Consider the correspondence:

$(P)P(a) \leftrightarrow (P)(\exists P_i)P_i(a)$

[e.g., for every property P there exists an instance of P, P_i, such that $P_i(a)$].

$(\exists P)P(a) \leftrightarrow (\exists P)(\exists P_i)P_i(a)$

[i.e., there exist a property P and an instance of P, P_i, such that $P_i(a)$].

Though standard logic on the left side of the arrows is exhausted in possibilities, in PPL there are two other quantifier combinations: namely,

$(P)(P_i)P_i(a)$ [i.e., for every property P and every instance of P, P_i, $P_i(a)$].

$(\exists P)(P_i)P_i(a)$ [i.e., there exists a property P such that for every instance of it, P_i, $P_i(a)$].

It is through attention to the full range of quantifier combinations in PPL, hidden from standard predicate logic, that a consistent comprehension axiom can be constructed for PPL which allows for some impredicative definitions as legitimate while avoiding others involved in the vicious-circle paradoxes.

For perspicuity and ease of presentation and use, though unnecessary theoretically, the existential quantifier has been included in PPL; its relationship to the universal quantifier is given in the object-language by the 'definition' (i.e., noncreative axiom) schema

D1. $(\exists a)A \equiv \neg(a)\neg A$.

Though likewise redundant in expressive power, for ease of use the logical constants of conjunction, disjunction, and the biconditional are included in the object-language and are assumed to be 'defined' in terms of $\supset$ and $\neg$ by axiom schemata of the standard forms.

The device of *extended binding* by a quantifier with an intension operator variable is an application of the principle of immanent instance realism (IR) and is one of the distinguishing features of this logic. Extended binding by intension quantifiers, along with standard binding by quantifiers of other types, is defined as follows. First, the *scope* of a quantifier (a), where a is any type of variable of PPL, is defined in the usual fashion: if $(a)A$ is such that A is a wff, then every symbol constituting $(a)A$ is within the *scope* of (a). For a wff $(a)A$, the universal quantifier (a) binds variables contained in A as follows:

(1) If a is an individual or global variable, or a full or limited instance variable, then (a) binds all occurrences of a within its scope with the exception that (a) does not bind occurrences of a within any subformula of A of the form $(a)B$.

(2) If a is an intension variable, R^n, then

  (i) (a) binds all occurrences of R^n within its scope, except those occurrences within a subformula of A of the form $(R^n)B$, and

  (ii) [*Extended binding*] (a) binds all and only the occurrences of the instance variables R^n_i, for any subscript i, within its scope that occur in subformulas of A of the form $(R^n_i)B$ or $(\exists R^n_i)B$, except when these subformulas occur within subformulas of A of the form $(R^n)C$.

The definitions of scope and extended binding are assumed to be extended mutatis mutandis to the existential quantifier.

A variable that is not bound in a wff is *free* in that wff. A wff containing no free variable is *closed*. If a quantifier binds no variable within its scope, then it is said to be *vacuous*.

Formalized in 2(ii) is the concept of extended binding whereby an intension variable binds instance variables with the same intension component and accomplishes this specifically through the mediation of an instance quantifier, the operator variable of which the intension variable binds. Consider the following examples. The symbols below a quantifier are repeated under occurrences of variables bound by the quantifier:

$$(P)(P_i)(x)[P_i(x) \supset (\exists P_i) A_1 (P_i,x)].$$

To fully appreciate the significance of 2(ii), consider the following example, again with the symbols placed below an item indicating what is bound by the respective quantifiers:

$$(P)(\exists P_j)(P)P_j(P).$$

By 2(ii), P_j in the subformula $(P)P_j(P)$ is not bound by the quantifier (P) of the subformula, since an intension quantifier only binds a corresponding instance variable if the latter is itself bound by an instance quantifier whose variable is bound by the intension quantifier. Because of this, the wff in the last example is equivalent to $(P)(\exists P_j)(Q)P_j(Q)$. If a wff such as $(P)P_i(x)$ the quantifier (P) is vacuous. In short, an intension quantifier $(\mathbf{P})$ binds corresponding full instance variables $\mathbf{P}_i$ within their scope only through the mediation of a full instance quantifier $(\mathbf{P}_i)$ or $(\exists \mathbf{P}_i)$.

Extended binding makes explicit what is implicit in the understanding of standard predicate logics. There we rely constantly upon recognizing the presence of instances of the same universals in order to carry through even the simplest of derivations. For example, consider

$$(P)[P(a) \lor \neg P(a)].$$

In order to drop the quantifier (P) and instantiate each occurrence of P within its scope, we must recognize the latter to be the same *kind* of symbol—more precisely, to be an instance or token of the same printed type. Extended binding makes this usage explicit in PPL. Indeed, extended binding simply codifies explicitly in PPL the epistemic necessity essential to any knowledge: recognizing entities as exemplifying a common intension.

Transformation rules:

For wffs **A** and **B** of PPL,

Rules of inference:

R1. If ⊢ **A** and ⊢ **A** ⊃ **B**, then ⊢ **B**.

R2. If **a** is any variable and ⊢ **A**, then ⊢ (**a**)**A**.

Axiom schemata:

A1. **A** ⊃ (**B** ⊃ **A**).

A2. (**A** ⊃ (**B** ⊃ **C**)) ⊃ ((**A** ⊃ **B**) ⊃ (**A** ⊃ **C**)).

A3. (¬**A** ⊃ ¬**B**) ⊃ (**B** ⊃ **A**).

A4. (**a**)(**A** ⊃ **B**) ⊃ (**A** ⊃ (**a**)**B**), where **a** is a variable of any kind, and (**a**) does not bind a variable in **A**.

The following axiom schema is that of universal instantiation. It is stated in such a manner as to render PPL free of existential presuppositions in regard to limited instance variables and instance constants. Without restriction, A5 would permit the derivation of conditionals of the form (**a**)**A** ⊃ (∃**a**)**A**, which requires that there exists at least one entity of the type **a**. This is not a problem for intensions, for the axiom of comprehension (AC) that will follow asserts the existence of at least one n-place intension for every n-place propositional function that is not illegitimately impredicative. Nor do I see a problem with making the assumption that at least one individual exists, though purists could easily modify the following axiom in a standard way to eliminate the need for this assumption. What must be avoided is the requirement that for every intension constant—say, B—there is at least one instance of its kind, B_i. This necessity would follow from conditionals analogous to $(B_i)B_i(a) \supset (\exists B_i)B_i(a)$ if the latter were derivable in PPL. Yet, we want PPL to formalize a semantics in which there are intensions (e.g., corresponding to x is round and is square, or x is a unicorn) that are not instantiated—that is, have no instances. For this reason, A5(III), which describes the instantiation of universal quantifiers by limited instance variables or instance constants, will be formulated with an antecedent conditional of the form '(∃**a**)(**a** = **b**) ⊃'.

A5 (I) (a)$\mathbf{A} \supset \mathbf{B}$, where:

a is (1) an individual variable or (2) a global variable or (3) a full instance variable $\mathbf{R}_i^n$, and **B** results from **A** by replacing all free occurrences of **a** in **A** by a term **b** which is, respectively,

(1′) an individual variable or constant,

e.g., $(x)(\exists A_i)A_i(x) \supset (\exists A_i)A_i(b)$;

(2′) a variable or constant of any type other than a limited instance variable or instance constant,

e.g., $(\alpha)(\exists P)(\exists P_i)P_i(\alpha) \supset (\exists P)(\exists P_i)P_i(Q)$;

(3′) a full instance variable $\mathbf{P}_j^n$,

e.g., $(P_i)(Q_j)[P_i(x) \supset \neg Q_j(x)] \supset (Q_j)[R_k(x) \supset \neg Q_j(x)]$;

In all cases, **b** is such that it must not become bound in **B** at a place where **a** is not bound in **A**.

(II) (a)$\mathbf{A} \supset \mathbf{B}$ where **a** is an intension variable, $\mathbf{R}^n$, and **B** is the result of substituting as **b** an intension variable or constant, $\mathbf{P}^n$, for each free occurrence of $\mathbf{R}^n$ in **A** and substituting a full or limited instance variable $\mathbf{P}_j^n$, respectively, for each occurrence of an $\mathbf{R}_i^n$ bound by the initial quantifier (**a**). The substitutens must be so chosen as not to become bound where the variable substituted for was not.

Under extended binding, (II) allows instantiations where, for example, one can go from antecedent

$(P)[(\exists P_i)P_i(P) \vee (P_j)\neg P_j(P)]$

to consequent

$(\exists A_i)A_i(A) \vee (A_j)\neg A_j(A)$

or to consequent

$(\exists S_i)S_i(S) \vee (S_j)\neg S_j(S)$,

where P has been instantiated with intension constant A or intension variable S, respectively.

(III) $(\exists a)(a = b) \supset [(a)\mathbf{A} \supset \mathbf{B}]$ where **a** is (1) a full or (2) a limited instance variable $\mathbf{R}_i^n$, or (3) a global variable, and **B** results from **A** by replacing all free occurrences of **a** in **A** by a term **b** that is, respectively, (1′) either a limited instance variable $\mathbf{P}_j^n$ or an instance constant $\mathbf{P}_r^n$, r a natural number; (2′) a limited instance variable $\mathbf{R}_j^n$ or an instance constant $\mathbf{R}_r^n$, r a natural number; or (3′) any limited instance variable or instance constant,

e.g., $(\exists R_i)(R_i = B_j) \supset [(R_i)R_i(a) \supset B_j(a)]$.

Note that in all cases, if $(\mathbf{a})$ is vacuous for $\mathbf{A}$, then $\mathbf{B}$ is the same as $\mathbf{A}$.

Finally, we shall introduce an axiom for *identity*:

A6. $(\mathbf{a})(\mathbf{b})\{(\exists Id_i^2)Id_i^2(\mathbf{a},\mathbf{b}) \equiv (\mathbf{P}^1)(\mathbf{P}_j^1)[\mathbf{P}_j^1(\mathbf{a}) \equiv \mathbf{P}_j^1(\mathbf{b})]\}$.

In A6 we have a refined specification of the identity relation, Id, the advantage of which will become apparent in chapter 10 when it will be constrasted with a definition of the indiscernibility relation, a here formalizable distinction not possible on standard predicate logics. It should be noted that with identity so specified, it is not possible to treat identity as merely a convenient abbreviation of the metalanguage. For the left main bijunct of A6 asserts existence, whereas the right main bijunct does not. A6 is a 'creative' axiom schema of PPL. Moreover, we cannot look to an anticipated axiom of comprehension to supply A6, since, as we shall see, in order to avoid self-referential paradox, a proper formulation of such an axiom presupposes the identity relation as given.

In what follows, I shall, for ease of expression, abbreviate instances of the schema

$(\exists Id_i)Id_i(\mathbf{a},\mathbf{b})$

as simply

$\mathbf{a} = \mathbf{b}$,

and instances of the schema

$\neg (\exists Id_i)Id_i(\mathbf{a},\mathbf{b})$

as

$\mathbf{a} \neq \mathbf{b}$.

The system formalized so far, which does not include an axiom of comprehension will be referred to as *restricted* PPL.

Given consistency proofs—for example, by D. A. Bochvar and more recently by Nino Cocchiarella—of extended predicate logics without an axiom (schema) of comprehension, we have good reason to expect the above refined instance logic to be likewise provably consistent.[11] We shall see presently that this is in fact the case. What must then follow as both crucial and enlightening is a formulation of an axiom of comprehension that will provide a consistent extension of the above. So extended, the system will constitute (*full*) PPL.

Consistency of Restricted PPL

The following consistency proof of restricted PPL utilizes a standard syntactical reduction technique used to prove the consistency of second-order logic.[12] The technique employs the extended propositional calculus, EPC, which is the standard propositional calculus extended to include quantification over propositions. Every wff **A** of PPL has a set of associated formulas of the EPC—referred to by the acronym 'afeps'—which are identical in logical form and are determined as follows. First, delete all subject position symbols and their enclosing parentheses in **A**. Next, delete all quantifiers with intension variables, then all other quantifiers that do not now bind a variable—that is, those that at this stage of the reduction are vacuous. At this point all that will remain of **A** are predicate position instance constants and variables and quantifiers having the latter as operator variables. Finally, replace each remaining, distinct instance variable and constant by a distinct lowercase Latin letter, or 'proposition' variable or constant, respectively. We reserve 'p' . . . 'z' and 'a' . . . 'o' as proposition variables and constants, respectively, and these with or without numerical subscripts. The result will be an afep of **A**, designated '**A**''.

For example, let **A** be

$$(P)(P_i)(x)(Q_j)[P_i(x,Q_j) \vee \neg P_i(x,Q_j) \vee C_2(x)].$$

Dropping all but predicate terms in predicate positions and their instance quantifiers we have

$$(P_i)[P_i \vee \neg P_i \vee C_2].$$

Replacing P_i with a proposition variable p and C_2 with a proposition constant c, then an afep **A**' of **A** is

$$(p)[p \vee \neg p \vee c].$$

It is clear that the afeps corresponding to a given wff **A** are *identical* in logical form, differing only in choice of variables or constants. It is only this form that is relevant to the method of true-value resolution described below; because they are identical in form, however, all afeps of a given wff **A** will resolve in an identical manner to the same truth-value. Hence any particular afep from the set of afeps associated with a wff of PPL can represent that wff in the following analysis.

In order to demonstrate the syntactical consistency of restricted PPL, it is necessary to show that instances of the axioms have valid afeps and that any propositional form derivable by the rules of inference from a propositional form with valid afeps will also have valid afeps, but that not *every* expression of PPL has valid afeps; for example, the afeps of form **A** · ¬**A** are not valid. If PPL were inconsistent, then every proposition would be inferable, including propositions with invalid afeps. To prove consistency, then, it is first necessary to show that every wff that is an instance of the axiom schemata of PPL has *valid* afeps; that is, each is a tautology or comes out true, T, for all proper assignments of Ts and Fs to its proposition variables. These assignments of truth-values are determined as follows. For any wff of the EPC of the form $(\mathbf{p})\phi(\mathbf{p})$, $(\mathbf{p})\phi(\mathbf{p})$ is valid if and only if $[\phi(T){\cdot}\phi(F)]$ is valid—that is, if the conjunction consisting of ϕ with all occurrences of **p** replaced with T conjoined to ϕ with all occurrences of **p** replaced by F is valid. If $\phi(\mathbf{p})$ is an expression of EPC with **p** as a free variable, then it is treated as if it were of the form $(\mathbf{p})\phi(\mathbf{p})$; that is, $\phi(\mathbf{p})$ is valid if and only if $[\phi(T){\cdot}\phi(F)]$ is valid. With the existential quantifier also in the object-language, some wffs of PPL will have afeps of the form $(\exists\mathbf{p})\phi(\mathbf{p})$, and these are valid if and only if $[\phi(T) \vee \phi(F)]$ is valid. An afep consisting of a propositional constant **c** or its negation ¬**c** will be treated as if it were an existentially quantified expression of the form $(\exists\mathbf{p})\mathbf{p}$ or $(\exists\mathbf{p})\neg\mathbf{p}$, respectively, where **p** is some proposition variable. Note that $(\exists\mathbf{p})\mathbf{p}$ or $(\exists\mathbf{p})\neg\mathbf{p}$ is valid if and only if $(T \vee F)$ or $(\neg T \vee \neg F)$, respectively, is valid. Finally, an expression containing only Ts and Fs and logical connectives is valid if and only if its resulting value is T according to the standard truth-table definitions of the connectives. We shall call an expression that results from substituting Ts and Fs according to the above specifications for a propositional variable **p** in a wff $\phi(\mathbf{p})$ a *truth-value expansion* of ϕ on **p**. When all the proposition variables of a wff ψ of EPC have been expanded in this way, the resulting expression is said to be a truth-value expansion of ψ. The process of deriving a single truth-value from the truth-value expansion of an expression ψ of EPC is said to be a truth-value resolution of ψ.

With the help of this translation scheme, it is now possible to prove the consistency of restricted PPL. In doing so, I shall attempt to hold the 'symboleeze' to a minimum. First, observe that the afeps of any instances of the axiom schemata A1–A6 are instances, respectively, of the following afep schemata:

al. $\mathbf{A'} \supset (\mathbf{B'} \supset \mathbf{A'})$.

a2. $(\mathbf{A'} \supset (\mathbf{B'} \supset \mathbf{C'})) \supset ((\mathbf{A'} \supset \mathbf{B'}) \supset (\mathbf{A'} \supset \mathbf{C'}))$.

a3. $(\neg\mathbf{A'} \supset \neg\mathbf{B'}) \supset (\mathbf{B'} \supset \mathbf{A'})$.

a4.   (i)   If **a** does not bind a predicate variable in **B**, then afeps of A4 have the form

$$(\mathbf{A'} \supset \mathbf{B'}) \supset (\mathbf{A'} \supset \mathbf{B'}).$$

E.g., $(P_j)[(S_i)S_i(x) \supset (\exists Q_i)Q_i(P_j)] \supset [(S_i)S_i(x) \supset (\exists Q_i)Q_i(P_j)]$ has as an afep

$$[(s)s \supset (\exists q)q] \supset [(s)s \supset (\exists q)q].$$

If (**a**) does bind a predicate position variable in **B**, then **a** is an instance variable or an intension variable, hence:

(ii)   If **a** is an instance variable, then afeps of A4 have the form

$$(\mathbf{p})(\mathbf{A'} \supset \mathbf{B'}) \supset (\mathbf{A'} \supset (\mathbf{p})\mathbf{B'}),$$

where **p** is the proposition variable substituted for **a**. $\mathbf{A'}$ will not contain a free occurrence of **p**.

E.g., $(P_j)[(S_i)S_i(x) \supset P_j(x)] \supset [(S_i)S_i(x) \supset (P_j)P_j(x)]$ has as an afep

$$(p)[(s)s \supset p] \supset [(s)s \supset (p)p].$$

(iii)   If **a** is an intension variable, then the afeps of A4 have the form

$$(\mathbf{A'} \supset \mathbf{B'}) \supset (\mathbf{A'} \supset \mathbf{B'}).$$

E.g., $(P)[(\exists S_i)S_i(x) \supset (\exists P_j)P_j(x)] \supset [(\exists S_i)S_i(x) \supset (P)(\exists P_j)P_j(x)]$ has a corresponding afep

$$[(\exists s)s \supset (p)p] \supset [(\exists s)s \supset (p)p].$$

a5.   (i)   If (**a**) does not bind a predicate position variable in **A**, then afeps of A5 have the form

$\mathbf{A}' \supset \mathbf{A}'$.

E.g., $(S_i)R_j(S_i) \supset R_j(S_2)$ has as an afep $r \supset r$.

If (a) does bind a predicate position variable in $\mathbf{A}$, then $\mathbf{a}$ is an instance variable or an intension variable, hence:

(ii) If $\mathbf{a}$ is (1) a full instance variable or (2) a limited instance variable such that (a) binds predicate position variables in $\mathbf{A}$, then the afeps of A5(I) or A5(III) are either of the form

(1′) $(\mathbf{p})\mathbf{A}' \supset \mathbf{B}'$

or

(2′) $<$afep of $(\exists \mathbf{a})(\mathbf{a} = \mathbf{b})> \supset [(\mathbf{p})\mathbf{A}' \supset \mathbf{B}'],$

where $\mathbf{p}$ is the proposition variable substituted for $\mathbf{a}$ in $\mathbf{A}$, and $\mathbf{B}'$ differs from $\mathbf{A}'$ at most in containing a proposition variable $\mathbf{q}$ or constant $\mathbf{a}$ at all positions where $\mathbf{A}'$ contains $\mathbf{p}$.

E.g., $(R_i)[A_1(R) \cdot R_i(x)] \supset [A_1(R) \cdot Q_i(x)]$ has as an afep

$(r)[a \cdot r] \supset [a \cdot q]$.

Or $(\exists A_i)(A_i = A_1) \supset [(A_i)(A_i(c) \vee \neg A_i(c)) \supset (A_1(c) \vee \neg A_1(c))]$ has afeps of the form

$<$afep of $(\exists A_i)(A_i = A_1)> \supset [(\mathbf{p})(\mathbf{p} \vee \neg \mathbf{p}) \supset ((\exists \mathbf{q})\mathbf{q} \vee (\exists \mathbf{q})\neg \mathbf{q})],$

where constant A_1 is first replaced by a proposition constant $\mathbf{a}$, and then $\mathbf{a}$ is replaced by an existentially quantified variable.

(iii) If $\mathbf{a}$ is an intension variable, the afeps of A5 have the form

$\mathbf{A}' \supset \mathbf{B}'$,

where $\mathbf{A}'$ and $\mathbf{B}'$ are identical in form with the possible exception of having different but corresponding proposition variables, but in this case the different proposition variables will be bound by the same type of quantifier. This is so because under the formation rules an intension variable only binds an instance variable through the mediation of an instance quantifier.

E.g., $(R)[(A_1(R) \vee R_j(a)) \cdot (\exists R_i)R_i(x)] \supset [(A_1(R) \vee R_j(a)) \cdot (\exists Q_i)Q_i(x)]$ has as an afep

$$[(a \vee s) \cdot (\exists r)r] \supset [(a \vee s) \cdot (\exists q)q].$$

(Note that R_j of the previous example is not bound by the initial quantifier (R), so is unaffected by the instantiation of R by Q that produces the consequent of the example.)

a6. $(\exists \mathbf{p})\mathbf{p} \equiv (\mathbf{q})[\mathbf{q} \equiv \mathbf{q}]$,

   where $\mathbf{p}$ and $\mathbf{q}$ are any proposition variables.

It is not difficult to determine that any afep as an instance of the above forms a1–a6 is valid. The only nonobvious cases are a5(ii) and (iii) and a6. Consider first a6. Its truth-value expansion would be:

$$(T \vee T) \equiv [(T \equiv T) \cdot (F \equiv F)],$$

which resolves first to $T \equiv T$, then to T, and hence is valid. In the consistency proof that follows, it is necessary to recall that an expression of the form $\mathbf{a} = \mathbf{b}$ is an abbreviation for $(\exists Id_i)Id_i(\mathbf{a},\mathbf{b})$, and that the latter has afeps of the form $(\exists \mathbf{p})\mathbf{p}$, which resolves to T. Similarly for $\mathbf{a} \neq \mathbf{b}$, which is an abbreviation of $\neg (\exists Id_i)Id_i(\mathbf{a},\mathbf{b})$, the corresponding afep is $\neg (\exists \mathbf{p})\mathbf{p}$, which resolves to $\neg T$, then to F.

As to a5(ii)(1′), in the process of the truth-value expansion of $(\mathbf{p})\mathbf{A}' \supset \mathbf{B}'$ there will result a finite set of conjuncts each of which will have one of two forms: '$(\mathbf{p})[\ ] \supset T$' or '$(\mathbf{p})[\ ] \supset F$', where T or F represent the results of a process of truth-value resolution of $\mathbf{B}'$, and '$(\mathbf{p})[\ ]$' represents a partial resolution of A' consisting in a logical matrix of truth-functional connectives among truth-values and $\mathbf{p}$, all other proposition variables and constants having had truth-values substituted for them. For example, consider the afep

$$(p)\,(r \cdot p) \supset (r \cdot q),$$

whose resolution proceeds as

$$[(p)(T \cdot p) \supset (T \cdot q)] \cdot [(p)(F \cdot p) \supset (F \cdot q)]$$
$$[(p)(T \cdot p) \supset (T \cdot T)] \cdot [(p)(F \cdot p) \supset (F \cdot T)] \cdot [(p)(T \cdot p) \supset (T \cdot F)] \cdot [(p)(F \cdot p)$$
$$\supset (F \cdot F)]$$
$$[(p)(T \cdot p) \supset T] \cdot [(p)(F \cdot p) \supset F] \cdot [(p)(T \cdot p) \supset F] \cdot [(p)(F \cdot p) \supset F].$$

Now all conjuncts of the form '$(\mathbf{p})[\ ] \supset T$' resolve to T independent of the truth-value of '$(\mathbf{p})[\ ]$'. Conjuncts of the form '$(\mathbf{p})[\ ] \supset F$' will also resolve to T for the following reason. Because $\mathbf{A}'$ and $\mathbf{B}'$ are identical in form, except that $\mathbf{B}'$ contains a proposition variable **q** or constant **c** where **A′** contains **p**, then any conjunct '(**p**)[ ] ⊃ *F*' in the resolution process is such as to derive from a conjunct of the form '(**p**)[ ] ⊃ { }', where [ ] and { } are identical truth-functionally, { } containing only truth-functional connectives among truth-values, and the two differing only in the fact that { } will have a truth-value substituted for **q** or **c** in all the places where [ ] retains **p**. We are now working with the case where { } has the value of *F* on this truth-value assignment. Hence, when (**p**)[ ] is resolved to the conjunction [.*T*.] · [.*F*.], where first *T*, then *F*, is substituted for **p** in [ ], one of these conjuncts will be identical to { } and hence likewise have a value of *F*. With the resolutant to the antecedent of (**p**)[ ] ⊃ *F* being *F*, the entire conjunction has the value *T*. Hence, an afep of the form (**p**)**A′** ⊃ **B′** resolves to a finite set of conjuncts each one of which has value *T*, thus the afep is valid.

Afeps corresponding to a5(ii)(2′)—that is, of the form <afep of (∃**a**)(**a** = **b**)> ⊃ [(**p**)**A′** ⊃ **B′**]—are thus also valid, since the antecedent resolves to *T*, as does the consequent on the previous analysis.

As for the validity of the afeps of a5(iii), recall that these are of the form **A′** ⊃ **B′**, where **A′** and **B′** are identical in form with the possible exception of containing different proposition variables; but if this is the case, these corresponding variables will always be quantified identically. The example given above was:

$$(R)[A_1(R) \vee R_j(a)) \cdot (\exists R_i)R_i(x)] \supset [(A_1(R) \vee R_j(a)) \cdot (\exists Q_i)Q_i(x)],$$

which has as an afep

$$[(a \vee s) \cdot (\exists r)r] \supset [(a \vee s) \cdot (\exists q)q].$$

Because all such conditional afeps will consist in an antecedent and a consequent that are identical, except possibly for the choice of variable of quantification, and because the truth-value resolution of quantified expressions that are identical except for the variable of quantification—for example, $(\exists r)r$ and $(\exists q)q$—is the same, then, upon complete truth-value resolution, these conditional afeps will resolve to a finite conjunction of conditionals each of which has an antecedent and a consequent with the same truth-value; hence each resolves to *T*. Thus, all such afeps are valid.

The second step in proving the consistency of restricted PPL is the necessity of showing that the rules of inference of PPL preserve the property of having a valid afep, that is, any wff that can be inferred by the rules of inference from wffs that have valid afeps will itself have valid afeps.

For inference rule R1,

if ⊢ **A** and ⊢ **A** ⊃ **B**, then ⊢ **B**,

if **A**′ and (**A** ⊃ **B**)′ are valid afeps, then so is **B**′. Assume **A**′ and (**A** ⊃ **B**)′ have the value T upon their truth-value resolutions. Then, since (**A** ⊃ **B**)′ is identical to **A**′ ⊃ **B**′, **A**′ ⊃ **B**′ will have the value T upon its truth-value resolution. But, for **A**′ and **A**′ ⊃ **B**′ to resolve to T implies that **B**′ must resolve to T.

For inference rule R2,

if **a** is any variable, if ⊢ **A** then ⊢ (**a**)**A**,

if (**a**) does not bind a variable in predicate position in **A**, then, by the rules for constructing afeps, **A**′ and ((**a**)**A**)′ are identical, and validity is preserved. For example, for **A** as $(P_i)P_i(x)$ and (**a**)**A** as $(x)(P_i)P_i(x)$, an afep of both is (p)p. If (**a**) does bind a predicate position variable in **A**, then **a** is either an instance variable or an intension variable:

(i) if **a** is an instance variable, e.g.,

for **A** as $P_i(..)$ and (**a**)**A** as $(P_i)P_i(..)$,

then the truth-value expansions of **A**′ and ((**a**)**A**)′ are identical; hence validity is preserved, since **a** in **A** is a free variable in predicate position which, by the rules for constructing afeps, requires the proposition variable substituted for **a** in **A** to be universally quantified. In the example, constructing **A**′, we go from $P_i(..)$ to p to (p)p, which is identical to ((**a**)**A**)′, the form of afeps of $(P_i)P_i(..)$.

(ii) if **a** is an intension variable, e.g.,

for **A** as $(P_i)P_i(..)$ and (**a**)**A** as $(P)(P_i)P_i(..)$,

then again the truth-value expansions of **A**′ and ((**a**)**A**)′ are identical; hence validity is preserved, since the construction of afeps requires the deletion of intension variables. In the example, **A**′ has the form of (p)p, which is identical to ((**a**)**A**)′, the form of afeps of $(P)(P_i)P_i(..)$.

We have now shown that all instances of the axiom schemata A1–A6 of PPL have valid afeps and that the rules of inference guarantee that any wff inferred by these rules from the axioms has valid afeps. It follows that without an axiom of comprehension the restricted PPL is consistent, in that it can be shown that there are wffs of restricted PPL that are not theorems of restricted PPL. If the system were inconsistent, then any proposition would be derivable in it. Consider all wffs of restricted PPL of the form $\mathbf{A} \cdot \neg \mathbf{A}$—for example, $(P_i)P_i(x) \cdot \neg(P_i)P_i(x)$. The afeps of all such wffs would be of the form $\mathbf{A}' \cdot \neg \mathbf{A}'$ and would be invalid, hence no wff of the form $\mathbf{A} \cdot \neg \mathbf{A}$ can be a theorem of restricted PPL.

An Axiom of Comprehension and the Consistency of Full PPL

Let us now turn to the crucial problem of formulating for PPL a consistent axiom (schema) of comprehension (AC), an axiom that specifies the conditions for defining properties and relations in the object-language. The axiom will be a modification of the instance analog of the standard formulation; that is, it will be a modification of

(9.1) $(\exists R^n)(\mathbf{b}_1)(\mathbf{b}_2) \ldots (\mathbf{b}_m)[(\exists \mathbf{R}_i^n)\mathbf{R}_i^n(\mathbf{a}_1, \mathbf{a}_2, \ldots, \mathbf{a}_n) \equiv \phi].$

Note that, because of the device of extended binding, for 9.1 to be a closed wff of PPL, the list of variables $\mathbf{b}_1, \mathbf{b}_2, \ldots, \mathbf{b}_m$ must contain the variables $\mathbf{a}_1, \mathbf{a}_2, \ldots, \mathbf{a}_n$, as well as any full intension variable $\mathbf{P}$ not contained in the list of **a**s when one or more corresponding instances $\mathbf{P}_j$ are contained in the list of **a**s. Of course, 9.1 must be modified so as to avoid self-referential contradiction and be, so one would hope, a provably consistent extension of restricted PPL.

It is the axiom (schema) of comprehension of a system which, relative to the background semantics, specifies how intensions and their instances can be defined in terms of logical compounds of other such entities. For given conditions of the definiens, ϕ, the axiom guarantees the existence of a corresponding intension $\mathbf{R}$ and possibly some of its instances $\mathbf{R}_i$ as definienda. Because of this, a comprehension axiom warrants the introduction into the object-language of new intension constants and their instances—for example, Russell's property. The latter definitions are added to the object-language as 'noncreative' axioms, in the sense that they add to the vocabulary of the logic constants that name entities whose existence is already guaranteed by the comprehension axiom. In regard to existence, nothing can be proved in the system with the addition of these constants that could not have been proved without them.

What is essential, then, are restrictions on the formulation of definiens ϕ

such as will avoid the inconsistencies of the classical self-referential paradoxes of logic and semantics. To the extent that an ontology and its corresponding logic can distinguish with precision illegitimate from legitimate impredicative specifications and preclude the former in an other than ad hoc manner, to that extent, we have an indirect but powerful argument for the truth of the motivating semantics. We shall see below that the refinement of instance ontology and its logic, PPL, diagnose and dissolve a representative core of the classical paradoxes while at the same time allowing for legitimate impredicative definitions.

To provide the insights necessary for a consistent reformulation of an axiom of comprehension, we will examine Russell's property paradox in light of its PPL formulation. The paradox arises from the seemingly legitimate property of *not being self-predicative*. Some properties do not apply to themselves—for example, being red, being triangular, being prime—whereas others apparently do apply to themselves—for example, being a property, being abstract, being a concept, being a vague concept. In standard extended predicate logic, Russell's property, Rus, is defined as

(9.2) $(P)[Rus(P) \equiv \neg P(P)]$.

This is standardly classified as an 'impredicative' definition, due to the fact that the definiens contains a universally quantified predicate position variable that ranges over the class containing the same entity being defined as the predicate in the definiendum. Definition 9.2 is a paradigm example of a subclass of impredicative definitions that renders the entire genre suspect. For, instantiating P with Rus, we have the contradiction:

$Rus(Rus) \equiv \neg Rus(Rus)$.

A common reaction is that though there is no such property as specified in 9.2, nonetheless, intuitively, there would seem to be a property that we are aiming at but miss because some refinement is wanting in our ontological/logical analysis. It is my point to show that relation instances and their logic constitute such a refinement. Translated into PPL, 9.2 becomes

(9.3) $(P)[(\exists Rus_i)Rus_i(P) \equiv (P_j)\neg P_j(P)]$.

In English, for every property (universal) P, there exists an instance of Russell's property that applies to P if and only if no instance of P applies to P. However, as stated in 9.3, one can yet derive a contradiction when P is replaced by Rus:

$(\exists \text{Rus}_i)\text{Rus}_i(\text{Rus}) \equiv (\text{Rus}_j) \neg \text{Rus}_j(\text{Rus})$.

Hence, there can exist no intension corresponding to Rus as defined in 9.3. This correct conclusion can be derived formally within PPL by modifying 9.1 to

(9.4) $(\mathbf{R}^n)\{(\exists \mathbf{Q}^n)(\mathbf{Q}^n = \mathbf{R}^n) \equiv (\mathbf{b}_1)(\mathbf{b}_2) \ldots (\mathbf{b}_m)[(\exists \mathbf{R}_i^n)\mathbf{R}_i^n(\mathbf{a}_1, \mathbf{a}_2, \ldots, \mathbf{a}_n) \equiv \phi]\}$.

Then, for the particular case of the proposed Russell property,

(9.5) $(\exists Q)(Q = \text{Rus}) \equiv (P)[(\exists \text{Rus}_i)\text{Rus}_i(P) \equiv (P_j) \neg P_j(P)]$.

The falsity of the right-hand side of the main biconditional in 9.5 implies the falsity of the left-hand side; that is, there is no intension identical to Rus.

Though an axiom of comprehension of the form 9.4 would render PPL consistent, it does not provide an insight into the self-referential mechanism involved in Russell's property whereby the intuitive, legitimate concept we attempt to grasp by it can be freed from contradiction. One of our goals here is to distinguish legitimate from illegitimate impredicative reasoning and to eschew the latter within PPL. To this end, I suggest that the requisite insight is close at hand. Concentrating upon the portion of 9.5 that is 9.3, we observe that if the universal instance quantifier of the definiens on the right, (Rus_j), is restricted to range over every instance of Rus except the instance of the definiendum on the left, Rus_i, then the universal denial of the definiens would be restricted so as to exempt the particular assertion of the definiendum, and thus no self-contradiction would result. Such a restriction captures the positive, classic condition on all definitions: that the definiendum not be defined *idem per idem*— that is, not in terms of itself. The necessary restriction can be accomplished by introducing the formal device of a 'bridging' variable, Rus_h, and rewriting 9.3 as

(9.6) $(P)(\text{Rus}_h)\{(\exists \text{Rus}_i)[\text{Rus}_i(P) \cdot \text{Rus}_i = \text{Rus}_h] \equiv (P_j)[P_j \neq \text{Rus}_h \supset \neg P_j(P)]\}$.

Instantiating P with Rus, we get

(9.7) $(\text{Rus}_h)\{(\exists \text{Rus}_i)[\text{Rus}_i(\text{Rus}) \cdot \text{Rus}_i = \text{Rus}_h] \equiv (\text{Rus}_j)[\text{Rus}_j \neq \text{Rus}_h \supset \neg \text{Rus}_j(\text{Rus})]\}$.

What 9.7 says is that in the limiting, impredicative case of P = Rus, if every instance of Rus, except any that takes Rus as a subject, does not have Rus as a subject, then there is an instance of Rus that has Rus as a subject. It follows that

Rus applies to Rus. This is seen clearly from the fact that no self-contradiction is involved in 9.6.

Assume that Rus does not apply to itself:

(a) $(Rus_i) \neg Rus_i(Rus)$.

Then by analogs in PPL of inferences sanctioned by standard predicate logic,

(b) $(Rus_i)(\neg Rus_i(Rus) \vee \neg(Rus_i = Rus_i))$.
(c) $\neg (\exists Rus_i)(Rus_i(Rus) \cdot Rus_i = Rus_i)$.
(d) $\neg (Rus_j)[Rus_j \neq Rus_i \supset Rus_j(Rus)]$ instantion and negation on 9.6
(e) $(\exists Rus_j)[Rus_j \neq Rus_i \cdot Rus_j(Rus)]$.
(f) $(\exists Rus_j)Rus_j(Rus)$.

Yet (f) contradicts (a). Assume, now, that Rus does apply to itself; then

(g) $(\exists Rus_i)Rus_i(Rus)$.

Let Rus_1 be any instance such that $Rus_1(Rus)$, then by 9.6,

(h) $(Rus_j)[Rus_j \neq Rus_1 \supset \neg Rus_j(Rus)]$.

But here (h) does not contradict the assumption (g). Hence, Russell's property as defined in 9.6 is not self-contradictory; indeed, by the last result, it is predicable of itself.[13]

Despite this success, however, 9.6 as is will not do. To see why, let $Rus_1(Tri)$ and $Rus_2(Sqr)$ be the statements, respectively, that Rus_1 applies to the intension Triangle and Rus_2 to the intension Square, statements which are true since neither Triangle nor Square apply (i.e., have instances which apply) to themselves as intensions. Now it is possible to instantiate 9.6 to yield

$$(\exists Rus_i)[Rus_i(Sqr) \cdot Rus_i = Rus_1] \equiv (Sqr_j)[Sqr_j \neq Rus_1 \supset \neg Sqr_j(Sqr)].$$

Because the right bijunct is true, it follows that

$$(\exists Rus_i)[Rus_i(Sqr) \cdot Rus_i = Rus_1],$$

and hence that

$Rus_1(Sqr)$.

Now we have $Rus_1(Tri)$ and $Rus_1(Sqr)$: that is, the same instance of Rus applying to two distinct subjects, which means that Rus_1 has the character of a universal, not that of an unrepeatable instance. Yet, it was precisely the goal of the PPL formalization to maintain the rigid distinction of the motivating semantics between recurrent intensions and their occurrent instances, as stated in the principle of subject uniqueness (SU). It is not difficult, however, to modify 9.6 in order to avoid these difficulties. We need only eliminate the biconditional in favor of two conditionals in the form of:

(9.8) $(P)(Rus_h)\{[(\exists Rus_i)[Rus_i(P) \cdot Rus_i = Rus_h] \supset (P_j)[P_j \neq Rus_h \supset \neg P_j(P)]] \cdot [(P_j)[P_j \neq Rus_h \supset \neg P_j(P)] \supset (\exists Rus_i)Rus_i(P)]\}.$

This, together with the given

$(Sqr_j)[Sqr_j \neq Rus_1 \supset \neg Sqr_j(Sqr)],$

renders only

$(\exists Rus_i)Rus_i(Sqr),$

with no implication that any such Rus_i is Rus_1.

Moreover, as the reader can verify, in the cases where $P \neq Rus$ and hence $P_j \neq Rus_h$ is true for all P_j and Rus_h, 9.8 implies

(9.9) $(\exists Rus_i)Rus_i(P) \equiv (P_j)\neg P_j(P).$

In view of these results, we could use the analogy that refined PPL is to standard predicate logic as relativity mechanics is to classical mechanics, and that the complications of 9.8 play the role of 'Lorenz transformations' in PPL. In the 'ordinary' predicative case of $P \neq Rus$, the form of 9.8 reduces to that of 9.9, the classic definitional form specifying Russell's property.

Note that 9.8 is logically equivalent to 9.7 in the limiting case of $Rus = P$, and thus the above demonstration that Rus is noncontradictory and applies to itself remains unchanged. Also note that if 9.8 were added as an axiom to restricted PPL, the extended system would remain consistent. For, a corresponding afep of 9.8 is

$[(\exists r)(r \cdot T) \supset (p)(F \supset \neg p)] \cdot [(p)(F \supset \neg p) \supset (\exists r)r].$

The truth-value resolution is then, first,

$\{[(T \cdot T) \vee (F \cdot T)] \supset [(F \supset \neg T) \cdot (F \supset \neg F)]\} \cdot \{[(F \supset \neg T) \cdot (F \supset \neg F)] \supset T\},$

which resolves to T.

I note in passing that the latter, instance analysis of Russell's property paradox would extend mutatis mutandis to, and thus avoid the contradiction within, Russell's relation paradox—'the relation that relates all and only those relations that do not relate themselves'.[14]

The above instance analysis of Russell's property paradox suggests the following axiom of comprehension for PPL:

Axiom (Schema) of Comprehension (AC):
$$(\mathbf{R}^n)\{(\exists \mathbf{Q}^n)(\mathbf{Q}^n = \mathbf{R}^n) \equiv (\mathbf{b}_1)(\mathbf{b}_2) \ldots (\mathbf{b}_m)(\mathbf{R}_h^n)\{[(\exists \mathbf{R}_i^n)[\mathbf{R}_i^n(\mathbf{a}_1, \mathbf{a}_2, \ldots, \mathbf{a}_n) \cdot \mathbf{R}_i^n = \mathbf{R}_h^n] \supset \phi] \cdot [\phi \supset (\exists \mathbf{R}_i^n)\mathbf{R}_i^n(\mathbf{a}_1, \mathbf{a}_2, \ldots, \mathbf{a}_n)]\}\},$$

where AC is a closed wff of PPL such that:

(i) $\mathbf{R}^n$ is not free in ϕ;

(ii) the only variables of ϕ are $\mathbf{a}_1, \mathbf{a}_2, \ldots, \mathbf{a}_n$ and possibly instance variables that by extended binding by a quantifier having a member of $\mathbf{a}_1, \mathbf{a}_2, \ldots, \mathbf{a}_n$ as an operator variable are also bound in ϕ,

   e.g., $\ldots \equiv (P)(R_h)\{[(\exists R_i)[R_i(P) \cdot R_i = R_h] \supset (\exists P_j)P_j(P)] \cdot \ldots$;

(iii) there are no instance quantifiers among $(\mathbf{b}_1)(\mathbf{b}_2) \ldots (\mathbf{b}_m)$ that bind instance variables in predicate position in ϕ (this implies that all instance quantifiers binding instance variables in ϕ are themselves in ϕ);

(iv) all occurrences of negation in ϕ are within literals;

(v) all *existential* instance quantifiers (full or limited) of ϕ binding variables in predicate positions will be at the level of literals (i.e., the only wff within the scope of an existential quantifier, besides the quantifier itself, is a literal);

(vi) all *universal* instance quantifiers $(\mathbf{P}_j^m)$ of ϕ (full or limited) binding variables in predicate position will have occurrences of the form $(\mathbf{P}_j^m)(\mathbf{P}_j^m \neq \mathbf{R}_h^n \supset \psi)$, where ψ is a literal.

By extension, we shall continue to refer to expressions taking the place of ϕ as the definiens and the instances of $\mathbf{R}_i^n$ and, through them, the intensions $\mathbf{R}^n$, as definienda.

It is important to note that if ϕ is such as to fall under (v) above—that is, if it contains only predicate position variables quantified by existential instance quantifiers—then the instance of AC containing such a ϕ is a simple extension of 9.1, specifically the form 9.4:

$$(\mathbf{R}^n)\{(\exists \mathbf{Q}^n)(\mathbf{Q}^n = \mathbf{R}^n) \equiv (\mathbf{b}_1)(\mathbf{b}_2) \ldots (\mathbf{b}_m)\{(\exists \mathbf{R}_i^n)\mathbf{R}_i^n(\mathbf{a}_1, \mathbf{a}_2, \ldots, \mathbf{a}_n) \equiv \phi\}\}.$$

This is the PPL analog of the axiom of comprehension formulated for standard predicate logics. In this fact one observes the limiting case status of classical predicate logic. By analogy, standard predicate logic is to instance logic as the study of visible light is to the study of the entire electromagnetic spectrum. Or, returning to the analogy introduced above, 9.1 is to AC as classical mechanics is to relativity mechanics, and just as standard predicate logics, like classical mechanics, are sufficient for most ordinary purposes, so the self-referential paradoxes, similar to the aberrations in the orbit of the planet Mercury, signal a grossness in want of a more general, minutely controlled theory. It is the precision of predicate instances that makes it possible to prevent definitions idem per idem, yet save our intuitions concerning the legitimacy of certain impredicative definitions.

It is a simple matter to determine that all instances of AC yield only valid afeps, where any afep of an instance of AC will have the form

$$\{T \equiv \{[(\exists \mathbf{r})[\mathbf{r} \cdot T] \supset \phi'] \cdot [\phi' \supset (\exists \mathbf{r})\mathbf{r}]\}\},$$

where ϕ' is the afep of ϕ. First, recall that the translation procedure from wffs of PPL to wffs of EPC retains only *predicate* position instance constants, or instance variables and their quantifiers, and then substitutes distinct proposition constants or variables, respectively, for distinct instance symbols. By conditions (i)–(vi) of AC, the afep ϕ' will consist in only truth-functionally combined expressions of the possible forms $(\exists \mathbf{p})\mathbf{p}$, $(\exists \mathbf{p})\neg \mathbf{p}$, $(\mathbf{q})[F \supset \mathbf{q}]$, $(\mathbf{q})[F \supset \neg \mathbf{q}]$, $(\exists \mathbf{p})\mathbf{p}$ and $(\exists \mathbf{p})\neg \mathbf{p}$, which correspond, respectively, to possible subformulas of ϕ of the forms $(\exists \mathbf{P}_j)\mathbf{P}_j(..)$, $(\exists \mathbf{P}_j)\neg \mathbf{P}_j(..)$, $(\mathbf{Q}_k)[\mathbf{Q}_k \neq \mathbf{R}_h \supset \mathbf{Q}_k(..)]$, $(\mathbf{Q}_k)[\mathbf{Q}_k \neq \mathbf{R}_h \supset \neg \mathbf{Q}_k(..)]$, $\mathbf{C}_n(..)$ or $\neg \mathbf{C}_n(..)$, where $\mathbf{C}_n$ is an instance constant (i.e., n is natural number). Recall that negation occurs only at the level of literals in ϕ, so it will occur in any corresponding afep only at the level of atomic proposition variables, not compounds—for example, not as in $\neg(\mathbf{p} \cdot \mathbf{q})$.

In outline, any instance of AC would have afeps with at most components of the schematic form

(I) $\{T \equiv \{[(\exists \mathbf{r})[\mathbf{r} \cdot T] \supset [..(\exists \mathbf{p})\mathbf{p}..(\exists \mathbf{p})\neg \mathbf{p}..(\mathbf{q})[F \supset \mathbf{q})..(\mathbf{q})[F \supset \neg \mathbf{q})..]] \cdot [[..(\exists \mathbf{p})\mathbf{p}..(\exists \mathbf{p})\neg \mathbf{p}..(\mathbf{q})[F \supset \mathbf{q})..(\mathbf{q})[F \supset \neg \mathbf{q})..] \supset T]\}\},$

where both expressions with the ellipses are abbreviations for an expression of EPC with one or more occurrences of one or more expressions of the indicated forms, and ellipses represent truth-functional combination, if any, by only the binary logical connectives ($\cdot$, $\vee$, $\supset$, $\equiv$), with *no* occurrences of negation, $\neg$. Because the truth-value resolution of the forms $(\exists \mathbf{p})\mathbf{p}$, $(\exists \mathbf{p})\neg \mathbf{p}$, $(\mathbf{q})[F \supset \mathbf{q})$, and $(\mathbf{q})[F \supset \neg \mathbf{q})$ are each T, (I) resolves first to

$$\{T \equiv \{[((T \cdot T) \vee (T \cdot F)) \supset [..T..T..T..T..]] \cdot [[..T..T..T..T..] \supset T]\}\}.$$

And again, because the ellipses represent groupings of truth-functional combination by means of only the binary logical connectives, $\cdot$, $\vee$, $\supset$, and $\equiv$, with *no* occurrences of negation, $\neg$, the entire expression resolves to T. Hence, all instances of AC have valid afeps, so AC is a consistent addition to the already consistent restricted PPL.

This is a significant result. With a logic inspired by an instance ontology, and in particular under the seemingly simplest comprehension axiom AC necessitated by it, it is possible to include in the language of PPL both ordinary and innocuous nonimpredicative, as well as some formerly impugned impredicative, definitions of intensions and their instances. This is possible in the following way. First, note that section (vi) of AC precludes any definiens from containing expressions of the forms $(\mathbf{P}^m)[..(\mathbf{P}_j^m)\mathbf{P}_j^m(..)..]$, $(\mathbf{P}^m)[..(\mathbf{P}_j^m)\neg \mathbf{P}_j^m(..)..]$, $(\exists \mathbf{P}^m)[..(\mathbf{P}_j^m)\mathbf{P}_j^m(..)..]$, $(\exists \mathbf{P}^m)[..(\mathbf{P}_j^m)\neg \mathbf{P}_j^m(..)..]$, $(\mathbf{C}_i^m)\mathbf{C}_i^m(..)$, $(\mathbf{C}_i^m)\neg \mathbf{C}_i^m(..)$, where $\mathbf{C}_i^m$ is a limited intension variable. Intuitively, the first two types of expressions would fall under the definition of 'impredicative' when extended to take into account the refinement of predicate instances. I shall consider it so extended; that is, a definition is *impredicative in PPL* if and only if the definiens contains predicate position instance variables bound by both a universal instance quantifier and, through extended binding, a universal intension quantifier. Definitions containing occurrences of expressions of the first two forms above are *illegitimately* impredicative in PPL, whereas definitions conforming to section (vi) of AC, where the prescribed clause $\mathbf{P}_j^m \neq \mathbf{R}_h^n \supset ..$ prevents idem per idem definitions, are *legitimately* impredicative in PPL. With definitions containing expressions of the form $(\mathbf{P}_j^m)[\mathbf{P}_j^m \neq \mathbf{R}_h^n \supset \psi]$, at the point of instantiation where $\mathbf{P}_j^m = \mathbf{R}_h^n$, these expressions have truth-values of T independent of the truth-value of ψ, and at this point the truth-value of $\mathbf{R}_i^n(..)$ of the definiendum ceases to be a function of itself or its negation. The remaining four forms of expression listed above likewise require the preventative clause (vi) in order to enforce the requirement against definition idem per idem in interpretations with a domain of one intension (this single intension would have to be the identity intension, Id).

The above AC can then be viewed as substantiating Gödel's conjecture that

It might even turn out that it is possible to assume every concept to be significant everywhere except for certain "singular points" or "limiting points," so that the paradoxes would appear as something analogous to dividing by zero. Such a system would be most satisfactory in the following respect: our logical intuitions would then remain correct up to certain minor correcitons, i.e., they could then be considered to give an essentially correct, only somewhat "blurred" picture of the real state of affairs.[15]

In the refined logic of PPL, to 'divide by zero' is to define an instance $\mathbf{R}_i$ in terms of itself. In PPL, 'division by terms not zero' is to define $\mathbf{R}_i$ in terms of instances $\mathbf{R}_j$ not identical to $\mathbf{R}_i$.

Regarding Gödel's visual analogy of the 'blurred', what the above shows is that it is not our logical sight which is defective and in need of correction with pragmatic 'type-focal lenses'; our logical intuitions are correct in their ordinary field of focus. What is needed for some minute purposes (e.g., avoiding illegitimate impredicative contradictions or formally distinguishing identity from indiscernibility) is the microscopic amplification of relation instances.

There is another feature of the AC that deserves comment: this concerns the restriction of instance quantifiers of the definiens to the level of literals. That is, besides the inductive weight of rendering a consistency proof possible, what rationale is there for restricting instance quantifiers to the level of literals? Certainly by instance analogs of standard rules of quantifier distribution (or 'rules of passage'), it is possible to infer from expressions allowed in the definiens of AC to expressions with instance quantifiers not at the level of literals— for example, from $(\exists R_i)R_i(x) \vee (\exists R_i)R_i(y)$ to infer $(\exists R_i)[R_i(x) \vee R_i(y)]$, and conversely. Note, however, that, as usual, we cannot infer from $(\exists R_i)R_i(x) \cdot (\exists R_i)R_i(y)$ to $(\exists R_i)[R_i(x) \cdot R_i(y)]$. Moreover, under the motivating instance ontology, the latter expression asserts that there exists an instance that is identical as a predicate to what, without special restrictions, are two distinct individuals, x and y; that is, it contradicts the principle of subject uniqueness (SU) characteristic of instance ontology—that no relation instance can have more than one relata n-tuple. By requiring instance quantifiers at least to 'begin' at the level of literals, the definiens of AC prevents the violation of SU.

As a final point concerning the formulation of AC, note that the restricting clauses of the definiens, $P_i^n \neq R_j^m \supset ..$, are such that it is not necessary that n equal m. Of course, under the intended ontology no two instances of intensions with different polyacity could be identical. But this would have to be added as an additional axiom (schema). Would this be a nonlogical axiom? It would seem not, and here again logic and ontology would appear to be indistinguishable.

Extending this last point, some philosophers have claimed that it is with the axiom of comprehension that one slides across the boundary from logic to ontology. The argument is that with such an axiom one asserts the existence of intensions and, in PPL, possibly instances thereof, and that it is the province of ontology, not logic, to warrant such claims. I have previously maintained that ontology and logic coincide at a point prior to existential claims; namely, at the point where logic embodies syntactically, as formal predication, the presupposed semantics of an ontic theory of material predication. To this extent, predicate logic is a formalized ontology. Even so, logic proper is not free of existential claims. Because of its universality, a priori necessity, and cognitive status only, it is difficult to deny that the relation of identity, Id, is a logical relation. If it is, then logic is committed to the existence of at least one specific intension. Moreover, with the additional refinement of relation instances, under axiom A6, logic is committed not only to the explicitly assertable existence of the identity intension but also to the existence of an instance thereof; $(\exists Id_i)Id_i(Id,Id)$. Claims of existence do not necessarily exclude one from the domain of logic. The overall point is that there is no sharp boundary between logic and ontology, but rather a symbiosis at a root level that is primarily a theory of ontic predication. Predicate logic is not topic-neutral in the sense of being free of ontic commitments; the claim to the contrary made of first-order predicate logic is an illusion resulting from the latter's relative unsophistication in spelling out the nature of predication, abetted by the traditional neglect of the issue as a topic of ontological analysis. In refined contrast, PPL embodies in its formation rules the ontic principles of instance predicates, IP (only unrepeatable relation instances are ontic predicates), and immanent instance realism, IR (distinct instances $\mathbf{R}_i^n$, $\mathbf{R}_j^n$, . . . share a numerically identical aspect $\mathbf{R}^n$). Note that if PPL were extended to include the principles of subject uniqueness (SU) and instance uniqueness (IU), then, because their corresponding afeps are valid (as the reader can easily verify), this extension of PPL would be consistent.

The above formulation of PPL was inspired and guided by the 'informal' intensional semantics argued for previously. However, there is no apparent reason why a formalized model-theoretic semantics could not be devised for PPL. Presumably, it would be but a straightforward modification of existing formalized semantics for logics of nominalized predicates (e.g., that of Cocchiarella[16]). Paralleling results from these existing systems, soundness and completeness theorems for PPL would be forthcoming. I shall not attempt such a formalization here, however.

Diagnosing and Preventing Self-Referential Paradox

Despite a vast literature on the self-referential paradoxes and a variety of admirably ingenious but ad hoc devices for getting round them, there is still no widely accepted 'solution'.[17] A solution would have to address satisfactorily what Charles Chihara has distinguished as the diagnostic and preventative problems: "The diagnostic problem is to seek out that which is deceiving us and, if possible, explain why we have been deceived. The preventative problem, briefly put, is the problem of how to set up, with the least loss of expressive and deductive power, logical systems or, perhaps, languages, within which such paradoxes cannot arise."[18]

Presumably, what Chihara has in mind as a solution to the diagnostic problem is that it satisfy Russell's criterion that, to avoid being ad hoc, it "result naturally and inevitably from our positive doctrines," being consonant with our logical common sense.[19] Russell's criterion for a solution to the preventative problem was, in addition to the elimination of contradictions, the retention of as much of mathematics as possible. The difficulty specific to mathematics is the apparent noneliminability of impredicative definitions from widely accepted results ranging from those essential to the defining of natural numbers to central theorems of real analysis (e.g., the Bolzano–Weierstrass theorem) to the 'diagonal reasoning' of Cantor's theorem and the self-reference of Gödel's theorems. Because of the profoundly suspect nature of impredicative definitions in general, some theorists—for instance, Herman Weyl—have been willing to sacrifice parts of classical mathematics dependent upon them. Similarly, because of the pivotal use of an impredicatively defined set, Henri Poincaré rejected Cantor's theorem—the proof that the power set of a set s has a greater cardinality than s.

The absence of a uniform solution, despite years of effort, has produced despair in some quarters and desperate acts in others—for example, statements that the liar sentence or the sentence 'The Russell set is a member of itself' are both true and false.[20] The situation has been assessed as a "massive failure on the part of the logical community."[21] This assessment is made, of course, against a background assumption that our intuitions concerning the offending properties, relations, sets, truth-predicates, and so forth are essentially correct, though flawed in some yet to be detected detail. Others—for example, Quine—make the more radical assessment that in these matters our intuitions are bankrupt and that we must take a pragmatic approach to avoiding contradiction and explicating basic concepts. However, the success above in diagnosing Russell's property paradox with only minimum adjustments to our logical intuitions gives us warrant to think that failure to uniformly diagnose and prevent the impredicative paradoxes is due to the lack hitherto of a refined analytic instrument such as PPL. In conceptual analysis, as in brain surgery, the work that can be done is delimited by the refinement of our tools. Limits on the scope of standard predicate logics are widely recognized: problems of intensional contexts, predicate modifiers (e.g., adverbs), distinguishing identity from indiscernibility, and so on. Those who insist upon these 'classical logics' as canonical, like those on the ontological side who cling to individuals and their properties and relations (whether taken as real or as syncategoremata only) as exhaustive, cut themselves off not only from potential solutions but even from clear formulations of the problems.

In the following I shall focus upon what I take to be three further, representative types of self-referential paradox: Russell's set paradox, the generalized Fitch–Curry paradox, and the simple liar paradox and its strengthened and divine liar kin.[22] In each case, when the offending property or relation is defined with the refinement of instances under the restrictions of AC, no contradictions arise; respectively, Russell's set is found to be an element of itself, a Fitch–Curry relation does not allow the derivation of any proposition whatsoever, and the liar and strengthened liar propositions are false, and the divine liar is disarmed.

Russell's Set Paradox

Consider first the paradox of Russell's set, r, the set of all sets that are not elements of themselves. When parsed in standard predicate logic, with $\in$, the element-of relation, we have

$$(9.10)\quad (x)[\in(x,r) \equiv \neg \in(x,x)],$$

which, when $x = r$, results in the contradiction $\in(r,r) \equiv \neg \in(r,r)$. Analogous to the above definition under AC of Russell's property, with the help of *instances* of the element-of relation, Russell's set would be defined as

(9.11) $(x)(\in_h)\{[(\exists\in_i)[\in_i(x,r) \cdot \in_i = \in_h] \supset (\in_k)[\in_k \neq \in_h \supset \neg\in_k(x,x)]] \cdot$
   $[(\in_k)[\in_k \neq \in_h \supset \neg\in_k(x,x)] \supset (\exists\in_i)\in_i(x,r)]\}.$

I have here left understood the relevant subsuming biconditional

$\{(\exists Q^2)(Q^2 = \in^2) \equiv \dots\}$

that makes AC as applied to the present analysis. Because this expansion adds nothing to the analysis of the self-reference involved in the paradoxes to be considered below, I shall continue to leave it unstated.

Now 9.11 does not lead to a contradiction, but rather to the result that Russell's set as so defined is an element of itself.

(i) Assume that r is not an element of itself, that is,

(9.12) $\neg(\exists\in_i)\in_i(r,r)$ or $(\in_i)\neg\in_i(r,r).$

This together with the proper instantiation of 9.12 yields

a. $(\exists\in_k)[\in_k \neq \in_i \cdot \in_k(r,r)]$

and hence

b. $(\exists\in_k)\in_k(r,r),$

which contradicts assumption (i).

(ii) Now on the other hand, assume that r is an element of itself, that is,

(9.13) $(\exists\in_i)\in_i(r,r).$

As with the analogous assumption of Russell's property under AC, no contradiction appears. For, with the proper instantiation of 9.11, it would follow only that

a. $(\in_k)[\in_k \neq \in_i \supset \neg\in_k(r,r)],$

and no contradiction arises at the dangerous and limiting ('division by zero') case $\in_k = \in_i$.

What is significant about this analysis of Russell's set paradox is its assigning the crux of the problem to the previously unobservable fact that in defining a class we *simultaneously specify the existence of instances of the element-of relation*. Here we have the extensional analog of the thesis that the definition of an intension is the simultaneous specification of its potential instances. And in this paradox, as in all the paradoxes that will be analyzed here, it is through instances of relations that the exact mechanisms of legitimate versus contradictory self-predication become apparent. Contrary to a standard assessment, Russell's set is a symptom not of our inadequate understanding of the concept of set or the element-of relation, but rather of a lack of refinement in our concept of predication.

The Generalized Fitch–Curry Paradox

The Fitch–Curry paradox is instructive because its formulation does not contain the negation operator, $\neg$, and so is said to show the limited value of proposed solutions to the paradoxes that restrict themselves to modifying our understanding of negation in some way.[23] From the propositional function $\in(x,x) \supset p$, assuming that it determines a class f, it is possible to prove p, where p is any arbitrarily chosen proposition—for instance, $q \cdot \neg q$. The reasoning can be extended to what I shall call the generalized Fitch–Curry paradox by substituting for the element-of relation, $\in$, any binary relation, R. In standard first-order predicate logic containing proposition variables (extended predicate logic is not needed here), let R and f be such that

(9.14) $(x)[R(x,f) \equiv R(x,x) \supset p]$.

Then,

(a)	$R(f,f)$	assumption
(b)	$R(f,f) \supset p$	(a) and 9.14
(c)	p	*modus ponens* on (a) and (b)
(d)	$R(f,f) \supset p$	conditional proof on (a)–(c)
(e)	$R(f,f)$	(d) and 9.14
(f)	p	modus ponens on (d) and (e).

What this shows is that there cannot exist a relation R and an entity f (individual, set, etc.) that satisfy 9.14; otherwise, any proposition p follows. Yet, under the naive axiom of set comprehension, it was thought that there must exist a set f for R = $\in$. The Fitch–Curry paradox is avoided, however, when relation instances are used in a manner similar to how they were used in the previous paradoxes. Then 9.14 would be rewritten as

(9.15) $(x)(R_h)\{[(\exists R_i)[R_i(x,f) \cdot R_i = R_h] \supset (R_k)[R_k \neq R_h \supset (R_k(x,x) \supset p)]] \cdot$
$[(R_k)[R_k \neq R_h \supset (R_k(x,x) \supset p)] \supset (\exists R_i)R_i(x,f)]\}$.

To see that p does not follow from this, we parallel the above proof by first instantiating 9.15 and separating the left conjunct as

(a) $(\exists R_i)[R_i(f,f) \cdot R_i = R_i] \supset (R_k)[R_k \neq R_i \supset (R_k(f,f) \supset p)]$.

(b) $(\exists R_i)R_i(f,f)$ assumption

(c) $R_i(f,f)$ existential instantiation on (b)

(d) $(\exists R_i)[R_i(f,f) \cdot R_i = R_i]$ addition on (b) and existential gener-
                                                                 alization

(e) $(R_k)[R_k \neq R_i \supset (R_k(f,f) \supset p)]$ modus ponens on (a) and (d)

(f) $R_i \neq R_i \supset (R_i(f,f) \supset p)$ universal instantiation on (e)

The antecedent of the conditional in line (f) prevents (f) and (c) from otherwise resulting in a further line (g) containing p only. Note that even if there were such a line (g), discharging the assumption in (b) we would have only $(\exists R_i)(R_i(f,f) \supset$ p; but this is not the right-hand side of (a), hence we cannot get $(\exists R_i)R_i(f,f)$, so cannot conclude to a final line p.

The Liar Paradox and Its Kin

Let us now turn the application of instance analysis under PPL to the ancient, paradigmatic semantic paradox of the simple liar and show how it and, by direct extension, some of its variants can be solved in the same manner as the Russell and the Fitch–Curry paradoxes and their variants. In particular, it will be seen that with the analytic tool of relation instances, the liar, the strengthened liar, the divine liar, and, by implied extension, the cyclic liar as well are each analogously disarmed without the need of any of the distorting devices of a Tarski/Kripkean language/metalanguage hierarchy, truth-value gaps, truth-value gluts, or many-value logics.[24]

The simple liar is:

(L) This sentence is false.

Or,

L = L is false.

If L is true, then it is false, and if false, then it is true.

It is often argued that what the liar and its semantic kin show is that our ordinary conception of truth (and falsity), reference, or negation is naive and inadequate, and that what is needed is a rigorous semantic theory correcting our grosser intuitions.[25] Such a theory is said to be of the utmost urgency since there are no concepts more global and fundamental to all rationality than those of turth, reference, and negation. Though the latter point is well taken, we shall see in this section that, to the contrary, the liar and the like are not symptomatic of our confused understanding of these concepts. It is not our concepts of truth, reference, or negation that must be refined; rather, it is the underlying theory of predication that must be sharpened to include relation instances. Once instances are admitted, the axiom of comprehension (AC) surfaces, and under it the resulting, consistent definition of truth displays no relevant difference from the definitions of the predicates involved in the other impredicative paradoxes examined, each requiring simply the same type of exclusionary clauses in the respective definitions in order to avoid the limiting self-contradictory case. Hence, we have stronger warrant for the thesis that PPL will be able to give a uniform analysis of all the classical self-referential paradoxes and in this confirm the widely held belief (held by Russell, e.g.) that the often repeated Peano–Ramsey distinction between *logical* (Russell's, Cantor's, Burali–Forti, etc.) and *semantical* antinomies (liar, Richard's, Berry's, etc.) is superficial, turning upon nothing specific to the intensions involved.

Before bringing PPL to bear upon the simple liar, it is worth rehearsing briefly three standard proposals for disarming L and the like, along with their shortcomings. Consider first a close relative of the simple liar known as the strengthened liar:

(SL) This sentence is not true.

The strengthened liar arises as a rebuff to theories which attempt to prevent the simple liar by claiming that our underlying semantics should be modified to allow L to have either no truth-value (truth-gap theories) or some third truth-value. With these maneuvers, though L no longer leads to contradiction, the problem of inconsistency is simply pushed back one step to the seemingly meaningful SL; if SL is true, then it is false, and if false or neither true nor false, it is true.

A second standard suggestion for parrying the liar group of paradoxes is to claim that L and the like express *no propositions*, the latter being truth-bearers in the primary sense. If L expresses no proposition, then there is nothing to be either true or false, hence no contradiction arises. A major difficulty with this approach is that it has remained a bare assertion—that is, there is no developed theory to explain why self-referential sentences like L lack corresponding propositions whereas sentences analogous to them do. For example, consider

(F) This sentence is not in French,

which, though likewise self-referential, is nevertheless innocuously true. A more telling example is that of the propositional liar:

(PL) PL expresses no true proposition,

which again is true if false, and false if true.[26] To disarm PL, the propositionalist would have to claim that PL expresses no proposition—that is, be committed to the truth of the *proposition* expressed by

(PL′) PL expresses no true proposition.

Yet PL and PL′ are *identical* except for their clerical labeling. What distinguishes PL from PL′ so that PL expresses no proposition, whereas PL′ does? Is it the direct self-reference of PL and not PL′? This question brings up a more general criticism: what on the face of it is demanded is not a parochial solution peculiar to the liar and its semantic cousins; but rather, a uniform, comprehensive theory that will diagnose and eliminate all the classic self-referential paradoxes precisely as self-referential in some flawed manner. Any program that could resolve all the liar-type paradoxes would remain incomplete until it was shown how it fits into a comprehensive theory that distinguishes licit for illicit self-reference. It may in fact be the case that there are no propositions corresponding to the liar and like sentences, but this is an issue distinct from the broader problem of illegitimate self-reference.

A third classic device for avoiding the liar-type paradoxes is the adoption of a Tarskian hierarchy of languages; for a given language L_n, true-in-L_n is defined only in the distinct metalanguage L_{n+1}. With semantical concepts such as truth (and falsity) removed to the higher metalanguage L_{n+1}, there is no self-referential attribution of the truth-predicates in a given language L, hence no contradiction of the liar type. This approach has the serious drawback of fragmenting the intuitively global notion of truth into infinitely many analogous but regional truth-predicates. Not only is this counter-intuitive and contrary to usage in natural languages; it requires giving up certain fundamental, intuitively true global applications of truth-predicates, as in the principle of bivalance, for example:

Every proposition is either true or false,

and in the principle of noncontradiction:

No proposition is both true and false.

As observed by Tarski, any adequate theory of truth must be both *formally correct* (free from contradiction) and *materially adequate* (capturing our basic intuitions concerning the meaning of the truth-predicates). One of the most obvious of the latter intuitions is thought to have been put succinctly by Aristotle in the famous passage: "To say of what is that it is not, or of what is not that it is, is false, while to say of what is that it is, or of what is not that it is not, is true" (*Metaphysics* 1011b26–29). Summarizing this intuition, Tarski proposed his famous T-schema as a criterion for any proposed definition of truth. A definition of truth for language *L* is materially adequate if it implies every instance of the schema

(T) ψ is true if and only if ϕ,

where ψ is a quotation name of ϕ, and ϕ is a sentence of language *L*. Hence the famous example

'Snow is white' is true if and only if snow is white.

Under T, our untutored intuitions, which allow for the simple liar sentence L, are shown to be inadequate, since

'L is false' is true if and only if L is false,

and since L = 'L is false', then

L is true if and only if L is false.

It was Tarski's conclusion that the least drastic way to salvage the vague intuitions motivating the T-schema is to require instances of T to be in a metalanguage, where the sentence quoted by ψ is in the object-language, and ϕ is a metalanguage translation of this quoted sentence. The T-schema itself is not questioned. Yet it will be precisely the lesson of the PPL analysis below that it is not our intuitions concerning truth that are inadequate but rather it is the inadequacy of the T-schema itself as a criterion of adequacy. Indeed, the criterion of adequacy for a *definition* of truth must, like any definition in PPL, comply with the formal restrictions imposed by the axiom of comprehension.

When these necessary strictures are applied, truth-in-the-object-language can be defined in the object-language in a consistent manner.

Parenthetically, philosophers have criticized Aristotle's dictum and its formulation in the T-schema as trivial, observing that instances of it reveal next to nothing about the nature or essence of truth, particularly concerning the commonsense, intuitive correspondence theory. Particular instances of the T-schema—for example, " 'Snow is white' is true if and only if snow is white"— simply restate the correspondence theory for a particular proposition; here the proposition for 'snow is white' is said to be true because it corresponds to the fact that snow is white. The nature of the correspondence is not addressed. But to criticize the T-schema thus is to take a logical criterion of adequacy and confuse it with a deeper, underlying ontological explication, a distinction of which Tarski was acutely aware. Some critics, finding the existing standard ontic analyses inadequate to sustain a correspondence theory and the alternative theories of coherence and pragmatism subject to fundamental weaknesses, have proposed that the T-schema gives all that need be said about a theory of truth. This is the so-called 'minimalist conception', whose supposed deflationary virtue is that it demystifies the concept of truth. One is here reminded of the person who extols the virtues of poverty because he has found no way to escape it. Rather than resign ourselves to the poverty of a minimalist conception of truth, we would do better to work for the explanatory wealth inherent in an expanded underlying ontology. The arguments that I have proposed to advance instance ontology provide capital for such a theory. As a first, loose approximation, one not yet formulated in the language of PPL and incorporating the necessary restrictions of AC, but sufficient to illustrate the implications of instance ontology, consider the following basic-case definitions of True and False. For a sentence in a natural language of the form $\ulcorner F^n(a_1, \ldots, a_n)\urcorner$,

> $\ulcorner F^n(a_1, \ldots, a_n)\urcorner$ is true if and only if there exists an instance of F that is *predicative* among the entities of the ordered n-tuple $\langle a_1, \ldots, a_n \rangle$; that is, there is a structure among $a_1, \ldots, a_n$ caused by the interlinking of some instance F_i. That $\ulcorner F^n(a_1, \ldots, a_n)\urcorner$ is false if and only if there does not exist an instance of F predicative among $a_1, \ldots, a_n$.

The complex consisting of some-instance-of-F-linking-relata-$a_1, \ldots, a_n$ is the traditional fact or state of affairs, with true propositions corresponding *in this sense* to facts, false propositions corresponding to no *complex* as described.

Facts, precisely as integrated complexes, are given immediately in experience or are inferred as in, for example, scientific theories. What exist objectively, 'in the world', whether the world of the intellect or extra-conceptually, are structures both simple and hierarchically complex, and truth is when propositions correspond to the implied relation instance structures.

Returning to the liar and like paradoxes and their instance analysis, it is essential to extend PPL so as to allow reference to truth-bearers corresponding to wffs of PPL. In the classic Tarskian treatment, truth-bearers of closed wffs are the wffs themselves—that is, sentences of the language. Yet there are simple but strong arguments for positing complex intensions of a special sort, the standard 'propositions', as truth-bearers in the primary sense—for example, that multiple, varying sentences, in the same or in different languages, can express and so be true or false of the same content.[27] Sentences are truth-bearers only in a derivative, secondary sense. This distinction is of relevance to an instance analysis of the liar and the like. Consider the sentences that result if the liar, L, is substituted for itself repeatedly:

L is false.
(L is false) is false.
((L is false) is false) is false.
And so on.

Though there is here produced iteratively an increasingly large number of distinct sentences, if L has a corresponding proposition, then, by substitution of expressions with the same referent, each sentence in the list will nevertheless assert the *same* proposition. In terms of instances of properties, when specific instances of False are assigned to the predicates in the above list, we have

$F_1(L)$.
$F_2(F_1(L))$.
$F_3(F_2(F_1(L)))$.
And so on.

Since $L = F_1(L)$, all the outermost instances, F_1, F_2, F_3, . . . , have the same subject L; so, by the motivating ontology, $F_1 = F_2 = F_3 = \ldots$.

We shall now extend PPL so as to associate with each wff of the language a corresponding proposition that will bear instances of either True or False. This extension will be called PPL*. In PPL* the formation rules of PPL are extended to include a proposition-referring function designated by the asterisk locution "* . . .*". The asterisk function will map *closed* wffs—that is, sentences—that occur (or will occur with the instatiation of variables) between the asterisks to a corresponding proposition. The concomitant adjustments in the formal semantics need not detain us here. The ability to refer to propositions corresponding to their wffs, together with the subsequent definitions *in* PPL* of the predicates True and False, renders PPL* a *closed language* in a sense analogous to that of Tarski. Yet, Tarskian pessimism concerning such languages notwithstanding, PPL* is consistent.

The amplification of PPL to PPL* with the addition of the asterisk function requires that the formation rules of PPL be extended in the following manner:

(1) ***P*** is a wff of PPL* if and only if **P** is a wff of PPL*.

(2) All other formation rules of PPL are modified to allow wffs of the form ***P*** to occupy any position that an individual constant can occupy.

The motivation behind (2) is that, being neither predicative, as are instances, nor the abstracted intension of such instances, propositions are of the same semantic category as individuals.

We can now define in PPL* and in accordance with AC the predicates of True, T, and False, F. These definitions are given recursively as constituents of the object-language PPL* but are stated schematically in the metalanguage as follows: For wffs of PPL* such that $\{\mathbf{a}_1, \ldots, \mathbf{a}_n\} \subset \{\mathbf{b}_1, \ldots, \mathbf{b}_n\}$, where ψ is any sentence of PPL*,

(a) $(\mathbf{R}^n)(\mathbf{R}_j^n)(\mathbf{b}_1) \ldots (\mathbf{b}_m)(T_h)\{[[(\exists T_i)[T_i(*\mathbf{R}_j^n(\mathbf{a}_1, \ldots, \mathbf{a}_n)*) \cdot T_i = T_h] \supset [\mathbf{R}_j^n \neq T_h \supset \mathbf{R}_j^n(\mathbf{a}_1, \ldots, \mathbf{a}_n)]] \cdot [[\mathbf{R}_j^n \neq T_h \supset \mathbf{R}_j^n(\mathbf{a}_1, \ldots, \mathbf{a}_n)] \supset (\exists T_i)T_i(*\mathbf{R}_j^n(\mathbf{a}_1, \ldots, \mathbf{a}_n)*)]\}.$

(b) $(\mathbf{R}^n)(\mathbf{R}_j^n)(\mathbf{b}_1) \ldots (\mathbf{b}_m)(F_h)\{[[(\exists F_i)[F_i(*\mathbf{R}_j^n(\mathbf{a}_1, \ldots, \mathbf{a}_n)*) \cdot F_i = F_h] \supset [\mathbf{R}_j^n \neq F_h \supset \neg\mathbf{R}_j^n(\mathbf{a}_1, \ldots, \mathbf{a}_n)]] \cdot [[\mathbf{R}_j^n \neq F_h \supset \neg\mathbf{R}_j^n(\mathbf{a}_1, \ldots, \mathbf{a}_n)] \supset (\exists F_i)[F_i(*\mathbf{R}_j^n(\mathbf{a}_1, \ldots, \mathbf{a}_n)*)]\}.$

(c) $(..)..(..)[(\exists T_i)T_i(*\neg\psi*) \equiv (\exists F_j)F_j(*\psi*)]$

(d) $(..)..(..)[(\exists F_i)F_i(*\neg\psi*) \equiv (\exists T_j)T_j(*\psi*)].$

For ψ with free occurrences of **a**,

(e) $(..)..(..)[(\exists T_i)T_i(*(\mathbf{a})\psi*) \equiv (\mathbf{a})(\exists T_j)T_j(*\psi*)].$
(f) $(..)..(..)[(\exists F_i)F_i(*(\mathbf{a})\psi*) \equiv (\exists \mathbf{a})(\exists F_j)F_j(*\psi*)].$
(g) $(..)..(..)[(\exists T_i)T_i(*(\exists \mathbf{a})\psi*) \equiv (\exists \mathbf{a})(\exists T_j)T_j(*\psi*)].$
(h) $(..)..(..)[(\exists F_i)F_i(*(\exists \mathbf{a})\psi*) \equiv (\mathbf{a})(\exists F_j)F_j(*\psi*)].$

Definitions for T and F of wffs of the forms $\phi \cdot \psi$, $\phi \vee \psi$, $\phi \supset \psi$, and $\phi \equiv \psi$ can be defined in the manner corresponding to the standard truth-table definition of the respective connective. All these definitions correspond to the strictures of AC, so are consistent additions to a consistent base. Hence, the above definitions are collectively the analog of Tarski's T-schema and show that PPL* is a language that can consistently contain its metalanguage truth-predicate (i.e., PPL* is a *closed language*). Tarski's theorem, which denies the definability of a truth-predicate in standard formal systems, is thus defeated at the deeper analytical level of PPL*.

For positive sentence literals, the principle of noncontradiction follows from (a) and (b), and by the subsequent clauses (c)–(h) and so on, the principle would apply to any sentence of PPL*.

Let us now apply the relevant clauses above to an analysis of the simple liar. Parsed in PPL*, L above would be rendered

$l = *(\exists F_i)F_i(l)*.$

(i) Assume l is true—that is, $(\exists T_j)T_j(l)$, which, by definition, is equivalent to

$(\exists T_j)T_j(*(\exists F_i)F_i(l)*).$

Then, by (g),

$(\exists F_i)(\exists T_j)T_j(*F_i(l)*).$

instantiating F_i with, say F_1, we have

$(\exists T_j)T_j(*F_1(l)*).$

Since $F_1(l)$ is a sentence of PPL*, then, by (a), wherein T_i is instantiated with T_1,

$F_1 \neq T_1 \supset F_1(l),$

which, because the antecedent is true, implies

$F_1(l).$

Yet the latter statement together with the present assumption (i) asserts that there are instances of both T and F which apply to the same sentence l, a violation of the principle of noncontradiction.

(ii) Assume l is false—that is, $(\exists F_i)F_i(l)$, which, by definition, is equivalent to

$$(\exists F_j)F_j(*(\exists F_i)F_i(l)*).$$

By (h),

$$(F_i)(\exists F_j)F_j(*F_i(l)*).$$

Instantiating F_i with, say, F_a, subscript a denoting any integer,

$$(\exists F_j)F_j(*F_a(l)*).$$

From this, the left major conjunct of (b) wherein F_h is instantiated with F_a, it follows that

$$F_a \neq F_a \supset \neg F_a(l).$$

Because the antecedent is false, the biconditional is true but does not contradict the initial assumption that l is false, and this for any instance F_a.

Hence, because only assumption (i) leads to contradiction, the simple liar, l, is merely false, not contradictory.

Consider next the strengthened liar, SL, which translates into PPL* as

$$(sl) \quad \neg(\exists T_i)T_i(sl).$$

The assumption that sl is true—that is, that $(\exists T_j)T_j(* \neg(\exists T_i)T_i(sl)*)$—leads to contradiction, as the reader may determine. However, the assumption that sl is false does not result in contradiction:

Assume that sl is false—that is, $(\exists F_j)F_j(sl)$. Then,

$$(\exists F_j)F_j(* \neg(\exists T_i)T_i(sl)*).$$
$$(\exists T_j)T_j(*(\exists T_i)T_i(sl)*) \text{ by (d).}$$
$$(\exists T_i)(\exists T_k)T_k(*T_i(sl)*) \text{ by (g).}$$

Instantiating T_i with T_1,

$$(\exists T_k)T_k(*T_1(sl)*).$$

By (a), this implies that

$$T_1 \neq T_k \supset T_1(sl).$$

This contradicts the present assumption only if $T_1 \neq T_k$ is true. Yet, nothing compels us to assert this nonidentity; indeed, given the above observation concerning the liar and the sameness of instance $F_1 = F_2 = F_3 = \ldots$ despite iterations of $..F_3(F_2(F_1(l)))..$, we would expect $T_1 = T_k$; in other words, that 'SL is true' and '(SL is true) is true' corresponds to the same proposition.

I note in passing that similar analyses of other versions of the liar—for example, cyclic liars—likewise produce noncontradictory results. The shortest cyclic liar is:

(A) The truth-bearer of B is true.

(B) The truth-bearer of A is false.

With True and False defined as above, the PPL* translation and analysis ends with A being true and B false, as the reader can verify.

It is also easy to verify that the truth-teller sentence

(T) This truth-bearer is true,

whose PPL* rendering is

(t) $(\exists T_i)T_i(t),$

is not contradictory under either assumption as to its truth or falsity. This corresponds to what has been claimed as the basic intuition, that the truth-value for t is 'up for grabs'.[28]

We note that the fact that a consistent truth-predicate can be defined in a language adopting PPL as its underlying logic runs counter to the Gödel–Tarski theorem, which asserts that there is no formal definition of a truth-predicate for languages whose logic is standard predicate logic.[29] This theorem involves reasoning parallel to that of Gödel's incompleteness theorems, and its defeat in PPL raises suspicions that the incompleteness theorems may prove to be likewise non sequiturs in PPL. We shall see shortly that this is the case.

Directly relevant to the above analysis of the liar paradox is Patrick Grim's recent, interesting extrapolation of the liar, which purports to show the impossibility of an omniscient being.[30] Let us consider this briefly. The impossibility of an omniscient being is one of three similar impredicative arguments which

Grim constructs, the other two being the supposed demonstration of the impossibility of a totality of all truths and the impossibility of possible worlds conceived as sets of maximally consistent propositions. Grim offers these arguments as contributing to a cluster of logical results (e.g., Gödel's incompleteness theorems) that purportedly demonstrate the incoherence of the notions of *all* truth or *total* knowledge. To reinforce this conclusion, Grim also constructs a Cantorian diagonalization argument intended to elicit a contradiction inherent in the concept of the set of all truths. The argument can be modified to show, it is claimed, the impossibility of either the set of all falsehoods or the set of all propositions.[31] Below I shall argue that the impredicative specification essential to the diagonalization argument of Cantor's theorem is illegitimate by the previous analysis, but that, modified to a legitimate impredicative specification, it renders the argument a non sequitur. As an exact analog, Grim's diagonalization argument against the set of all truths would likewise fail.

Against the concept of an omniscient being, Grim offers the following divine liar:

(D) God believes that D is false,

which, leaving the 'is false' predicate nonformalized for purposes of perspicuity, parses into PPL* as

(d) $(\exists \text{Bel}_i)\text{Bel}_i(g, {}^*d \text{ is false}^*)$,

where g designates God. If d is true, then God holds a false belief and cannot be omniscient. If d is false, then the denial of d must be true—that is, God does not believe that d is false. Hence, there is a truth—that d is false—that God does not believe, and again God is not omniscient.

Under PPL*, however, the divine liar can be disarmed by observing the restrictions of AC as applied to the definition of divine belief of false propositions. In the special case of the doxastic states of the Divine Mind, there cannot, by definition, be error. This absolute veracity condition implies, as a first approximation, the following biconditional, which in turn results in a by now familiar self-contradiction. That is,

(9.16) $(\exists \text{Bel}_i)\text{Bel}_i(g, {}^{**}(\exists R_j)R_j(a_1, \ldots, a_n)^* \text{ is false}^*) \equiv$
$(R_k)\neg R_k(a_1, \ldots, a_n).$

For the specific proposition d,

$$(\exists \mathrm{Bel}_i)\mathrm{Bel}_i(g, {}^*(\exists \mathrm{Bel}_j)\mathrm{Bel}_j(g, {}^*d \text{ is false}{}^*){}^*) \equiv (\mathrm{Bel}_k)\neg\,\mathrm{Bel}_k(g,d).$$

Since $d = {}^*(\exists \mathrm{Bel}_j)\mathrm{Bel}_j(g, {}^*d \text{ is false}{}^*){}^*$, then

$$(9.17) \quad (\exists \mathrm{Bel}_i)\mathrm{Bel}_i(g,d) \equiv (\mathrm{Bel}_k)\neg\,\mathrm{Bel}_k(g,d).$$

Just as exact analogs of contradiction 9.17 have been disarmed by the application of the refined AC, so here, 9.17 is removed when 9.16, in particular its right bijunct, is modified in accordance with AC.

Defeating Gödel's Incompleteness Theorems in PPL

A further observation and one that is extraordinary and far-reaching in its consequences, is the defeat in the refined logic of PPL of Gödel's incompleteness theorems.[32] Given the above neutralization of the impredicatively induced paradoxes, the defeat of Gödel's theorems in systems adopting PPL as their underlying logic may perhaps be of little surprise to the reader familiar with the first incompleteness theorem's essential impredicative use of the predicate Provable-in-F in establishing the incompleteness of formal system F. Let us examine the relevant details.

Gödel's original 1931 paper presented the incompleteness theorems in the following form:

(I) If Peano's axioms are combined with the higher-order predicate logic of *Principia Mathematica*, there results a formal system F which is incomplete; that is, there is a sentence S of F such that neither S nor $\neg$S is provable in (derivable by the rules of) F.

And following as a corollary from (I):

(II) For any formal system F as described in (I), the consistency of F cannot be proved within (established by the methods of deduction of) F.

Though originally proved by Gödel for higher-order systems and their equivalents (e.g., Zermelo–Fraenkel set theory), the reasoning can be extended to systems of first-order Peano arithmetic, whose underlying logic is elementary predicate logic with identity.

For perpiscuity, I shall here appeal to the 'semantic analog' of Gödel's original purely syntactical proof of theorem I. That is, system F will be considered interpreted in a model, and will be assumed *sound* relative to the model.

By means of Gödel's ingenious *arithmetization* technique, it is possible to show how for a formal system F consisting of at least first-order predicate logic and containing Peano arithmetic one can model in (the arithmetic expressions of) F its syntactical metalanguage predicates such as those of variable, formula, axiom, and, especially, proof. Further—and the key to the negative results of theorem I—is the possibility of identifying in F an expression g which, because of the arithmetic modeling of predicates of the metalanguage, says of itself when interpreted in the metalanguage that it is unprovable in F; that is,

(g) g is not provable in F.

Now, if the system F in which g is formulated is sound, then it follows that F cannot be complete, since, specifically, neither g nor $\neg g$ is provable in F. To see this, assume first that $\neg g$ is provable in F. Since F is assumed to be sound, then it must be the case that $\neg g$ is true. But $\neg g$ asserts that g is provable in F, hence contradicts the assumption. Next, assume that g is provable in F. Then because F is sound, then g must be true; that is, what it asserts must be the case, and it asserts that g is not provable in F. But this contradicts the assumption. Hence, neither g nor $\neg g$ is provable in F. Moreover, since g is not provable in F and this is what g asserts, then we have here a sentence of F whose truth has been established informally outside F but which cannot be proved by means inherent in F.

For the relevant details, let F be an interpreted formal language whose deductive core is a standard predicate logic and has the following characteristics. First, by a device in the metalanguage it is the case that certain terms in F are, in the metalanguage, names for expressions of F. Gödel's device is to provide each expression with a unique *Gödel number* which then serves as its name. Specifically here, we shall use bold corner quotes, "$\ulcorner\psi\urcorner$", to indicate the expression in F that in the metalanguage names expression ψ; for example "$\ulcorner Rx\urcorner$" is an expression of F that names the sentence resulting from substituting an intension constant for 'R' and an individual constant for 'x'. Also, let F be sufficient to contain a definition of a predicate Prov, such that,

$\mathrm{Prov}(\ulcorner\psi\urcorner) \equiv \Phi$,

where, established in the metalanguage, $\mathrm{Prov}(\ulcorner\psi\urcorner)$ is true in F if and only if ψ is provable in F. For Gödel, $\ulcorner\psi\urcorner$ ranges over numerals for Gödel numbers of expressions of the language, and Φ is a complex expression of elementary arithmetic, the culmination of a series of forty-six carefully crafted definitions. Now, with '$\vdash_F$' standing for 'is provable (derivable) in F', any legitimate definition Φ of the predicate Prov must be such that

(a) if F is *sound*, then for every sentence ψ of F,
   if $\vdash_F \text{Prov}(\ulcorner\psi\urcorner)$, then $\vdash_F \psi$;

and

(b) if F is *complete*, then for every sentence ψ of F,
   if $\vdash_F \psi$, then $\vdash_F \text{Prov}(\ulcorner\psi\urcorner)$.

Hence if F is both sound and complete,

(c) $\vdash_F \text{Prov}(\ulcorner\psi\urcorner)$ if and only if $\vdash_F \psi$.

It follows from the above and the assumption of $\vdash_F \text{Prov}(\ulcorner\psi\urcorner)$ that

(d) $\vdash_F \text{Prov}(\ulcorner\psi\urcorner) \equiv \psi$.

Finally, let it be possible to construct the following sentence in F:

(G) $\neg\text{Prov}(\ulcorner G\urcorner)$.

Gödel's work showed how in any formal system consisting of standard first- (or higher-) order predicate logic and containing Peano's axioms for arithmetic it is possible to construct the analog of G. Self-referentially, G says of itself that it is not provable in F. Assume G is provable in F, so $\vdash_F \text{Prov}(\ulcorner G\urcorner)$ and by (d)

$\vdash_F \text{Prov}(\ulcorner G\urcorner) \equiv G$,

and thus

$\vdash_F \text{Prov}(\ulcorner G\urcorner) \equiv \neg\text{Prov}(\ulcorner G\urcorner)$.

The only way to avoid this contradiction and retain the crucial attribute of soundness (a) is to deny completeness (b) of system F in regard to proposition G. But if $\ulcorner G\urcorner$ does not have the property Prov, then $\neg\text{Prov}(\ulcorner G\urcorner)$ is the case, which is to say that G is true. So, G is true but $\ulcorner G\urcorner$ does not have the property Prov, which means in the metalanguage that G is not provable in L; thus we have established the equivalent of incompleteness theorem I for formal language L.

   In the refined logic of PPL, however, the analog of

$\vdash_F \text{Prov}(\ulcorner\psi\urcorner) \equiv \vdash_F \psi$

does *not* obtain. That is, where $\psi = g$ and

(g) $(\text{Prov}_k) \neg \text{Prov}_k(\ulcorner g \urcorner)$,

it is *not* the case that

$\vdash_{\text{PPL}} (\exists \text{Prov}_k) \text{Prov}_k(\ulcorner g \urcorner) \equiv (\text{Prov}_k) \neg \text{Prov}_k(\ulcorner g \urcorner)$,

which is, of course, a contradiction.

In a language incorporating PPL as the underlying logic, there is no analog of the definition

$\text{Prov}(\ulcorner \psi \urcorner) \equiv \Phi$,

whether Φ is a proposition of arithmetic or whatever, and where Prov can be interpreted in the metalanguage as Provable-in-F. This is so because such a definition would have to be legitimately impredicative in conformity with the axiom of comprehension (AC) of PPL and thus contain the requisite preventative clauses. That is, for expressions of the form $\ulcorner (R_k) \neg R_k(x) \urcorner$, a proposed definition of the predicate Prov (and its instances), Prov intended in the object-language to capture the meaning of Provable-in-F of the metalanguage, and for an object-language assumed to be sound and also complete, would have to imply

$(R)(x)(\text{Prov}_h)\{[(\exists \text{Prov}_i)[\text{Prov}_i(\ulcorner (R_k) \neg R_k(x) \urcorner) \cdot \text{Prov}_i = \text{Prov}_h] \supset$
$(R_j)[R_j \neq \text{Prov}_h \supset \neg R_j(x)]] \cdot [(R_j)[R_j \neq \text{Prov}_h \supset \neg R_j(x)] \supset$
$(\exists \text{Prov}_i)\text{Prov}_i(\ulcorner (R_k) \neg R_k(x) \urcorner)]\}$.

But with this, no contradiction arises within F. For the particular case of $g = \psi$, it becomes

(9.18) $(\text{Prov}_h)\{[(\exists \text{Prov}_i)[\text{Prov}_i(\ulcorner (\text{Prov}_k) \neg \text{Prov}_k(\ulcorner g \urcorner) \urcorner) \cdot \text{Prov}_i = \text{Prov}_h] \supset$
$(\text{Prov}_j)[\text{Prov}_j \neq \text{Prov}_h \supset \neg \text{Prov}_j(\ulcorner g \urcorner)]] \cdot [(\text{Prov}_j)[\text{Prov}_j \neq \text{Prov}_h \supset$
$\neg \text{Prov}_j(\ulcorner g \urcorner)] \supset (\exists \text{Prov}_i)\text{Prov}_i(\ulcorner (\text{Prov}_k) \neg \text{Prov}_k(\ulcorner g \urcorner) \urcorner)]\}$.

Now, substituting g for $(\text{Prov}_k) \neg \text{Prov}_k(\ulcorner g \urcorner)$, there results

$(\text{Prov}_h)\{[(\exists \text{Prov}_i)[\text{Prov}_i(\ulcorner g \urcorner) \cdot \text{Prov}_i = \text{Prov}_h] \supset (\text{Prov}_j)[\text{Prov}_j \neq \text{Prov}_h \supset$
$\neg \text{Prov}_j(\ulcorner g \urcorner)]] \cdot [(\text{Prov}_j)[\text{Prov}_j \neq \text{Prov}_h \supset \neg \text{Prov}_j(\ulcorner g \urcorner)] \supset (\exists \text{Prov}_i)\text{Prov}_i(\ulcorner g \urcorner)]\}$.

In keeping with the results for the analyses of the previous paradoxes, the assertion g is simply false, not contradictory. This would mean that g, as interpreted in the metalanguage, is provable in system L. By extension, the inference to the analog of incompleteness theorem II is likewise blocked.

In the substitution form of 9.18 above, $\text{Prov}_j = \text{Prov}_h$ corresponds to the 'singular point', analogous to the limiting case of division by zero, that, as we have noted, Gödel conjectured was responsible for illicit self-reference. It is ironic that for a formal system F precise enough to verify Gödel's conjecture and to enforce the prohibition implied in the conjecture, it is impossible to derive Gödel's theorems relative to F.

In sum, with PPL as the underlying logic, it is possible to distinguish within a language (and metalanguage) legitimate from illegitimate impredicative definitions. Containing the subtlety of relation instances, a definition of Prov and its instances must have the form, to a first approximation, of

(9.19) $(\exists \text{Prov}_i)\text{Prov}_i(\ulcorner \psi \urcorner) \equiv \Phi$.

Whether Φ is a complex arithmetical expression or whatever, it must contain the provisos for preventing the instance of Prov specified in the definiendum from being denied as a predicate in the definiens, Φ. That is, Φ, and indeed all of 9.19, must be rewritten so as to yield 9.18 in the case of $\psi = g$. And again, whether stated as an expression of arithmetic or not, the metalanguage interpretation of the resulting expression will be such as not to yield a contradiction or in turn imply that the language in question is incomplete. Rather, what has been shown here is that standard predicate logics are 'incomplete' in the sense that they cannot distinguish between correct and incorrect forms of impredicative specifications.

Defeating Cantorian Diagonal-Type Arguments in PPL

As previously alluded to, because of the close affinity between some of the paradoxes and the Cantorian diagonal-type reasoning, a few mathematicians and logicians have openly questioned the latter's validity,[33] while a few others have simply expressed concern that we do not have as yet sufficient understanding of the reasoning involved to be able to pronounce diagonal reasoning safe.[34] In the following critique I shall examine as a paradigm case the diagonal reasoning of Cantor's theorem: that for any set s, the power set of s, $P(s)$, has a greater cardinality than does s. Because Cantor's proof involves impredicative specifications, Poincaré rejected it,[35] and it was in attempting to discover a flaw in the proof that Russell discovered his set paradox.[36]

One of the standard but indirect objections to the reasoning in Cantor's theorem is the fact that it seemingly conflicts with the Löwenheim–Skolem theorem. The latter states that any satisfiable first-order theory (e.g., Zermelo–Fraenkel set theory) has a countable model; that is, no such theory can have only nondenumerable models. Yet Cantor's theorem purports to demonstrate that there are sets in our theory that are nondenumerable in all models of the theory. A standard interpretation, put forth by Skolem, is that we have here only an apparent conflict. A set s is nondenumerable only in a *relative* sense; the members of s cannot be put into one-to-one correspondence with the natural numbers by any relation in the *model*. The set s can be proved denumerable, however, under a one-to-one correspondence outside the model, in a 'higher' system. Skolem concludes that "the notion of 'finite', 'infinite', 'simply infinite sequence', and so forth turn out to be merely relative within axiomatic set theory."[37] Elsewhere Skolem expressed the opinion that "one can doubt that there is any justification for the actual infinite or the transfinite."[38] In response to this relativity, von Neumann remarks: "Of all the cardinalities only the finite ones and the denumerable one remain. Only these have real meaning; everything else is formalistic fiction."[39] He concludes that according to the Löwenheim–Skolem theorem every axiomatic set theory has the 'mark of unreality'.[40] At the very least, the theorem is taken to show that the intended interpretation of set theory, our 'intuitive notion of set', is not captured by our axiom systems.[41]

A third, but weaker, objection to Cantor's theorem is the fact that two well-known predicate logics developed explicitly to avoid the self-referential paradoxes but at the same time to mitigate some of the ad hoc features of type theory, Quine's *New Foundations* and Wang's system Σ, turn out to be such that Cantor's theorem cannot be proved in them.[42] Wang's system Σ, for example, has the interesting properties of including its own consistency proof, immunity from Gödel's incompleteness argument, and the denumerability of all its sets (i.e., Cantor's theorem does not hold).[43] Wang contends with regard to the latter that there is no loss to ordinary mathematics and, in general, that there is "no clear reason why mathematics could not dispense with impredicative or absolutely indenumerable sets."[44]

Let us now examine the nature of diagonal-type reasoning through its use in the famous Cantor theorem. Cantor's theorem purports to show that, for any set s, the assumption that s is equinumerous (can be put into one-to-one correspondence) with its power set, $P(s)$, yields a contradiction. The argument can be broken down into the following steps:

(1) Assume that there exists a one-to-one correspondence f between s and its power set $P(s)$, $f: s \rightarrow P(s)$.
(2) Let c be the set of all the elements of s such that each of these elements x is mapped by f to a subset of s that does not contain x as an element; that is,

$$(9.20) \quad c = \{x \mid \neg(x \in f(x))\}.$$

(3) Because c is a subset of s, then, by hypothesis, there exists a $y \in s$ such that $f(y) = c$.
(4) Either $y \in c$ or $\neg(y \in c)$.
   (i) Assume $\neg(y \in c)$—that is, $\neg(y \in f(y))$, which, from the definition of c in 9.20, it follows that $y \in c$, a contradiction.
   (ii) Assume $y \in c$. By the definition of c, $\neg(y \in f(y))$, or, by substitution, $\neg(y \in c)$, again a contradiction.

The standard conclusion reached is that the initial assumption of a one-to-one correspondence f between any set s (finite or infinite) and its power set $P(s)$ is impossible. Because there is a one-to-one correspondence between the elements of s and a proper subset of s (i.e., $f: x \rightarrow \{x\}$), then $P(s)$ always has a greater cardinality than s.

To see that the generalized diagonal procedure utilizes the illegitimate impredicative specification identified above, we need only observe the definition of set c in 9.20 as parsed in PPL:

$$(9.21) \quad (x)\{(\exists \in_i)\in_i(x,c) \equiv (\in_k)[\neg \in_k(x, f(x))]\}.$$

To define set c thus is exactly analogous to the illegitimate definitions of Russell's set, Russell's property, falsehood, and so on above. Contradictory ab initio is the definition of c, as seen by instantiating x with c in 9.21. So viewed, Cantor's theorem does not indict the assumed existence of any one-to-one function f.

If we modify the illegitimate nonpredicative specification of c in 9.21 with the proper exclusionary clause, it becomes:

$$(9.22) \quad (x)(\in_h)\{[(\exists \in_i)[\in_i(x,c) \cdot \in_i = \in_h] \supset (\in_k)[\in_k \neq \in_h \supset \\ \neg \in_k(x, f(x))]] \cdot [(\in_k)[\in_k \neq \in_h \supset \neg \in_k(x, f(x))] \supset (\exists \in_i)\in_i(x,c)]\}.$$

Now, corresponding to (4) of Cantor's proof above, we test the following assumptions:

(i) Assume $\neg(y \in c)$; that is,

   (a) $(\in_i)\neg\in_i(y,c)$.
   (b) $(\in_i)\neg\in_i(y,f(y))$, substituting $f(y)$ for c.
   (c) $\neg(\exists\in_i)\in_i(y,f(y))$.
   (d) $\neg(\in_k)[\in_k \neq \in_h \supset \neg\in_k(y,f(y))]$, from (c) and 9.22.
   (e) $(\exists\in_k)\neg[\in_k \neq \in_h \supset \neg\in_k(y,f(y))]$.
   (f) $(\exists\in_k)[\in_k \neq \in_i \cdot \in_k(y,f(y))]$.
   (g) $(\exists\in_k)\in_k(y,f(y))$.

(b) and (g) contradict one another.

(ii) Assume $y \in c$; that is,

   (a) $(\exists\in_i)\in_i(y,c)$,

or

   (b) $(\exists\in_i)\in_i(y,f(y))$.
   (c) $(\exists\in_i)[\in_i(y,f(y)) \cdot \in_i = \in_i]$.

If we instantiate 9.22 to get

   (d) $(\in_k)[\in_k \neq \in_i \supset \neg\in_k(y,f(y))]$,

then no contradiction exists between lines ii(b) and ii(d).

What this shows is that when the set c is defined in a legitimate impredicative manner in PPL, we do not end in a contradiction, which would otherwise impugn the correspondence f. In short, it has *not* been shown that it is impossible to have a one-to-one correspondence between a set and its power set when the set is infinite. Interestingly, the set of all sets, S—a set that is paradoxical as 'too large' in Cantor's set theory—has a subset that can be put into one-to-one correspondence with its power set $P(S)$ simply by mapping each set that is an element of $P(S)$ onto itself in S.

Given the differentiation between legitimate and illegitimate impredicative reasoning revealed under PPL, it follows that Cantor's theorem is a non sequitur, derivable only if one allows the spurious impredicative specification of 9.21. We have not established, of course, that all forms of reasoning classified as 'diagonal'—for example, Cantor's proof of the nondenumerability of the real

	1	2	3	4	5	6	7	·	·	·
P_1	—	2	—	4	5	—	7	·	·	·
P_2	1	—	3	4	—	—	7	·	·	·
P_3	—	2	3	—	5	6	—	·	·	·
·										
·										
·										
P_n	—	2	3	—	5	·	·	n	·	·	·
·										
·										

Fig. 9.1. The decision matrix

numbers—are defeated analogously to that above. It is worth observing, however, the defeat in exactly parallel fashion of a diagonal-type argument used as an alternative proof of Gödel's incompleteness theorem I. The argument purports to show that there is no *decision procedure* for arithmetic truth—that is, no purely mechanical, algorithmic procedure for determining whether or not an arbitrary number predicate is true of an arbitrary natural number. This establishes Gödel's incompleteness theorem by the contrapositive: if there were a complete axiomatization of arithmetic, then, by this fact, there would be a decision procedure for arithmetic. Every true statement of arithmetic would be provable from the axioms, and any such proof would be a decision procedure. Let F be a formal system containing arithmetic, and assume that F has a decision procedure. We restrict our attention to one-place number predicates, P_n, where the subscript represents the nth place in some lexicographical ordering. Let f be the function that maps a number predicate to the set of natural numbers that satisfy the number predicate—$f: P_n \rightarrow \{x \mid P_n(x)$ is true$\}$. By our assumption, there is a decision procedure for determining whether or not a natural number is a member of any such set. In such a case the number predicate *represents* the corresponding set. The situation can be diagrammed as in figure 9.1. The set of numbers within each row represents the set of natural numbers satisfied by the number predicate of that row, on the left, whereas the blanks indicate those numbers not satisfied by the corresponding predicate. We now define a set c 'down the diagonal' as

$$c = \{x \mid \neg (x \in f(P_x))\}.$$

Given the relationships as schematized in figure 9.1, we have a decision procedure for determining whether an arbitrary natural number is an element of c or not. Now it can be shown through the medium of recursive functions that if there is a decision procedure for determining whether a given natural number belongs to a given set of natural numbers, then there is a number predicate that represents the set.[45] Hence there is some number predicate, P_m, for some natural number m, on the left-hand side of the figure such that $f(P_m) = c$. The question can now be asked: Is $m \in f(P_m)$ or not? Assume that $m \in f(P_m)$. Hence $m \in c$, which, by definition of c, yields the fact that $\neg (m \in f(P_m))$, a contradiction. Assume to the contrary that $\neg (m \in f(P_m))$. Then, by definition of c, $m \in c$, so $m \in f(P_m)$, a contradiction. From this we conclude that formal system F can have no decision procedure and consequently is not completely axiomatizable.

This argument is exactly parallel to that of Cantor's theorem above, and just as in the latter the set c parsed in PPL to 9.21, so the set c in the last argument parses with PPL into

$$(9.23) \quad (x)\{(\exists \in_i)\in_i(x,c) \equiv (\in_k)[\neg \in_k(x,f(P_x))]\}.$$

If there is a number m such that $f(P_m) = c$, then instantiating x with m in 9.23 produces the contradiction

$$(\exists \in_i)\in_i(m,c) \equiv (\in_k)[\neg \in_k(m,f(P_m))]$$
$$\equiv (\in_k)[\neg \in_k(m,c).$$

The violation of the strictures of AC of PPL is the same here as it was in Cantor's theorem, requiring the adjusted analog of 9.22:

$$(9.24) \quad (x)(\in_h)\{[(\exists \in_i)[\in_i(x,c) \cdot \in_i = \in_h] \supset (\in_k)[\in_k \neq \in_h \supset$$
$$\neg \in_k(x,f(P_x))]] \cdot [(\in_k)[\in_k \neq \in_h \supset \neg \in_k(x,f(P_x))] \supset (\exists \in_i)\in_i(x,c)]\}.$$

No contradiction arises from this legitimate impredicative definition of c, so this alternative route to Gödel's theorem is also defeated in PPL.

As one would expect from the implicational relationship between Turing's result and Gödel's first theorem, the defeat in PPL of the above argument extends to an exactly analogous diagonal argument for Turing's negative result concerning the halting problem—there is no general algorithm for deciding the question of the stopping of Turing machines. The latter is equivalent to the result of Church's theorem that there is no one algorithm that works to decide all mathematical questions. For details of the diagonal argument, I refer the reader to Roger Penrose's perspicuous exposition.[46] As above, an analog of 9.24 defeats Turing's argument in a formal system whose underlying logic is that of PPL.

The preceding results should have a humbling effect with regard to the presumptions that at times find their way into our philosophizing and, relevant here, into our inflated estimation of our analytic tools. Indicative is the formulation often given to Gödel's incompleteness theorem I:

> If *any formal theory* adequate to contain elementary arithmetic is consistent, then it is incomplete.[47]

So formulated, there is the implicit prejudice that all formal systems must have one of the present predicate logics (first- or higher-order) at its core, as if these formulations were finished and complete in capturing all the basic distinctions and subsequent modes of inference relevant to predication. One is reminded here of Kant's estimate of the Aristotelian logic of his time and of how, from its supposed complete list of forms of judgment, Kant thought himself warranted in deriving a complete set of synthesizing categories that give the structure and set the limits on all possible experience. Analogously, one lesson of this chapter is that the modern limitation theorems of Gödel, Tarski, and Turing are likewise a function of the limitations of our present standard predicate logics, and that there exists a refined, subsuming logic in which these theorems do not hold.

On a General Diagnosis and Solution of Self-Referential Paradox

In order to display more fully the analytic power of PPL, I have examined individually a selection of self-referential paradoxes. This was in lieu of an initial single analysis of some proposed common form of the paradoxes, a condensed effort that would certainly have been less convincing. I will conclude by considering a proposed general diagnosis of what must at least be considered a core of classical self-referential paradoxes.

In a 1905 essay, Russell gave what he considered to be the logical form of all the impredicative paradoxes: "Given a property ϕ and a function f, such that, if ϕ belongs to all members of $u, f(u)$ always exists, has the property ϕ, and is not a member of u; then the supposition that there is a class w of all terms having property ϕ and that $f(w)$ exists leads to the conclusion that $f(w)$ both has and has not the property ϕ."[48] Recently, Graham Priest has reexamined Russell's general diagnosis and has found it necessary to extend it slightly to the following form: The classic self-referential paradoxes involve properties ϕ and ψ, and a function δ, where

(1) $w = \{x \mid \phi(x)\}$ exists and $\psi(w)$, and

(2) if $x \subseteq w$ such that $\psi(x)$, then (a) $\delta(x) \notin x$ and (b) $\delta(x) \in w$.[49]

For example, Russell's paradox results from $\phi(x)$ being the property $\neg \in (x,x)$, w the set of all sets that are not elements of themselves, $\psi(x)$ the self-identity property $(\lambda x(x = x))$, and δ the identity function. The Burali–Forti paradox of the greatest ordinal results from $\phi(x)$ being x-is-an-ordinal, w the set of all ordinals, $\psi(x)$ the identity property, and $\delta(x)$ the least ordinal greater than every member of x. Berry's paradox of the least integer not nameable in fewer than nineteen syllables results from $\phi(x)$ being the property x-is-a-natural-number-definable-in-less-than-nineteen-words, w the set of all such numbers, and $\phi(x)$ the property x-is-definable-in-less-than-fourteen-words. $\delta(x)$ is the least ordinal not in x. Priest also shows how the Mirimanoff, Köing, Richard, liar, knower, and heterological paradoxes can be analyzed into the above form. I refer the reader to Priest for details.

The issue here is that all paradoxes having the aforementioned form, in particular, jointly satisfying 2(a) and 2(b), are illegitimately impredicative in a way paralleling that identified in our assay of Cantor's theorem and are likewise rendered legitimately impredicative in the manner given. For the combined conditions 2(a) and 2(b) parsed in PPL require

(9.25) $(\exists \in_i) \in_i (\delta(x),w) \equiv (\in_k) \neg \in_k (\delta(x),x)$.

And, for $x = w$,

$(\exists \in_i) \in_i (\delta(w),w) \equiv (\in_k) \neg \in_k (\delta(w),w)$,

which is a contradiction. Once again, the contradiction is removed when, in conformity with AC, the necessary restrictions are introduced into 9.25—that is,

(9.26) $(x)(\in_h)\{[(\exists \in_i)[\in_i(\delta(x),w) \cdot \in_i = \in_h] \supset (\in_k)[\in_k \neq \in_h \supset \neg \in_k(\delta(x),x))]] \cdot [(\in_k)[\in_k \neq \in_h \supset \neg \in_k(\delta(x),x)] \supset (\exists \in_i) \in_i(\delta(x),w)]\}$.

With this, all the paradoxes listed above are eliminated from a system whose underlying logic is PPL.

In summary, the PPL analyses of the above range of paradoxes give warrant to Gödel's conjecture that the self-referential contradictions arise at certain 'singular points' or 'limiting points' analogous to dividing by zero. This 'division by zero' is tantamount to allowing relation instances of the definiendum to be in the range of universal quantifiers of the definiens in such a fashion that the truth-value of the definiendum is in part required to be a function of itself. We have seen that it is possible within the refinements of PPL to distinguish and exclude destructive self-referential, impredicative specifications while allowing legitimate forms. Thereby a positively motivated diagnosis and an other than ad hoc prevention program is possible for the otherwise intractable self-referential paradoxes. Significantly, impredicative reasoning found illegitimate and excluded from PPL was observed to be the type of reasoning involved in Cantor's theorem, the celebrated imitation theorems of Tarski and Gödel, and, by extension, that of Turing. These theorems do not hold for any formal system with PPL as the underlying logic. This insight, that the classic limitation theorems are a function of the grossness of standard predicate logics, has profound implications for much prevalent philosophizing about the limitations of formal systems and the capacities of human reasoning. I shall not pursue these implications here but, rather, further reinforce the claim as to the veracity of instance ontology by demonstrating its analytic and problem-solving power in the areas of foundational mathematics and the theory of identity.

Instance Ontology and Logic Applied to the Foundations of Arithmetic and the Theory of Identity

In this final chapter I shall discuss two powerful examples of the problem-solving potential of instance ontology: one in the foundations of mathematics, the other in the theory of identity. The analytical fertility that gives rise to long sought-after results in these areas is offered as further inductive warrant for the truth of instance ontology and, in particular, the realist 'intensional' version partially formalized in PPL.

Natural Numbers and Instance Ontology

The *most difficult* problem confronting contemporary studies in the foundations of mathematics is this: How can we develop logic, if, on the one hand, we are to avoid the danger of the meaninglessness of impredicative definitions and, on the other hand, are to reconstruct satisfactorily the theory of real numbers.—Carnap, "The Logicist Foundations of Mathematics"

Fundamental to the philosophy of mathematics is an ontology and epistemology of the arithmetic of the natural numbers. No branch of mathematics is more universal in its range of attribution—to the actual and the possible, to the mental and the physical—or epistemically simpler—children master it. The fact that the domain of arithmetic is everything thinkable and, as such, coincides with that of logic was evidence for Frege that arithmetic is a subfield of logic.[1] The only rival to arithmetic in its extension, but, significantly, not in its epistemic simplicity and naturalness, is set theory. Consonant with the foregoing, I will argue that, notwithstanding their technical advantages for deductive formalizations, the various set-theoretical modelings of the natural numbers and their interrelationships, which constitute arithmetic, are philosophically inadequate proxies for what are in fact intensional entities and their mutual relations.

As worked out below, this thesis reinforces and corrects Frege's intensionalism, which forms the semantic underpinnings of his logicist program for reducing arithmetic to logic, a program that on the basis of Fregean ontology consists of a forced and misleading mixture (for reasons to be stated) of intensional and extensional elements. Cocchiarella makes the point that Frege's logicism is, at its core, a theory about reducing arithmetic to a theory of predication, as opposed to a theory of class membership, the now standard set-theoretical reduction.[2] A theory of predication is inherently intensional, and this is why Frege's logicism requires a logic that is at least second-order predicate logic, not a first-order theory of membership. Overtly, Frege's logicism failed because his logical system allowed for the derivation of Russell's paradox.[3] More subtly, it also failed as a convincing analysis of natural numbers, in that here numbers were identified with extensions of a certain kind, an error the nature of which I will explain shortly. Using PPL as the formalization of the proper analysis of predication, and assuming that the term 'logic' extends to it, I shall below preserve half the logicist program—namely, show how it is possible in PPL to generate definitions of the concepts '0', 'is a successor of', 'is a natural number', and others which are formally sufficient, as well as philosophically adequate to their explananda, for *stating* Peano's postulates. As to the *derivation* of the postulates in PPL, the second half of the logicist program, this is not possible. However, the postulates can be generated in analogs of known ways from the combination of PPL and the single additional axiom known as Hume's principle. Significantly, this extended system can be given a finite consistency proof.

The starting point for substantiating the above claims is the observation that cardinality is essential to the concept of natural number, and cardinal number is the measure of quantity—the amount of specified plurality, including the limiting case of an absence thereof, that is, 0 amount. Because plurality is central to number and is associated with extension, philosophers and mathematicians have often simply identified the notion of plurality with that of class or set and have then incorporated the concept of class into their definitions of cardinal numbers. These proposed definitions have been, variously:

(a) A natural number is a class of specific entities, where the cardinality of the class is equal to the number—for example, $3 = \{\{\{\phi\}\}\}$. (This is the historically influential view of Euclid and the tack taken in contemporary set theory, e.g., in the von Neumann and the Zermelo models.[4]

(b) A natural number is a class of equinumerous classes, each element class having the cardinality equal to the number—for example, 3 = set of all triplets. (This is the view of Russell in *Introduction to Mathematical Philosophy* [1919], but under his 'no class' theory only the formal model, not the philosophical definition, of number in *Principia Mathematica* (1910).[5])

(c) A natural number is a property of classes, all equinumerous classes having the same cardinal property. (This is the view of Georg Cantor and recently that of Penelopy Maddy.[6])

In contrast to (a) and (b), (c) represents some concession to intensions. There is, however, a third, fully intensional option close to what Frege argued in the early *Grundlagen der Arithmetik* (1884)[7] and the one argued for here, where the connection between number and plurality is mediated by a further property:

(d) Natural numbers are properties of properties, the attribution of the former being a function of the extension of the latter.

According to Russell's 'no class' theory, in which classes were eliminated in favor of propositional functions, the latter interpreted as properties and relations, (b) became (d) in *Principia Mathematica*, and (d) was reaffirmed in his summary work, *My Philosophical Development* (1959).[8] Reflecting his ambivalence, however, (b) is the preferred definition in *The Principles of Mathematics* (1903) and the *Introduction to Mathematical Philosophy* (1919).[9] Option (d) was also held by Hilbert and Ackermann in their *Principles of Mathematical Logic* (1938), in which they conclude: "Number thus appears as the properties of predicates, and in our calculus every number is represented as a predicate constant of second level."[10]

Within prevailing predicate logic, option (d) is usually construed as interpreting numbers as second-level numerical quantifiers. In this vein, David Bostock once proposed a formal system wherein numbers are treated as numerical quantifiers and, with the device of quantifying over quantifiers, derived Peano's postulates and hence arithmetic.[11] In the analysis that follows, however, because of the intension/instance distinction inherent in the refined logic of PPL, a more transparent, more explanatorily adequate treatment of numbers is possible. The device of extended binding in PPL is in a sense 'quantifying over quantifiers', though, beyond technical fertility, it is motivated by the common intension/exemplifying instance ontology. It is this latter distinction that allows numbers to be treated as both predicates ('numerical quantifiers') and nonpredicative 'objects', to use Frege's term, the importance of which will be seen below.

Option (a) in its modern form is widely and rightly held to have been discredited by a well-known argument of Paul Benacerraf.[12] The core of the argument is simply that it is possible to associate the natural numbers with classes of specific entities in different (indeed, infinitely many) ways. Thus in the Zermelo model $3 = \{\{\{\phi\}\}\}$, and in the von Neumann model $3 = \{\phi,\{\phi\},\{\phi,\{\phi\}\}\}$. However, there is no nonarbitrary means of deciding which classes really are the corresponding numbers. The insight to be gained here is that with option (a) numbers are identified with *particular* classes, yet cardinal numbers are what any one-to-one corresponded classes have *in common*, and shared commonality is characteristic of predicative properties, not nonpredicative classes. The number 3 cannot be identified with either set $\{\{\{\phi\}\}\}$ or set $\{\phi,\{\phi\},\{\phi,\{\phi\}\}\}$, for 3 is the quantity that both have in common due to the correspondence $\{\phi\} \leftrightarrow \phi$, $\{\{\phi\}\} \leftrightarrow \{\phi\}$, and $\{\{\{\phi\}\}\} \leftrightarrow \{\phi,\{\phi\}\}$. Numbers have the character of properties. Additional evidence for this is Benacerraf's own structuralist conclusion: there is no way to individuate numbers independent of their position in the ordinal progression 1, 2, 3, 4, 5, . . . (What I have claimed to be the more fundamental cardinal relationships are not considered.) He says: " 'Elements' of the structure have no properties other than those relating them to other 'elements' of the same structure. . . . *Any* object *can play the role of* 3; that is, any object can be the third element in some progression."[13] But this is further evidence that numbers are intensions; for, outside synonymy (which Benacerraf does not mention), there are likewise for intensions no specifiable identity conditions other than their relationships with other intensions, a point which was made against Quine in chapter 1. Moreover, in treating numbers as vacuous placeholders in the network of relations constituting a progression, Benacerraf has reduced them to bare particulars. But bare particulars are the illusory residue of a distillation that ignores intensions. Yet numbers must have (be) intensions if they are to explain the other than arbitrary assignment of relations making up the structural network that Benacerraf identifies with the ordinal numbers; for the obtaining of a relation between relata is a function of the compatibility of both the content of the relation (e.g., Is-Less-than) and the contents of the relata (say, 2 and 3).

It is interesting that Euclid's version of option (a), widely repeated in ancient Greek thought and popular thereafter as a philosophical analysis of number (e.g., in Locke and Hume[14]), is stronger in one sense than its modern counterparts. According to Euclid, "Number is a multitude composed of units."[15] The theory (usually implicit) is that any entity is a *unit* when every characteristic of it except its singularity has been abstracted away. Then 3, for example, is to be identified with the class of 3 units; no matter what triplets of whatever kinds of entities one considers, by this abstraction process we supposedly arrive at the same 3-membered class of abstract units. Unfortunately, as Frege observed,[16] to accomplish what the theory purports, units must be pure singularity with no other characteristics; that is, they must be 'bare singletons'. But, like bare particulars, such qualityless singletons are ontically indistinguishable, hence there can only be one such entity. All numbers, then, become identical to the class of one abstract unit, which is absurd.

Turning to option (b), as a philosophical explication that attempts to give not simply a technically useful analog but the exact nature of the entity, it is absurd on the face of it. It commits what could be called the 'fallacy of presupposed omniscience', a fallacy alluded to in chapter 6. If the number 3, for example, is literally identical to the class of all three-membered classes taken extensionally as an inventory of all triplets (which is what is intended!), then only an omniscient intellect could have knowledge of what is, independent of a specifying concept, an infinite list. The plausibility of this view derives from confusing the 'class concept' (Russell's term)—that is, the intension of 'class of all three-membered classes'—with the 'class', or extension. We understand perfectly well the intension Class-of-all-Three-Membered-Classes, and we understand the concept of it having an extension essentially *as a function of this intension* (Russell's 'definition by intension'[17]), such that proposed entities are considered elements of this extension on the basis of whether they satisfy the corresponding intension. By finite minds cannot comprehend an infinite list of triplets, which is what the class of all three-membered classes becomes when taken 'purely extensionally'. To claim that we have epistemic access to a cosmic catalog of triplets of entities of any type, some of which have yet to exist, is, to say the least, the most pretentious and discreditable form of Platonism. It is ironic that, in defense of (b), Russell in the *Introduction to Mathematical Philosophy* concluded: "It is therefore more prudent to content ourselves with the class of couples, which we are sure of, than to hunt for a problematical number 2 which must always remain elusive."[18] The only sense in which we are 'sure of' the class of couples is as a function of its class concept, which we comprehend, but the latter as an intension is what Russell claims to find 'elusive'. Finally, if it is countered that one could identify 3 with the above intension, then it is no longer (b) that is being supported, but rather something like a confused version of (c). Modeling numbers as classes of equinumerous classes is a useful logical fiction, but not to be confused with a philosophically accurate definition.

As for option (c), I shall argue against it in making the case for (d). In support of (d), in addition to affirming Frege's argument for it, I shall also argue along a different Fregean line, one corollary to the moderate realism advocated herein. To anticipate, the view that emerges is that natural numbers (e.g., 4) are intension contents of unit monadic properties (e.g., 4_i, 4_j, . . .), where the latter are predicative of further intensions (e.g., Frege's 'horse of the king's carriage', H— i.e., 4_i(H)). The truth condition for an applied number statement of the form '4_i(H)' is that the extension of intension H is in one-to-one correspondence with the first four ordinal numbers, the canonical measuring standard. Because of this, instances of number properties (other than instances of the number 1) are not predicative of property instances, say H_j, where H_j(Bucephalus). Pure arithmetic is constituted by number-theoretic (unit) relations among number intensions themselves—for example, 2 + 3 = 5, and 2 is an even divisor of 6.

In arguing for (d) we need look no further for a foundation than Frege's treatment of number in the *Grundlagen*. Here Frege puts forth the fundamental insight that central to the concept of cardinal number is that it answers the question: How many?, *and* that this is a compressed form of the question: How many Fs are there, for some concept F. That is, "the content of a statement of number is an assertion about a concept."[19] Frege points out that the same aggregate of entities is rightly numbered 500 men or 4 companies, depending upon how one considers them, this being a function of the categorizing concept chosen. Similarly, the same playing cards can be numbered as 52 cards, 4 suits, or 1 deck, depending upon the sortal intension employed. The implication is that numbers involve extensions tied essentially to defining intensions—there are no aggregates apart from delimiting concepts. Frege observes that this thesis gets strong warrant in the case of the number 0, there being no class but only a concept—for example, 'moon of Venus', to which the number 0 applies. Number, then, must make reference to some concept F; so Frege offers the following definition:[20]

(10.1)   The number of Fs is the extension of the concept 'equinumerous to F'; that is, $N_x[F(x)] = \{G | G \approx F\}$.

The expression '$N_x[..]$' is the now standard cardinal operator whose argument is for Frege a *concept* F, an objective, predicative entity corresponding to the linguistic predicate 'F(x)', and whose value is the number of entities that ex-emplify this quality. The symbol '$\approx$' refers to the relation existing between two properties when their extensions can be put into one-to-one correspondence. On the face of it, 10.1 seems to be a peculiar version of (a) and something of the inverse of (c)—here a number is a certain class (extension) of a property. Frege was careful to distinguish extensions from classes, however, tying the former closely to their corresponding intensions as the source of their unity, a view likewise advocated by Russell.[21] Frege states: "Assigning a number always goes along with naming a concept, not a group, an aggregate or such-like things; and that if a group or aggregate is named, it is always determined by a concept, that is to say, by the properties an object must have in order to belong to the group."[22] This thesis was argued in chapter 1.

The argument for the view that numbers are properties of properties can be strengthened by pursuing a further Fregean distinction, one whose implications have not been fully appreciated. Frege observed that statements of cardinal number fall into two classes: statements where the number terms are predica-tive or adjectival (A-type)—for example, 'Jupiter has four moons'—and those where the number terms are substantival or proper nouns (N-type)—for exam-ple, '19 is a prime number'. The latter are the proper statements of pure number theory, the science which Frege sought to put on a firm logical foundation. But if, as Frege claims, assertions of quantity involve numbers as (or *as parts of* for Frege) predicates, this would seem to give priority to A-type number state-ments. In fact, Frege reverses the priority by going on to state that all A-type statements of the form 'There are n Fs' are to be parsed as N-type equivalence statements of the form 'The number of Fs = n'—that is, $N_x[F(x)] = n$ (e.g., 'Jupiter has four moons' is to be parsed as 'The number of moons of Jupiter = four').

The point I wish to make, which goes to support option (d), is that, regardless of which type of number statement comes closest to the nature of cardinal number (A-type as assertions of quantity or N-type as relationships of arithme-tic as a science), we cannot, pace Frege, coherently reduce one type to the other. The argument is simple and turns upon a point which Frege did not address— the absolute modal difference between the contingent character of most A-type statements ('Jupiter has four moons', 'Henry VIII had seven wives') and the characteristic necessity of N-type number statements ('The number of Jupiter's moons = four', '2 + 3 = 5'). To force a reduction of one type to the other is, in many cases, to trade a given modal quality for its contradictory, a sure sign that such a reduction is misguided. What is required is a noneliminative account of both types. This is why numbers cannot be direct predicates of sets, option (c)—all such predication is *necessary*. The assertion, for example, that 'Jupiter has four moons' (assuming for the sake of argument that this is the case) cannot be construed as an assertion that the number 4 is a predicate of the set {$moon_1$, $moon_2$, $moon_3$, $moon_4$}; for if, in fact, there are exactly four moons of Jupiter, named by the terms within the set brackets, then *this* set could have no other number than 4. The set has the quantity of 4 *necessarily*, though the original proposition is *contingent*. Jupiter need not have four moons (and we now know it does not), let alone these four moons.

Consequently, it is a manifest constraint on any account of the content of number statements that it provide a basis for distinguishing the two types of number statements.[23] What ontology, then, as the content of such statements, will account for this difference between numbers as predicates and numbers as nonpredicative subjects? As outlined earlier, instance moderate realism is an obvious solution. To better appreciate that this is the case, we shall observe what can be construed as Frege's further efforts in this direction. First, it is to be noted that Frege's reason for reversing the seeming priority of A-type over N-type number statements has to do with a basic tenet of his ontology. The relevant ontological distinction is his bifurcation of entities into *concepts*—predicative, 'unsaturated', 'linking' entities—and *objects*—nonpredicative, 'saturated' entities, the subjects of predicative concepts. Frege sees this ontic division as rigidly paralleling a prior grammatical distinction between, respectively, incomplete grammatical predicates, 'F(..)', and substantival expressions that, grammatically, can be the subjects of linguistic predicates. In propositions (Frege's 'thoughts') corresponding to A-type statements, numbers occur predicatively (in the present literature as 'numerical quantifiers'), whereas in propositions corresponding to N-type statements, they occur as objects. Now, since number terms are substantives in true N-type statements, which have priority as statements of arithmetic as a science, these terms must refer to objects, and the only relevant candidates which capture the requisite notion of plurality are extensions, hence definition 10.1. Yet there are difficulties latent in Frege's principle that ontology strictly follows grammatical categories; for example, it commits him to such absurdities as the notorious 'The concept of a horse is not a concept'.[24] The phrase 'The concept of a horse' is a noun phrase, not a predicate, so must name an object, not a predicative concept. If the lesson of this absurdity had not been lost on Frege and he had allowed A-type number statements to suggest a definition for number, it would have been 10.1 modified to:

(10.2) The number of Fs is a concept of F determined by the equinumerosity of F with other concepts.

This is the equivalent of (d).

Indeed, Frege lays the foundations for the possibility of 10.2 and provides the means of reconciling nonreductively A- and N-type number statements through an undeveloped distinction in which he recognizes separate entities as the nominata of nominalized predicates, later called 'concept-correlates'.[25] That is, corresponding to a concept F(..) is its concept-correlate F, which is essentially F(..) but without the latter's predicative, 'unsaturated' character—the nonpredicative aspect being what is here called its intension. Clearly, in these we have an aspect of the moderate realism advanced previously, one that is directly applicable to the ontology of cardinal number. From this perspective, numbers are nonpredicative 'concept-correlates' abstracted from their predicative and individuated instances in propositions expressed in A-type statements. This explanation has the important advantage of not requiring the reduction of number predicates to numbers, or vice versa, and at the same time is consonant with the intuition that (cardinal) numbers are in their essence characteristic of quantity (answering the question: How many?) and so retains the priority of A-type statements.

In another way, Frege comes closer to a moderate realist treatment of numbers when he claims that, though numbers are objects, they occur as *part of* the numerical predicate in the propositions described by A-type number statements. For example and symbolically, [..4..] (moon of Jupiter(x)). The locution '[.. ..]' represents the predicative aspect of the predicate [..4..], where 4 is the common intension, the 'concept-correlate', the same content as, say, in the numerically distinct instance of the predicate [..4..] in the fact [..4..] (Apples in the bowl(x)). That Frege may have had something like this in mind is evident in an intriguing footnote he attaches to his definition of *the number of Fs* in the *Grundlagen*.[26] He states that he thinks it possible to substitute for 10.1 its intensional equivalent:

(10.3) The number which belongs to the concept F is the *concept* 'equinumerous to F'; that is, $N_x[F(x)] = H$, where $(X)\{[..H..](X) \equiv X \approx F\}$.

Among possible objections to 10.3, Frege cites its apparent inability to let us speak of multiple ones, twos, and so on in the plural. In this regard Frege presumably had in mind truths like 'The prime factors of 9 are 2 3s', where we make reference to multiple occurrences of the same number. He goes on to say that he is convinced that this and other stated objections to 10.3 can be met, though he does not pursue the issue. Now, it would seem that the only way to provide multiple instances of numbers, consistent with a nonreductive account of both A- and N-type number statements, is to require that numbers as predicates be numerically distinct instances—say 4_1, 4_2, 4_3, and so on—of the nonpredicative universal 4. So stated, the 'object' 4 is 'part of' each predicative instance 4_n. The form of the definition in 10.3 would then be modified to

(10.4) $N_x[F(x)] = H$, where $(X)(H_n(X) \equiv X \approx F)$, for some n uniquely correlated with X.

H would be a Fregean 'object' and concept-correlate to predicate instance and Fregean 'concept' H_n.

In summary, to account for both necessary and contingent modal qualities of number statements, it is necessary to retain cardinal numbers as predicates. But this must be reconciled with the nonpredicative, substantive occurrences of number terms ('objects' in Frege's sense) in statements of pure arithmetic. The independently motivated ontology that can coherently reconcile these demands, and in an epistemologically respectable manner as well, is the moderate realism that I have been arguing for. Instances of numbers—for example, 3_i—are predicates of concepts, some necessary (e.g., 3_i(Prime-Divisor-of-30)), some contingent (e.g., 3_i(Apples-in-the-Bowl)).

It is instructive and confirmatory of this moderate realist analysis of numbers to observe how it resolves the ambiguity of a specific modal inference made famous by Quine.[27] Consider the argument:

Necessarily, $9 > 7$.
The number of planets $= 9$.
_____
Necessarily, the number of planets > 7.

The premises are true, but the conclusion is false. Yet, the conclusion appears to be nothing more than the result of substituting for '9' in the first premise the extensionally identical 'the number of planets' from the second premise. This apparent failure of substitutivity in modal contexts—their being 'referentially opaque'—renders them, according to Quine, at best obscure and at worst wrongheaded.

Now a Fregean analysis of the above argument offers some preliminary clarification. With numbers as predicates of concepts, the above argument becomes:

Necessarily, 9 > 7.

The number of the concept of being a planet = 9.

Necessarily, the number of the concept of being a planet > 7.

It is possible to read the conclusion here as true. If we extend Frege's analysis to include number instances—for example, 9_i—not only is the conclusion true, but the nature of the difficulties in Quine's version becomes perspicuous. So rendered the argument is:

$(\exists >_i)[>_i(9,7) \cdot (\exists Nec_j)Nec_j(>_i)].$

$(\exists X)(\exists X_i)[(\exists NN_j)NN_j(X) \cdot X_i(\text{Planets}) \cdot X = 9].$

$(\exists X)(\exists X_i)[(\exists NN_j)NN_j(X) \cdot X_i(\text{Planets}) \cdot (\exists >_l)[>_l(X,7) \cdot (\exists Nec_k)Nec_k(>_l)]].$

Here substitutivity is retained. More important, note that if the conjunct

$(\exists >_l)[>_l(X,7) \cdot (\exists Nec_k)Nec_k(>_l)]$

is mistakenly read as

$(\exists >_l)[>_l(X_i,7) \cdot (\exists Nec_k)Nec_k(>_l)],$

where X_i is an instance of 9 predicated of the concept planet, then the entire conclusion would be equivalent to the original false conclusion that

Necessarily, the number of planets > 7.

Instance analysis removes the ambiguity. Necessity is a property of an instance of the Greater-than relation as it exists between *intension* 9 and intension 7; it is not a property of an instance of the Greater-than relation as it exists between the *instance of* 9 that is a predicate of the concept of being a planet and the intension 7.

On the above analysis, numbers of pure arithmetic—for example, 3—are not Platonic transcendent Forms to which, mysteriously, we have epistemic access, but, rather, are the abstracted intensions common to their instances, so have cognitive existence only. Instances of number predicates are themselves cognitive in ontic status, for they are properties of intensions, some of which, at least, are conceptual only, and a pure monadic property of a conceptual entity must be a conceptual entity. That is, the abstraction to number intensions is not Aristotelian (*Metaphysics* 1026a28); the mind does not abstract from the content of the sensibly given weight, hardness, heat, and so forth, to reveal as a contained residue a specific quantity; nor is this abstraction the modern relative proposed by Maddy, where one supposedly perceives numbers in the process of perceiving sets of which numbers are said to be properties.[28] The mind does not acquire a number intension or its predicative instances from the content of sense experience; they are, rather, a priori. A specific number instance arises conceptually as a predicate of a property P when the extension of P is understood to be in one-to-one correspondence with a subset of the ordinal numbers (the measuring standard); the corresponding number intension is then an abstraction from like instances. Number intensions and their instances are *abstract* in the strict sense of not being relata in spatiotemporal relations; but this is not, contrary to a common construal, an indictment of them. To be an abstract entity is not to be conceptually inaccessible if the entity is a concept (intension) itself.

We do not say, however, that the natural numbers are 'free creations of the human mind', the view, for example, of Richard Dedekind.[29] Though conceptual, these properties and relations are no more 'subjective' in the sense of being arbitrary and freely stipulated than are the concepts of truth, identity, or exemplification. For, once in existence, an intension determines the relations (and properties) it can have by the very content that it is, independent of its origin within or ontic dependence upon a mind. This is the source of the necessity and analytic character of these relations and of their objectivity. The naive, but widely held, proportion that the subjective is to the objective as the arbitrary is to the self-determinate is simple false.

Reiterating, pure arithmetic is the totality of statements expressing the properties and relations among numbers as universals, analogous to the Dretske–Tooley–Armstrong theory of causality, in which causal laws are nomic relations between universals. The relations of pure arithmetic are necessary, but, unlike causal laws, as purely conceptual, they are a priori, similar in this regard to the relations corresponding to the logical operators (e.g., $\supset$, $\vee$, $(\exists..)$) and constituting the science of logic. Contra Benacerraf, arithmetic relations form a structure whose relata terms are not simply blank place-holders; rather, they have contents, and these contents, at least for the first few natural numbers, are known by abstraction from their instances. From the intensions of small numbers and their cardinal and ordinal relationships of which we have direct epistemic access, theoretical arithmetic extrapolates to a posited infinite system of such intensions and their relations. The meta-structure of this system is modeled on the elementary algorithms that we use to manipulate the corresponding numeration, and it is this that can give us knowledge of specific relationships between larger finite number intensions to which we do not have direct access. It is in this sense that arithmetic is an *intensionally* 'idealized theory'; it is not, as Kitcher suggests, an *extensionally* idealized theory that extrapolates the two fundamental operations of collecting and pairwise ordering past the accidental limitations of finite human minds.[30] As the Piagetians insist, these cognitive operations may be necessary for the acquisition by humans of the related arithmetic abstractions, yet the operations are not these abstract intensions, and it is in the latter that theoretical arithmetic lies. In sum, it is instance moderate realism that gives ontic underpinning to arithmetic as a body of truths (a science), to their necessity and a priori status (objectivity), to how we can know them (accessibility) and how they apply to the material and conceptual world. It explains arithmetic's traditional association with rationalism and, in not having spatial and temporal relations, the Platonic status accorded to numbers. In presenting arithmetic as a system of relationships, partially given or posited, mostly consequential among posited cardinal intensions, the methodological role of proof is accounted for, something that neither empiricist nor Platonist theories can do.

A Formalization of Arithmetic and Its Consistency

I will now demonstrate how within a formal system containing PPL it is possible to generate definitions, conforming to the above instance ontology, of the concepts '0', 'is a successor of', 'is a natural number', and others, which, once secured and in the presence of one additional axiom—Hume's principle—yield Peano's postulates in a well-established manner. Once Peano's postulates[31] are secured, arithmetic of the natural numbers follows, and presumably that of integers, rationals, and real numbers in the usual ways. An important result here is the demonstration that the formal system consisting of PPL plus Hume's principle, and consequently arithmetic and all analysis thereby derivable, is provably consistent and is so by the elementary syntactic, 'finite' procedure used to demonstrate the consistency of PPL itself. Indeed, all that is necessary is to show that the PPL formulation of Hume's principle has a valid afep.

The significance of this consistency proof turns upon its character as 'finite', a desideratum sought by David Hilbert in his famous formalist program for the foundations of mathematics, a program intended primarily to safeguard mathematics against impredicatively induced self-referential paradox. Though 'finite' in this regard was not explicitly specified by Hilbert, it has been taken to mean a method involving no infinite searches, one that can be specified exhaustively in a finite number of words.[32] It has become a common, though not universal (see Detlefsen[33]), claim that Gödel's second incompleteness theorem shows the impossibility of proving the consistency of arithmetic by finitary means. Following from the first theorem, Gödel's second theorem says that if P is a consistent formal system equivalent to the logic of *Principia Mathematica* and containing Peano's postulates, and p is an 'arithmetized' formalization in P of the metalanguage statement that P is consistent, then p is not provable in P. An underlying assumption of the above claim is that all finitary proofs can be 'arithmetized' in the manner of Gödel and so be incorporated in P; hence the existence of a finitary consistency proof of P would mean that it is possible to prove the consistency of P in P—a violation of the second theorem.[34] Offered in confirmation is Gerhard Gentzen's famous 1936 consistency proof of arithmetic, which required the use of transfinite induction.[35] Gödel himself, however, was more cautious in his original 1931 paper, saying that the second theorem represented no contradiction to the formalistic standpoint of Hilbert, "for this standpoint presupposes only the existence of a consistency proof effected by finite means, and there might conceivably be finite proofs which *cannot* be stated in P."[36] This possibility is realized in the syntactical consistency proof of PPL plus Hume's principle, for parts of this proof pertain to refined formulae of PPL with expressions for both predicates and predicate instances, and these, a fortiori, cannot be stated in the grosser standard predicate logic of P. It is the refinement of predicate instances which, at bottom, makes this consistency proof possible, just as it rendered a non sequitur in PPL Gödel's first theorem, from which the second theorem would have followed.

In order to axiomatize arithmetic, Hume's principle must be added to the underlying logic of PPL. Hume's principle states:

(HP) The number of Fs is the number of Gs if and only if F ≈ G.

The symbol ≈ is read: has an extension in one-to-one correspondence with the extension of. The principle is so called because of Hume's statement in the

Treatise that "when two numbers are so combined, as that the one has always an unite answering to every unite of the other, we pronounce them equal."[37] That arithmetic can be generated from Hume's principle and standard predicate logic (at least second-order) has been demonstrated by both Crispin Wright and George Boolos,[38] the latter showing how, between the *Grundlagen* and the *Begriffsschrift*, Frege had the means to deduce from Hume's principle the equivalent of Peano's postulates. The inconsistency in Frege's system arises from the assumptions he used in deriving Hume's principle.[39]

In attempting to render Frege's logicist program consistent, Russell placed the blame for its inconsistency on impredicative definitions, which he then sought to eliminate with his complicating theory of types. Yet, the logical analysis of mathematics reveals many such definitions. Carnap gives what is perhaps the simplest, most fundamental example: the definition of *natural number*, NN.[40] In standard predicate logic the definition is given as:

$$(10.5) \quad NN(P) \equiv (X)\{[X(0) \cdot (Q)(X(Q) \supset X(S(Q)))] \supset X(P)\},$$

where $S(..)$ is the successor function, which will be defined precisely below. This definition was classified as 'impredicative' because the universal quantifier '(X)' of the definiens ranges over NN of the definiendum. What is more, in the derivation of elementary number theory, as in the *Principia*, it is sometimes necessary to substitute 'NN' for 'X' in 10.5.[41] It was Carnap's view that although 10.5 is impredicative, it is harmless. We shall see that when 10.5 is parsed in PPL, Carnap's opinion is substantiated (cf. the quote from Carnap introducing the first section of this chapter).

For reasons of perspicuity I shall first give versions of the standard definitions necessary for deriving Peano's postulates formulated in the language of simple extended predicate logic (with the exception of the components of the definition in PPL of equinumerosity, $\approx$, and the ancestral relation, Anc), from which the refined PPL equivalents can easily be obtained by inserting instance quantifiers. In the form of these definitions I shall be following a recent exposition by Charles Chihara.[42] For our purposes, it is necessary to give a precise definition in PPL of the equinumerosity relation between properties P and Q. First, I shall define what it means for a relation R to have the property of being a one-to-one correspondence, symbolized 'Cor':

$$(10.6) \quad (\exists Cor_i)Cor_i(R) \equiv (a)(b)(c)\{[((\exists R_i)R_i(a,b) \cdot (\exists R_j)R_j(a,c)) \supset b = c] \cdot [((\exists R_i)R_i(b,a) \cdot (\exists R_j)R_j(c,a)) \supset b = c]\}.$$

Important for the proof that HP can consistently be added to PPL, and hence the consistency proof of arithmetic, is the observation that the right bijunct of the definition of Cor has afeps of the form:

$$[((\exists r)r \cdot (\exists p)p) \supset T] \cdot [((\exists r)r \cdot (\exists p)p) \supset T],$$

which successively resolves to

$$[(T \cdot T) \supset T] \cdot [(T \cdot T) \supset T]$$
$$T \cdot T$$
$$T.$$

We can now define the relation of equinumerosity, $\approx$, in PPL:

(10.7) $P \approx Q \equiv (\exists R)\{(\exists Cor_i)Cor_i(R) \cdot (\alpha)[(\exists P_j)P_j(\alpha) \supset$
$[(\exists b)(\exists Q_k)Q_k(b) \cdot (\exists R_l)R_l(\alpha,b)]] \cdot (b)[(\exists Q_j)Q_j(b) \supset$
$[(\exists \alpha)(\exists P_k)P_k(\alpha) \cdot (\exists R_l)R_l(\alpha,b)]]\}.$

(Note that the left bijunct is an abbreviation for '$(\exists \approx_i)\approx_i(P,Q)$', though for present purposes the abbreviation is sufficient.) Again, for purposes of establishing the consistency of PPL + HP, we observe that the right bijunct of the last expression has as an afep:

$$\{<\text{afep for 'Cor'}> \cdot [(\exists p)p \supset [(\exists q)q \cdot (\exists r)r]] \cdot [(\exists q)q \supset [(\exists p)p \cdot (\exists r)r]]\},$$

which resolves successively to

$$\{T \cdot [T \supset [T \cdot T]] \cdot [T \supset [T \cdot T]]\}$$
$$\{T \cdot [T] \cdot [T]\}$$
$$T.$$

With this we can define what is meant by a *cardinal property*. First, we define the binary relation of Is-a-Cardinal-Property-of:

A property P is a cardinal property of X if and only if, for all properties Y, Y has property P if and only if Y is equinumerous with X.

Symbolically, this binary relation, CardR, is given as:

(10.8) $(P)(X)\{CardR(P,X) \equiv (Y)[P(Y) \equiv Y \approx X]\}.$

The corresponding monadic attribute, Card, is given by

P is a cardinal property if and only if there is some X such that P is the cardinal attribute of X.

Symbolically,

(10.9) $(P)\{Card(P) \equiv (\exists X)CardR(P,X)\}$.

Restricting the variables P, Q, R to cardinal properties but allowing variables X, Y, Z to range over all properties, the successor relation, $SR(.,.)$, and the corresponding successor function, $S(..)$, can be defined as follows:

Cardinal property Q is the successor of cardinal property P if and only if there exist a property X instantiating Q and there exist an entity α such that α instantiates X and there exist a property Y whose cardinal property is P such that any entity which instantiates X but is not identical to α instantiates Y and conversely.

Or,

(10.10) $(Q)(P)\{SR(Q,P) \equiv (\exists X)[Q(X) \cdot (\exists \alpha)(\exists Y)[X(\alpha) \cdot P(Y) \cdot (b)(Y(b) \equiv (X(b) \cdot b \neq \alpha))]]\}$.

The *successor function*, $S(..)$, is then defined as

(10.11) $(Q)(P)\{S(P) = Q \equiv SR(Q,P)\}$.

Zero is defined thus:

A cardinal property P has the property of zero, 0, if and only if P is instantiated by no entity.

Or,

(10.12) $0(X) \equiv (\alpha) \neg X(\alpha)$.

The property of being a *natural number* is then defined as 10.5 above.

As the reader can easily verify, definitions 10.8–10.11 are translated into the refined logic of PPL by simply replacing each property in predicate position by the corresponding instance variable and its existential quantifier. The resulting expression requires no preventative clauses dictated by the axiom of comprehension (AC) in order to avoid illegitimate impredicativity. More significantly, the same is true of the definition of natural number, 10.5, its PPL translation being

(10.13) $(\exists NN_i)NN_i(P) \equiv (X)\{[(\exists X_j)X_j(0) \cdot (Q)((\exists X_k)X_k(Q) \supset$
$(\exists X_l)X_l(S(Q))] \supset (\exists X_m)X_m(P)\}.$

Note that there are *no* universal instance quantifiers binding a predicate position instance; hence, by AC, 10.13 requires no preventative clauses. It is legitimately impredicative as is, and in this Carnap was correct.

What is interesting, however, is that the definition of 0 when parsed in PPL does require an instance restriction. 10.12 becomes:

(10.14) $(X)(0_h)\{[(\exists 0_i)[0_i(X) \cdot 0_i = 0_h] \supset (\alpha)(X_j)[(X_j \neq 0_h \supset \neg X_j(\alpha)]] \cdot$
$[(\alpha)(X_j)[(X_j \neq 0_h \supset \neg X_j(\alpha)] \supset (\exists 0_i)0_i(X)]\}.$

Here because of the universal quantifier '(X_j)' of the definiens, the latter must also include the restriction clause '$X_j \neq 0_h \supset$'.

In order to derive Peano's postulates in the Fregean manner, it is necessary to have the definition of the *ancestral relation*. As a preliminary, we define the property of being *hereditary*, Her:

(10.15) $(\exists Her_i)Her_i(P) \equiv (Q)[(\exists P_j)P_j(Q) \supset (\exists P_k)P_k(S(Q))].$

With this we can define the ancestral relation, Anc, as:

(10.16) $(\exists Anc_i)Anc_i(P,Q) \equiv (R)\{[(\exists Her_j)Her_j(R) \cdot (\exists R_k)R_k(P)] \supset$
$(\exists R_l)R_l(Q)\}.$

These definitions, together with Hume's principle, HP, as a single axiom yield Peano's postulates in the manner, for example, of Wright.[42] The reader is referred to Wright for detail. With the standard recursive definitions of addition and multiplication added, arithmetic can be generated in the usual way. Our present interest is to demonstrate that HP is a consistent addition to the logic of PPL, and that it is so by the 'finite' syntactical consistency proof used to demonstrate the consistency of PPL. All that is necessary to accomplish this is to show that HP formulated in the language of PPL has valid afeps. In PPL the HP axiom is rendered:

(HP) $(P)(Q)\{[(\exists NN_i)NN_i(P) \cdot (\exists NN_j)NN_j(Q)] \supset [P = Q \equiv P \approx Q]\}.$

Then all afeps of HP have the form of the representative afep

$\{[(\exists n)n \cdot (\exists m)m] \supset [<\text{afep of 'P} = \text{Q'}> \equiv <\text{afep of 'P} \approx \text{Q'}>]\}.$

We saw in chapter 9 that afeps of the relation of equality, here 'P = Q', resolve to *T*, and we observed above that the afeps of 'P ≈ Q' also resolves *T*. Hence, the afeps of HP resolve successively as:

$$\{[T \cdot T] \supset [T \equiv T]\}$$
$$T \supset T$$
$$T.$$

Hence HP is a consistent addition to the consistent logic of PPL, and it is demonstratively so by a finite syntactical consistency proof. Consequently we have demonstrated by finite means the consistency of arithmetic, as well as that of integers, rationals, and reals to the extent that they are derivable in well-known ways from natural numbers. What has made this possible are the refinements of PPL over standard predicate logics, the same refinements that, relevantly, defeat Gödel's incompleteness theorems in PPL.

Distinguishing Identity from Indiscernibility

As a final exercise, let us turn the light of instance ontology on a fundamental problem in the theory of identity. As described in chapter 1, much clarification has been achieved on the epistemic side of identity theory. These results were motivated in part by what has been called *Frege's Puzzle*: why identity statements of the form '*a* = *b*' are typically informative, contingent, and a posteriori, whereas statements of the form '*a* = *a*' are uninformative, necessary, and a priori. The most persuasive accounts are of a Fregean type, where informative statements of the form '*a* = *b*' record the cognition that two different senses or information contents—for example, that of being the Morning Star and that of being the Evening Star—can characterize the same entity.[44] The referent of *a* and of *b* was known initially through two different sets of properties—under different 'guises'—but with the judgment that *a* = *b*, we achieve the epistemic gain that there is a single referent having properties from *both* sets of senses.

Equally important, and on the ontic side, but getting less attention, is the crucial problem of distinguishing identity (absolute, numerical) from indiscernibility (relative identity). A well-known exception in this regard is the work of Peter Geach.[5] Geach argues, in effect, that a satisfactory account of identity and indiscernibility must give necessary and sufficient conditions for when predicates can be said to express what he takes to be these two distinct relations. He claims that proponents of identity in classical first-order predicate logic (e.g., Frege and Quine) have not done this but, rather, have promoted a definition whose definiens is too gross to distinguish these relations and thus at best can imply only the weaker indiscernibility. This was the point made against Quine in Chapter 1 in response to his criticism of intensions and their lack of identity conditions. Retaining the first-order formulation as the best available and arguing that all attempts to rectify it fail and *must* fail, Geach concludes that we must surrender the notion of strict identity as incoherent and, further, that we should adopt in its place a theory of 'relative identity' in which there are an indefinite number of relations of indiscernibility, each with respect to a given property—for example, x is the same A as y, where A is some property. The relative theory of identity has been variously criticized and is not directly relevant to the issues at hand.[46] What we must be clear about is that there is a real distinction between identity and indiscernibility and that this distinction cannot be stated in standard predicate logics.

In standard fashion, the identity predicate, Id, is added to first-order predicate logic with the following or equivalent axioms:

(10.17) $\mathrm{Id}(x,x)$.

(10.18) $(\mathrm{Id}(x,y) \cdot \mathbf{F}x) \supset \mathbf{F}y$.

10.18 is an axiom schema in which $\mathbf{F}$ is any one-place predicate in the language.[47] Geach's criticism is equally applicable, however, but for what follows more perspicuous when identity is formulated as a definition in second-order logic as Leibniz's law:

(10.19) $\mathrm{Id}(x,y) \equiv (\mathrm{P})(\mathrm{P}x \equiv \mathrm{P}y)$.

Geach calls a relation an I-predicate if and only if it can be substituted for 'Id' in 10.17 and 10.18 and the latter are true for all constructible predicates $\mathbf{F}$ of a theory T. Because 10.19 and the pair 10.17 and 10.18 yield analogous results in their respective logics, I shall extend the definition of an I-predicate to relations that satisfy the right-hand side, or definiens, of 10.19. In either logic, Geach's point is that, as part of the logic of a theory T in which individuals x and y share all their properties, it would be impossible to discriminate in T between cases where x and y are numerically identical and cases where they remain numerically distinct but indiscernible; that is, both identity and indiscernibility are I-predicates.

A standard means of focusing on this point is to divide 10.19 into the principles of the indiscernibility of identicals,

(10.20) $\text{Id}(x,y) \supset (F)(Fx \equiv Fy)$,

and the identity of indiscernibles,

(10.21) $(F)(Fx \equiv Fy) \supset \text{Id}(x,y)$.

Though 10.20 is generally uncontroversial, 10.21 in both its strong and its weak forms has been rightly criticized. According to the strong form of the identity of indiscernibles, if individuals agree in all their monadic properties (nonrelations), then they are identical. The weak form asserts that if individuals have all properties and relations in common, they are identical. To have a relation in common means to be the same nth relatum in an n-term relation with all other relata fixed—for example, being to the left of a. The latter are the previously referred-to relation-properties. Restating the strong form, it holds that two distinct individuals must differ in at least one monadic property. Yet it has been objected by several philosophers that there is no logical necessity for this. As Armstrong observes, it is perfectly conceivable that there exist, for example, two ball bearings distinct as spatially related but identical in all nonrelational properties. He refers approvingly to the thesis that, as far as we know, elementary particles of the same species are absolutely without difference internally, whether in the same atom or at opposite ends of the universe.[48]

These observations are not fatal to one who wishes to maintain the classic second-order definition of identity, 10.19, or its first-order analog; indeed, they suggest the following possible reply. A proponent of 10.19 might argue that the supposed problem results from confusing the strong and weak forms of the identity of indiscernibles. The strong form, they might argue, is indeed false; individuals may have all monadic properties in common and yet be distinct. By this very fact, any two such individuals are related by a legitimate relation of, say, 'internal indiscernibility'. Of course, such an equivalence relation is not an I-predicate (and hence is not that of numerical identity), since in specifying the shared qualities we are quantifying over monadic properties only, not also relation-properties with implicit polyacity. If we do not observe this difference of range of quantification, we may slide into the false belief that this bona fide indiscernibility relation exists between individuals satisfying the biconditional with the more general global quantifier—that is, the right-hand side of 10.21

interpreted *weakly*, rendering it then an I-predicate. Accepting the identity of indiscernibility principle, 10.21, in this, its weak, form as true, and the principle of indiscernibility of identicals, 10.20, as uncontroversial, we come to the false conclusion that we do indeed have two distinct relations, one of indiscernibility, the other of strict identity, which are indistinguishable as I-predicates satisfying the classic definition 10.19. The error is removed, it would be claimed, if we avoid this confusion of false strong with true weak indiscernibility, in which case there is only one I-predicate, strict identity, and Geach's objection dissolves.

This reply turns on the assumption that weak indiscernibility is logically true; but this is as doubtful as the necessity of strong indiscernibility. Restated, the weak form asserts that different particulars must differ in at least some relations. However, as Max Black has pointed out, it is not inconceivable that there exists a universe consisting of exactly two spheres identical in every property, relational and nonrelational.[49] Such discriminating relation-properties as involving 'being to the left of' would be absent in such a universe, in that they presuppose a third entity—namely, an observer. Black then extends this conception to a radically symmetric universe in which any complexity is mirrored through a mathematical center of symmetry such that entities have all the properties and relations on one side that they have on the other. In the same vein, A. J. Ayer asks us to consider the apparently meaningful, noncontradictory notion of a cyclical universe repeating itself exactly from and to infinity.[50] Each such repetition would produce a system of entities each with properties and relations indistinguishable from their counterpart in an infinity of distinct systems.

In sum, the above observations imply that Geach is correct; there are two distinct relations, identity and indiscernibility, both of which are I-predicates—that is, satisfy the definiens of the identity definition 10.19. Therefore, this definiens cannot imply identity, but only the weaker property of indiscernibility, Ind; that is,

(10.22) $(F)(Fx \equiv Fy) \supset \text{Ind}(x,y)$.

Strict identity awaits a further specification. Interestingly, however, David Widerker has given a proof based on the completeness theorem for first-order logic with identity that this logic cannot provide a stronger requirement for absolute identity than that given by the definitional axioms 10.17 and 10.18 or their equivalents.[51] In fact—and this is the essence of the problem—given what is required of the definitions of identity and indiscernibility, no standard predicate logic of any order could serve to distinguish these relations. This is so because, in order to conform to our pre-formalized but clear intuitions, the definitions of identity and indiscernibility must provide for the following:

(I.1) Identity and indiscernibility must be equivalence relations (i.e., reflexive, symmetric, and transitive) defined over every category of entities.

(I.2) For either identity or indiscernibility, any entities a and b will have this property if and only if they in some sense share all their properties. Here we have two different senses of 'share all their properties'.

(I.3) Identity must imply indiscernibility, but not vice versa.

The generalized Geach thesis that standard predicate logics are incapable of distinguishing between identity and indiscernibility follows from the impossibility of formulating definitions in these logics that can jointly satisfy I.2 and I.3. Specifically, the entire problem rests on distinguishing *two* senses in which entities a and b can share all their properties. Though two distinct definienda are required, the only way in such logics that the necessary and sufficient definiens requirement of 'sharing all properties' can be parsed is by the single '$(F)(Fa \equiv Fb)$' or its equivalent, and this guarantees *only* indiscernibility, not the finer numerical identity. In short, standard predicate logics are simply too gross to be capable of the necessary distinction. This must prove an embarrassment for Quineans, who self-righteously wield the slogan 'No entity without identity', since for the concept of identity itself we have no specifiable identity conditions that successfully distinguish it from indiscernibility, and 'No entity without indiscernibility' misses the mark completely.

Given this situation, our alternatives are (a), with Geach, to retain standard predicate logics as canonical and relinquish hope of a satisfactory account of absolute identity in favor of the weaker relative identity (i.e., indiscernibility relative to a given property), or (b) to provide definitions in a refined logic satisfying conditions I.1–I.3 above.

Option (b) is available to us in PPL. In chapter 9, as axiom A6 of PPL, identity was specified as:

(ID) $(a)(b)\{(\exists Id_i)Id_i(a,b) \equiv (P)(P_j)[P_j(a) \equiv P_j(b)]\}$,

where the global variables 'a' and 'b' range over entities of all three classes: individuals, intensions, and instances. In words, entity a is related by an instance of ID to entity b if and only if every instance P_i of every property P that belongs to a also belongs to b, and conversely. The uniqueness of the instance of identity Id_j is guaranteed by the principle of instance uniqueness (IU). In contrast to ID, indiscernibility, Ind, is defined through its instances by the axiom:

(IND) $(a)(b)[(\exists Ind_j)Ind_j(a,b) \equiv (P)[(\exists P_i)P_i(a) \equiv (\exists P_j)P_j(b)]]$.

In words, a is related by an instance of Ind to b if and only if for every property P, if there is an instance of P, P_i, that applies to a, then there exists an instance of P, P_j, that applies to b, and conversely. As so defined, Id and Ind satisfy conditions I.1–I.3. They are equivalence relations, Id implies Ind but not conversely, and, most important, we have the requisite two different senses in which entities a and b share 'the same properties'. Under ID we have the very strong condition that a and b are identical if and only if they share numerically the same instances of numerically the same property universals, whereas under IND we have the weaker condition that a and b are indiscernible if and only if they have instances of the same property universals, though not necessarily the same instances. The latter would be the case, for example, for all entities in Black's symmetric universes.

Instance ontology is perennial in the history of Western philosophy. Yet, despite its persistent recurrence, the doctrine has remained obscure in its tenets, lacking in explicit supporting arguments, and undeveloped in its ontological and logic implications. In this book I have attempted to go some way to remedy these deficiencies. The analytical results have, in many ways, been extraordinary. On the ontological side, we have seen the possibility of unit attributes understood in the manner of moderate realism constituting a single-category ontology that avoids the flaws of classic substance/attribute ontology. Arguments for relation instances have been presented, among the strongest following from an ontic analysis of relations, an area that, because of historical prejudices, has been generally neglected in ontology. Equally remarkable are the results on the side of formal logic. Formalization of the logic inherent in instance moderate realism has given rise to a refined analytical, inference tool, PPL, which allows the precision necessary to distinguish between legitimate and illegitimate impredicative specifications. As a result, the classic self-referential paradoxes have been diagnosed and prevented in the refined extended predicate logic that is PPL, all without the usual ad hoc maneuvers such as a system of types or restrictions on the standard rules of inference. The same analysis has revealed that the celebrated limitation theorems of Gödel and Tarski do not hold in PPL and, relatedly, that the same finite syntactical consistency proof that applied to PPL can be extended to establish the consistency of an 'intensional' formalization of arithmetic, an account of arithmetic well motivated by instance ontology. Finally, we observed how instance ontology formulated in PPL solves the fundamental problem of formally distinguishing between identity and indiscernibility. What further problem-solving capacities are latent in instance ontology plus PPL remain to be seen.

Notes

Chapter 1   Instance Ontology

1. P. F. Strawson, *Individuals* (London: Methuen, 1971), pp. 168–69, n. 1. To avoid complications, I have substituted 'John' where Strawson used the pronoun 'His'.
2. This tactic is suggested by D. M. Armstrong in *Nominalism and Realism* (Cambridge: Cambridge University Press, 1978), p. 80.
3. John Cook Wilson, *Statement and Inference*, vol. I (Oxford: Clarendon Press, 1926), p. 187 and n. 3; cf. p. 713. Other references to unit relations can be found in vol. 1, pp. 171, 199, 207–8, 233; vol. 2, pp. 665, 670–71, 713.
4. Ibid., vol. 1, p. 207.
5. For a less 'romantic' example, consider:

   a's distance from *b* is greater than *c*'s distance from *d*.

   Here it would seem that we are asserting a relation of Greater-than to exist between two instances of the Distance relation, which, not so related, would be affirmed by the grammatical forms '*a* is a distance from *b*' and '*c* is a distance from *d*'. For it cannot be the case that we are asserting that the universal Distance is greater than itself; nor can we evade the appeal to instances by saying that the Greater-than relation is between numbers that are measurements of the distances. Since the Greater-than relation is asymmetric, the numerical measurements must be nonidentical contraries which the Distance relation cannot simultaneously possess. However, instances of the Distance relation solve this problem.
6. Edmund Husserl, *Logical Investigations*, vol. 1, trans. J. Findlay (New York: Humanities Press, 1970), pp. 376–77.
7. Russell's early adherence to instance ontology is described by Thomas Foster, "Russell on Particularized Relations," *Russell: The Journal of the Bertrand Russell Archives* 3 (1983–84): 129–43.
8. Wilson, *Statement and Inference*. vol. 1, pp. 171, 187, 199, 207–8, 232; vol. 2, pp. 665, 670–71, 713.
9. Nicholas Wolterstorff, *On Universals* (Chicago: University of Chicago Press, 1970), pp. 90ff.
10. Strawson, *Individuals*, pp. 168–69, n. 1.
11. William of Ockham, *The Summa Logicae*, Part 1, trans. Michael Loux as *Ockham's Theory of Terms* (Notre Dame, Ind.: University of Notre Dame Press, 1974), p. 88.
12. G. F. Stout, "The Nature of Universals and Propositions," (1921), rpt. in *Studies in Philosophy and Psychology* (London: Macmillan, 1930), pp. 384–403.
13. D. C. Williams, "The Elements of Being," *Review of Metaphysics* 7 (1953): 3–18, 171–92. Keith Campbell, *Abstract Particulars* (Oxford: Basil Blackwell, 1990); id., "The Metaphysics of Abstract Particulars," in *The Foundations of Analytic Philosophy*, ed. P. French et al. (Minneapolis: University of Minnesota Press, 1981), pp. 477–88; id., "Abstract Particulars and the Philosophy of Mind," *Australasian Journal of Philosophy* 61 (1983): 129–41.
14. Armstrong, *Nominalism and Realism*, pp. 64ff.
15. Each of these types of nominalism is analyzed in detail in ibid.
16. Ibid. and Reinhardt Grossmann, *The Categorical Structure of the World* (Bloomington: Indiana University Press, 1983). A now classic rebuttal of resemblance nominalism (considered by some to

be the most defensible form of nominalism) is found in Arthur Pap, "Nominalism, Empiricism, and Universals," *Philosophical Quarterly* 9 (1959): 330–40, and Frank Jackson, "Statements about Universals," *Mind* 86 (1977): 427–29. See also D. M. Armstrong, *Universals: An Opinionated Introduction* (Boulder, Colo.: Westview Press, 1989). For a refutation of instance nominalism see Herbert Hochberg, "A Refutation of Moderate Nominalism," *Australasian Journal of Philosophy* 66, no. 2 (1988): 188–207. Part of Hochberg's argument is that no type of nominalism can account for the order inherent in asymmetric relations.

17. D. M. Armstrong, *What is a Law of Nature?* (Cambridge: Cambridge University Press, 1983), and Michael Tooley, *Causation: A Realist Approach* (Oxford: Clarendon Press, 1987).

18. Penelope Maddy, *Realism in Mathematics* (Oxford: Clarendon Press, 1990), and John Bigelow, *The Reality of Numbers* (Oxford: Clarendon Press, 1988).

19. Naturalism can be defined as the contemporary version of nominalistic empiricism, which holds that (a) all truths are contingent, (b) all objects are natural objects (spatiotemporally placed and constituting nodes in causal chains), and (c) all knowledge is acquired on the basis of the empirical methods of the natural sciences.

20. W. V. O. Quine, "Two Dogmas of Empiricism," 1951, rpt. in *From a Logical Point of View*, 2d ed. (New York: Harper & Row, 1961), id., *Word and Object* (Cambridge, Mass.: MIT Press, 1960). Ludwig Wittgenstein, *Philosophical Investigations* (Oxford: Basil Blackwell, 1953).

21. Jerrold Katz, *The Metaphysics of Meaning* (Cambridge, Mass.: MIT Press, 1990). See also id., *Language and Other Abstract Objects* (Tototwa, N.J.: Rowman & Littlefield, 1981).

22. Armstrong, *Nominalism*, p. 86.

23. Gottlob Frege, *Translations from the Philosophical Writings of Gottlob Frege*, ed. Peter Geach and Max Black (Oxford: Blackwell, 1970), p. 106. Bertrand Russell, *My Philosophical Development* (London: Allen & Unwin, 1959), p. 67.

24. Armstrong, *Universals*, p. 110.

25. William and Martha Kneale, *The Development of Logic* (Oxford: Clarendon Press, 1962), pp. 138ff.

26. Aristotle states that central to metaphysics, as among the most general attributes of the real, are sameness, contrariety, otherness, prior and posterior, genus and species, perfection and unity, whole and part (*Metaphysics* 1004b1–8, 1005a11–18).

27. Cf. Aristotle *Categories* 15b17ff. See also *Metaphysics* 1038b15ff. and *Physics* 210a14ff.

28. Leibniz, *Philosophical Papers and Letters*, 2d ed., ed. Leroy Loemker (Dordrecht: Reidel, 1969), p. 264. See also pp. 334 and 337.

29. Bertrand Russell, *The Principles of Mathematics*, 2d ed. (1903; rpt. ed., New York: Norton, 1938), pp. 221ff.

30. F. H. Bradley, *Collected Essays*, vol. 2 (Westport, Conn.: Greenwood Press, 1970), p. 638.

31. Leibniz, *Philosophical Papers*, p. 704.

32. Frank Lewis, *Substance and Predication in Aristotle* (Cambridge: Cambridge University Press, 1991), pp. 161ff.; also id., "Form and Predication in Aristotle's *Metaphysics*," in *How Things Are*, ed. J. Bogen and J. McGuire (Dordrecht: Reidel, 1985), pp. 58–86.

33. Armstrong, *Nominalism*, p. 111.

34. Ibid., p. 113.

35. Ibid., p. xiv.

36. Jerrold Katz, "Has the Description Theory of Names been Refuted?," in *Meaning and Method: Essays in Honor of Hilary Putnam*, ed. George Boolos (Cambridge: Cambridge University Press, 1990), pp. 31–61.

37. P. F. Strawson, *Subject and Predicate in Logic and Grammar* (London: Methuen, 1974), pp. 25ff.

38. Bertrand Russell, *Human Knowledge: Its Scope and Limits* (New York: Simon & Schuster, 1948), pp. 460ff., 250ff.; id., *The Problems of Philosophy* (Oxford: Oxford University Press, 1959), pp. 31ff. Hochberg has defended Russell's theory of structural realism against critics, arguing that if relations are taken intensionally, not extensionally, then the arguments of the critics fail. See Herbert Hochberg, "Causal Connections, Universals, and Russell's Hypothetico-Scientific Realism," *Monist* 77, no. 1 (1994): 71–92.

39. Russell, *Human Knowledge*, p. 468.

40. Katz, *Metaphysics of Meaning*.

41. W. V. O. Quine, "On the Individuation of Attributes" 1975, rpt. in *Theories and Things* (Cambridge, Mass.: Harvard University Press, Belknap Press, 1981), p. 102, my emphasis.

42. See Susan Haack, *Philosophy of Logics* (Cambridge: Cambridge University Press, 1978), pp. 173f.

43. W. V. O. Quine, "Logic and the Reification of Universals," in *From a Logical Point of View*, p. 103. See Haack, *Philosophy of Logics*, pp. 43ff.

44. Quine, "Two Dogmas of Empiricism," p. 21.

45. P. F. Strawson and H. P. Grice, "In Defense of a Dogma," *Philosophical Review* 65, no. 2 (1956): 141–58. The non sequitur character of Quine's circular argument is also observed by William Alston, "Quine on Meaning," in *The Philosophy of W. V. Quine*, ed. L. Hahn and P. Schilpp (LaSalle, Ill.: Open Court, 1986), pp. 54–55.

46. Strawson, *Subject and Predicate in Logic and Grammar*, p. 37.

47. Katz, *Metaphysics of Meaning*, p. 186.

48. Gottlob Frege, *The Foundations of Arithmetic*, 2d ed. (Evanston, Ill.: Northwestern University Press, 1968), p. 79.

49. For an analysis of the concept of identity see Thomas Morris, *Understanding Identity Statements* (Aberdeen: Aberdeen University Press, 1984).

50. For a balanced discussion of the substantivist versus the relationist conception of space/time in regard to modern physics see Lawrence Sklar, *Philosophy of Physics* (Boulder, Colo.: Westview Press, 1992), pp. 19ff., 72ff.

51. F. H. Bradley, *Appearance and Reality*, 2d ed. (Oxford: Clarendon Press, 1897), pp. 31–32. Bertrand Russell, *An Essay on the Foundation of Geometry* (Cambridge: Cambridge University Press, 1897), pp. 188ff. Evidence of the influence of Zeno's paradoxes on Leibniz is found in *Philosophical Papers*, p. 496.

52. Leibniz, *Philosophical Papers*, p. 682.

53. Campbell, *Abstract Particulars*, p. 127.

54. See Julius Weinberg, "The Concept of Relations: Some Observations on its History," in *Abstraction, Relation, and Induction* (Madison: University of Wisconsin Press, 1965), pp. 61–119, for a history of Bradley's regress argument.

55. Mark Henninger, *Relations: Medieval Theories, 1250–1325* (Oxford: Clarendon Press, 1989), pp. 153–54.

56. Weinberg, "Concept of Relations," pp. 112ff.

57. David Hume, *Enquiry Concerning Human Understanding*, IV. i. 25; 1777 ed., ed. P. H. Nidditch (Oxford: Clarendon Press, 1975), p. 29.

58. Ibid., VII. i. 50, p. 63.

59. David Hume, *A Treatise on Human Nature*, I. ii. 4; ed. T. H. Green and T. H. Grose (1886; rpt. ed., Germany: Scientia Verlag Aalen, 1964), p. 352.

60. Ibid., appendix, p. 559.

61. That we experience certain causal relations is asserted by D. M. Armstrong in his "Reply to

Menzies," in *Ontology, Causality, and Mind: Essays in Honour of D. M. Armstrong*, ed. J. Bacon, K. Campbell, and L. Reinhardt (Cambridge: Cambridge University Press, 1993), pp. 225–32. Armstrong cites A. Michotte, *The Perception of Causality*, trans. T. Miles (London: Methuen, 1963), as making a strong case for the direct perception of causal relations. Evan Fales provides arguments for the perception of causation and analyzes causation in a manner similar to that of Armstrong in *Causation and Universals* (New York: Routledge, 1990), pp. 11ff.

62. Campbell, *Abstract Particulars*, pp. 98ff.

63. Plotinus, *The Enneads*, trans. Stephen MacKenna, 3d ed. (New York: Pantheon), p. 525.

64. Leibniz, *Philosophical Papers*, p. 531.

65. Ibid., pp. 600–617. See also p. 34.

66. Ibid., p. 343. This quote is from a letter of Leibniz to Arnauld. He restates his thoughts on the distinction between unity per se and unity per accidens several times in his correspondence with Arnauld. See *The Leibniz–Arnauld Correspondence*, ed. and trans. H. T. Mason (New York: Barnes & Noble, 1967), pp. 88, 93–94, 121–22.

67. Bertrand Russell, "Some Explanations in Reply to Mr. Bradley," *Mind* 19 (1908): 374.

68. F. H. Bradley, "Reply to Mr. Russell's Explanation," *Mind* 20 (1911): 74.

69. Russell, *Principles of Mathematics*, p. 49.

70. Strawson, *Individuals*, pp. 167ff.

71. Hochberg, "Refutation of Moderate Nominalism."

72. Stout, *Studies in Philosophy and Psychology*, pp. 384ff.

73. Kurt Gödel, "What is Cantor's Continuum Problem?," in *Philosophy of Mathematics: Selected Readings*, 2d ed., ed. P. Benacerraf and H. Putnam (Cambridge: Cambridge University Press, 1983), p. 484, n. 26.

74. Michael Hallett, *Cantorian Set Theory and Limitation of Size* (Oxford: Clarendon Press, 1984), pp. 33–34.

75. Ibid., pp. 34ff.

76. D. M. Armstrong, "Classes as States-of-Affairs," *Mind* 100 (1991): 189–200.

77. Bigelow, *Reality of Numbers*, pp. 106f.; and id., "Sets as Haecceities," in *Ontology, Causality, and Mind*, ed. Bacon et al., pp. 73–76.

78. Max Black, *Caveats and Critiques* (Ithaca, N.Y.: Cornell University Press, 1975), p. 86.

79. Russell, *Principles of Mathematics*, p. 140.

80. Russell, *My Philosophical Development*, p. 67.

81. Frege, *Translations from the Philosophical Writings*, p. 106.

82. Bertrand Russell, *Introduction to Mathematical Philosophy* (1919; rpt. ed., New York: Simon & Schuster, 1971), p. 183.

83. Russell, *Principles of Mathematics*, p. 81.

84. Gottlob Frege, *Posthumous Writings*, ed. H. Hermes, F. Kambartel, and F. Kaulbach (Chicago: University of Chicago Press, 1979), p. 183; id., *Translations from the Philosophical Writings*, pp. 102, 104, 106.

85. The 1900 manuscript is entitled "Do Differences Differ?" In a prior unpublished manuscript of 1897, "An Analysis of Mathematical Reasoning," Russell argued for instances of certain relations (those of Good, Red, Heavy, and Causation) based on the spatial and/or temporal localization of their relata. The manuscripts are in the Russell Archives, McMaster University, Hamilton, Ontario.

86. Philip Kitcher, *The Nature of Mathematical Knowledge* (New York: Oxford University Press, 1984), pp. 133f., 145f.

87. Maddy, *Realism in Mathematics*, pp. 59ff.; Kurt Gödel, "Russell's Mathematical Logic," in *Philoso-*

phy of Mathematics, ed. Benacerraf and Putnam, p. 449; id., "What is Cantor's Continuum Problem?" p. 483.

88. Nelson Goodman, "The World of Individuals" (1956), rpt. in *Contemporary Philosophical Logic,* ed. I. Copi and J. Gould (New York: St. Martin's Press, 1978), pp. 177–90.

89. W. V. O. Quine, *Set Theory and Its Logic* (Cambridge, Mass.: Harvard University Press, 1963), p. 1.

90. Gottlob Frege, "On Concept and Object," in *Translations from the Philosophical Writings,* pp. 42–55. Frege made a peculiar distinction between aggregates composed of their elements and extensions of concepts which have their being 'in the concept'. There are no empty aggregates, only empty extensions.

Chapter 2 Traditional versus Instance Ontology

1. U2 a″ and b″ are, I propose, useful tools for interpreting scholastic moderate realism, rendering its obscure distinctions coherent and intelligible in marking real differences. Thus, Aquinas's representative view was that intensions—e.g., Man—are in themselves neither universal nor particular but are particular in their mode of inherence in individuals—e.g., in Socrates. Since being universal and being particular are apparently contradictory, in requiring the same entity to be both, scholastic realism is apparently incoherent. However, this contradiction is removed when, in keeping with the tradition, 'universal' is read as implying 'is multiply predicative', and, concomitantly, 'particular' in regard to intensions is read as 'predicative of only one subject'. Then, in being 'neither universal nor particular', an intension X is neither predicative of many nor predicative of one subject; i.e., X is not predicative at all, which is the assertion of U2 a″. Then, to say that an intension X is 'particular when inhering in a subject' can be consistently construed as meaning that X is an aspect of a unit property X_i, where the later is predicative of a single subject only. This is the assertion of U2 b″.

2. D. M. Armstrong, *Nominalism and Realism* (Cambridge: Cambridge University Press, 1978), pp. 12ff.

3. Translated by Paul Spade in *Five Texts on the Mediaeval Problem of Universals* (Indianapolis: Hackett, 1994), p. 172.

4. D. M. Armstrong, *Universals: An Opinionated Introduction* (Boulder, Colo.: Westview Press, 1989), p. 17.

5. William of Ockham, *Ockham's Theory of Terms: Part 1 of the Summa Logicae,* trans. by Michael Loux (Notre Dame, Ind.: University of Notre Dame Press, 1974), pp. 162ff.

6. Ibid., p. 170.

7. Ibid.

8. Keith Campbell, *Abstract Particulars* (Oxford: Basil Blackwell, 1990), pp. 98–99.

9. These and other objections are found in James Van Cleve, "Three Versions of the Bundle Theory," *Philosophical Studies* 47 (1985): 95–107.

10. Max Black, "Identity of Indiscernibles," in *Universals and Particulars: Readings in Ontology,* ed. Michael Loux (Notre Dame, Ind.: University of Notre Dame Press, 1976), pp. 250–62, and A. J. Ayer, "The Identity of Indiscernibles," ibid., pp. 263–70.

11. Bertrand Russell, *An Inquiry into Meaning and Truth* (London: Allen & Unwin, 1940), pp. 231, 240, 337; id., *Human Knowledge: Its Scope and Limits* (New York: Simon & Schuster, 1948), pp. 292–308. Campbell, *Abstract Particulars,* pp. 68–69, 130–33. Nelson Goodman, *The Structure of Appearance,* 2d ed. (Indianapolis: Bobbs-Merrill, 1966), pp. 200–211.

12. C. R. Harris, *Duns Scotus,* vol. 2 (New York: Humanities Press, 1959), pp. 94f.

13. Campbell, *Abstract Particulars,* p. 9.

14. In reply to these arguments, an advocate of bare particulars has responded that Campbell and I have misunderstood the nature of bare particulars. Such an entity, it is said, has properties and relations but does not have an essence or nature of its own. But this seems not to differ from the conception that has been impugned here, for presumably, to so characterize a bare particular means that every specification of it is accidental to it—i.e., it would be what it is independent of *any* attribution predicated of it. This, however, is what Campbell and I are arguing is incoherent.

15. Russell, *Inquiry into Meaning and Truth*, p. 98.

16. See the essays collected in Donald Davidson, *Essays on Actions and Events* (Oxford: Clarendon Press, 1980). Barry Taylor, *Modes of Occurrence* (Oxford: Basil Blackwell, 1985).

17. Jaegwon Kim, "Events as Property Exemplification," in *Action Theory*, ed. M. Brand and D. Walton (Dordrecht: Reidel, 1976), pp. 159–77. Also in the same volume see Myles Brand, "Particulars, Events, and Actions," and R. M. Martin, "Events and Actions: Some Comments on Brand and Kim."

18. D. M. Armstrong, *What is a Law of Nature?* (Cambridge: Cambridge University Press, 1983), pp. 88ff.

19. Bas van Fraassen, *Laws and Symmetry* (Oxford: Clarendon Press, 1989), pp. 103ff.

20. See Peter Menzies, "Laws of Nature, Modality, and Humean Supervenience," in *Ontology, Causality and Mind: Essays in Honour of D. M. Armstrong*, ed. J. Bacon, K. Campbell, and L. Reinhardt (Cambridge: Cambridge University Press, 1993), pp. 194ff.

21. Campbell, *Abstract Particulars*, p. 146. For an overview of the standard view of fields as relational structures, see Harold Oliver, *A Relational Metaphysics* (The Hague: Martinus Nijhoff, 1991).

22. Alfred North Whitehead, *Process and Reality: An Essay in Cosmology* (New York: The Free Press, 1978). For a detailed analysis of Whitehead's ontology, see F. B. Wallack, *The Epochal Nature of Process in Whitehead's Metaphysics* (Albany, N.Y.: SUNY Press, 1980). Also promoting Whiteheadian metaphysics is Oliver, *Relational Metaphysics*.

23. This is the repeated theme in Whitehead's *The Concept of Nature* (Cambridge: Cambridge University Press, 1920).

24. Whitehead, *Process and Reality*, p. 20; cf. p. 27.

25. Ibid., p. 73.

26. Ervin Laszlo, *Introduction to Systems Philosophy* (New York: Gordon and Breach, 1972), and Ludwig von Bertalanffy, *General Systems Theory* (New York: George Braziller, 1968).

27. I. Blauber, V. Sadovsky, and E. Yudin, *Systems Theory: Philosophical and Methodological Problems* (Moscow: Progress Publishers, 1977), p. 119.

28. Ibid., p. 127.

29. J. H. Marchal, "On the Concept of System," *Philosophy of Science* 42 (1975): 448–68.

Chapter 3   Plato and Aristotle on Instance Ontology

1. For references both for and against a category of property instances in Plato, see the dissenting view of David Gallop, *Plato: Phaedo* (Oxford: Clarendon Press, 1975).

2. Raphael Demos, "Note on Plato's Theory of Ideas," *Philosophy and Phenomenological Research* 8 (1947–48): 456–60. R. S. Bluck, *Plato's Phaedo* (London: Routledge & Kegan Paul, 1955), pp. 17–18. G. Vlastos, "Reasons and Causes in the Phaedo," *Philosophical Review* 78 (1969): 291–325.

3. From the translation by H. Tredennick in *The Collected Dialogues of Plato*, ed. Edith Hamilton (New York: Random House, 1961), pp. 83–84.

4. Evidently this puzzle over the fact that a person can be both short and tall was prominent in philosophical circles, it reportedly being found in the fifth century B.C. Greek comic poet and Pythagorean Epicharmos. I have not had access to the text so as to verify the reference, however.

5. Hector-Nero Castañeda, "Leibniz and Plato's *Phaedo* Theory of Relations and Predication," in *Leibniz: Critical and Interpretive Essays*, ed. M. Hooker (Minneapolis: University of Minnesota Press, 1982), pp. 124–59. Also id., "Plato's *Phaedo* Theory of Relations," *Journal of Philosophical Logic* 1, nos. 3–4 (1972): 467–80. See also Mohan Matthen, "Plato's Treatment of Relational Statements in the Phaedo," *Phronesis* 27, no. 1 (1982): 90–100; Mark McPherran, "Matthen on Castañeda and Plato's Treatment of Relational Statements in the *Phaedo*," *Phronesis* 28, no. 3 (1983): 298–306.

6. Julius Weinberg, "The Concept of Relation: Some Observations on Its History," in *Abstraction, Relation, and Induction: Three Essays in the History of Thought* (Madison: University of Wisconsin Press, 1965), pp. 61–119.

7. Constantine Cavarnos, *The Classical Theory of Relations* (Belmont, Mass.: Institute for Byzantine and Modern Greek Studies, 1973), pp. 14, 43.

8. Bertrand Russell, *Principles of Mathematics*, 2d ed. (New York: Norton, 1938), rpt. from 1903 ed., p. 222.

9. G. W. Leibniz, *Philosophical Papers and Letters*, 2d ed., ed. Leroy Loemker (Dordrecht: Reidel, 1969), p. 704.

10. Reinhardt Grossmann, *The Categorical Structure of the World* (Bloomington: Indiana University Press, 1983), pp. 159ff.

11. Ibid., p. 162.

12. Castañeda, "Leibniz and Plato's *Phaedo* Theory of Relations and Predication," p. 126.

13. See Mark Henninger, *Relations: Medieval Theories, 1250–1325* (Oxford: Clarendon Press, 1989).

14. Francis M. Cornford, *Plato's Theory of Knowledge* (Indianapolis: Bobbs-Merrill, 1957), pp. 43–45.

15. Ibid., p. 159, n. 1.

16. James Lesher, "Aristotle on Form, Substance, and Universals: A Dilemma," *Phronesis* 16, no. 2 (1971): 169–78. See also Rogers Albritton, "Forms of Particular Substances in Aristotle's *Metaphysics*," *Journal of Philosophy* 54, no. 22 (1957): 699–708. For an overview of the contrast between Aristotle's view on substance in the *Categories* and that in the *Metaphysics*, see Edwin Hartmann, "Aristotle on the Identity of Substance and Essence," *Philosophical Review* 85, no. 4 (1976): 545–61.

17. Werner Jaeger, *Aristotle*, trans. Richard Robinson (Oxford: Clarendon University Press, 1934), pp. 40 and 46–47, n. 3. See also Robert Turnbull, "Aristotle's Debt to the 'Natural Philosophy' of the *Phaedo*," *Philosophical Quarterly* 8 (1958): 131–43.

18. Frank Lewis, *Substance and Predication in Aristotle* (Cambridge: Cambridge University Press, 1991), pp. 278ff.

19. J. L. Ackrill, *Aristotle's* Categories *and* De Interpretatione (Oxford: Clarendon Press, 1963), p. 4.

20. Lewis, *Substance*, p. 55.

21. W. D. Ross, *Aristotle's* Metaphysics (Oxford: Clarendon Press, 1924), 1:lxxxiii. Ross observes that Aristotle draws ontological distinctions where grammar does not and ignores some distinctions that grammar does draw.

22. Ackrill, *Aristotle's* Categories, pp. 74ff.

23. Wilfred Sellars, "Substance and Form in Aristotle," *Journal of Philosophy* 54, no. 21 (1957): 688–99.

24. Ackrill, *Aristotle's* Categories, pp. 74f. According to Ackrill, Aristotle may also be alluding to property instances at *Categories* 4a10ff. W. D. Ross, *Aristotle*, 4th ed. (London: Methuen, 1953), pp. 23–24. Hippocrates Apostle, *Aristotle's Categories and Propositions* (Grinnell, Iowa: Peripatetic Press, 1980), pp. 54ff. See also R. J. Jones, "Are the Qualities of Particular Things Universal or

Particular?," *Philosophical Reviw* 58, no. 1 (1949): 152–70; G. Matthews and S. M. Cohen, "The One and the Many," *Review of Metaphysics* 21 (1968): 630–55. For an overview of the controversy and detailed textual arguments in support of the thesis that Aristotle held the doctrine of unit properties, see Robert Heinaman, "Non-substantial Individuals in the *Categories*," *Phronesis* 26, no. 3 (1981): 295–307. For another overview of the Ackrill versus Owen debate, see J. M. E. Moravcsik, "Aristotle on Predication," *Philosophical Review* 76 (1967): 80–96.

25. G. E. L. Owen, *Logic, Science and Dialectic* (Ithaca, N.Y.: Cornell University Press, 1986), pp. 252ff. Michael Frede, *Essays in Ancient Philosophy* (Minneapolis: University of Minnesota Press, 1987), pp. 58ff. Lewis, *Substance*, pp. 66ff.

26. R. E. Allen, "Individual Properties in Aristotle's *Categories*," *Phronesis* 14, no. 1 (1969): 31–39.

27. For an overview of the issues and difficulties, see Frede, *Essays*, pp. 63ff., 78ff. Likewise, as well as for the view that Aristotle did not advocate a doctrine of unit attributes in *Metaphysics* Z and H, see Michael Loux, *Primary Ousia; An Essay on Aristotle's* Metaphysics *Z and H* (Ithaca, N.Y.: Cornell University Press, 1991), pp. 197ff.

28. Ross, *Aristotle's* Metaphysics, 1:cii.

29. This is the second stage in the two-stage process of *aphairesis*. See Ross, *Aristotle's* Metaphysics, 2:165. See also Lewis, *Substance*, pp. 282ff.

30. Mary Gill, *Aristotle on Substance* (Princeton, N.J.: Princeton University Press, 1989). See also Ross, *Aristotle's* Metaphysics, 1:cxvi–cxix, and Albritton, "Forms of Particular Substances in Aristotle's *Metaphysics.*"

31. See the papers by J. Lukasiewicz, G. E. Anscombe, and K. R. Popper under "The Principle of Individuation," in *Aristotelian Society Supplement* 27 (1953): 69–120.

32. Joseph Owens, "Matter and Predication in Aristotle," in *The Concept of Matter in Greek and Medieval Philosophy*, ed. Ernan McMullin (Notre Dame, Ind.: University of Notre Dame Press, 1963), pp. 79–93.

33. Gill, *Aristotle on Substance*, pp. 31–34. See also John Cooper, *Reason and Human Good in Aristotle* (Cambridge, Mass.: Harvard University Press, 1975), pp. 28ff.

34. See Lesher, "Aristotle on Form, Substance, and Universals."

35. See David Ross, *Aristotle*, 4th ed. (London: Methuen, 1953), p. 172.

36. Frank Lewis, "Form and Predication in Aristotle's *Metaphysics*," in *How Things Are*, ed. J. Bogen and J. McGuire (Dordrecht: Reidel, 1985), pp. 59–83.

37. Gottlob Frege, *Translations from the Philosophical Writings of Gottlob Frege*, ed. P. Geach and M. Black (Oxford: Basil Blackwell, 1970), pp. 54–55.

38. Ibid.

39. Ibid.

40. See Henninger, *Relations*, p. 8.

41. See Cavarnos, *Classical Theory of Relations*, p. 49.

42. Ibid., pp. 56ff.

43. Henninger, *Relations*, pp. 66ff.

44. Cavarnos, *Classical Theory of Relations*, pp. 92, 104f.

Chapter 4   Some Medieval and Early Modern Views

1. Maurice de Wulf, *History of Medieval Philosophy*, vol. 1, trans. E. Messenger (New York: Nelson & Sons, 1951), p. 139.

2. For the text see Richard McKeon, *Selections from Medieval Philosophers*, 1:97ff. For discussion see de Wulf, *Medieval Philosophy*, p. 141.

3. McKeon, *Selections*, p. 97.

4. Jorge J. E. Gracia, *Introduction to the Problem of Individuation in the Early Middle Ages* (Washington, D.C.: Catholic University Press, 1984), p. 78. Gracia provides an excellent analysis and translation of relevant texts.

5. Ibid., p. 83.

6. Ibid.

7. Ibid., p. 67.

8. Parviz Morewedge, *The* Metaphysica *of Avicenna* (New York: Columbia University Press, 1973), p. 33.

9. Ibid.

10. Ibid.

11. Ibid., p. 34.

12. Ibid., p. 33.

13. Michael Marmura, "Avicenna's Chapter, 'On the Relative,' in *Metaphysics* of the *Schifa*," in *Essays on Islamic Philosophy and Science*, ed. George Hourani (Albany, N.Y.: SUNY Press, 1975), pp. 87–88, my emphasis.

14. Ibid., p. 88.

15. Ibid.

16. Ibid.

17. Thomas Aquinas, *Summa Contra Gentiles*, trans. Anton Pegis (Garden City, N.Y.: Doubleday, 1955), p. 127. For commentary see Frederick Copleston, *A History of Philosophy* (Garden City, N.Y.: Doubleday, 1962), vol. 2, pt. II, pp. 172ff. For a detailed description of Aquinas's and scholastic modern realism, see Peter Coffey, *Epistemology*, vol. 1 (Gloucester, Mass.: Peter Smith, 1958), pp. 268–83. For an excellent exposition of the ontological positions concerning universals and individuation taken by various medieval philosophers, see Jorge Gracia, ed., *Individuation in Scholasticism: The Later Middle Ages and Counter-Reformation, 1150–1650* (Albany, N.Y.: SUNY Press, 1994).

18. Thomas Aquinas, *On Being and Essence*, trans. Armand Maurer, 2d ed. (Toronto: Pontifical Institute of Mediaeval Studies, 1968), pp. 36–37.

19. Ibid., p. 37, n. 11.

20. Copleston, *History*, vol. 2, pt. II, pp. 46–47, 239.

21. C. R. S. Harris, *Duns Scotus*, vol. 2 (New York: Humanities Press, 1959), p. 92.

22. Maurice de Wulf, *An Introduction to Scholastic Philosophy*, trans. P. Coffey (New York: Dover, 1956), pp. 107ff. See also J. R. Rosenberg, "Individuation," in *The New Catholic Encyclopedia*, vol. 7 (New York: McGraw-Hill, 1967), pp. 475–78.

23. Harris, *Duns Scotus*, p. 96.

24. Ibid., p. 95.

25. Disputation V of Saurez's *Disputationes metaphysicae* is translated in Jorge Gracia, *Suarez on Individuation* (Milwaukee, Wis.: Marquette University Press, 1982), pp. 121–22.

26. Trans. Michael Ewbank in "The Route to Substance in Suarez's *Disputationes Metaphysicae*," *Proceedings of the American Catholic Philosophical Association* 61 (1987): 103.

27. For Suarez a per se unity is the intrinsic unit necessary to form a complete essence of a certain genus. Re Suarez's argument for hylomorphism, see John Kronen, "The Importance of the Concept

of Substantial Unity in Suarez's Argument for Hylomorphism," *American Catholic Philosophical Quarterly* 65, no. 3 (1991): 335–60.

28. Trans. Jorge Gracia in "Suarez's Conception of Metaphysics: A Step in the Direction of Mentalism?," *American Catholic Philosophical Quarterly* 65, no. 3 (1991): 287–309.

29. Ibid., pp. 276–77.

30. Trans. Gracia in *Suarez on Individuation*, pp. 32–33. Having said this, Suarez at VI. 2. 9 muddies the water further, saying, "For, if the nature [of universality] were not in some way one, then it would not be universal at all, but would be a multitude or aggregate of things. If, however, it were not capable of being in many, it would not be universal, but singular. And it is indeed necessary that it be in many things in a manner opposed to singularity or individuality, that is, that it be in many inferiors which can be multiplied and enumerated under this common notion. Therefore, these two, namely, unity and community, are to be explained in such a way that it will be clear that the aspect (*rationem*) properly constitutive of the universal is not to be found in things apart from the intellect" (ibid., p. 277).

31. De Wulf, *History*, pp. 147ff.

32. William of Ockham, *Summa totius logicae*, 1. C. XIV. Trans. in Richard J. Van Iten, *The Problem of Universals* (New York: Appleton-Century-Crofts, 1970), p. 71.

33. See Marilyn Adams, "Universals in the Early Fourteenth Century," in *The Cambridge History of Latin Medieval Philosophy*, ed. N. Kretzmann, A. Kenny, and J. Pinborg (Cambridge: Cambridge University Press, 1982), pp. 411–39.

34. Van Iten, *Universals*, pp. 69 and 72.

35. Ibid., pp. 74–75.

36. Calvin Normore, "Buridan's Ontology," in *How Things Are*, ed. J. Bogen and J. McGuire (Dordrecht: Reidel, 1985), pp. 180–203.

37. In Buridan's *Questiones in metaphysicam aristoteles*, V, q. 8, fols. 31, 33. Portions translated by Normore, "Buridan's Ontology," p. 198.

38. Julius Weinberg, "The Concept of Relation: Some Observations on Its History," in *Abstraction, Relation, and Induction: Three Essays in the History of Thought* (Madison: University of Wisconsin Press, 1965), pp. 79ff.

39. Ockham, *Ockham's Theory of Terms*, trans. Michael Loux (Notre Dame, Ind.: University of Notre Dame Press, 1974), p. 170.

40. Weinberg, "Concept of Relations," p. 93. Reference to Avicenna, *Metaphysica*, iii, chap. 10.

41. Mark Henninger, *Relations: Medieval Theories, 1250–1325* (Oxford: Clarendon Press, 1989), pp. 19ff.

42. Ibid., pp. 152ff.

43. Ibid., pp. 85–86. See also Weinberg, "Concept of Relations."

44. Henninger, *Relations*, pp. 16–17.

45. Ibid., pp. 34–35.

46. G. W. Leibniz, *New Essays Concerning Human Understanding*, trans. A. Langley (La Salle, Ill.: Open Court, 1949), II, 25, par. 10, p. 236; hereafter abbreviated *NE*.

47. Nicholas Rescher, *Leibniz's Metaphysics of Nature* (Dordrecht: Reidel, 1981), pp. 56ff.

48. Gottfried Wilhelm Leibniz, *Philosophical Papers and Letters*, 2d ed., ed. Leroy Loemker (Dordrecht: Reidel, 1969), pp. 445 and 609; hereafter abbreviated *L*. See also *NE* II, 25, part. 1, p. 235.

49. John Locke, *Essay Concerning Human Understanding*, II. xxv. 8; ed. P. Nidditch (Oxford: Clarendon Press, 1975), p. 322.

50. David Hume, *A Treatise on Human Nature*, I. i. 4; ed. T. H. Green and T. H. Grose (1886; rpt. ed., Germany: Scientia Verlag Aalen, 1964), p. 320.

51. Laurence McCullough, "Leibniz and Traditional Philosophy," *Studia Leibnitiana* 10, no. 2 (1978): 254–70. See also id., "Leibniz's Principle of Individuation in His *Disputatio metaphysica de principio individui* of 1663," in *Individuation and Identity in Early Modern Philosophy*, ed. K. Barber and J. Gracia (Albany, N.Y.: SUNY Press, 1994), pp. 201–17; Kenneth Clatterbaugh, *Leibniz's Doctrine of Individual Accidents*, in *Studia Leibnitiana*, special issue no. 4 (Wiesbaden: Steiner, 1973); id., "Leibniz's Principle of the Identity of Indiscernibles," *Studia Leibnitiana* 3, no. 4 (1971): 241–52. Unlike some of his near-contemporaries, Leibniz admired much of scholastic philosophy, describing it in one place as a "great treasure of very important and strictly demonstrative truths." See *L* 309.

52. Gottfried Wilhelm Leibniz, *Disputatio metaphysica de principio individui*, in *Sämtliche Schriften und Briefe*, 6th ser., vol. 1 (Darmstadt: Otto Reich Verlag, 1930). There is a French translation, "*Disputation metaphysique sur le principle d'individuation* de G. W. Leibniz," *Les Études philosophiques* 1 (1979): 79–105.

53. Gottfried Martin, *Leibniz: Logic and Metaphysics*, trans. K. Northcott and P. Lucas (Manchester: Manchester University Press, 1964), pp. 133ff. Benson Mates, *The Philosophy of Leibniz* (Oxford: Oxford University Press, 1986), pp. 170ff.

54. McCullough, "Leibniz's Principle of Individuation," pp. 208–209.

55. Suarez's discussion of Scotus is at *Disputationes metaphysicae*, VI. 1. 2. On Suarez's misrepresenting Scotus, see Copleston, *History*, vol. 2, pt. II, p. 234.

56. In this regard Leibniz was leery of 'abstract entities', holding that knowledge of concrete things is always prior to that of abstract entities (*NE* II, 13, par. 6, p. 148).

57. Bertrand Russell, *A Critical Exposition of the Philosophy of Leibniz* (London: Allen & Unwin, 1900). C. D. Broad, *Leibniz: An Introduction* (London: Cambridge University Press, 1975), p. 37.

58. Mates, *Philosophy of Leibniz*, pp. 216ff.

59. Hide Ishiguro, *Leibniz's Philosophy of Logic and Language* (Ithaca, N.Y.: Cornell University Press, 1972), pp. 94ff.

60. Ibid., p. 101.

61. G. W. Leibniz, *Die Philosophischen Schriften*, 7 vols., ed. C. I. Gerhardt (Berlin, 1857–90; rpt. Hildesheim: Olms, 1965), 2:517; hereafter abbreviated *G*. Trans. in Mates, *Philosophy of Leibniz*, p. 225.

62. E. Bodemann, *Die Leibniz-Handschriften der Königlichen öffentlichen Bibliothek zu Hannover* (Hanover, 1895; rpt. Hildesheim: Olms, 1966, IV. viii. 60r. Trans. in Mates, *Philosophy of Leibniz*, p. 224.

63. Translation is that of Mates, *Philosophy of Leibniz*, p. 235. See also *NE* II, 12, par. 5, p. 148.

64. E.g., see *L* 307, 309, 267, and G. H. R. Parkinson, *Leibniz: Logical Papers* (Oxford: Clarendon Press, 1966), p. 77.

65. Also at *L* 308 and 649.

66. Hector-Nero Castañeda, "Leibniz and Plato's *Phaedo* Theory of Relations and Predication," in *Leibniz: Critical and Interpretive Essays*, ed. M. Hooker (Minneapolis: University of Minnesota Press, 1982), pp. 124–59.

67. Trans. Castañeda, ibid., p. 125. From *Nouvelles lettres et opuscules inédits de Leibniz*, ed. A. Foucher de Careil (Paris: Durand, 1857), p. 108.

68. Trans. Castañeda, ibid., p. 127. From *Elementa philosophiae de summa rerum*, ed. I. Jagodinski (Kasan, 1913), p. 122.

69. See Mates, *Philosophy of Leibniz*, pp. 218ff.

70. Louis Couturat, ed., *Opuscules et fragments inédits de Leibniz: Extraits des manuscrits de la biblio-thèque royale de Hanovre* (Paris, 1903; rpt. Hildesheim: Olms, 1961, pp. 520 and 521; hereafter abbreviated *C*. Translations are in Mates, *Philosophy of Leibniz*, pp. 225 and 226. See also *L* 268.

71. Excerpts of the logical papers are found in Parkinson, *Leibniz: Logical Papers*, pp. 12ff. See also *NE* IV, 17, par. 4, p. 560.

72. Trans. in Parkinson, *Leibniz: Logical Papers*, p. 14.

73. Trans. in Parkinson, *Leibniz: Logical Papers*, p. 12.

74. Whether, as I have assumed, Leibniz intended that the connective referred to by 'to the extent that' be identical with that of 'and by that very fact' is irrelevant to the basic issues discussed here.

75. Trans. by Ishiguro, *Leibniz's Philosophy*, p. 23.

76. Trans. by Parkinson, *Leibniz: Logical Papers*, p. 13. Leibniz here refers to the logician Joachim Jungius (1587–1657), who he compared to Descartes and even Aristotle, and whose logic text, *Logica Hamburgensis* (Hamburg: 1638; rpt. Hamburg, 1957) was Leibniz's favorite (see *L* 223). In the *Logica*, in a section on relations, Jungius gives the standard parsing of relation sentences: e.g., that the friendship between Orestes and Pylades is such that "the friendship that Orestes feels toward Pylades is one thing, and that which Pylades feels toward Orestes is another" (trans. by Mates, *Philosophy of Leibniz*, p. 212). What is interesting about the Jungius connection, as Mates points out, is that in the *Logica* he makes the statement that "In fact nothing exists in reality besides singulars; universals depend upon our way of understanding" (p. 55, #14; Mates, p. 212, n. 15). Moreover, he seems to hold the view that at least some relations are entia rationis.

77. This is Rescher's interpretation, *Leibniz's Metaphysics*, p. 46.

78. Jaakko Hintikka, "Leibniz on Plenitude, Relations, and the 'Reign of Law'," in *Leibniz: A Collection of Critical Essays*, ed. H. Frankfurt (Notre Dame, Ind.: University of Notre Dame Press, 1972), pp. 155–90.

79. Mates, *Philosophy of Leibniz*, pp. 217ff.

80. Russell, *Critical Exposition*; Broad, *Leibniz*, p. 37.

81. This is the view of Clatterbaugh in *Leibniz's Doctrine of Individual Accidents* (1973). However, in his earlier article, "Leibniz's Principle of the Identity of Indiscernibles" (1971), Clatterbaugh interpreted Leibniz as holding that no two individual accidents exactly resemble one another, so there are no shared universals.

Chapter 5 Some Modern Views of Unit Attributes

1. John Cook Wilson, *Statement and Inference*, vol. 2 (Oxford: Clarendon Press, 1926), p. 713.

2. Bertrand Russell, "An Analysis of Mathematical Reasoning" (1897) and "Do Differences Differ?" (1900), manuscripts in Russell Archives, McMaster University. A relevant analysis of these manuscripts is given by Thomas Foster, "Russell on Particularized Relations," *Russell: The Journal of the Bertrand Russell Archives* 3 (1983–84): 129–43. Nicholas Wolterstorff, *On Universals* (Chicago: University of Chicago Press, 1970), pp. 90ff.

3. Rpt. in Robert Marsh, ed., *Bertrand Russell: Logic and Knowledge* (New York: Putnam's Sons, 1971), pp. 105–24.

4. Ibid., p. 124.

5. Wolterstorff, *On Universals*, pp. 96ff.

6. Ibid., p. 102.

7. Ibid., pp. 102–3.

8. G. F. Stout, "The Nature of Universals and Propositions" (1921), rpt. in *Studies in Philosophy and Psychology* (London: Macmillan, 1930), pp. 384–403. D. C. Williams, "The Elements of Being," *Review of Metaphysics* 7 (1953): pp. 3–18, 171–92. Keith Campbell, *Abstract Particulars* (Oxford: Basil Blackwell, 1990); id., "The Metaphysics of Abstract Particulars," in *The Foundations of Analytic Philosophy*, ed. P. French et al. (Minneapolis: University of Minnesota Press, 1981), pp. 477–88; id., "Abstract Particulars and the Philosophy of Mind," *Australasian Journal of Philosophy* 61 (1983): 129–41.

9. Campbell, *Abstract Particulars*, p. xi.

10. Ibid., p. 58.

11. Ibid., p. 90.

12. Ibid., p. 99.

13. D. M. Armstrong, *Universals: An Opinionated Introduction* (Boulder, Colo.: Westview Press, 1989), p. 127.

14. Campbell, *Abstract Particulars*, p. 100.

15. Ibid., p. 24.

16. Ibid., p. 121.

17. Ibid., p. 56.

18. James Moreland, *Universals, Qualities, and Quality-Instances* (New York: University Press of America, 1985).

19. Campbell, *Abstract Particulars*, pp. 53 and 135.

20. James Moreland, "Keith Campbell and the Trope View of Predication," *Australasian Journal of Philosophy* 67, no. 4 (1989): 379–93.

21. Campbell, *Abstract Particulars*, p. 68.

22. Ibid., p. 69.

23. Ibid.

Chapter 6 The Irreducibility of Relations

1. This point is made by Herbert Hochberg in "A Refutation of Moderate Nominalism," *Australasian Journal of Philosophy* 66, no. 2 (1988): 188–207.

2. Bertrand Russell, *The Principles of Mathematics*, 2d ed. (New York: Norton, 1938), pp. 221ff. This is a reprint of the 1903 edition.

3. Keith Campbell, *Abstract Particulars* (Oxford: Basil Blackwell, 1990), p. 102.

4. Ibid., pp. 103–4.

5. Ibid., p. 100.

6. C. Lewis and C. Langford, *Symbolic Logic*, 2d ed. (New York: Dover, 1959), pp. 387–88.

7. Campbell, *Abstract Particulars*, p. 110.

8. Mario Bunge, *Treatise on Basic Philosophy, Semantics I: Sense and Reference* (Dordrecht: Reidel, 1974), pp. 155ff.

9. Herbert Hochberg, "The Wiener–Kuratowski Procedure and the Analysis of Order," *Analysis* 41 (1981): 161–63; id., "Russell's Early Analysis of Relational Predication and the Asymmetry of the Predication Relation," *Philosophia* 17, no. 4 (1987): 439–59; id., "A Refutation of Moderate Nominalism."

10. D. M. Armstrong, "In Defence of Structural Universals," *Australasian Journal of Philosophy* 64, no. 1 (1986): 85–91.

11. Panayot Butchvarov, *Being Qua Being* (Bloomington: Indiana University Press, 1979), pp. 239ff.

Chapter 7 Specious Arguments against Relation Instances

1. D. M. Armstrong, *Nominalism and Realism* (Cambridge: Cambridge University Press, 1978), pp. 77–78. Reinhardt Grossmann, *The Categorical Structure of the World* (Bloomington: Indiana University Press, 1983), pp. 102–16.
2. Armstrong makes this summary explicit in the companion volume to *Nominalism* entitled *A Theory of Universals* (Cambridge: Cambridge University Press, 1978), p. 2.
3. Gilbert Ryle, "Plato's 'Parmenides'," *Mind* 48 (1939), rpt. in *Studies in Plato's Metaphysics*, ed. R. Allen (New York: Humanities Press, 1965), pp. 97–147.
4. Armstrong, *Nominalism and Realism*, pp. 16, 69–70.
5. Bertrand Russell, *Principles of Mathematics*, 2d ed. (New York: Norton, 1938), pp. 51–52.
6. Ryle, "Plato's 'Parmenides'," pp. 106–7.
7. Alan Donagan, "Universals and Metaphysical Realism," *Monist* 47 (1963), rpt. in *Universals and Particulars: Readings in Ontology*, rev. ed., ed. Michael Loux (Notre Dame, Ind.: University of Notre Dame Press, 1976), pp. 136–39.
8. Nicholas Wolterstorff, *On Universals* (Chicago: University of Chicago Press, 1970), pp. 89–95.
9. Ibid., pp. 87–94.
10. Armstrong, *Nominalism and Realism*, pp. 70–71.
11. Donagan, "Universals," p. 137.
12. Ryle, "Plato's 'Parmenides'," p. 104.
13. Armstrong, *Nominalism and Realism*, pp. 72–73.
14. Russell, *Principles of Mathematics*, p. 51.
15. I take this infinite process of instances of the same relation to be a sign of the conceptual mode of the relation universal Exp. This is apparently the position of Aquinas, for whom such a relation is a *relatio rationis tantum.* See Julius Weinberg, "The Concept of Relation: Some Observations on Its History," in *Abstraction, Relation, and Induction* (Madison: University of Wisconsin Press, 1965), p. 95.
16. Morris Weitz, "Analysis and the Unity of Russell's Philosophy," in *The Philosophy of Bertrand Russell*, ed. P. Schilpp (Evanston, Ill.: Library of Living Philosophers, 1946), p. 68. For Russell's reservations and for conflicts between his unparticularization thesis and others of his doctrines, see William Winslade, "Russell's Theory of Relations," in *Essays on Bertrand Russell*, ed. E. Klemke (Urbana, Ill.: University of Illinois Press, 1970), pp. 95–101.
17. Bertrand Russell, "Reply to Criticism," in *Philosophy of Bertrand Russell*, ed. Schilpp, p. 648.
18. Russell, *Principles of Mathematics*, pp. 51–52.
19. Weitz, "Russell's Philosophy," pp. 68–69.
20. Russell, *Principles of Mathematics*, p. 52.
21. Armstrong, *Nominalism and Realism*, pp. 86–87; Brand Blanshard, *The Nature of Thought* (London: Allen & Unwin, 1939), 1:595–96, n. 1.
22. Armstrong, *Nominalism and Realism*, p. 111.

Chapter 8 Bradley's Regress and Further Arguments for Relation Instances

1. Russell's early adherence to the instance doctrine is described in Thomas Foster, "Russell on Particularized Relations," *Russell: The Journal of the Bertrand Russell Archives* 3 (1983–84): 129–43. Russell argued for the doctrine in two unpublished papers, "An Analysis of Mathematical Reasoning" (1897) and "Do Differences Differ?" (1900), now in the Russell Archives, McMaster

University. Nicholas Wolterstorff, *On Universals* (Chicago: University of Chicago Press, 1970), pp. 90ff.

2. For a critique of Russell's and Wolterstorff's arguments for instances based upon a Bradley-type regress, see my "Particularism, Exemplification, and Bradley's Regress," *Journal of Speculative Philosophy* 1, no. 3 (1987): 177–205.

3. D. M. Armstrong, "In Defence of Structural Universals," *Australasian Journal of Philosophy* 64, no. 1 (1986): 85–88. See also his *Universals: An Opinionated Introduction* (Boulder, Colo.: Westview Press, 1989), pp. 90–91, 110.

4. David Lewis, "Against Structural Universals," *Australasian Journal of Philosophy* 64, no. 1 (1986): 25–46, and id., "Comment on Armstrong and Forrest," ibid., pp. 92–93.

5. Armstrong, "Defence of Structural Universals," pp. 85–86.

6. F. H. Bradley, "Relations," in *Collected Essays*, vol. 2 (Westport, Conn.: Greenwood Press, 1970), p. 642. Bradley was working on this manuscript at the time of his death; it is important in that he intended it to express the sum of his thought on relations. It is to be noted that Bradley's view of relations was not that of other British idealists of the period—e.g., he was preceded by the idealist T. H. Green, who argued extensively against the empiricism of Locke and Hume precisely on the grounds that this empiricism could not account for relations, and that without relations no knowledge, experience, or conceptualization was possible. See *Works of Thomas Hill Green*, vol. 1 (New York: Longmans, Green & Co., 1906). For a context and overview of Green's arguments, see Peter Hylton, *Russell, Idealism, and the Emergence of Analytic Philosophy* (Oxford: Clarendon Press, 1990).

7. Bradley, "Relations," p. 634. In short, the erroneous side of the regress dialectic is Bradley's treating subject and predicate as two subjects, an error that Peter Geach finds in Aristotle and rightly characterizes as a disaster for logic comparable to the Fall of Adam. My point is that it is a comparable disaster for ontology. See Peter Geach, "History of the Corruption of Logic," in *Logic Matters* (Berkeley: University of California Press, 1972), pp. 44–61.

8. Bradley, "Relations," p. 644.

9. Ibid., p. 634.

10. Reinhardt Grossmann, *The Categorical Structure of the World* (Bloomington: Indiana University Press, 1983), p. 169.

11. Bertrand Russell, "Some Explanations in Reply to Mr. Bradley," *Mind* 19 (1908): 374. Russell also makes repeated use of the description 'relating relations' in the 1913 unpublished manuscript that became *Theory of Knowledge* (London: Allen & Unwin, 1984).

12. Bertrand Russell, *Principles of Mathematics*, 2d ed. (New York: Norton, 1938), pp. 140–41.

13. See Julius Weinberg, "The Concept of Relation: Some Observations on Its History," in *Abstraction, Relation, and Induction* (Madison: University of Wisconsin Press, 1965), pp. 93, 95.

14. Gustav Bergmann, *Realism* (Madison: University of Wisconsin Press, 1967), pp. 9, 42ff. Herbert Hochberg, "A Refutation of Moderate Nominalism," *Australasian Journal of Philosophy* 66, no. 2 (1988): 188–207. P. F. Strawson, *Individuals* (London: Methuen, 1971), pp. 168ff.

15. Something like this line of argument for instances was proposed by Alexius Meinong, though it was not developed; its weakness is pointed out by Grossmann, *Categorical Structure*, pp. 107f. My argument makes up the lacuna and does, I contend, meet Grossmann's objections.

16. D. M. Armstrong, *Nominalism and Realism* (Cambridge: Cambridge University Press, 1978), p. 115.

17. Frege, "Compound Thoughts," in *Essays on Frege*, ed. E. Klemke (Urbana, Ill.: University of Illinois Press), p. 538.

18. There is a similar paradox or near-paradox with the very concept of *unrepeatability*, which is

resolved in the same way. Individual a is unrepeatable and individual b is unrepeatable, but in this they have something in common, *unrepeatability*. In short, unrepeatability is repeatable. Intuitively, however, the unrepeatability-of-a is truly unrepeatable and nonidentical with the unrepeatability-of-b. This is now understood as $\text{Unrep}_1(a)$ and $\text{Unrep}_2(b)$, $\text{Unrep}_1 \neq \text{Unrep}_2$, and neither is identical to the common universal *Unrep*.

19. Armstrong, "Defence of Structural Universals," and id., *Nominalism and Realism*, pp. 116ff. John Bigelow and Robert Pargetter, "A Theory of Structural Universals," *Australasian Journal of Philosophy* 67, no. 1 (1989): 1–11. See also Lewis, "Against Structural Universals," pp. 25–26.

20. Armstrong, "Defence of Structural Universals," p. 88.

Chapter 9 Formalization of a Particularized Predicate Logic

1. Gödel's 'theory of concepts' view of logic is reported by Hao Wang in *Reflections of Kurt Gödel* (Cambridge, Mass.: MIT Press, 1987), p. 297, and *Beyond Analytic Philosophy* (Cambridge, Mass.: MIT Press, 1986), pp. 5 and 73. For an overview of the scholastic thesis that logic is a science of 'second intensions', see Anton Dumitriu, *History of Logic*, vol. 2 (Tunbridge Wells, Kent: Abacus Press, 1977), pp. 51–61.

2. Alonzo Church, *Introduction to Mathematical Logic* (Princeton: Princeton University Press, 1956), pp. 180ff.; 306ff.

3. Frederic Fitch, "Universal Metalanguages for Philosophy," *Review of Metaphysics*, 17, no. 3 (1964): 396–402.

4. This is in contrast to 'intensional logic' as logicians often use the term now, which contains no direct reference to intensions but includes the study of deductive systems for tense, modality, and conditionals.

5. Bertrand Russell, "Mathematical Logic as Based on the Theory of Types" (1908), rpt. in *Logic and Knowledge*, ed. R. Marsh (London: Allen & Unwin, 1956), p. 75. See Charles Chihara, *Ontology and the Vicious Circle Principle* (Ithaca, N.Y.: Cornell University Press, 1973), pp. 3ff.

6. Alonzo Church, "The Need for Abstract Entities," *American Academy of Arts and Sciences Proceedings* 80 (1951): 100–113, rpt. as "Intensional Semantics," in *The Philosophy of Language*, ed. A. P. Martinich (Oxford: Oxford University Press, 1985), pp. 40–47.

7. Hao Wang, *Reflections of Kurt Gödel*, p. 297, and *Beyond Analytic Philosophy*, pp. 5 and 73.

8. Nino Cocchiarella, *Logical Investigations of Predication Theory and the Problem of Universals* (Naples: Bibliopolis, 1986), pp. 165ff.

9. George Bealer, *Quality and Concept* (Oxford: Clarendon Press, 1982), pp. 42ff.

10. Church, *Mathematical Logic*.

11. D. A. Bochvar, "To the Question of Paradoxes of the Mathematical Logic and Theory of Sets," *Recueil mathématique* 15 (57), no. 13 (1944): 383–84. Nino Cocchiarella, "Whither Russell's Paradox of Predication," in *Logic and Ontology*, ed. M. Munitz (New York: New York University Press, 1973), pp. 133–58.

12. Church, *Mathematical Logic*, pp. 306ff.; Cocchiarella, "Russell's Paradox," pp. 140ff. Cocchiarella uses the syntactical technique to prove the consistency of an extended predicate logic (without refinement of instances), pp. 140ff.

13. Interestingly, Jaakko Hintikka has shown that the analogous prohibition which proves successful here is unsuccessful in avoiding contradiction in unrefined predicate logic. See his "Identity, Variables, and Impredicative Definitions," *Journal of Symbolic Logic*, 21, no. 3 (1956): 239–49, and id., "Vicious Circle Principle and the Paradoxes," ibid. 22, no. 3 (1957): 245–49. Instead of the

restriction in the definiens of 9.7, 'Rus$_j$ ≠ Rus$_h$ ⊃', Hintikka formulates Russell's property in standard predicate logic with the restriction 'P ≠ Rus ⊃'. In investigating Russell's vicious circle principle, the relevant formulation being that 'whatever contains an apparent variable must not be a possible value of that variable', Hintikka observed the set analog of the fact that the simplest implied restriction on the impredicative specification of Russell's property would be:

(a) (P)[Rus(P) ≡ (P ≠ Rus ⊃ ¬P(P))].

However, Hintikka proved (the set analog of the fact) that on a universe of at least two properties it is possible to derive a contradiction from (a). He concludes that on a very natural interpretation the vicious circle principle is false. With regard to (a), one is also reminded of Frege's similar but unsuccessful attempt to avoid Russell's set paradox, the property analog being

(b) (P)[P ≠ Rus ⊃ (Rus(P) ≡ ¬P(P))].

14. Bertrand Russell and Alfred North Whitehead, *Principia Mathematica*, vol. 1 (Cambridge: Cambridge University Press, 1910), p. 60.

15. Kurt Gödel, "Russell's Mathematical Logic" (1944), rpt. in *Philosophy of Mathematics: Selected Readings*, 2d ed., ed. P. Benacerraf and H. Putnam (Cambridge: Cambridge University Press, 1983), pp. 466–67.

16. Cocchiarella, *Logical Investigations*. For an instructive overview of the Henkin completeness proof for first-order logic, see John Pollock, *Technical Methods in Philosophy* (Boulder, Colo.: Westview Press, 1990), pp. 77ff.

17. For an excellent analysis of the self-reflections involved in paradoxes carried out within the limitations of standard predicate logic, see L. Goddard and M. Johnson, "The Nature of Reflexive Paradoxes: Part I," *Notre Dame Journal of Symbolic Logic* 24 (1983): 491–508, and "Part II," ibid. 25 (1984): 27–58. Also instructive is the analysis of Anton Dumitriu, "The Antinomy of the Theory of Types and the Solution of Logico-Mathematical Paradoxes," *International Logic Review* 5, no. 1 (1974): 83–102. Dumitriu argues that the self-referential paradoxes and others he proposes are due not to a particular value of the argument of a predicate, which is the focus of restriction within the theory of types, but rather to a value of the predicate position. This is the same conclusion that I draw here. Dumitriu claims that the paradoxes arise because mathematical logic does not observe carefully enough the prohibitions of classical logic against definitions being either contradictory or idem per idem. I use the designation 'idem per idem' in a broader sense than Dumitriu to mean any definition in which the truth-value of the definiendum (the obtaining of an instance of an *n*-place relation among a specific *n*-tuple of subjects) is made to be a function of itself as part of the definiens.

18. Charles Chihara, "A Diagnosis of the Liar and Other Semantical Vicious-Circle Paradoxes," in *Bertrand Russell Memorial Volume*, ed. G. Roberts (New York: Humanities Press, 1979), p. 53.

19. Russell, "Mathematical Logic as Based on the Theory of Types," p. 63.

20. Graham Priest, "The Logic of Paradox," *Journal of Philosophical Logic* 8 (1979): 219–41.

21. Ibid., p. 220.

22. For a description of the classic self-referential paradoxes, see Russell and Whitehead, *Principia Mathematica*, pp. 60ff. These and others are included in Evert Beth, *The Foundations of Mathematics* (Amsterdam: North-Holland, 1968), pp. 481ff.

23. Frederic Fitch, *Symbolic Logic* (New York: Ronald Press, 1952), pp. 106ff.

24. For a good overview of the standard devices for avoiding the liar paradox and its kin, as well as three new, interesting extensions for the liar, see Patrick Grim, *The Incomplete Universe* (Cambridge, Mass.: MIT Press, 1991).

25. For a recent assessment of the liar paradox as displaying a weakness in our conceptions of truth, reference, or negation, see Jon Barwise and John Etchemendy, *The Liar: An Essay on Truth and Circularity* (Oxford: Oxford University Press, 1987), p. 22.

26. Grim, *Incomplete Universe*, p. 21.

27. Arguments for propositions as truth-bearers are found variously in the literature; for a good synthesis, see Raymond Bradley and Norman Swartz, *Possible Worlds: An Introduction to Logic and Its Philosophy* (Indianapolis: Hackett, 1979), pp. 65ff. See also Alonzo Church, "Propositions and Sentences," in *Readings in the Philosophy of Language*, ed. J. Rosenberg and C. Travis (Englewood Cliffs, N.J.: Prentice-Hall, 1971), pp. 276–82. I reject the view that propositions are 'abstract' in the sense of existing independently of minds.

28. Barwise and Etchemendy, *Liar*, p. 22.

29. See C. Smorynski, *Self-Reference and Modal Logic* (New York: Springer, 1985), pp. 6–8. See also Robert Rogers, *Mathematical Logic and Formalized Theories* (Amsterdam: North-Holland, 1971), pp. 210–14.

30. Grim, *Incomplete Universe*, pp. 8–9. It is interesting to note that medieval philosophers and theologians argued over the self-referring proposition 'There is no truth' (*Nulla veritas est*), some holding that the proposition implied a proof for the existence of God. Assumed true, there is a truth; assumed false, a contradiction results. Hence, there is at least one truth. Since God is the author of all truth, then God exists. See W. Charron and J. Doyle, "On the Self-Refuting Statement 'There is no Truth': A Medieval Treatment," *Vivarium* 31, no. 2 (1993): 241–66.

31. Ibid., pp. 92ff.

32. Kurt Gödel, "On Formally Undecidable Propositions of *Principia Mathematica* and Related Systems" (1931), rpt. in *From Frege to Gödel: A Source Book in Mathematical Logic, 1870–1931*, ed. Jean van Heijenoort (Cambridge, Mass.: Harvard University Press, 1967), pp. 596–616.

33. For a description and critical assessment of Cantor's diagonal arguments, see Felix Kaufmann, *The Infinite in Mathematics* (Dordrecht: Reidel, 1978).

34. Henri Poincaré, *Mathematics and Science: Last Essays* (New York: Dover, 1963), p. 61.

35. Roger Penrose expresses this caution, saying, "Why should we accept the Gödel and Turing arguments, whereas we have had to reject the reasoning leading to the Russell paradox? The former are much more clear-cut, and are unexceptionable as mathematical arguments, whereas the Russell paradox depends upon more nebulous reasoning involving 'enormous' sets. But it must be admitted that the distinctions are not really as clear as one would like them to be. . . . To my mind the issue is still unresolved" (*The Emperor's New Mind* [Oxford: Oxford University Press, 1989], p. 111).

36. Bertrand Russell, *Introduction to Mathematical Philosophy* (1919; rpt. ed., New York: Simon & Schuster, 1971), p. 136.

37. Thoralf Skolem, "Some Remarks on Axiomatized Set Theory," in *From Frege to Gödel*, p. 295.

38. Thoralf Skolem, "The Foundations of Elementary Arithmetic," in *From Frege to Gödel*, p. 332.

39. John von Neumann, "An Axiomatization of Set Theory," in *From Frege to Gödel*, p. 408.

40. Ibid., p. 409.

41. Putnam has pushed Skolem's line of reasoning to the more general conclusion that "the *total use of the language* [our 'understanding'] does not 'fix' a unique 'intended interpretation' any more than axiomatic set theory by itself"—i.e., we do not have a single intuitive notion of set, in that our delimiting concepts are diversely modeled. See Hilary Putnam, "Models and Reality," in *Philosophy of Mathematics*, ed. Benacerraf and Putnam, p. 424.

42. These systems are described in A. Fraenkel, Y. Bar-Hillel, and A. Levy, *Foundations of Set Theory* (Amsterdam: North-Holland, 1973), pp. 161ff.

43. Hao Wang, *Survey of Mathematical Logic* (Amsterdam: North-Holland, 1964), pp. 559ff. For an attempt to develop mathematics from a predicative nominalist's interpretation of Wang's system Σ, including a description of Σ, see Chihara, *Ontology and Vicious Circle Principle*, pp. 173ff. and appendix. An overview of system Σ is found in Fraenkel et al., *Foundations of Set Theory*, pp. 175ff.

44. Wang, *Survey of Mathematical Logic*, p. 562.

45. A classic text on recursive functions is Stephen Kleene, *Introduction to Metamathematics* (Princeton: Van Nostrand, 1952). A more perspicuous presentation is found in Geoffrey Hunter, *Metalogic: An Introduction to the Metatheory of Standard First Order Logic* (Berkeley: University of California Press, 1971), pp. 232–49.

46. Penrose, *Emperor's New Mind*, pp. 57ff.

47. This formulation is given, e.g., in the popular exposition of Morris Kline, *Mathematics: The Loss of Certainty* (Oxford: Oxford University Press, 1980), p. 261.

48. Bertrand Russell, "On Some Difficulties in the Theory of Transfinite Numbers and Order Types," *Proceedings of the London Mathematical Society*, 2d ser., 4 (1905): rpt. in *Essays in Analysis*, ed. D. Lackey (London: Allen & Unwin, 1973), p. 141.

49. Graham Priest, "The Structure of the Paradoxes of Self-Reference," *Mind* 103, no. 409 (1994): 25–34.

Chapter 10 Instance Ontology and Logic Applied to the Foundations of Arithmetic and Theory of Identity

1. Gottlob Frege, *Foundations of Arithmetic*, 2d ed., trans. J. Austin (Evanston, Ill.: Northwestern University Press), p. 21.

2. Nino Cocchiarella, *Logical Studies in Early Analytic Philosophy* (Columbus: Ohio State University, 1987), pp. 65ff.

3. For details of how Frege's logic gives rise to contradiction, see Michael Resnik, *Frege and the Philosophy of Mathematics* (Ithaca, N.Y.: Cornell University Press, 1980), pp. 211ff.

4. Euclid's *Elements*, vol. 2, bk. VII, 2d ed., trans. T. L. Heath (New York: Dover, 1956), p. 277; cf. p. 280. For a discussion of the von Neumann and Zermelo models, see the classic Paul Benacerraf, "What Numbers Could Not Be," in *Philosophy of Mathematics: Selected Readings*, 2d ed., ed., P. Benacerraf and H. Putnam (Cambridge: Cambridge University Press, 1983), pp. 272–94. On Benacerraf, see Penelopy Maddy, *Realism in Mathematics* (Oxford: Clarendon Press, 1990), pp. 81ff.

5. Bertrand Russell, *Introduction to Mathematical Philosophy* (1919; rpt. ed., New York: Simon & Schuster, 1971), p. 12. Bertrand Russell and Alfred North Whitehead, *Principia Mathematica*, vol. 1 (Cambridge: Cambridge University Press, 1910).

6. Georg Cantor states this position in his review of Frege's *Grundlagen*; the relevant passage is translated by Reinhardt Grossmann in *The Categorical Structure of the World* (Bloomington: Indiana University Press, 1983), p. 304, and is from Cantor's *Gesammelte Abhandlungen* (Hildesheim: Olms, 1962). For critiques of views (a)–(d) on the nature of numbers, see Grossmann, *Categorical Structure*, pp. 293ff. Maddy, *Realism in Mathematics*.

7. Frege, *Foundations of Arithmetic*, pp. 79ff.

8. Bertrand Russell, *My Philosophical Development* (London: Allen & Unwin, 1959), p. 54.

9. Bertrand Russell, *The Principles of Mathematics*, 2d ed. (1903; rpt. ed., New York: Norton, 1938), pp. 115–16; id., *Introduction to Mathematical Philosophy*, p. 18.

10. D. Hilbert and W. Ackermann, *Principles of Mathematical Logic*, 2d ed., trans. L. Hammond, G. Leckie, and F. Steinhardt (New York: Chelsea, 1950), p. 136.

11. David Bostock, *Logic and Arithmetic* (Oxford: Clarendon Press, 1974).

12. Benacerraf, "What Numbers Could Not Be."

13. Ibid., p. 291.

14. John Locke, *An Essay Concerning Human Understanding*, ed. P. Nidditch (Oxford: Clarendon Press, 1975), pp. 205ff. David Hume, *A Treatise of Human Nature*, vol. 1, ed. T. H. Green and T. H. Grose (1886; rpt. ed., Germany: Scientia Verlag Aalen, 1964), pp. 337f.

15. Euclid, *Elements*, p. 277.

16. Frege, *Foundations of Arithmetic*, pp. 44ff.

17. Russell, *Introduction to Mathematical Philosophy*, p. 12.

18. Ibid., p. 18.

19. Frege, *Foundations of Arithmetic*, p. 59.

20. Ibid., pp. 79–80.

21. Russell, *My Philosophical Development*, pp. 55 and 67.

22. Gottlob Frege, "Translations of Parts of Frege's *Grundgesetze der Arithmetik*," in *Translations from the Philosophical Writings of Gottlob Frege*, ed. Peter Geach and Max Black (Oxford: Blackwell, 1970), p. 140.

23. This is the conclusion of Crispin Wright, though his reasons are left unstated. See his *Frege's Conception of Numbers as Objects* (Aberdeen: Aberdeen University Press, 1983), p. 36.

24. Gottlob Frege, "On Concept and Object," in *Translations*, ed. Geach and Black, pp. 42ff.

25. Ibid., p. 45. See Rulon Wells, "Frege's Ontology," in *Essays on Frege*, ed. E. Klemke (Urbana, Ill.: University of Illinois Press, 1968), pp. 16–17.

26. Frege, *Foundations of Arithmetic*, p. 80.

27. W. V. O. Quine, "Notes on Existence and Necessity," *Journal of Philosophy* 40 (1943): 113–27. See also *From a Logical Point of View*, 2d ed. (New York: Harper & Row, 1963), pp. 139ff.

28. Maddy, *Realism in Mathematics*, pp. 86ff.

29. Richard Dedekind, *Essays on the Theory of Numbers*, trans. W. Behman (New York: Dover, 1963), p. 31.

30. Philip Kitcher, *The Nature of Mathematical Knowledge* (New York: Oxford University Press, 1984), pp. 107ff.

31. Peano's postulates are:

    (1) 0 is a number.
    (2) The successor of any number is a number.
    (3) No two numbers have the same successor.
    (4) 0 is not the successor of any number.
    (5) (*Mathematical induction*) Any property that belongs to 0 and also to the successor of any number that has that property belongs to all numbers.

32. This summary is that of Rudy Rucker, *Infinity and the Mind* (New York: Bantam Books, 1983), pp. 300–301. A fuller statement is given by the French Hilbertian Jacques Herbrand in a 1931 article entitled "On the Consistency of Arithmetic," in which he gives a finitary consistency proof for a fragment of arithmetic. He states in a footnote: "By an intuitionistic [= finitary] argument we understand an argument satisfying the following conditions: in it we never consider anything but a given finite number of objects and of functions; these functions are well-defined, their definition allowing the computation of their value in a univocal way; we never state that an object exists without giving the means of constructing it; we never consider the totality of all the objects x of an infinite collection; and when we say that an argument (or a theorem) is true for all these x, we mean

that, for each x taken by itself, it is possible to repeat the general argument in question, which should be considered to be merely the prototype of these particular arguments" (rpt. in *From Frege to Gödel: A Source Book in Mathematical Logic, 1870–1931*, ed. Jean van Heijenoort (Cambridge, Mass.: Harvard University Press, 1967), p. 622.

33. Michael Detlefsen, *Hilbert's Program* (Dordrecht: Reidel, 1986).

34. Robert Rogers, *Mathematical Logic and Formalized Theories* (Amsterdam: North-Holland, 1971), pp. 207–8.

35. Stephen Kleene, *Introduction to Metamathematics* (Princeton: Van Nostrand, 1952), pp. 476ff.

36. Kurt Gödel, "On Formally Undecidable Propositions of *Principia Mathematica* and Related Systems" (1931), rpt. in *From Frege to Gödel*, p. 615.

37. Hume, *Treatise on Human Nature*, I. iii. 1, p. 374.

38. Wright, *Frege's Conception of Numbers*, pp. 154ff. George Boolos, "The Consistency of Frege's *Foundations of Arithmetic*," in *On Being and Saying: Essays for Richard Cartwright*, ed. Judith Thomson (Cambridge, Mass.: MIT Press, 1987), pp. 3–20. See also id., "The Standard of Equality of Numbers," in *Meaning and Method: Essays in Honor of Hilary Putnam*, ed. George Boolos (Cambridge: Cambridge University Press, 1990), pp. 261–77.

39. Resnik, *Frege and the Philosophy of Mathematics*, pp. 211ff.

40. Rudolf Carnap, "The Logicist Foundations of Mathematics," in *Philosophy of Mathematics: Selected Readings*, 2d ed., ed. P. Benacerraf and H. Putnam (Cambridge: Cambridge University Press, 1983), pp. 50ff.

41. Mark Steiner, *Mathematical Knowledge* (Ithaca, N.Y.: Cornell University Press, 1975), p. 34.

42. Charles Chihara, *Constructibility and Mathematical Existence* (Oxford: Clarendon Press, 1990), pp. 80ff.

43. Wright, *Frege's Conception of Numbers*, pp. 154ff.

44. See Thomas Morris, *Understanding Identity Statements* (Aberdeen: Aberdeen University Press, 1984), and Nathan Salmon, *Frege's Puzzle* (Cambridge, Mass.: MIT Press, 1986).

45. Peter Geach, "Identity," *Review of Metaphysics* 21, no. 1 (1967): 3–12; rpt. with a reply in Geach, *Logic Matters* (Berkeley: University of California Press, 1972), pp. 238–49.

46. John Perry, "Relative Identity and Number," *Canadian Journal of Philosophy* 8, no. 1 (1978): 1–14; William Alston and Jonathan Bennett, "Identity and Carinality: Geach and Frege," *Philosophical Review* 93, no. 4 (1984): 553–67.

47. Geach uses the equivalent axiom: $Fa \equiv (x)(Fx \bullet x = a)$ in *Logic Matters*, p. 239.

48. D. M. Armstrong, *Nominalism and Realism* (Cambridge: Cambridge University Press, 1978), pp. 93–94.

49. Max Black, "The Identity of Indiscernibles," in *Universals and Particulars: Readings in Ontology*, 2d ed., ed. Michael Loux (Notre Dame, Ind.: University of Notre Dame Press, 1976), pp. 250–62.

50. A. J. Ayer, "The Identity of Indiscernibles," in *Universals and Particulars*, ed. Loux, pp. 263–70.

51. David Widerker, "Identity, Indiscernibility and Geach," *Logique et analyse* 24 (1981): 211–21.

Index